THE • KIDS • CAN • PRESS JUMBO BOOK OF Easy Crafts

Written by Judy Ann Sadler
Illustrated by Caroline Price

Kids Can Press

To little crafters everywhere – *JAS*

Kids Can Press acknowledges the financial support of the Government of Canada, through the BPIDP, for our publishing activity.

Published in Canada by
Kids Can Press Ltd.
29 Birch Avenue
Toronto, ON M4V 1E2

Published in the U.S. by
Kids Can Press Ltd.
2250 Military Road
Tonawanda, NY 14150

Edited by Laurie Wark
Designed by Marie Bartholomew
Printed and bound in Canada by Webcom Limited
Model photography by Ray Boudreau
Craft photography by Frank Baldassarra

CM PA 01 0 9 8 7 6 5 4 3 2 1

Canadian Cataloguing in Publication Data
Sadler, Judy Ann, 1959–
The Kids Can Press jumbo book of easy crafts

(The Kids Can Press jumbo book series)
Includes index.
ISBN 1-55074-811-4

1. Handicraft – Juvenile literature. I. Price, Caroline. II. Title.
III. Title: Jumbo book of easy crafts. IV. Series.

TT160.S229 2001 j745.5 C00-931791-0

NELVANA

Kids Can Press is a Nelvana company

Contents

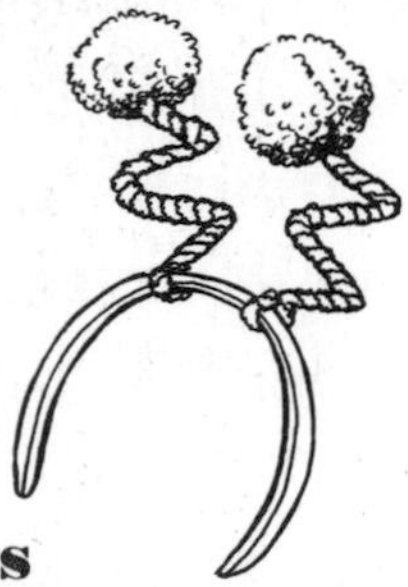

Introduction

Can you imagine a clothespin turning into a dragonfly? An egg carton becoming a raccoon? How about jar lids transforming into a marionette or a walnut into a sailboat? These are just a few of 175 fun, easy crafts you'll find in this book. There are animals, nature crafts, games, gifts, toys and works of art just waiting to be started. And finding what you want to make is simple. Got a pack of pipe cleaners? Look through the table of contents under "P" for pipe cleaners (where you'll also find paint, paper plates, pasta, pom-poms and more!) and choose your project. Or you can simply flip through the book and look for the pipe-cleaner pictures down the side of the page. A bag of buttons? Look under "B" in the contents or find the handy button symbol.

There are so many great reasons to make crafts together. It's wonderful to be with someone who shares your love of making stuff. Let the craft materials tickle your senses – see the colors and shapes in a handful of beads, feel the softness of felt, smell aromatic beeswax and hear the snip of scissors cutting through paper. Take time to play with these materials and let your imagination run free. Before you know it, you'll be happily cutting, gluing, coloring, twisting and decorating your way through this idea-packed book. Your refrigerator door and the rest of your home will soon be filled with your creations. Enjoy!

Materials

You will find some useful craft materials, such as egg cartons and cereal boxes, around your home. Gather other basic items, such as glue, safety scissors, paper, a pencil and a ruler. Keep them in a drawer, box or plastic bin along with some of the other materials you see in the table of contents. Use only non-toxic materials and keep scissors and small items, such as beads, beans and buttons, out of the reach of babies and toddlers. Adult supervision is necessary when the instructions call for the use of an iron, stove or anything sharp. Wear an old shirt and cover your work surface with newspaper whenever you're using paint, glue or other messy materials.

- **glue**
  Many crafts call for clear-drying, non-toxic liquid white craft glue. You can use a glue stick as an option for some crafts.
- **paper**
  You will need plain white paper, construction paper and scrap paper for some of the projects in this book.
- **cardboard**
  When a craft calls for "thin cardboard," this means cardboard from a cereal or cracker box. "Corrugated cardboard" is cardboard from a packing box.
- **pencils, crayons and markers**
  For some crafts, you'll need pencils, crayons and markers for decorating. Items such as stickers, glitter, ribbon, sequins and feathers are great for decorating crafts, too.

Magic wand

You don't need to draw a perfect star for this wand.

1. Draw a star shape onto the cardboard and cut it out.

2. Trace the star onto the dull side of the foil, flip the star over and trace it again. Cut out both foil stars.

3. Staple the straw to the cardboard star.

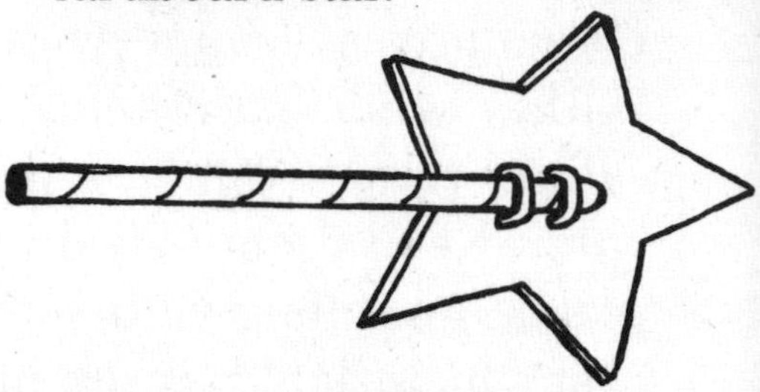

4. Glue a foil star onto each side of the cardboard star so the shiny sides show. Decorate the wand with ribbons or yarn.

You will need

a pencil, scissors, a stapler and white craft glue

◎

thin cardboard (from a cereal box)

◎

aluminum foil

◎

a plastic drinking straw

◎

yarn or curling ribbon

Magic mirror

Trace two different-sized round items, such as bowls, plastic lids or plates, to make this mirror. Decorate the mirror with beads, buttons, stickers or whatever else you can find.

1. Place the larger round item near the top of the cardboard and trace it. Draw a handle for the mirror, attached to the circle.

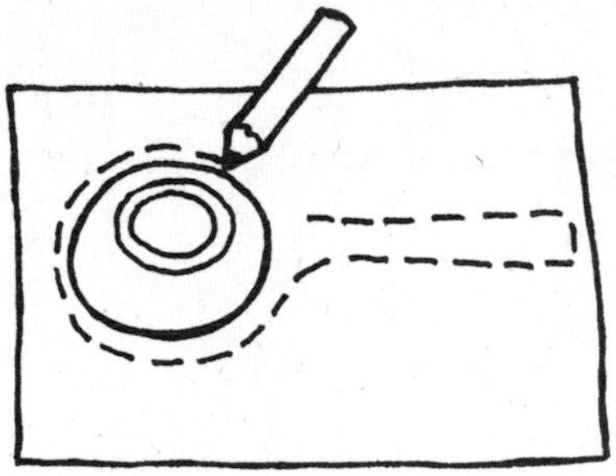

2. Cut out the mirror. You can cut away pieces of the handle to make it a comfortable shape to hold.

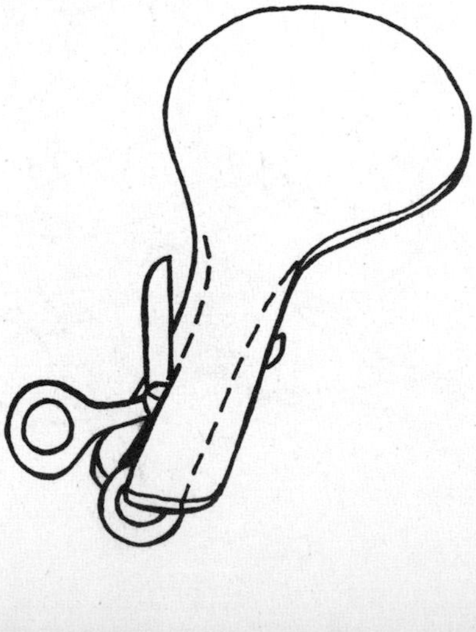

3. Trace this mirror shape onto a sheet of construction paper. Cut it out and glue it onto the cardboard mirror.

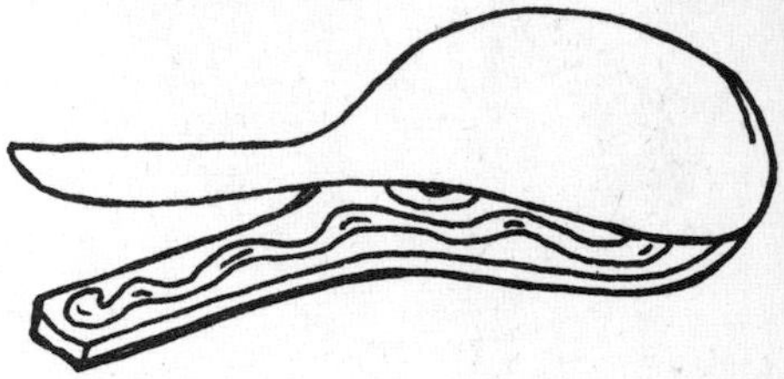

4. Use the smaller round item to trace a circle onto the dull side of the foil. Cut it out and glue it in place, shiny side out.

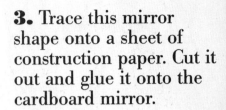

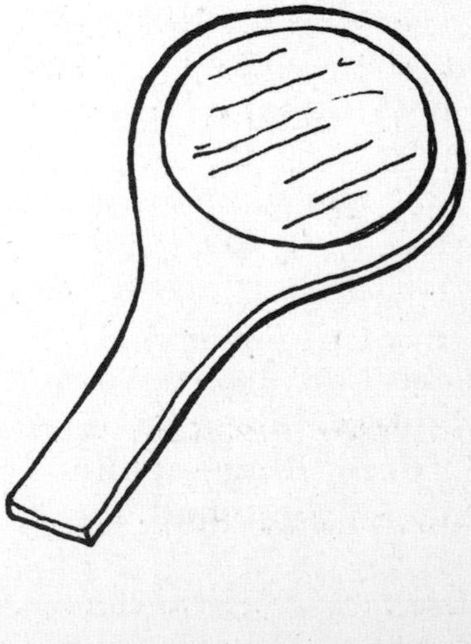

You will need

thin cardboard (from a cereal box)

two round items to trace

a pencil, scissors and white craft glue

construction paper

aluminum foil

beads, buttons or stickers

Decorated basket

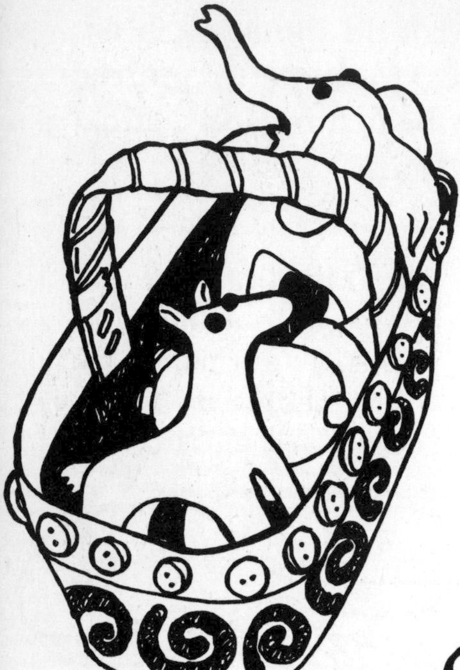

Transform a cardboard fruit basket into a terrific toy-carrier or gift basket.

1. If you are going to store small items, such as buttons and beads, in your basket, smoothly tape over the corner openings on the inside and outside.

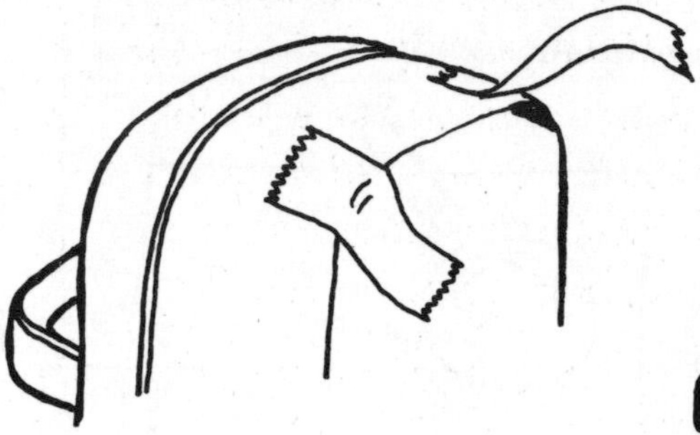

2. Paint the basket all in one color. Allow it to dry.

3. Paint on designs, such as stripes, swirls or flowers. Or glue on buttons, beads or other small, interesting items. You can wrap yarn, ribbon or strips of fabric around the handle.

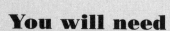

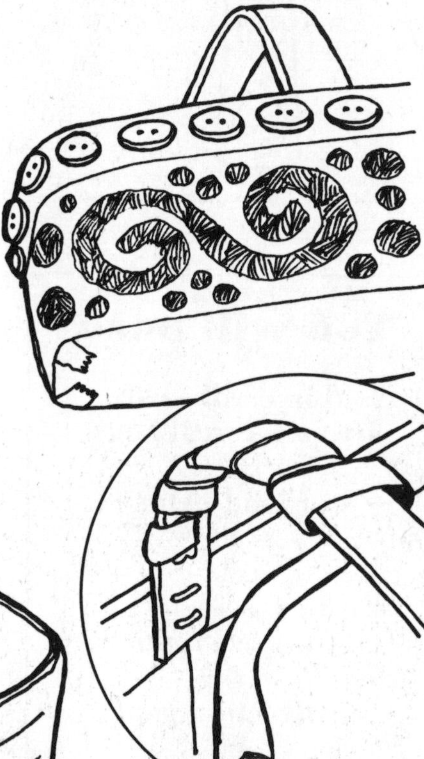

You will need

a clean fruit basket

masking tape (optional)

acrylic paint

a paint brush

buttons, beads, yarn, ribbon, fabric or other decorating supplies (optional)

M◎re basket fun

Art caddy

Place yogurt cups and other plastic containers in your decorated basket and fill them with crayons, markers, pencils, stickers and other craft supplies. Leave enough space for a small pad of paper. Now you can be creative everywhere you go!

Baby doll bed

Place a piece of felt or soft fabric, such as fleece, in the bottom of the basket. Use a bandanna, felt or fleece for a blanket. Give your doll something to play with by tying a small plastic toy from the handle of the basket. You can decorate another basket to carry doll clothes, bottles and other accessories.

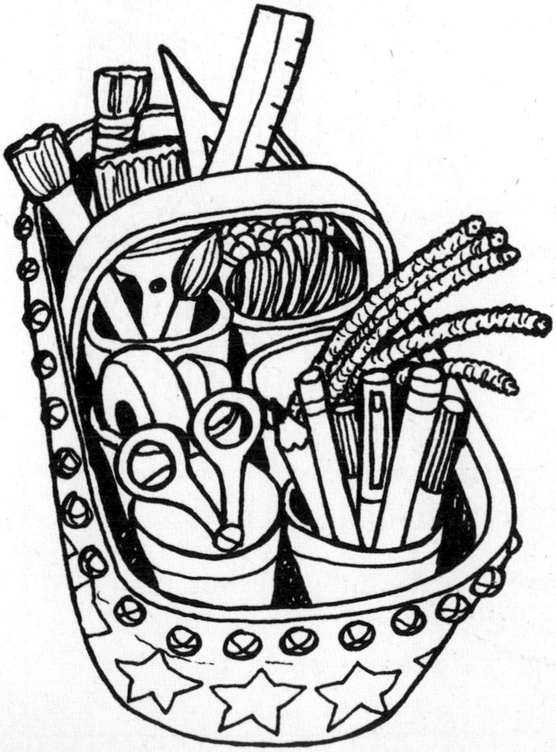

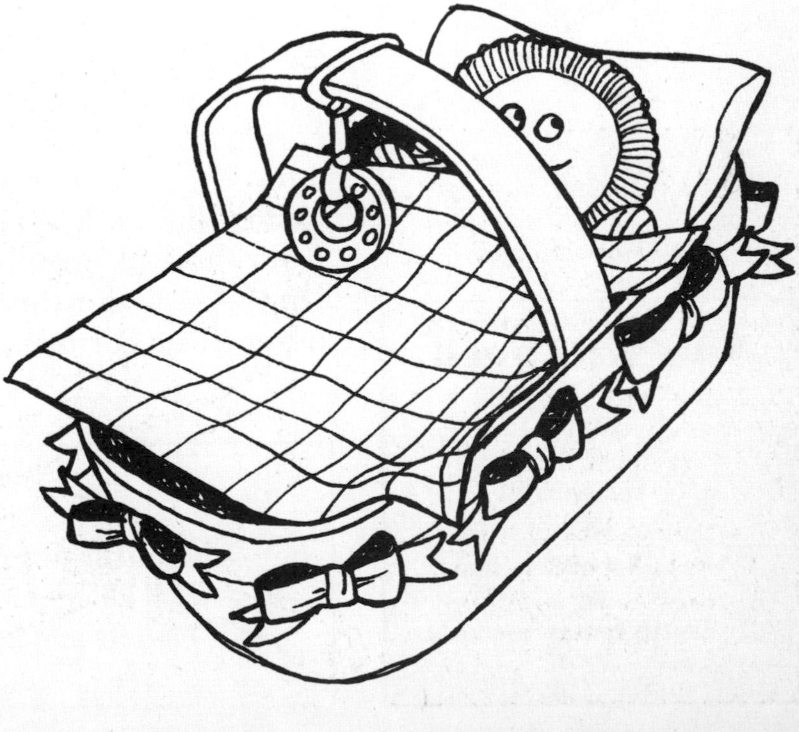

Berry-basket organizer

For this craft, use small, plastic berry baskets. Hang this handy organizer on a nail or doorknob and fill it with lightweight toys.

1. Cut eight pieces of yarn, each about 40 cm (16 in.) long.

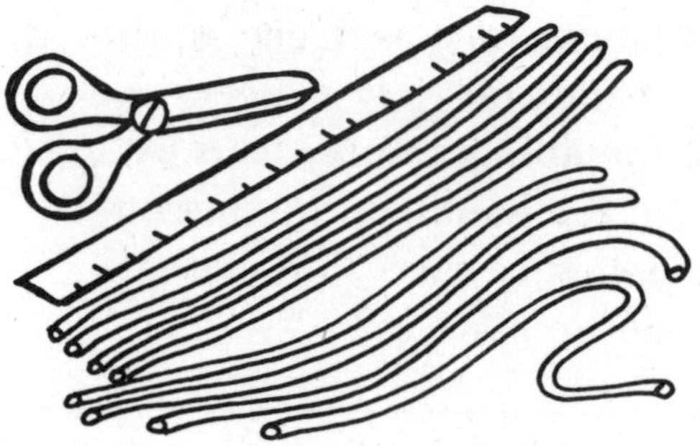

2. Thread a piece of yarn from a bottom corner of one basket to a top corner of the other basket and back again. Knot the ends together. Do the same for the other three corners.

3. Thread a piece of yarn into each of the other top corners. Bring all eight ends together and fasten them in an overhand knot as shown.

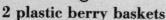

You will need

yarn
◎
scissors
◎
a ruler
◎
2 plastic berry baskets

More ideas

Add one or two more baskets and get even more organized! Or try fastening together two sets of three or four baskets and hanging them one above the other.

Egg basket

Here's a fun way to make a colorful basket for eggs, treats or any other treasures.

1. Twist together the pipe cleaners to make a handle. Fasten it to the sides of the basket.

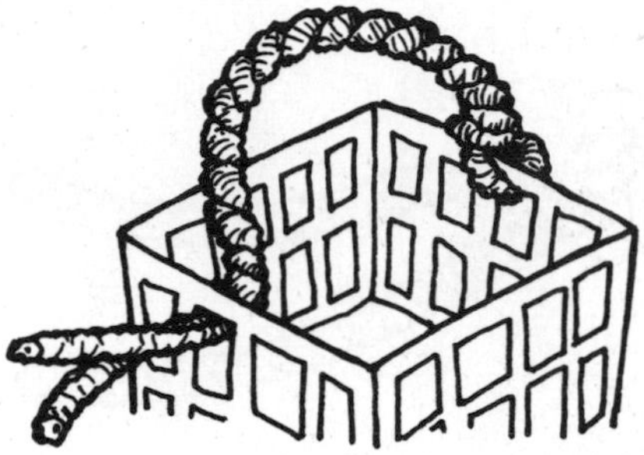

2. Wind a length of tape, sticky side out, along the outside top edge of the basket.

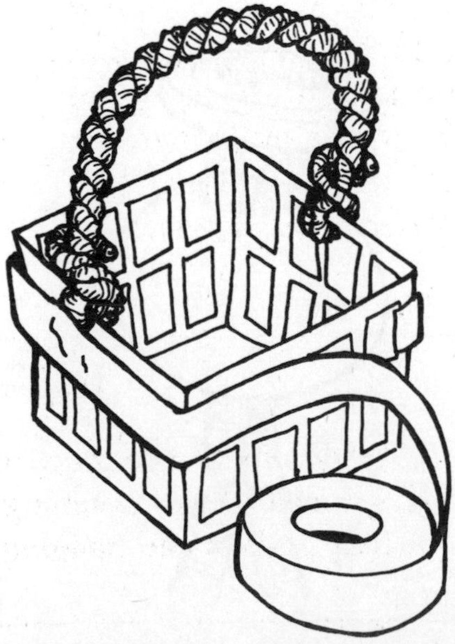

3. Cut many small pieces of tissue, each about 5 cm (2 in.) square.

4. Poke the eraser end of the pencil into the center of a square of tissue paper. Scrunch the tissue around the pencil and press it firmly onto the taped part of the basket. Keep going until the tape is covered. Add more tape and tissue if you wish.

You will need

2 different-colored pipe cleaners

◎

a plastic berry basket

◎

masking tape and scissors

◎

lots of colors of tissue paper

◎

a ruler

◎

an unsharpened pencil with an eraser

Bead buddies

These instructions are for making one bead buddy, but with beads in a variety of colors, shapes and sizes, you can create dozens of different buddies.

You will need

1½ pipe cleaners

a large button

a large bead

small and medium-sized beads

yarn

scissors

paint and a brush or permanent markers

1. Fold the long pipe cleaner in half and thread on the button. This is the hat.

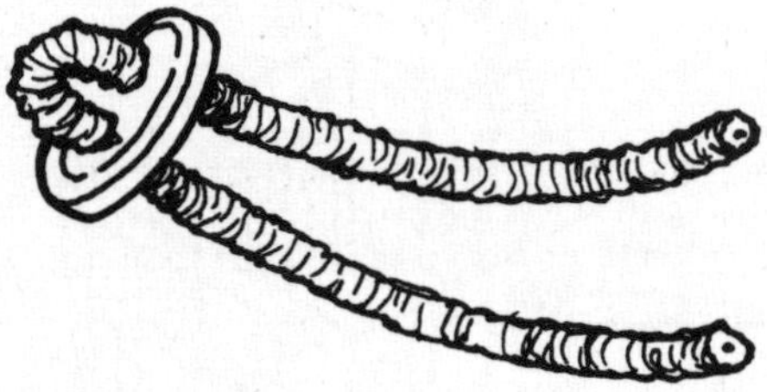

2. Thread the large bead onto both ends of the pipe cleaner and slide it up to the hat.

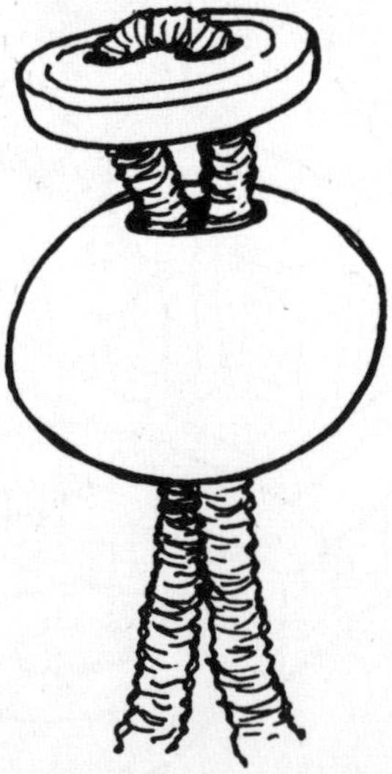

3. For the arms, place the short pipe cleaner between the folded one, just below the large head bead.

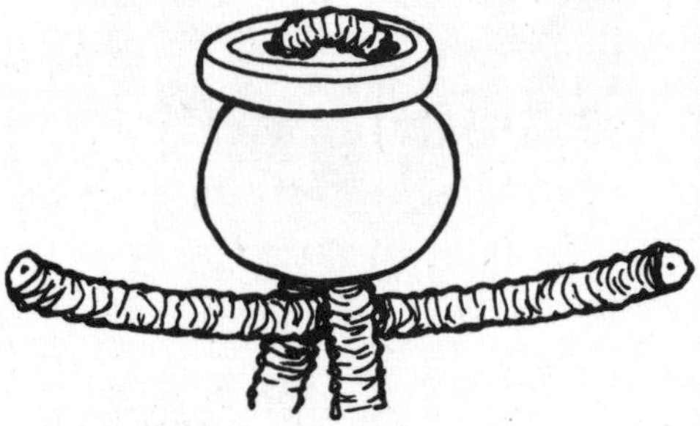

4. Thread a few beads with large holes up both pipe cleaner legs to make the body.

5. Separate the legs and thread on beads. Leave enough space on the ends to make small loops. Bend them up to look like feet.

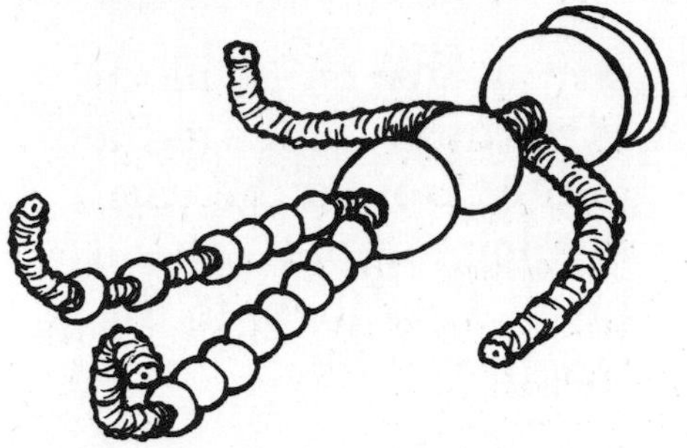

6. Bead the arms, too, leaving enough space to make loops for hands.

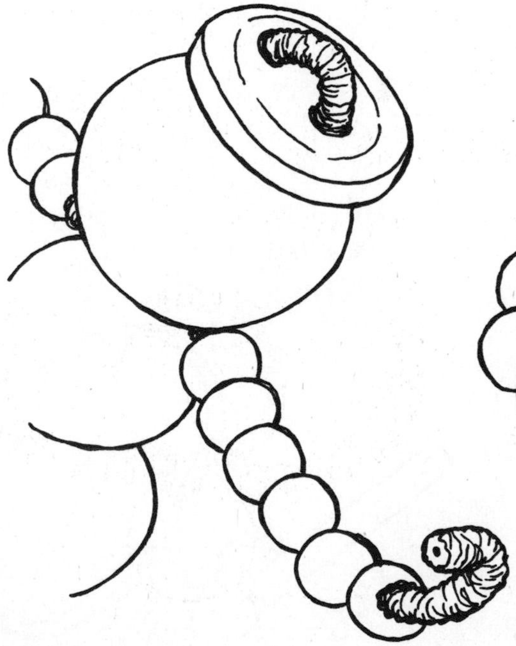

7. Cut two or three strands of yarn for the hair. Tie the yarn under the button hat. Style the hair by braiding, twisting or unraveling it.

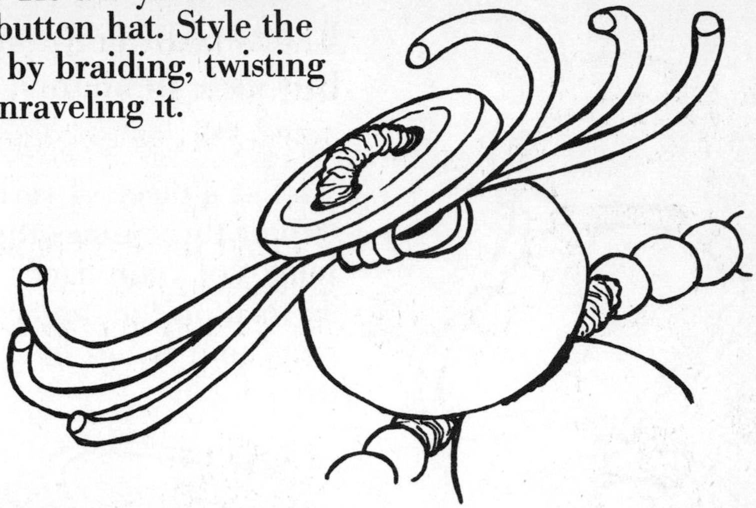

8. Draw or paint on a face. Name your new buddy!

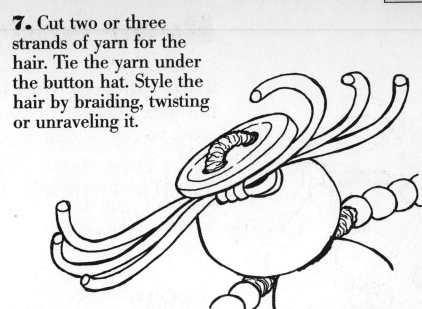

Bead-baby necklace

Use two different-sized beads with large holes for this cute pendant.

1. Cut a piece of yarn two or three times the length of your arm. Thread on the larger bead so it hangs in the center.

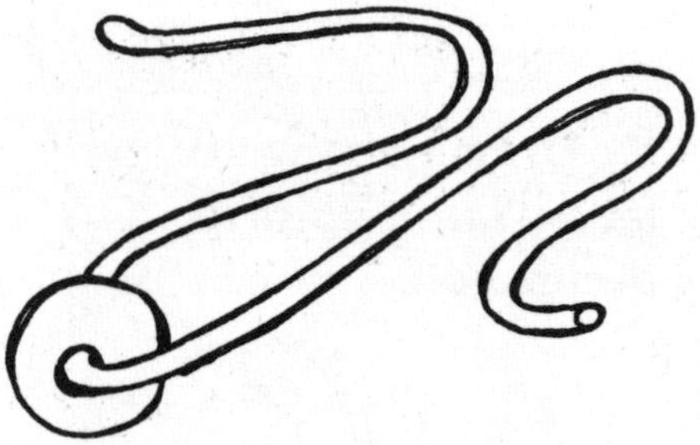

2. Hold the yarn ends together and thread both of them through the smaller head bead.

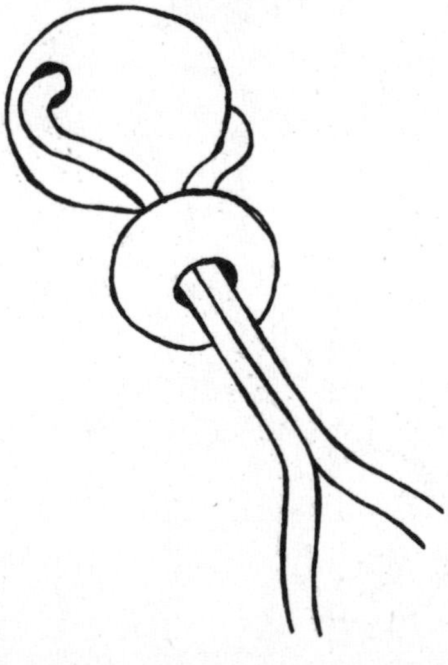

3. Cut five or six pieces of yarn for hair. Tie them tightly around the yarn coming out of the head bead. Trim them to the length you like.

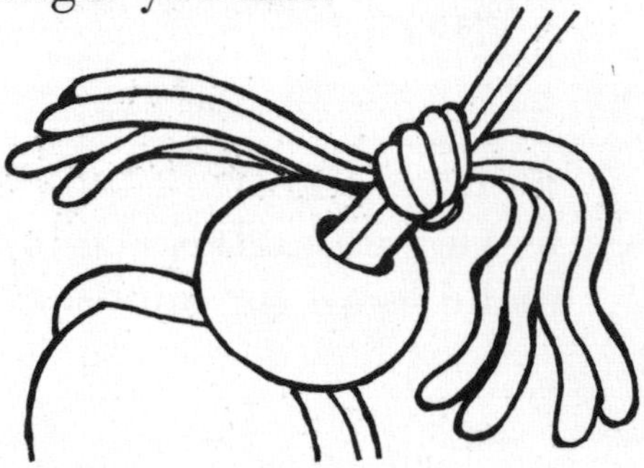

4. Draw or paint on a face. Try the necklace around your neck. Knot and trim the yarn so you can easily get it off and on.

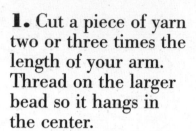

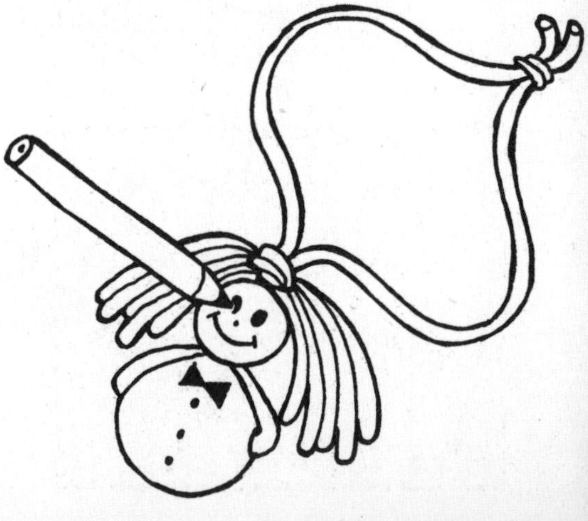

You will need

yarn

scissors

2 different-sized beads

paint and a brush, markers or small roly eyes

Beaded jewelry

By using elastic thread for this bracelet, necklace or anklet, you do not need a clasp.

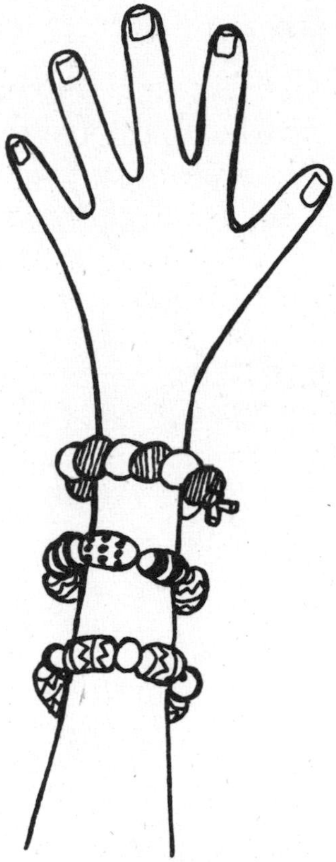

1. Cut a length of elastic thread about 30 cm (12 in.) long for a bracelet or anklet or at least 75 cm (30 in.) long for a necklace.

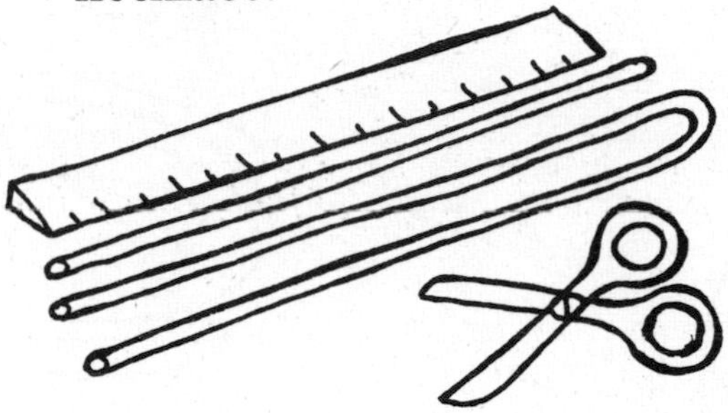

2. Thread on a bead and tie it near the end of the elastic thread.

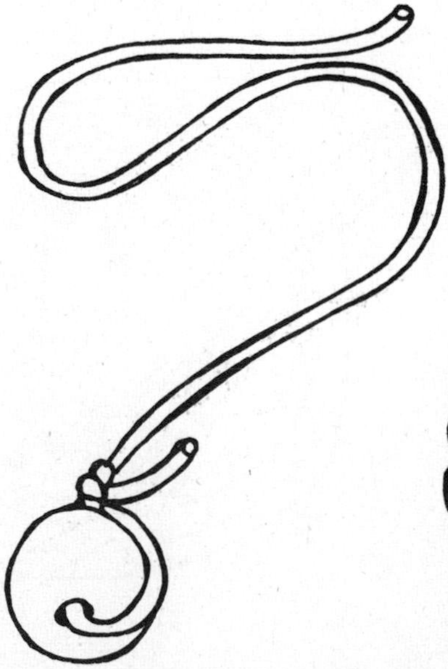

3. Thread on more beads. If your elastic thread frays, trim off the end and keep going.

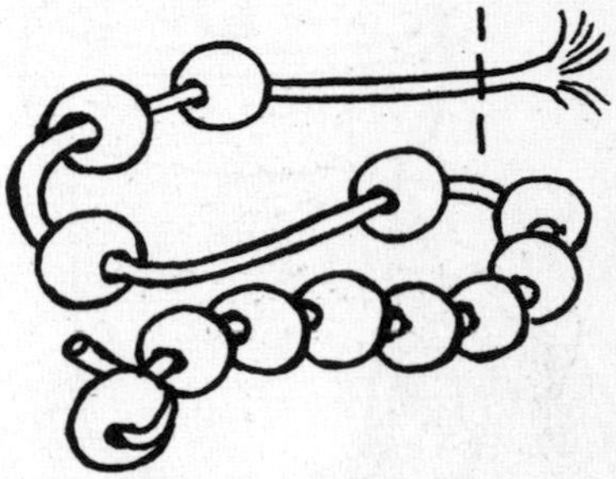

4. Try on your piece of jewelry. Take off or add on beads until it fits. Tightly knot the ends together.

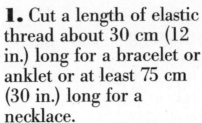

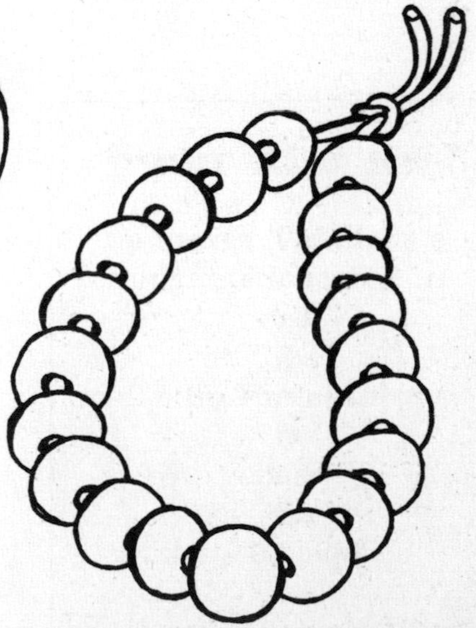

You will need

elastic thread or cord
◎
scissors and a ruler
◎
a variety of beads

Plant coaster

This coaster can be used for a cup, vase or potted plant. You can use beads that are different colors, but they should be the same size.

1. Spread a layer of glue in the lid.

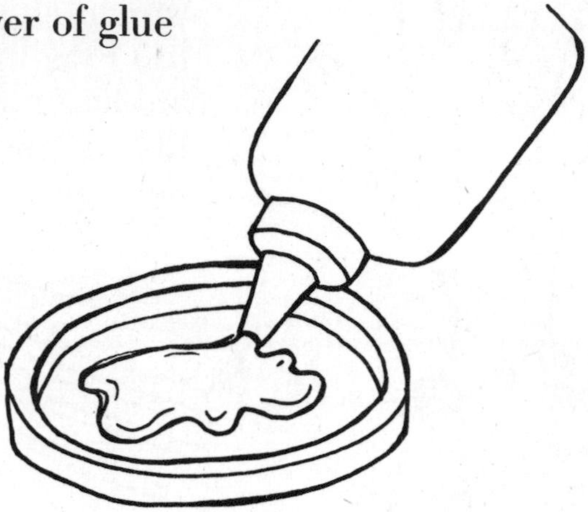

2. Pour in the beads. Move them around so there are no empty spaces. Allow the glue to dry overnight.

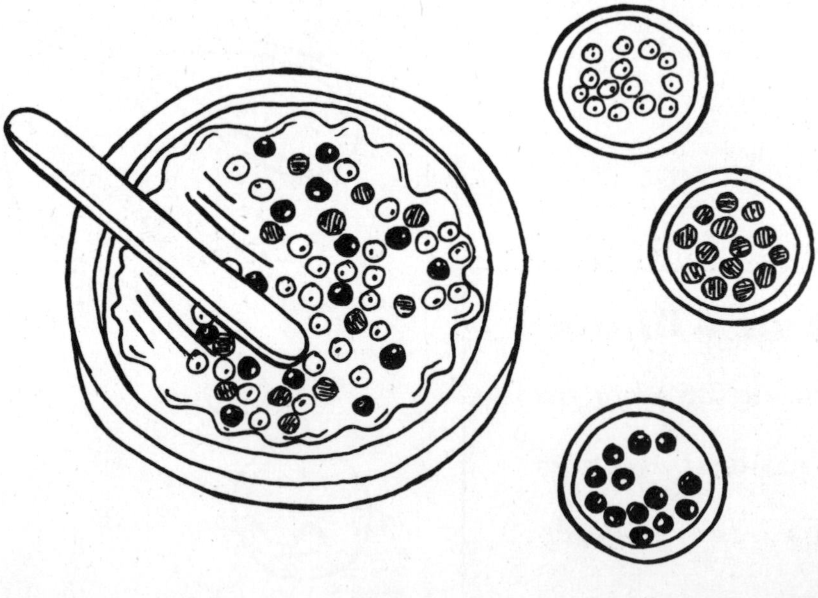

You will need

a shallow lid from a yogurt or margarine tub

white craft glue

beads

a Popsicle stick

Beaded star

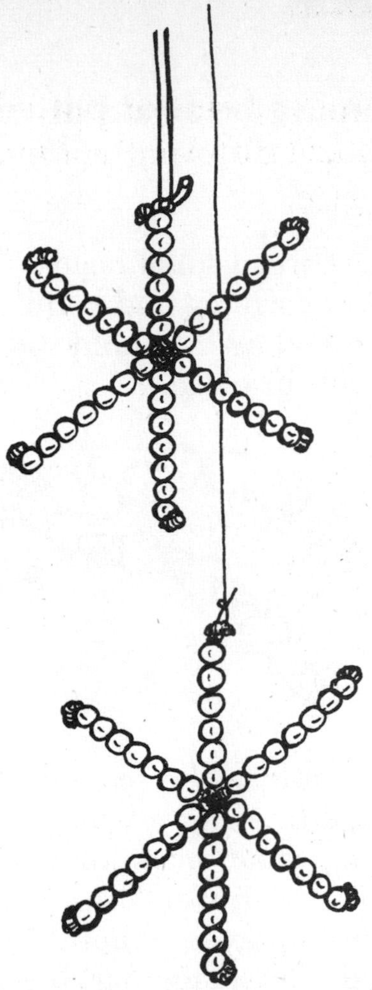

Once you've made this star, try using white beads on white or blue pipe cleaners to make a snowflake.

1. Cut both pipe cleaners in half. Set one half piece aside for a different project.

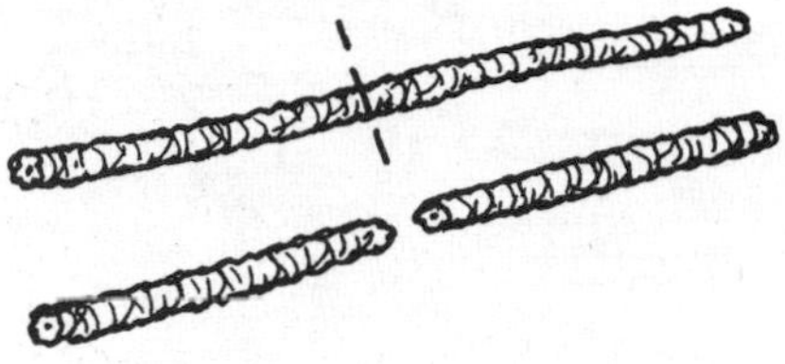

2. Hold the three pipe-cleaner pieces so the ends are even. Twist them together in the center. Spread the pipe cleaners apart to make a star shape.

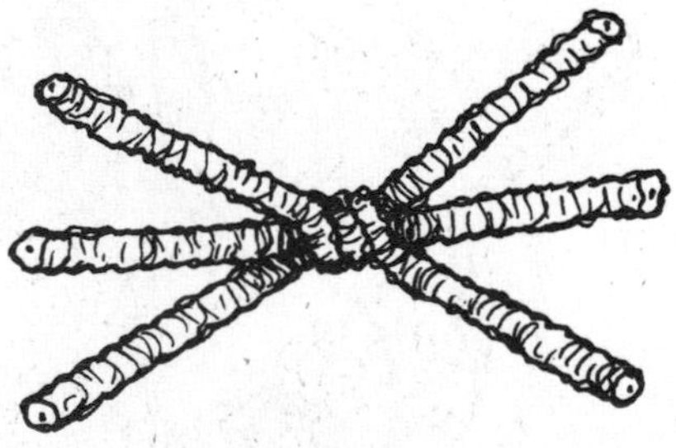

3. Thread beads on one point of the star. Fold over the end of the pipe cleaner to keep the beads in place. Bead the other five points the same way.

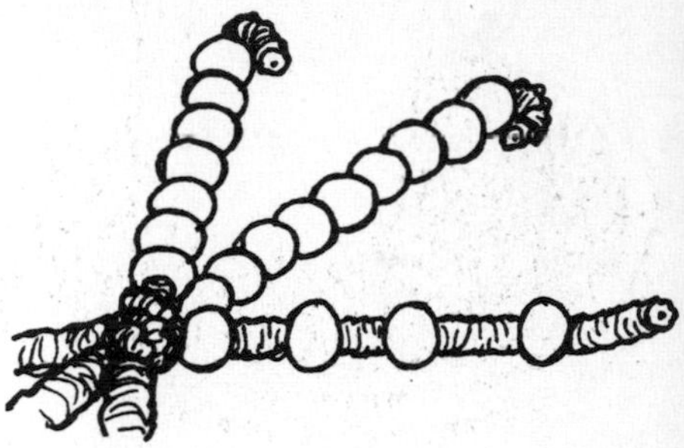

4. To hang up your star, tie thread or fishing line on one of the points. It looks nice in a window.

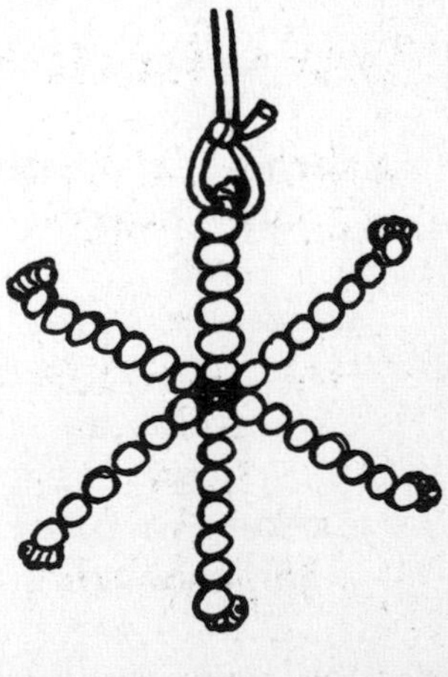

You will need

2 pipe cleaners
◎
scissors
◎
sparkling beads
◎
thread or fishing line

Beady spider

Not even Little Miss Muffet would be afraid of this cute spider!

1. Cut the pipe cleaners in half. Twist them together in the center. Spread some glue on the center area.

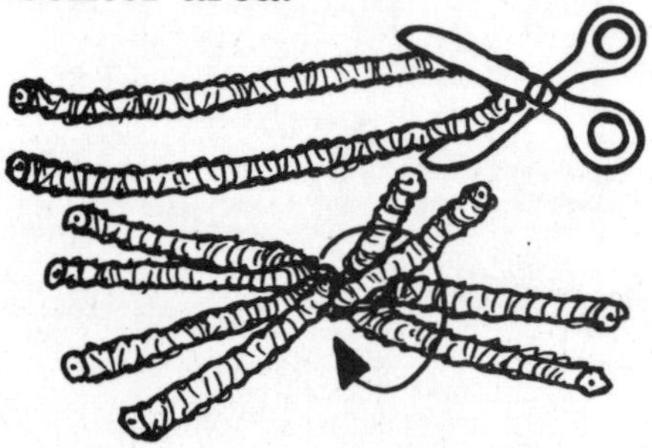

2. Thread a large bead onto the pipe-cleaner legs until it reaches the glue in the center. Spread the legs out.

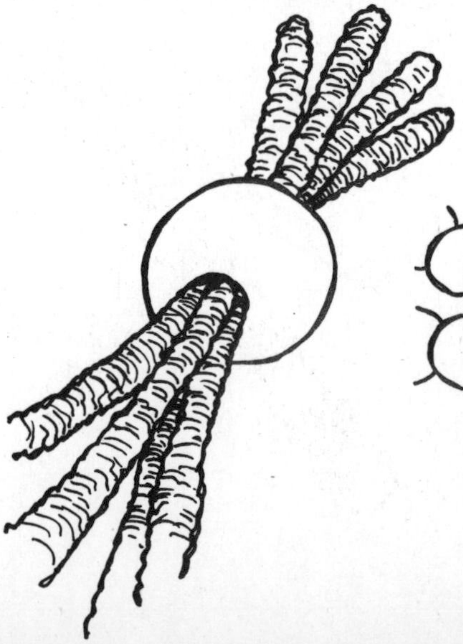

3. Thread small beads onto each leg and bend the end over to hold the beads in place.

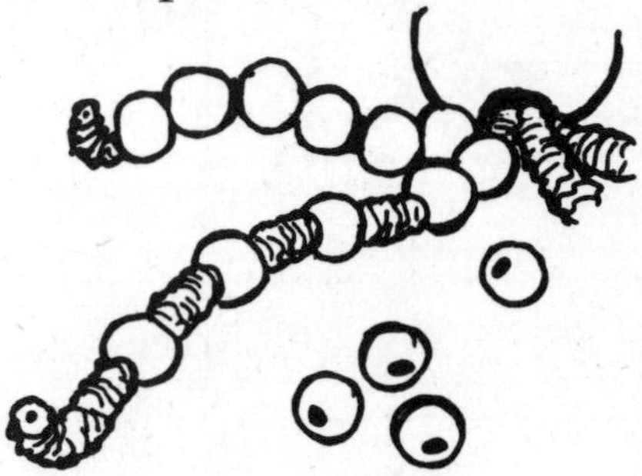

4. Glue on the second large bead for a head and a small bead for a nose, as shown. Draw or paint on eyes, a mouth and interesting markings.

You will need

2 pipe cleaners

scissors

2 large beads with large holes

white craft glue

small beads

markers or paint and a brush

Striped snake

If you don't have narrow ribbon, you can use yarn, embroidery floss or other thin, strong cord. You can use different colors than the ones in these instructions.

1. Thread a yellow bead onto the ribbon so it hangs in the center.

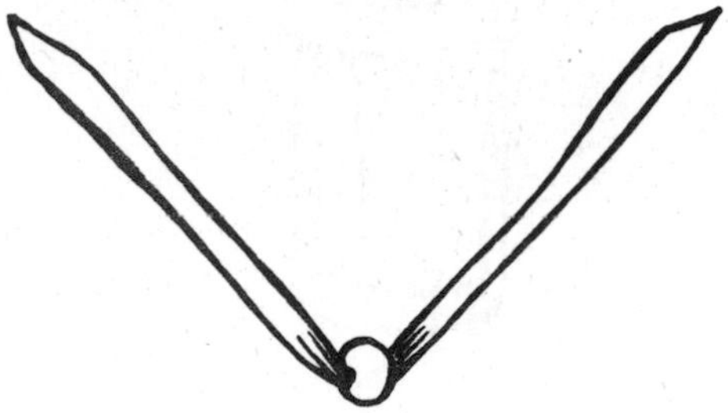

2. Hold both ribbon ends together and thread on a red bead, a yellow bead, a red bead and so on until you have about 10 of each color.

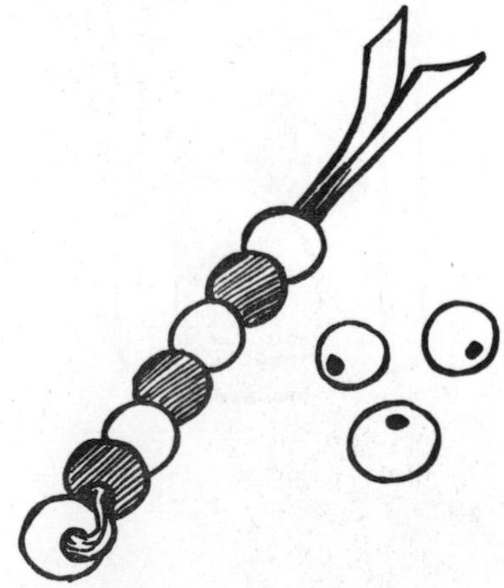

3. To make the head, separate the ribbon ends and thread three yellow beads onto each end.

4. Knot the ribbon ends together to hold on the beads. Trim them to look like a snake's tongue. Draw on eyes.

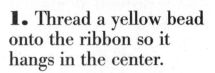

You will need

- about 50 cm (20 in.) of narrow red ribbon
- wooden or pony beads in red and yellow
- scissors
- a permanent marker

Growing beans

Use a clear plastic cup or small jar to hold this natural wonder.

1. Wet the paper towel. Place it in the container so it is pressed all around the inside.

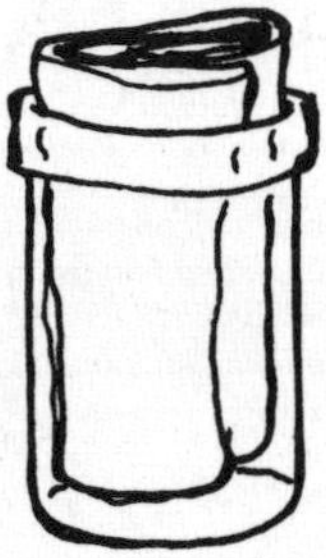

2. Place one or two bean seeds between the container and the paper towel.

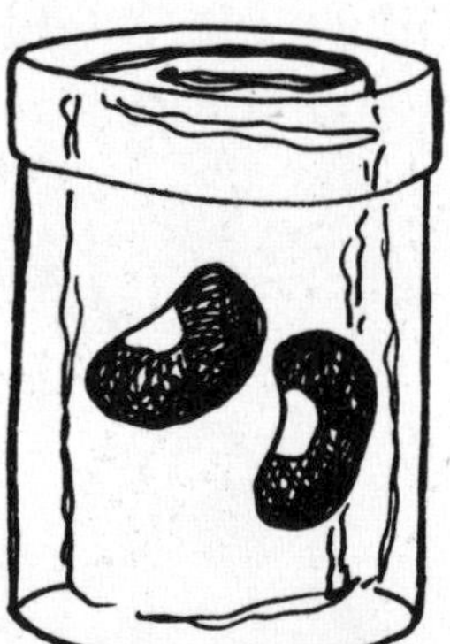

3. Place the container where you can see it. Wet the paper towel when it begins to get dry.

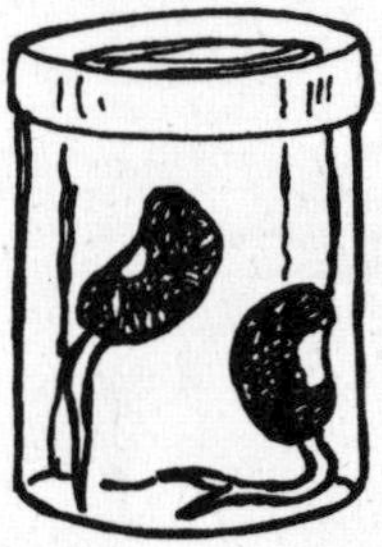

4. After the bean seeds sprout and have a few leaves, you can plant them outside in good weather, or inside in a pot with soil.

You will need

a paper towel or a small clean cloth

a clear container

bean seeds

Mosaics

For this project, use a variety of beans, such as white navy, red kidney and soybeans.

1. Draw a simple picture on the cardboard.

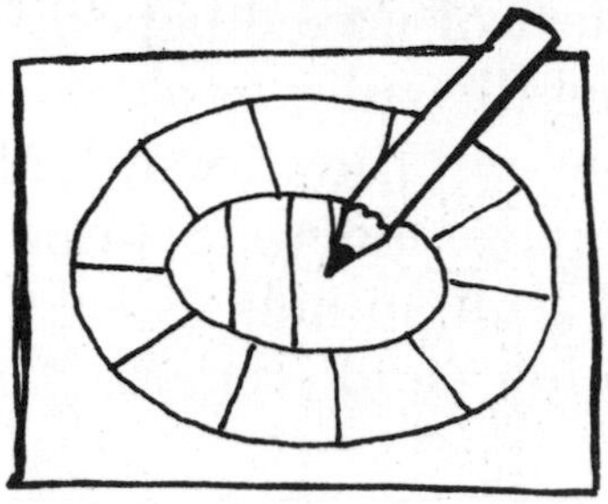

2. Experiment with different bean sizes, shapes and colors on all areas of your picture.

3. Glue the beans in place. Allow the picture to dry completely before you hang it up.

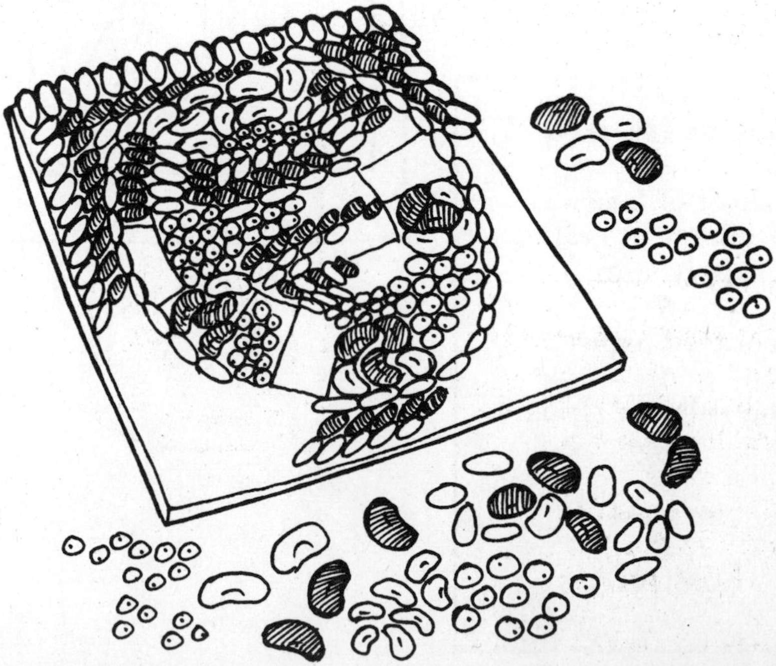

You will need

a pencil and white craft glue

◎

thin cardboard (from a cereal box)

◎

beans

Beeswax candles

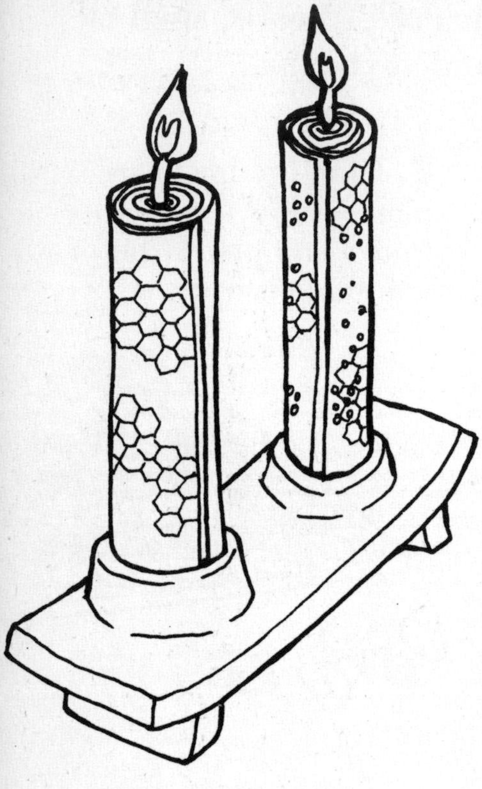

These beautiful, naturally sweet-smelling candles are easy to make. Roll them in glitter for sparkly candles.

1. Place the beeswax on a sheet of waxed paper. Using the ruler as a guide, cut the wax in half along the length. Set one half aside to make another candle later.

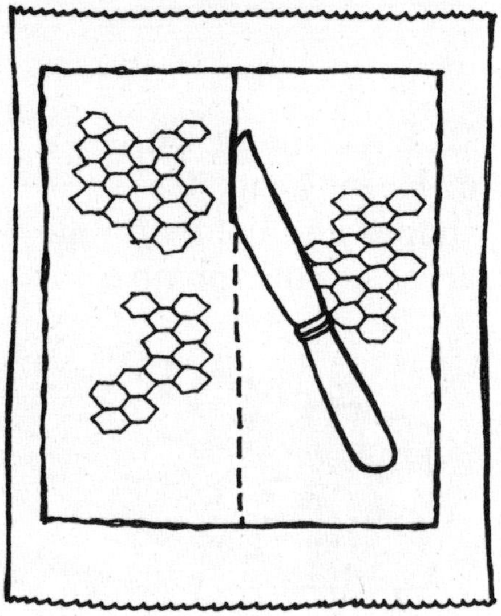

2. Cut a piece of candlewick about 5 cm (2 in.) longer than the short end of the wax. Place the wick along one end so that some of it hangs over at each side.

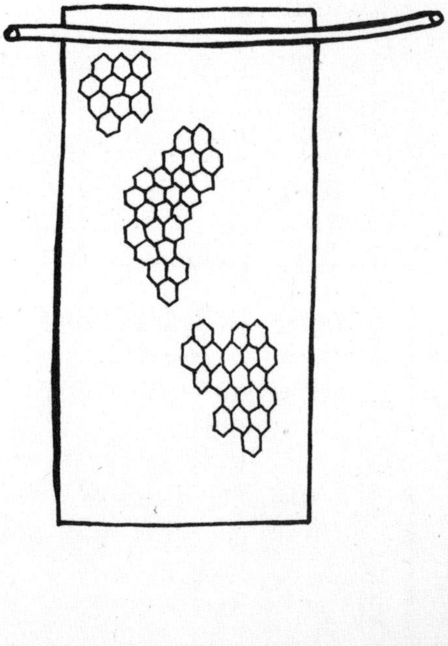

You will need

a sheet of beeswax (available at craft-supply stores)

waxed paper

a long ruler or straight edge

scissors

candlewick

3. Roll and press the edge of the wax onto the wick. It helps if your hands are warm. If the wax cracks, press it firmly over the wick and it will stick.

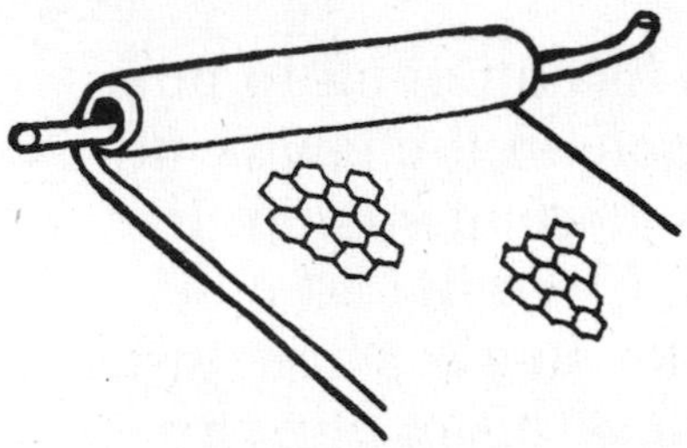

4. Tightly roll the wax. Try to keep both side edges even.

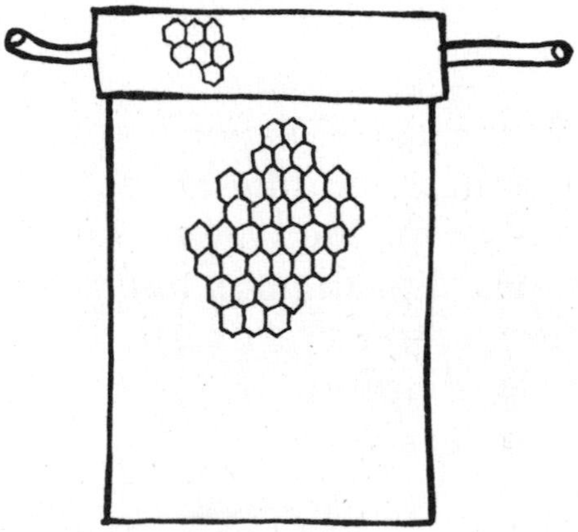

5. As you finish rolling the wax, press the end firmly onto the candle. (If it doesn't stick, blow it with a hair dryer to soften it a little.)

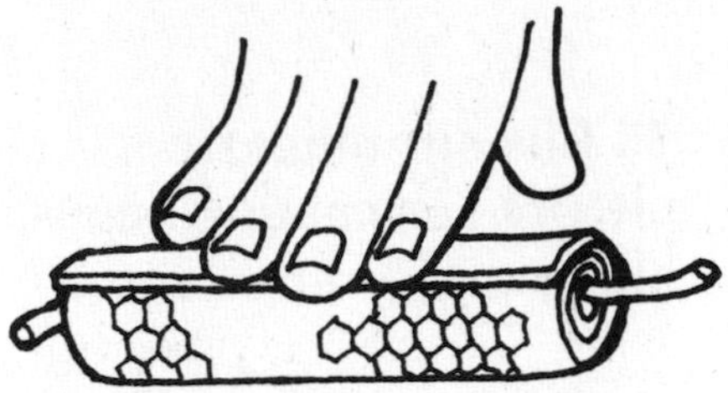

6. Decide which end of your candle will be the top. Trim off the wick at the bottom. Trim the wick to about 1 cm (1/2 in.) at the top.

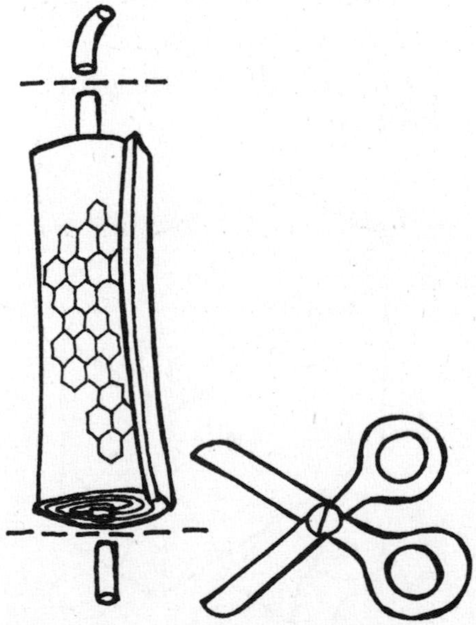

7. Place the candle in a holder that can fit different-sized candles. Have an adult light the candle. Remember to blow it out before you leave the room.

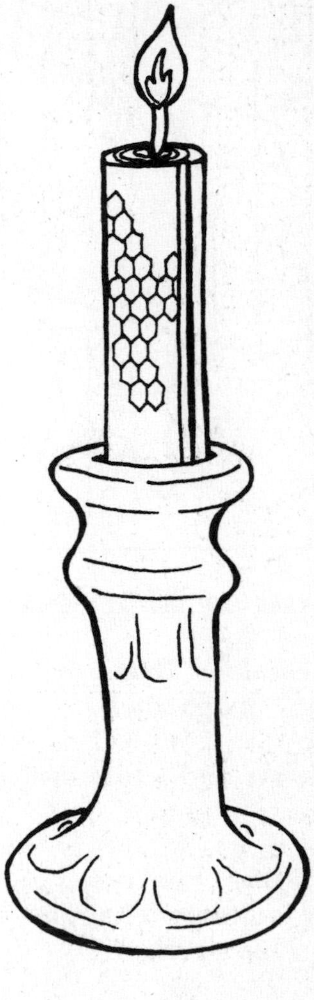

Flip-top toy box

Try using toy ads from flyers and catalogs to cover a laundry-detergent box. If your box has a handle, leave it uncovered.

1. Cut out magazine pictures or catalog pages of toys.

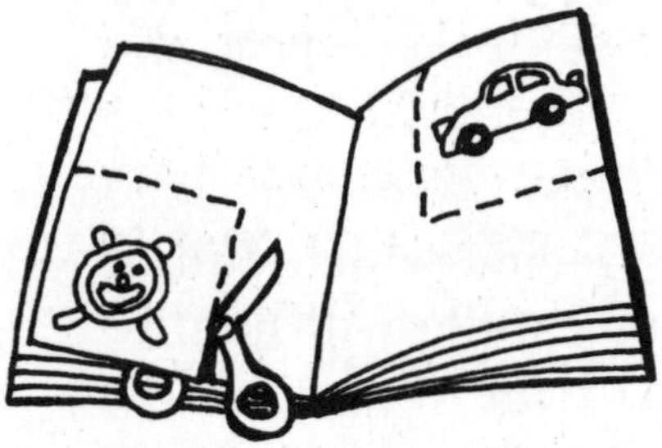

2. Glue the pictures all over the box in any direction. Overlap them so they look like a collage. Allow the glue to dry.

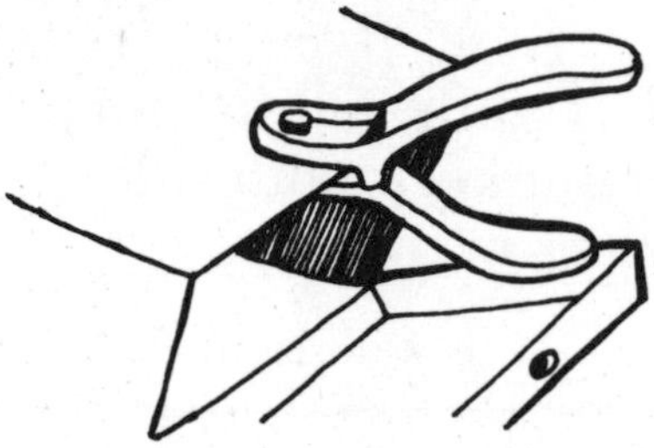

3. Ask an adult to poke a hole in the center of the bottom edge of the lid. Close the lid and poke another hole just below this one in the front of the box.

4. Insert the paper fasteners into the holes, and cover the backs with tape. Shut the box and tie it closed with yarn wound around the fasteners.

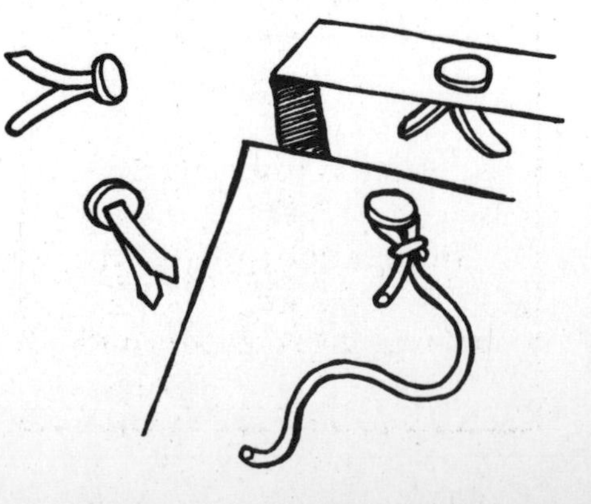

You will need

catalogs, flyers or magazines
◎
scissors and white craft glue
◎
a flip-top box, any size (a laundry-detergent box works well)
◎
2 paper fasteners
◎
strong tape, such as duct tape
◎
yarn

Shoebox wagon

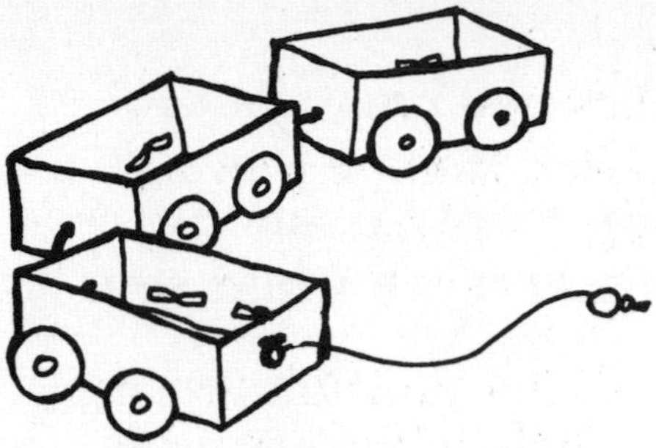

When you pull this wagon on a carpet, the wheels really go around! If you want to pull something heavy in the wagon, glue together two circles of cardboard for each wheel. You can make a train by tying more wagons to the first one.

1. Place the cup or lid on the cardboard, trace it four times and cut out the circles.

You will need

thin cardboard (from a cereal box)

a cup or lid for tracing

a pencil, an eraser and scissors

a shoebox

4 paper fasteners

string, cord or twine

a large bead (optional)

2. Place a cardboard wheel on the eraser and use the pencil to poke a hole into its center. (The eraser makes it easier to poke into the cardboard.) Repeat this with the other wheels.

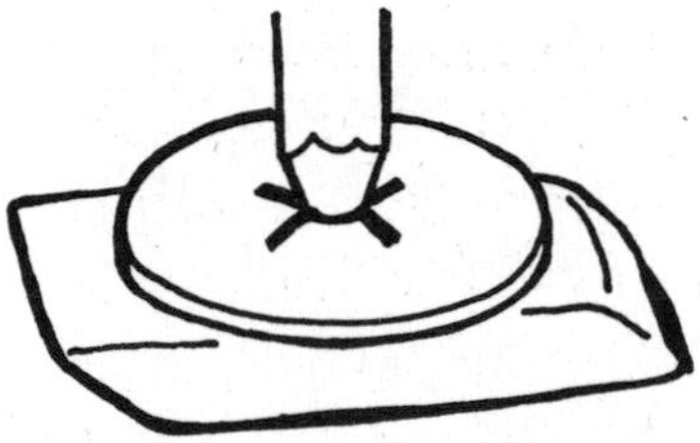

3. Hold a wheel against the side of the shoebox so that a little of it is below the bottom of the box. Poke a hole in the box through the hole in the wheel. Do the same for the other three wheels and attach all of them with the paper fasteners.

4. Poke a hole near the top of one end of the box and thread a pull string through it. Knot the string in place. If you like, tie a bead onto the other end of the string.

Tissue-box dollhouse

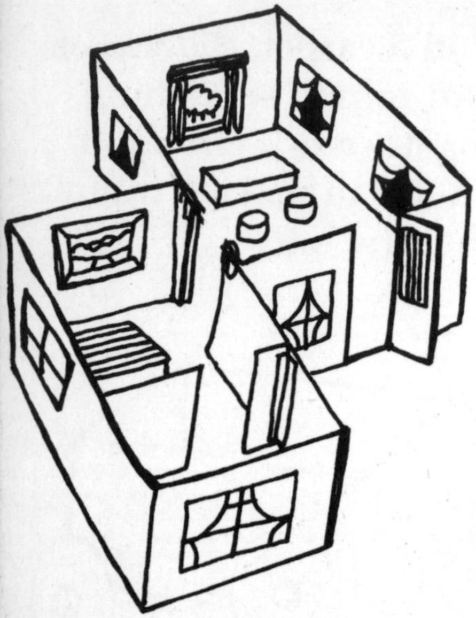

This dollhouse is made from empty tissue boxes. Begin with two rooms and add more when you have other empty boxes.

1. Cut the tops off the boxes.

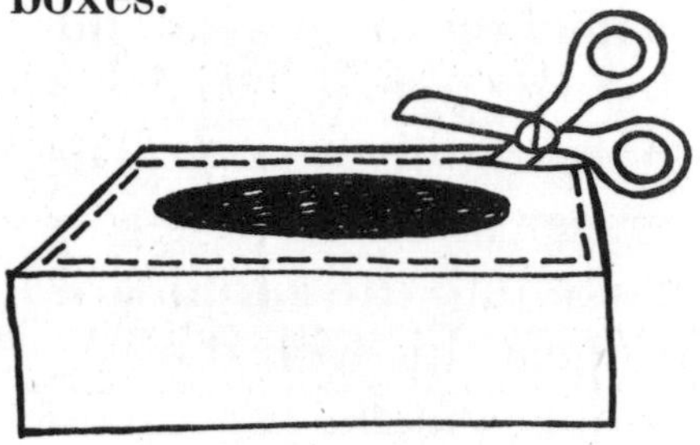

2. Use the paper clips to fasten the boxes together side by side or end to end.

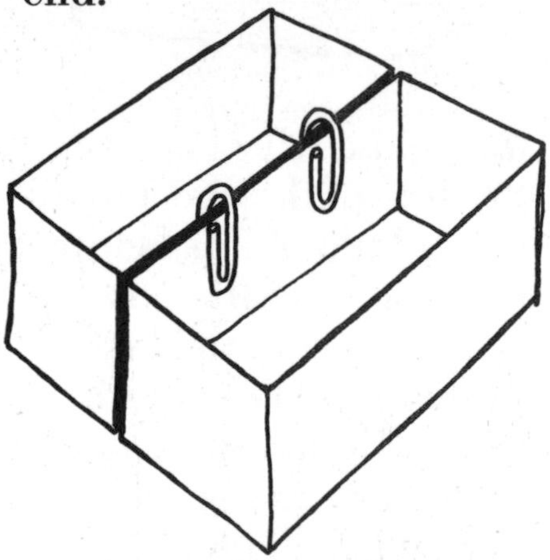

3. Make doorways between the rooms by cutting out pieces of the boxes. (You will need to unfasten the boxes to cut along the bottom edges.)

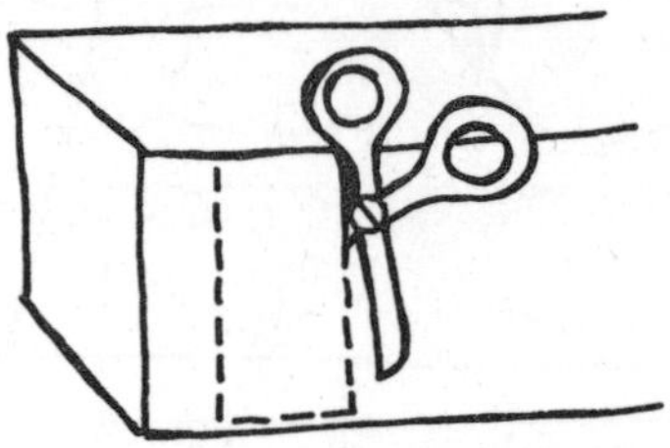

4. Create an outside door by making a cut down the side of one of the boxes. Also cut it across the bottom edge to the size you want. Fold back the door so it looks hinged.

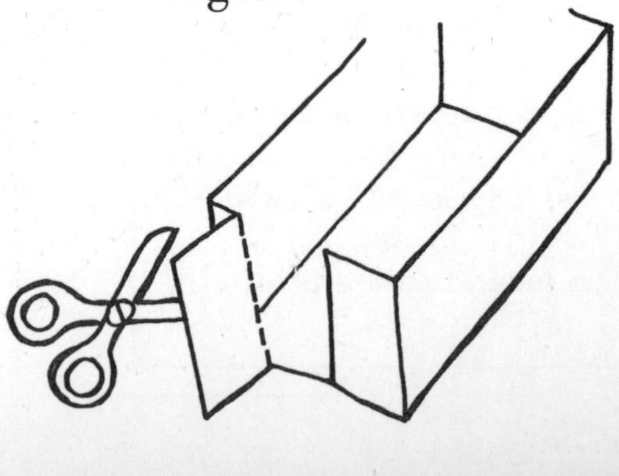

You will need

2 or more empty tissue boxes
◎
large paper clips
◎
scissors
◎
catalog pictures, white craft glue and other craft supplies (see step 5)

5. Now comes the fun part – decorating the rooms! Here are some ideas:

• Paint the walls or paste on construction paper, fabric or leftover wallpaper.

• Use fun fur, felt, fleece or carpet scraps for floor coverings.

• Decorate wooden blocks to make dressers, counters or a TV.

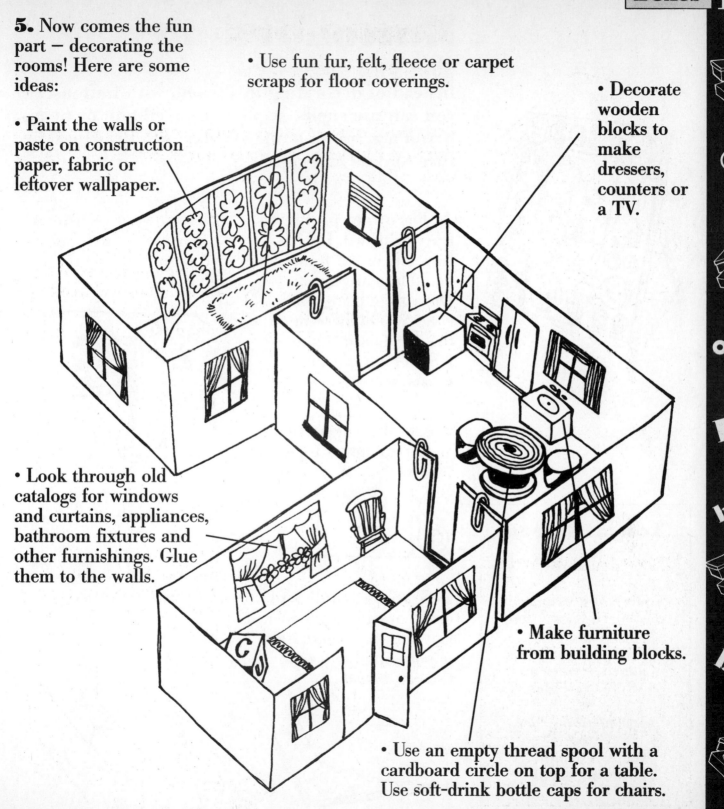

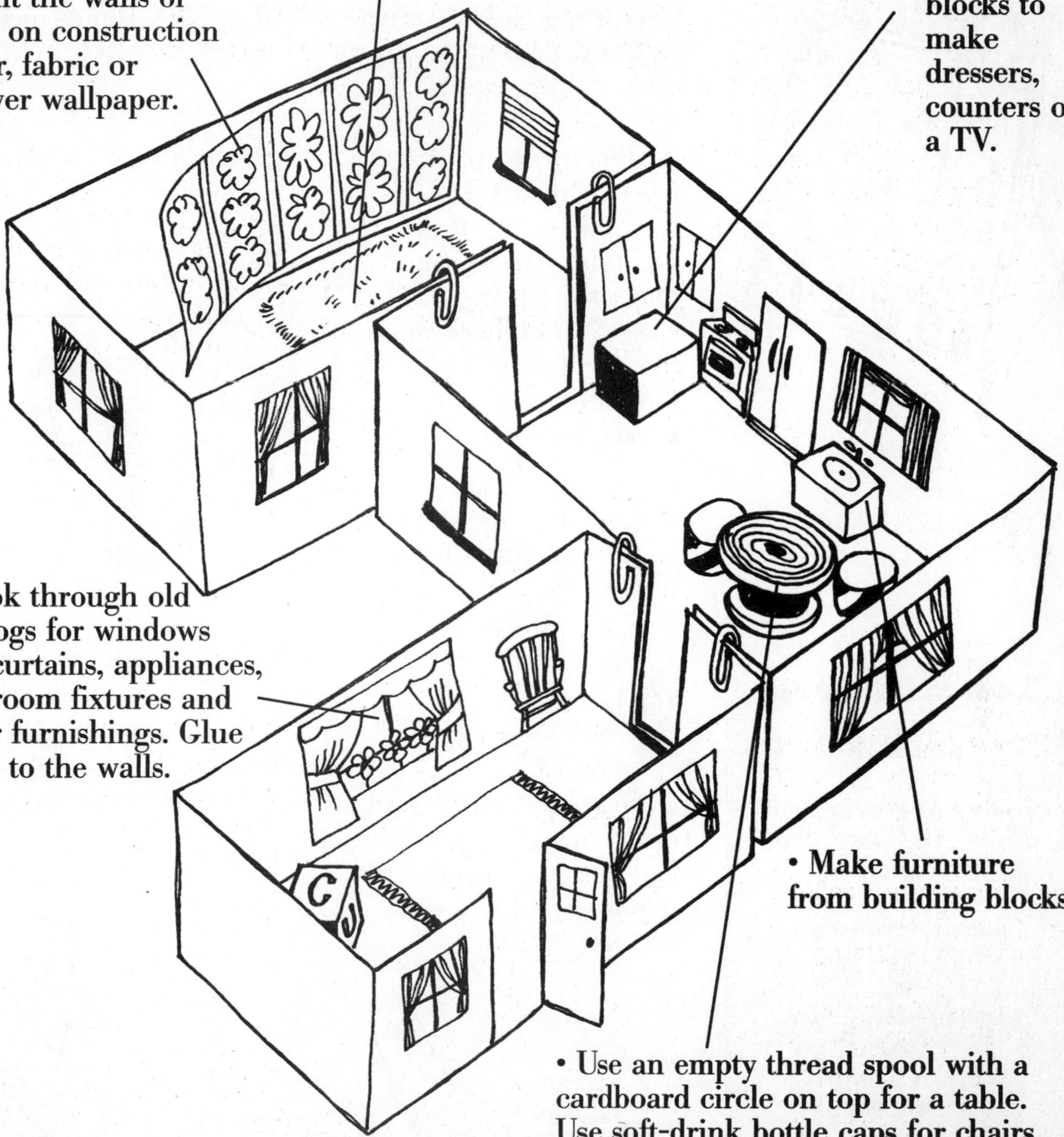

• Look through old catalogs for windows and curtains, appliances, bathroom fixtures and other furnishings. Glue them to the walls.

• Make furniture from building blocks.

• Use an empty thread spool with a cardboard circle on top for a table. Use soft-drink bottle caps for chairs.

Button frame

Instead of decorating this frame with buttons, you can use shells, sequins, lace, ribbon or beans. If you are framing one of your own drawings, be sure to date and sign it.

1. Place your picture on the cardboard. Decide how much of a frame you'd like around it. Draw lines using the ruler as a guide. Cut out the cardboard frame. (Do not cut out the center area.)

2. Trace the cardboard onto construction paper. Cut out the construction paper and glue it onto the cardboard.

3. Glue your picture in the center. Glue buttons all around it. Let the glue dry.

4. For a stand, cut a strip of cardboard almost as tall as the frame. Fold it about one-third from the top and glue the bent part to the center top area of the back of the frame.

You will need

a picture

◎

a piece of corrugated cardboard larger than your picture

◎

a pencil, a ruler and white craft glue

◎

construction paper

◎

buttons or other decorating supplies

Button castanets

Make two of these and join the band!

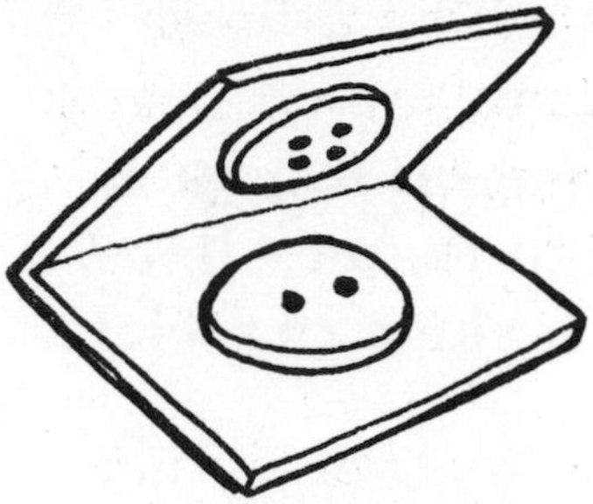

1. Fold the cardboard in half by bending it over the edge of a table so the fold line is straight. Trim the cardboard ends so they are even.

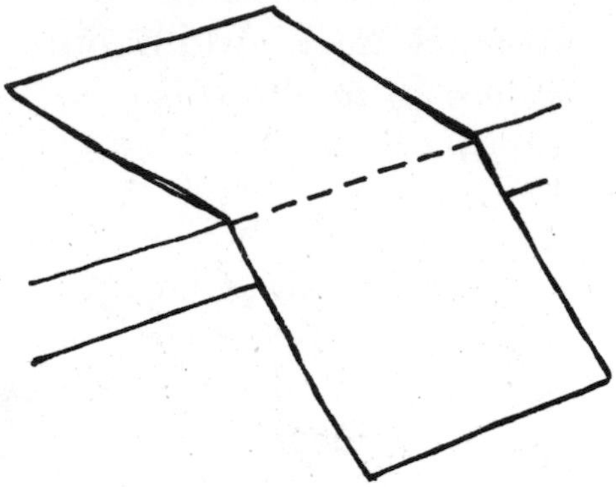

2. Unfold the cardboard. Glue one or more buttons at each end. Allow the glue to dry.

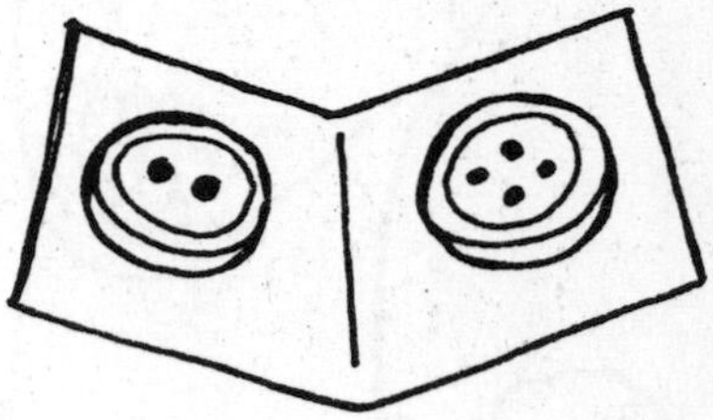

3. Fold the cardboard again and start clacking!

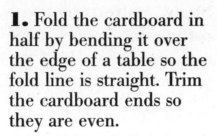

You will need

a strip of cardboard about 15 cm (6 in.) long
◎
scissors
◎
2 or more flat buttons
◎
white craft glue

Stuffed animal collar

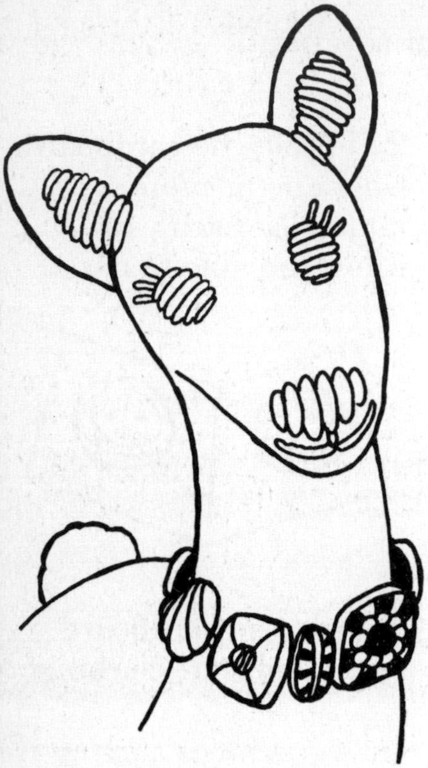

Shank buttons have a looped piece on the back rather than holes straight through them. After making this collar for your toy, make a bracelet or necklace for yourself!

1. Loosely measure the elastic cord around your animal's neck. Add about 15 cm (6 in.) to this length.

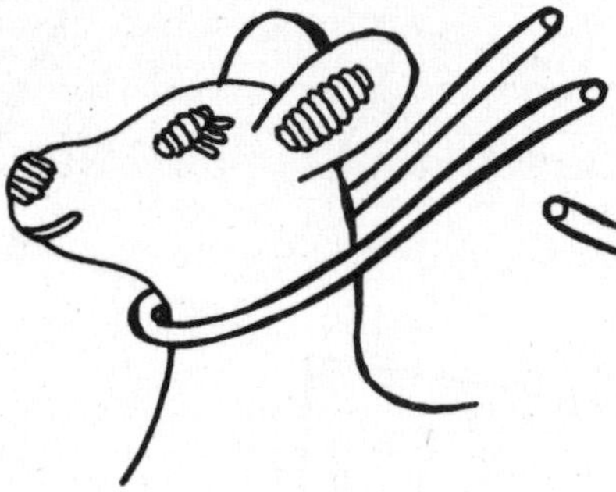

2. Knot a button onto one end of the elastic cord. Leave a tail about 8 cm (3 in.) long.

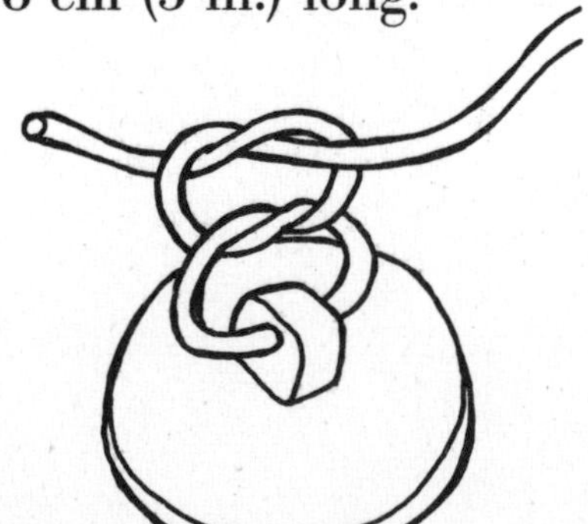

3. Thread on more buttons. If your cord begins to fray, trim off the end and keep going.

4. Try the button collar around your animal's neck. Add more buttons or remove them so the collar fits. Knot the ends together and trim them.

You will need

elastic cord or thread

a ruler and scissors

shank buttons

Button bouquet

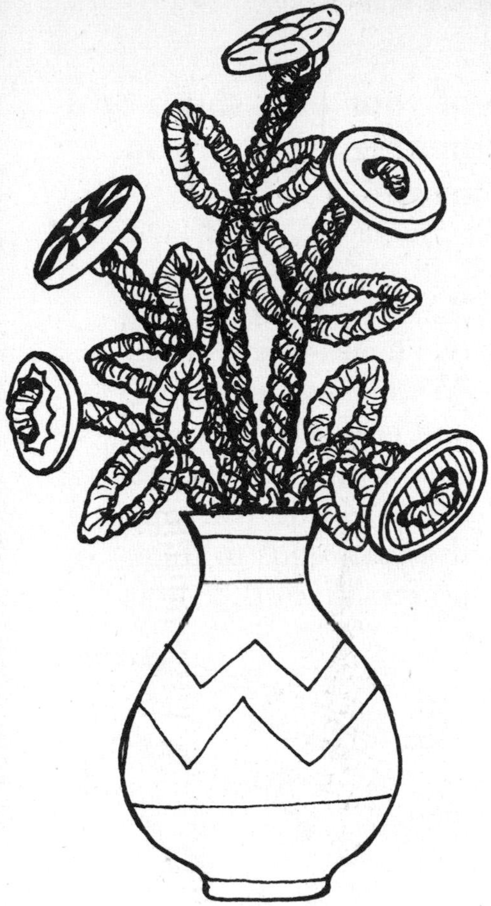

Here's a chance to use some of those extra-large buttons from the button box.

1. Fold a pipe cleaner in half. Thread on a button so it sits at the bent end of the pipe cleaner.

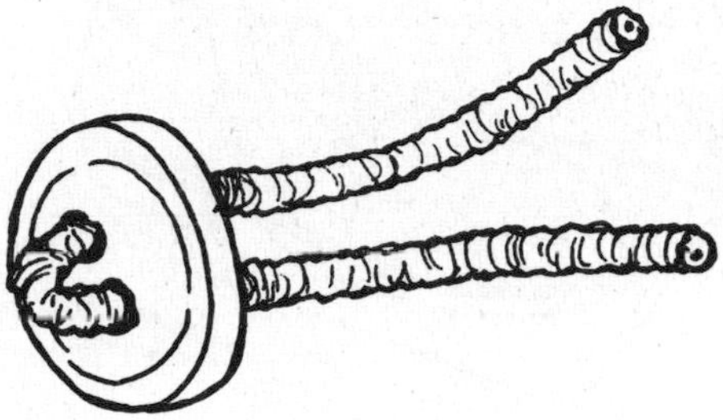

2. Twist the folded pipe cleaner together all the way down its length.

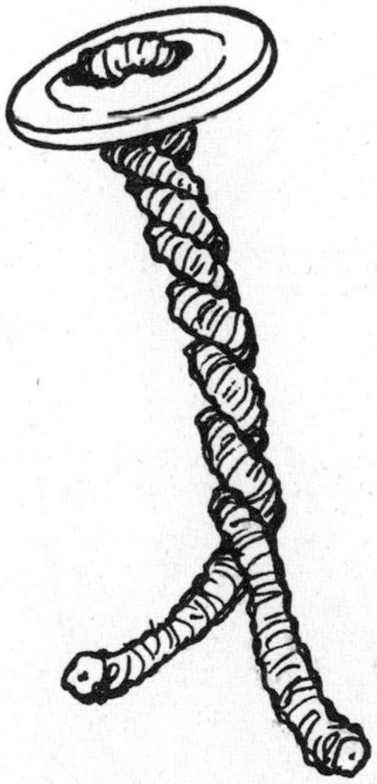

3. To make leaves, twist a green pipe cleaner around the stem. Shape the ends into leaves.

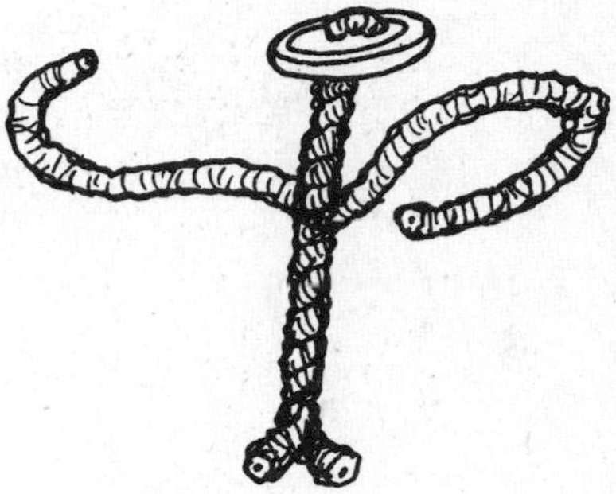

4. Make more button flowers. Tie them together with a ribbon if you like or place them in a vase.

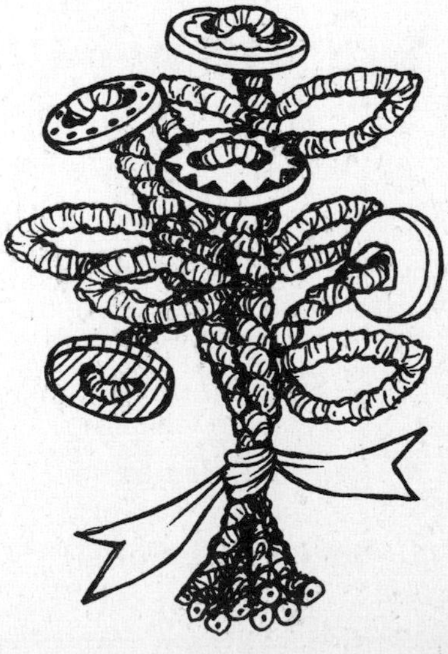

You will need

pipe cleaners

large buttons

ribbon (optional)

Lace-up shoe

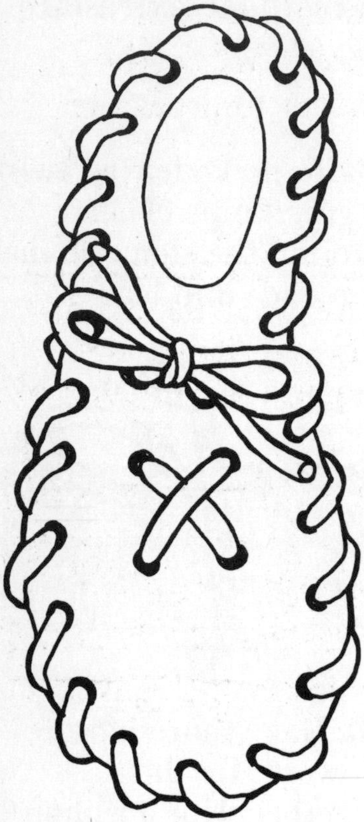

For this project, trace one of your own shoes or a shoe that belongs to someone bigger than you. Then practice tying your laces!

1. Trace a shoe on the cardboard and cut it out.

2. Punch holes around the outside of the shoe. Punch six holes in the center where the lace will go.

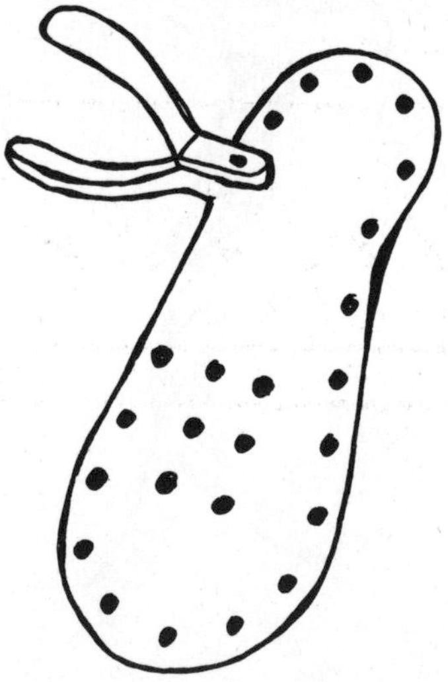

3. Cut a piece of yarn two arm lengths long. Wrap a little tape on one end and "stitch" all the way around the shoe. When you finish, tape the yarn ends to the underside of the shoe.

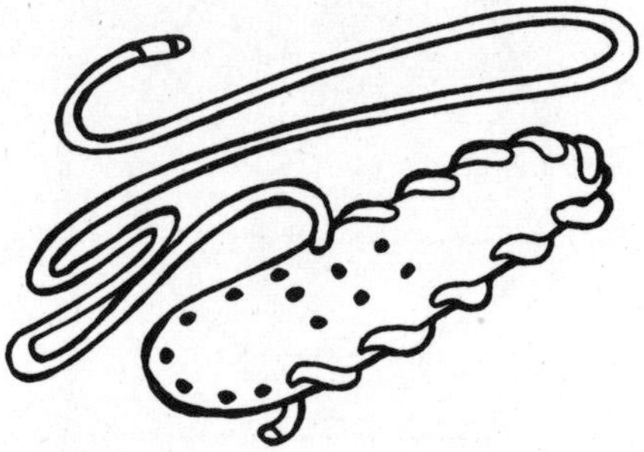

4. Lace up your shoe with yarn or a shoelace and see if you can tie a bow.

You will need

a pencil, scissors and tape

thin cardboard (from a cereal box)

a hole punch

yarn or ribbon

a shoelace (optional)

Royal crown

By using a paper clip to hold this crown together, you can adjust the size. When the clip is removed, the crown is flat and easy to put away.

1. Draw a crown shape onto the cardboard. Cut it out.

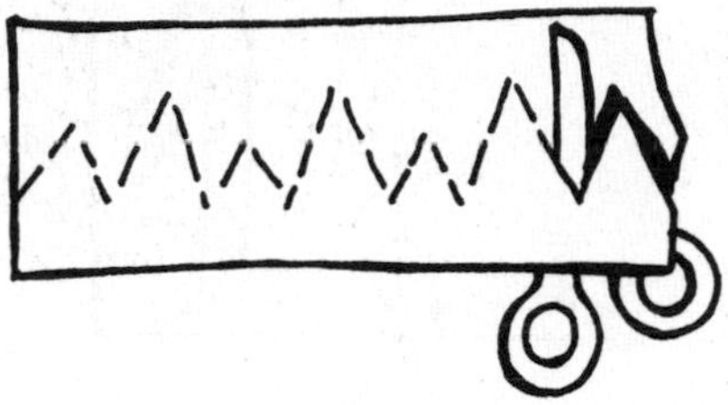

2. Spread glue on the cardboard. Place it glue side down on a strip of fabric or felt. Allow the glue to dry.

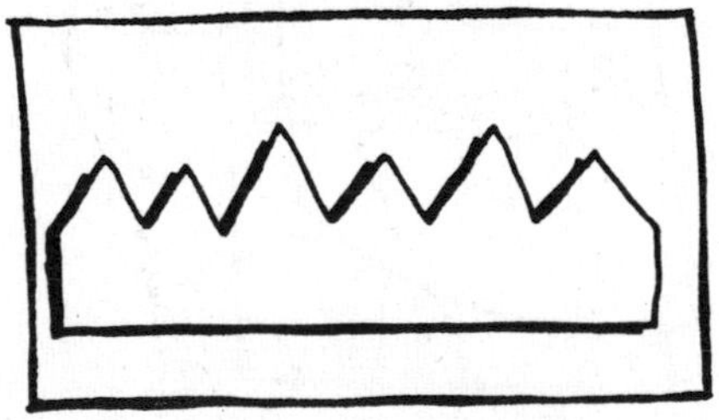

3. Cut out the fabric or felt around the crown. Glue on rhinestones, sequins, lace or other trim.

4. Try on the crown and hold it together with one or two paper clips.

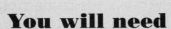

You will need

a pencil, scissors and white craft glue

thin cardboard or poster board, about 64 cm (25 in.) long

plain fabric or felt

supplies for decorating (see step 3)

1 or 2 large paper clips

Scrapbook

Make this scrapbook for cutouts, drawings, stickers and other stuff you wish to keep.

1. Cut two cardboard covers a little larger than a sheet of construction paper.

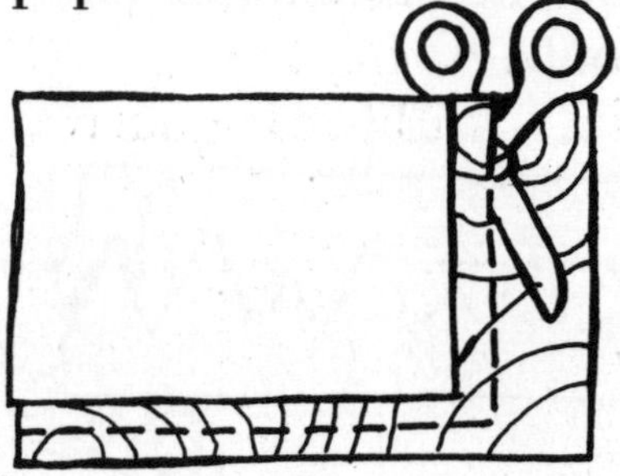

2. Cover the printed sides of the cardboard covers with construction paper.

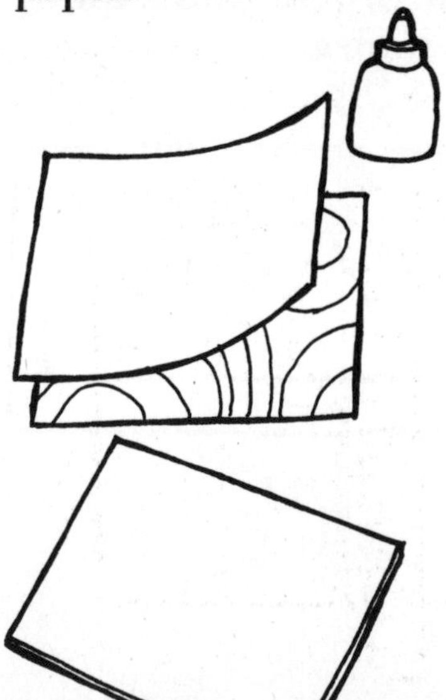

3. Ask an adult to help you hole-punch the covers with three holes each. Use them as a guide to hole-punch 10 or more sheets of construction paper.

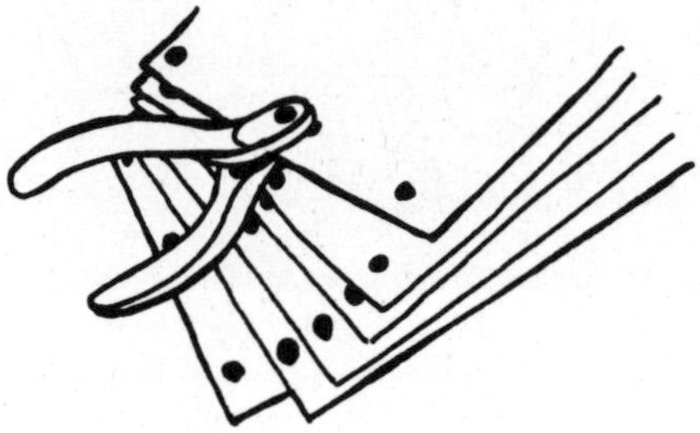

4. Fasten the scrapbook together with ribbon or rings. Decorate the cover.

You will need

thin cardboard (from a cereal box)

scissors, white craft glue and markers or crayons

construction paper

a hole punch

ribbon or binder rings

Tic-tac-toe

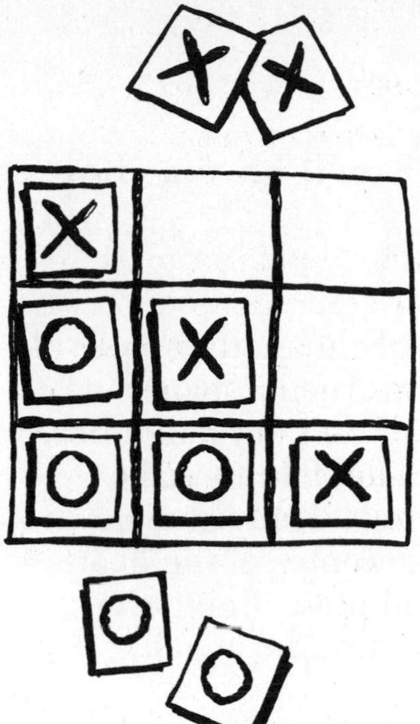

To play this game, one person has the "O" cards and the other has the "X" cards. Take turns placing one of your cards in a square. Whoever gets a row first – up and down, across or corner to corner – wins.

1. Glue construction paper onto a 23 cm (9 in.) cardboard square.

2. Use the ruler as a guide to draw lines on the square to make nine smaller squares.

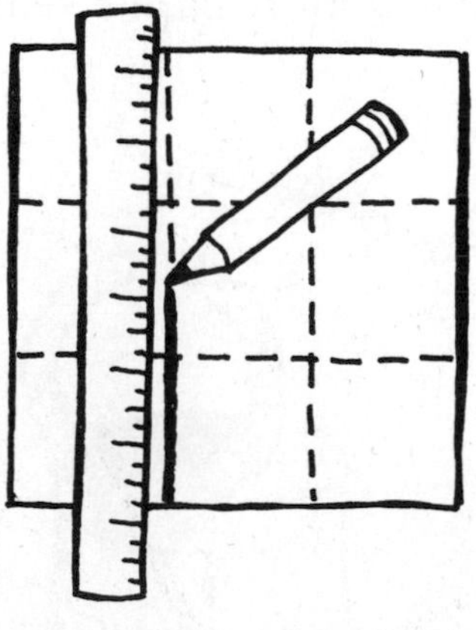

3. Cut 10 small, square pieces of cardboard.

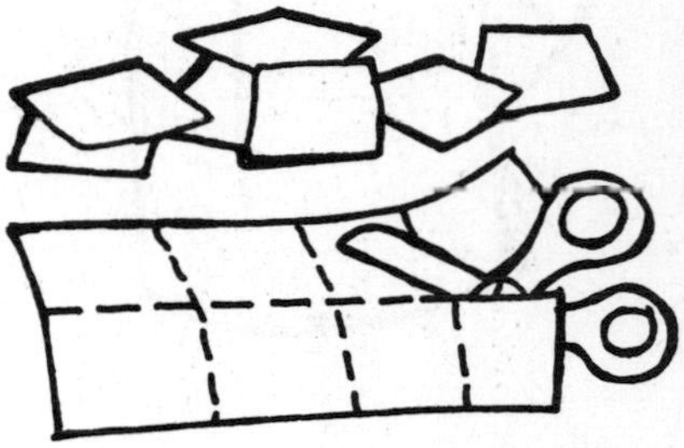

4. Draw a large "O" on five of the squares and an "X" on the other five. Now you're ready to play.

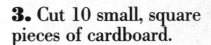

You will need

thin cardboard (from a cereal box)

construction paper

scissors, white craft glue and a ruler

markers

Cardboard-tube angel

If you make a few of these, you'll have a choir of angels.

1. Cut a strip of construction paper big enough to wrap around the roll. Glue or tape it in place.

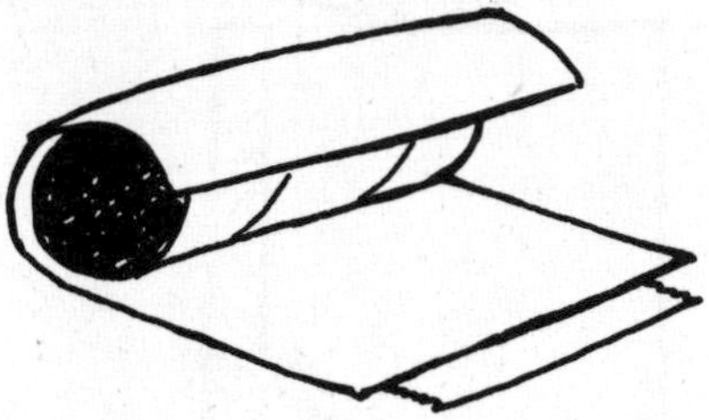

2. For a halo, shape part of a pipe cleaner into a circle with a short tail. Tape it to the back of the roll, along the construction paper seam.

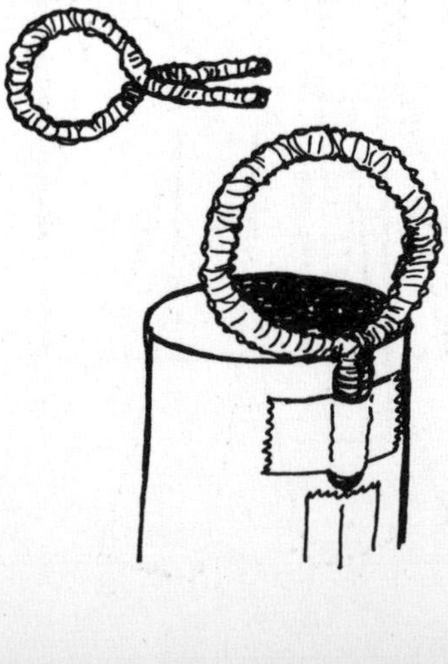

3. Fold another color of construction paper in half. Cut out half a heart on the fold to make wings. Apply glue down the center of the heart and press it onto the back of the angel.

4. Draw on a face and other features if you wish.

You will need

a toilet-paper roll

construction paper

scissors, white craft glue and masking tape

a tinsel or regular pipe cleaner

crayons or markers

Crazy-eight octopus

You won't believe how fast you can make this interesting octopus.

1. For the legs, make eight evenly-spaced cuts two-thirds of the way up the roll.

2. Bend and curl the eight legs so they are spread out.

3. Draw on a face and markings.

You will need

a toilet-paper roll

◎

scissors

◎

crayons or markers

Fishing game

For the fishing rod, use a stick, ruler, unsharpened pencil or whatever else you can find.

1. Cut two slits opposite each other in one end of a roll. Cut a triangle of construction paper and slide it into these slits to make a tail.

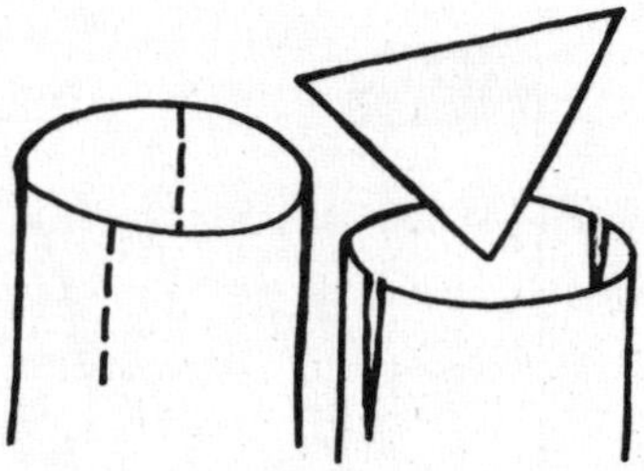

2. Punch holes around the other end of the roll. Draw on eyes, fins and other markings. Make more fish.

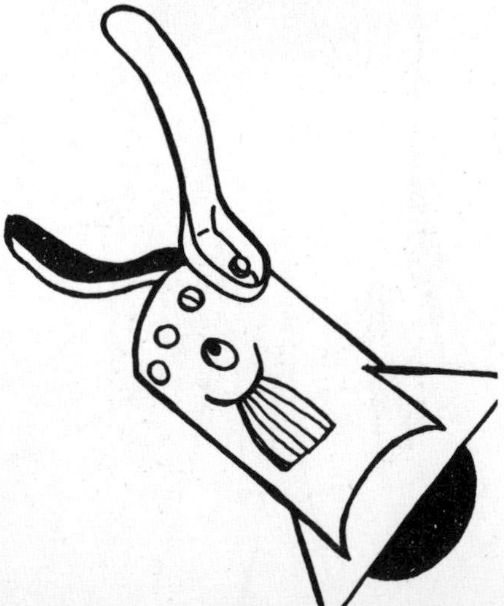

3. Open the paper clip and shape it as shown. Tie it onto one end of the yarn. Tie the other end of the yarn to the rod stick.

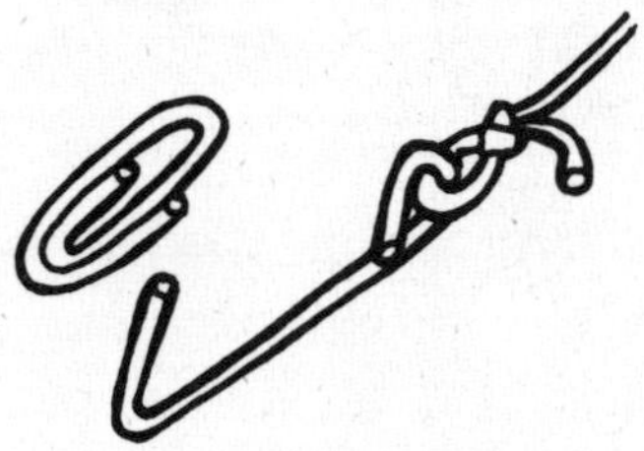

4. Go fishing! See if you can hook a fish through the holes in its mouth.

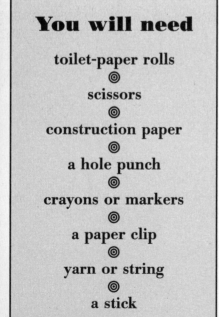

You will need

toilet-paper rolls
◎
scissors
◎
construction paper
◎
a hole punch
◎
crayons or markers
◎
a paper clip
◎
yarn or string
◎
a stick

Hummer

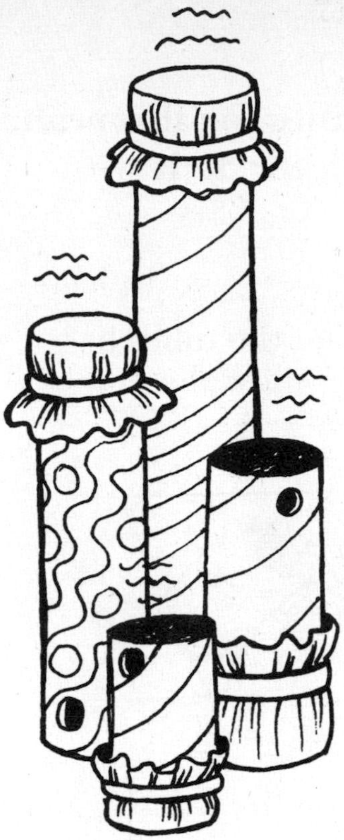

To make this hummer work, you need to hum a tune loudly into it.

1. Smoothly cover one end of the roll with waxed paper. Hold the waxed paper in place with the rubber band.

2. Use the hole punch to make a hole in the roll at the opposite end.

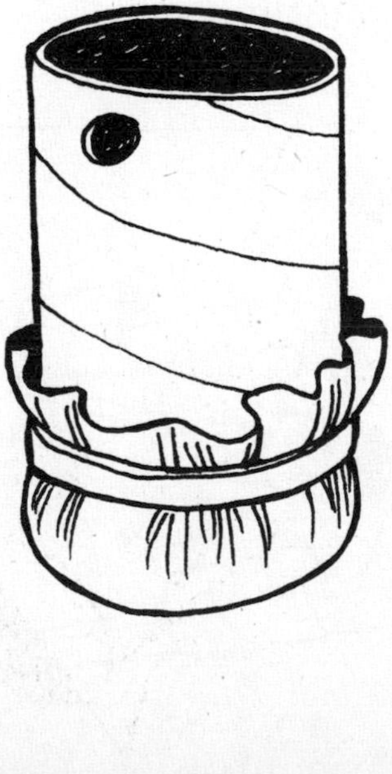

3. Decorate your hummer and start humming!

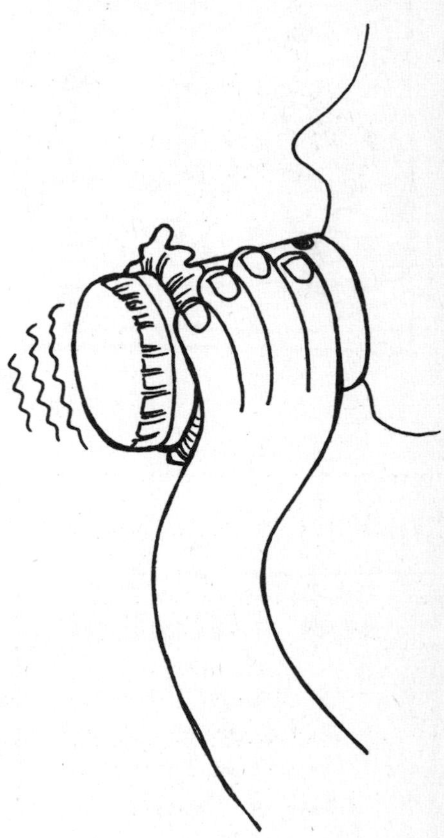

You will need

waxed paper

a toilet-paper roll

a rubber band

a hole punch

crayons, markers or stickers

Marble maze

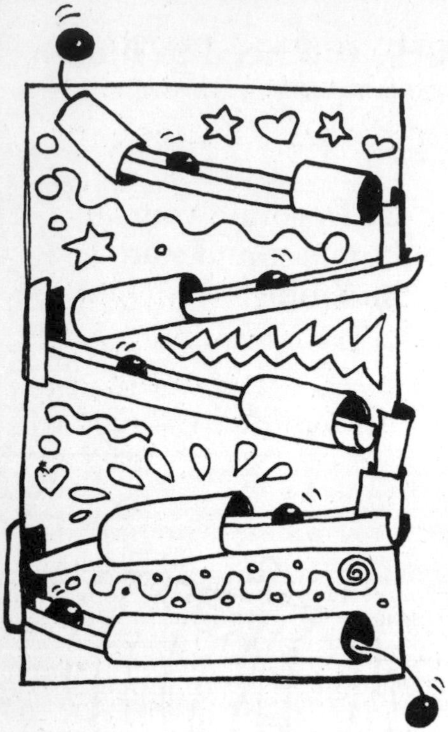

You'll need lots of cardboard tubes for this craft. After you've made your maze, decorate it with stickers, markers or crayons.

1. Cut the tubes into different sizes and shapes.

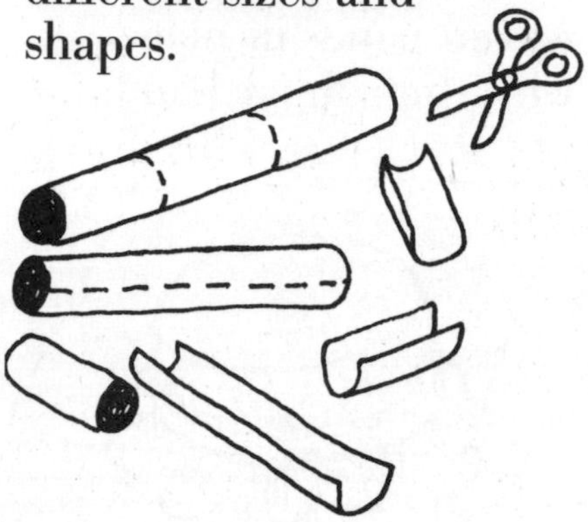

2. Lay the tubes on the large cardboard so that they are all slanted slightly downward. Each tube should empty into the next tube.

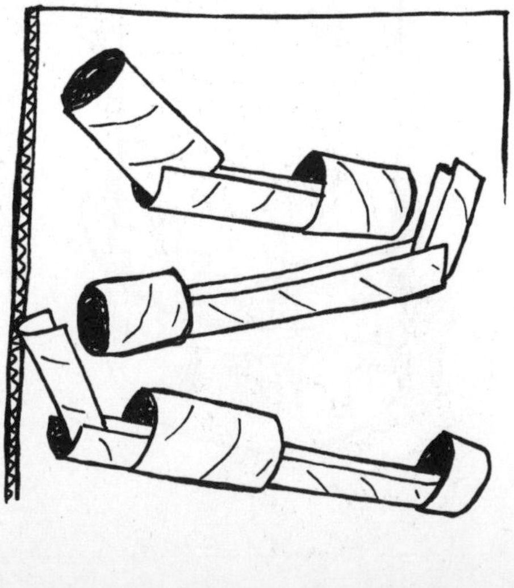

3. Glue the tubes in place. Allow the glue to dry.

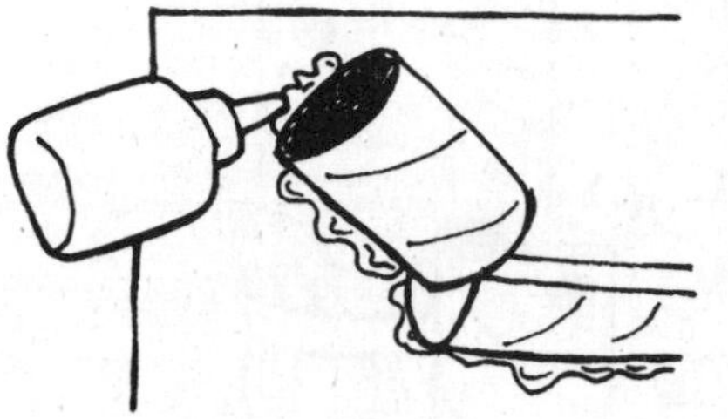

4. Prop the maze against a wall and test it with a marble. If a marble jumps out of the maze, glue or tape on pieces of tubes to fix it.

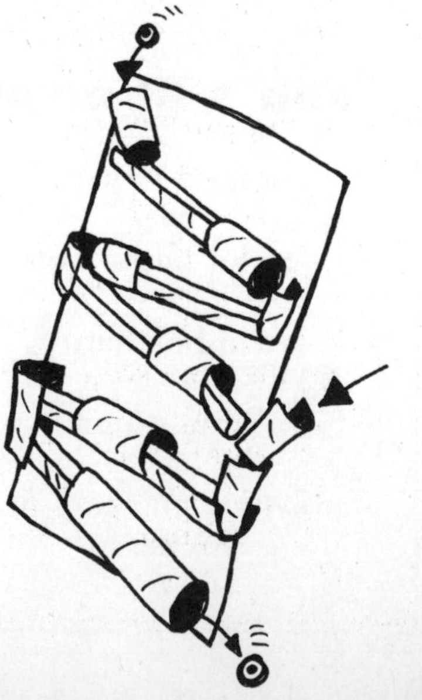

You will need

cardboard tubes

scissors and white craft glue or tape

a large piece of corrugated cardboard

marbles

stickers, markers or crayons (optional)

Party favors

For your next birthday party, make a bunch of these and give them out instead of loot bags. See page 67 for how to make a gift tag to attach to your party favor.

1. Cover one end of the roll with a small piece of wrapping paper. Hold the paper in place with the rubber band.

2. Fill the roll with treats, such as wrapped candies, plastic animals, stickers, marbles or craft supplies.

3. Wrap the roll with a strip of wrapping paper so there is extra paper on each end. Tape the paper in place, leaving the ends open.

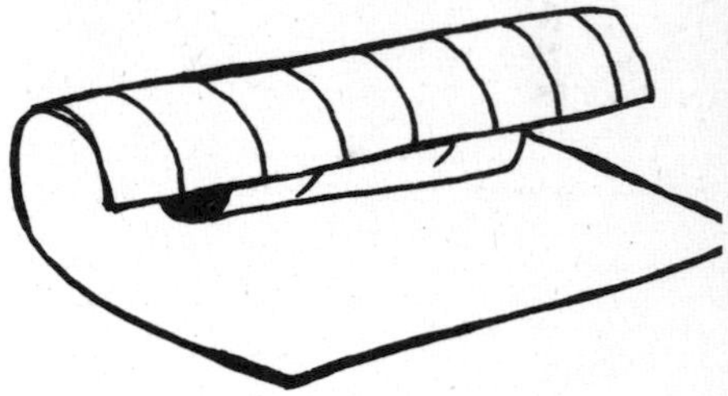

4. Tie a piece of ribbon at each end of the roll to close it.

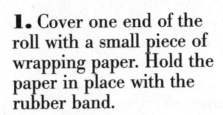

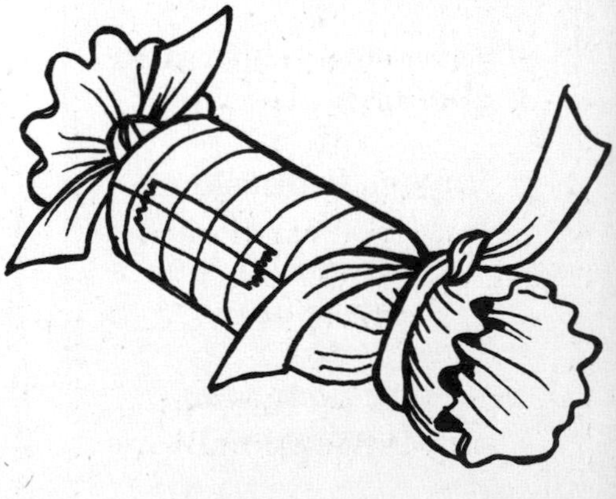

You will need

a toilet-paper or paper-towel roll

wrapping paper

scissors

a rubber band

treats (see step 2)

clear tape

ribbon

Toilet-paper roll creatures

There are many creatures you can make. All it takes is a toilet-paper roll and your imagination. These instructions are for making a bunny.

1. Cut a strip of construction paper big enough to wrap around the roll. Glue it in place.

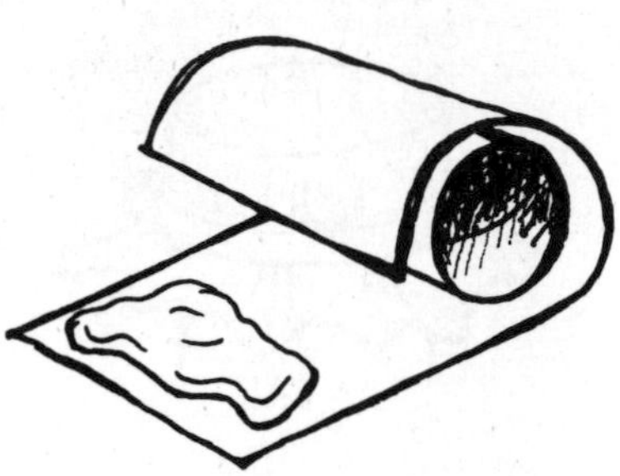

2. Cut the roll in half. (You'll need to shape the pieces so they are round again.) Glue the two halves together as shown.

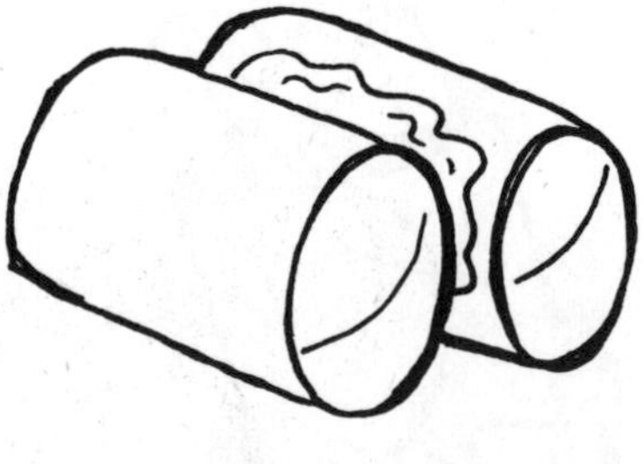

3. Draw on a face and glue on a tiny pom-pom nose if you have one.

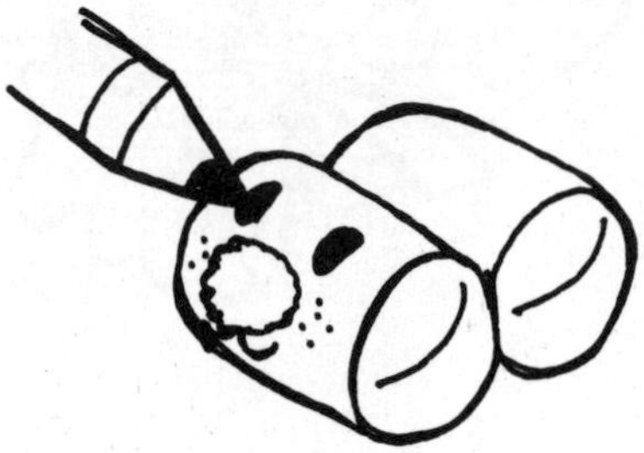

4. Cut out long ears from more construction paper. Glue them in the space between the two halves of the roll.

You will need

a toilet-paper roll

construction paper

scissors and white craft glue or a glue stick

crayons or markers

a cotton ball or pom-pom

a tiny pom-pom (optional)

5. Cut out feet and glue them under the head.

More ideas

Make other animals by changing the colors of the construction paper and shaping different ears, tails and paws. Poke in pipe cleaners for legs, antennae or a curly tail. Use yarn for a mane or a long tail. Try sitting your animal upright. If your creature falls over, glue it to a small cardboard base.

6. Glue on the cotton ball or pom-pom tail.

Flash cards

After you've made these flash cards for the alphabet, try simple words or numbers.

1. Write each letter of the alphabet on its own card in capital and small letters.

2. Go through the catalogs and magazines to find and cut out pictures of things that begin with each letter of the alphabet.

3. Glue each picture onto the back of the matching letter card.

4. Quiz your family and friends to see if they can guess the right letter for each picture.

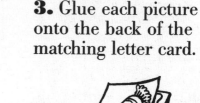

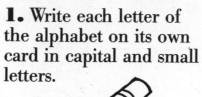

You will need

old catalogs and magazines

scissors and white craft glue or a glue stick

small index cards

crayons or markers

Memory game

Use old catalogs and magazines to find good pictures for your memory cards. If you don't have recipe or index cards, use squares of thin cardboard.

1. Cut out pairs of small pictures of things that are similar, for example, two pictures of clocks, dolls, birds or cars. Cut out about 20 pairs.

2. Cut the index cards in half and glue the pictures onto them.

3. To make it easier to pick up these thin cards, it's best to play this game on a floor with a carpet. Mix up the cards and place them face down in rows. The first player turns over two cards. If the cards match, she takes the pair. If the cards do not match, she turns them back over. The other players try to remember where the matching cards are so when they have a turn, they will be able to find a matching pair. The player with the most pairs of cards at the end of the game wins.

You will need

catalogs and magazines

scissors and white craft glue or a glue stick

index cards about 7.5 cm x 13 cm (3 in. x 5 in.)

Catalog mix and match

Old catalogs are lots of fun for cut and paste crafts.

1. Cut out pictures of babies, children and adults.

2. Cut out lots of hats, shoes, boots, sports equipment and other things to wear.

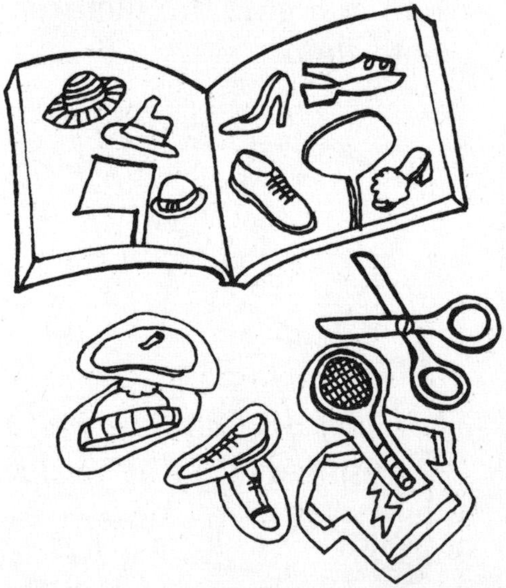

3. Mix everything up on the sheets of paper. Glue a huge pair of boots onto a girl in a bathing suit. Give a boy in sports clothing the head of a baby. Put a woman in a business suit on a playground slide. Make up lots of silly combinations.

You will need

old catalogs

scissors and white craft glue

sheets of paper

Puzzles

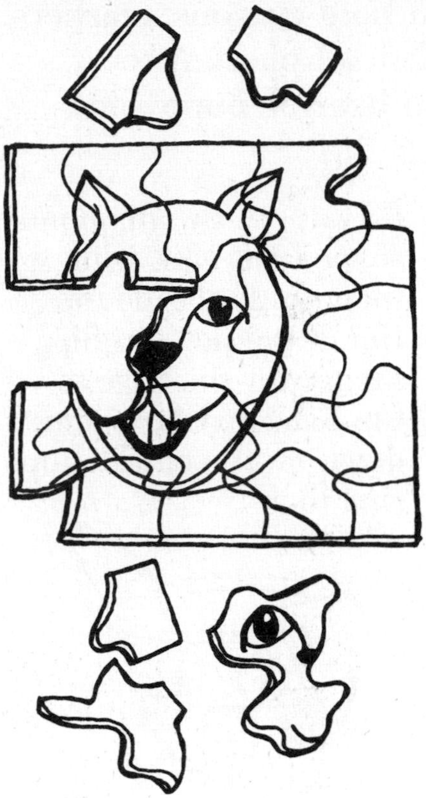

Sports and wildlife magazines often have full-page pictures that are fun to make into puzzles. Calendar pictures are great, too.

1. Glue the picture onto the paper.

2. On the back of the paper, draw curvy lines to create pieces of the puzzle. Cut along the lines.

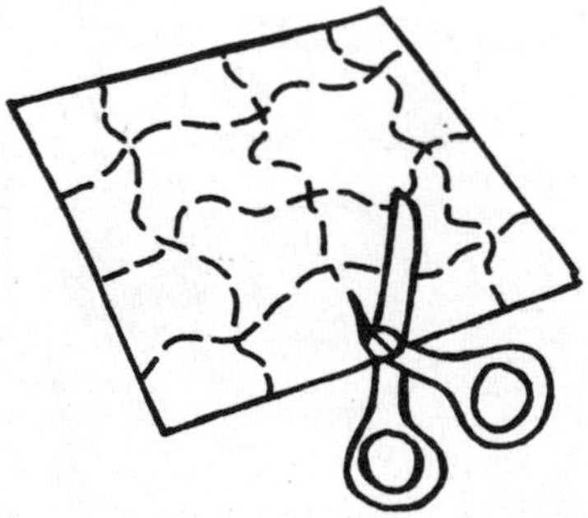

3. It's best to put this type of puzzle together on a smooth table or counter rather than on a carpet. Store the puzzle pieces in the envelope.

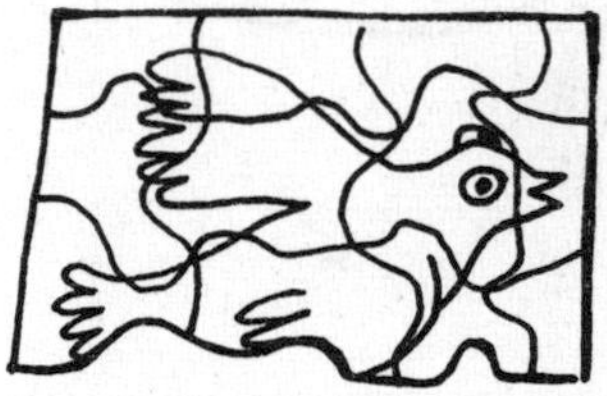

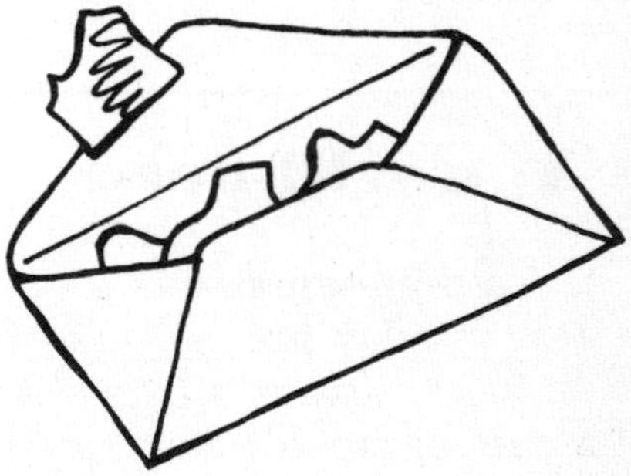

You will need

a large picture
◎
heavy paper
◎
white craft glue or a glue stick, a pencil and scissors
◎
an envelope

More ideas

To make your puzzle more challenging, glue a picture onto each side of the paper. It will get confusing trying to figure out which side of the puzzle piece to use.

Piggy pot

This decorated clay pot can hold crayons, markers, wrapped candies, keys or a small plant. After making this piggy pot, try a bear or puppy pot.

1. Glue on the eyes and button nose.

2. Draw on a mouth and cheeks with markers.

3. Cut out two diamond-shaped felt ears. Glue them to the inside top rim of the pot and flip them over the edge to the outside. Glue them down on the outside top rim, too.

4. Coil the pipe cleaner by wrapping it around a pencil. Glue the pipe cleaner to the back of the pot for a tail. (If it won't stay in place, tape it until the glue dries.)

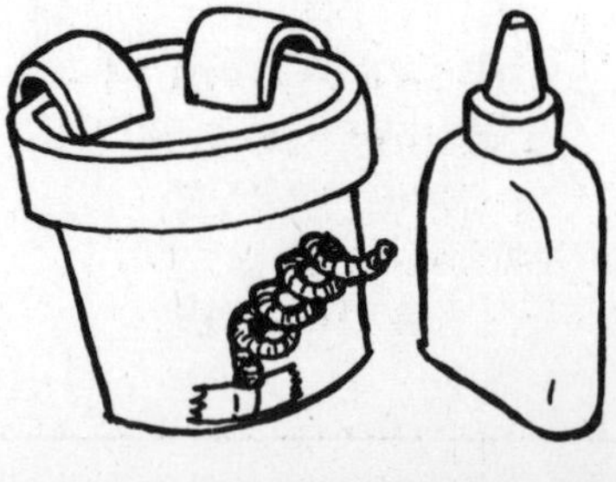

You will need

a medium-sized clay pot

a pair of small beads or roly eyes

a pencil, scissors, white craft glue and markers

a 2-hole button

scraps of felt

a short pipe cleaner

Decorated pot

If you like, you can paint the pot with acrylic craft paint before you begin gluing on decorations.

1. Wrap the ribbon around the top rim of the pot and tie it in a bow. You may wish to dab glue on the bow to keep it from coming undone later. Trim the ends of the ribbon.

2. Glue pretty buttons or beads around the pot. Or glue many of them in a design such as a flower or heart. Allow the glue to dry.

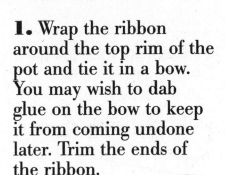

You will need

a clay pot, any size

a ribbon

an assortment of buttons and beads

scissors and white craft glue

More ideas

Use sponge shapes dipped in acrylic craft paint to decorate a pot. Or glue small cut pieces of tissue paper, wrapping paper or fabric all over it.

Clothespin flyer

You will need a clothespin with a spring for this airplane. The propeller really spins! You can color the airplane with markers or paint after you've put it together.

1. Cut a small propeller from the cardboard. It can be straight or propeller-shaped.

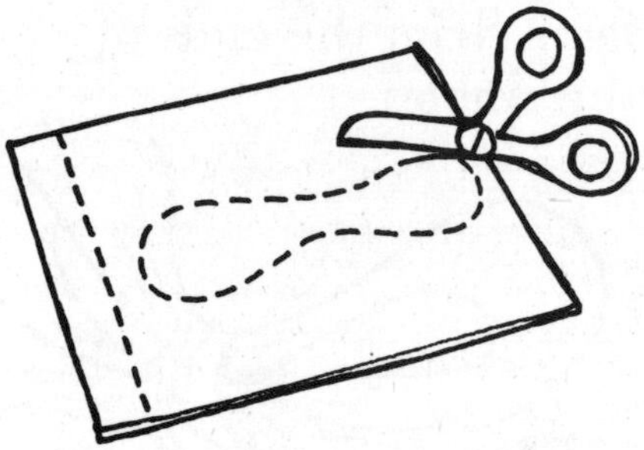

2. Place the propeller on the eraser. Have an adult poke into the propeller's center with the pin. Wiggle the pin in the propeller hole to make it bigger.

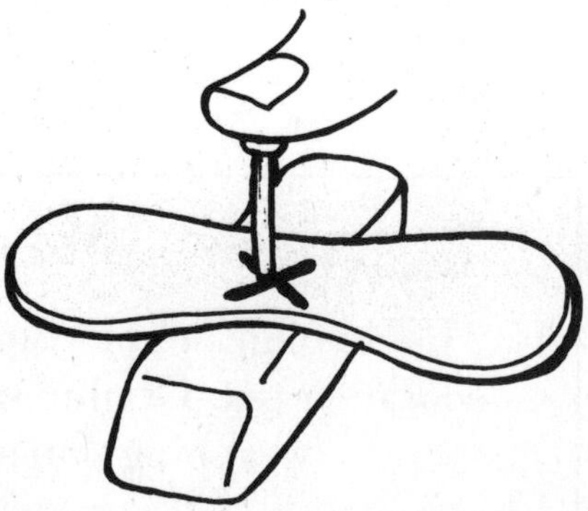

3. Squeeze the clothespin open and spread lots of glue on the open, inside area. Place the pin in the glue and close the clothespin. Adjust the pin so the propeller can spin freely.

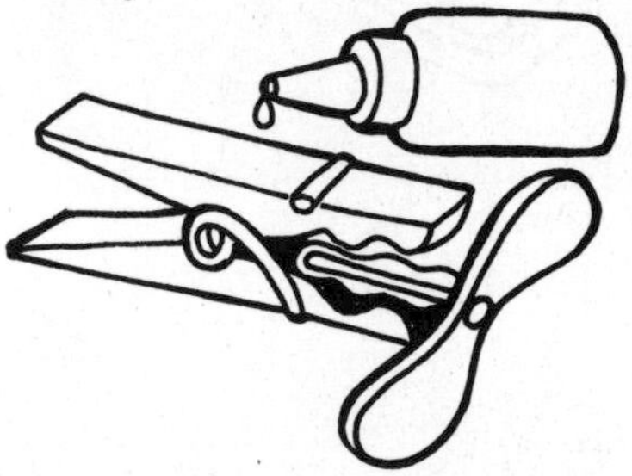

4. Glue two of the Popsicle sticks to the upper side of the clothespin and allow the glue to dry. Glue two more sticks to the under side. Allow the glue on all parts of the airplane to dry completely.

You will need

a scrap of thin cardboard

scissors, an eraser and white craft glue

a straight pin

a spring-action clothespin

4 Popsicle sticks

Clothespin pal

You'll want to make a whole gang of these! For a puppet, leave off the stand and glue a stick between the legs.

1. Draw pants, a shirt and shoes on the clothespin. You can color just the front or all around the clothespin. Draw on a face, too.

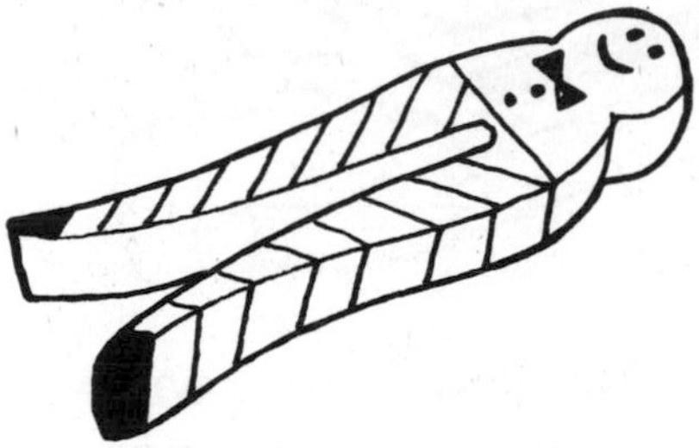

2. Wrap the pipe cleaner around the waist for a belt. Twist it twice at the back and bring the ends to the front for arms. Fold over the tips of the pipe cleaner to make hands.

3. Cut a few pieces of yarn for hair. Spread glue on top of the head and place the yarn in it. If the yarn hair is long, you may wish to style it.

4. To make a stand, cut a strip of thin cardboard about 18 cm (7 in.) long. Fold it in half and place it between the legs. Bend the ends upward so your clothespin pal can stand.

You will need

a flat craft clothespin

markers and white craft glue

a short pipe cleaner

yarn

thin cardboard

Dragonfly

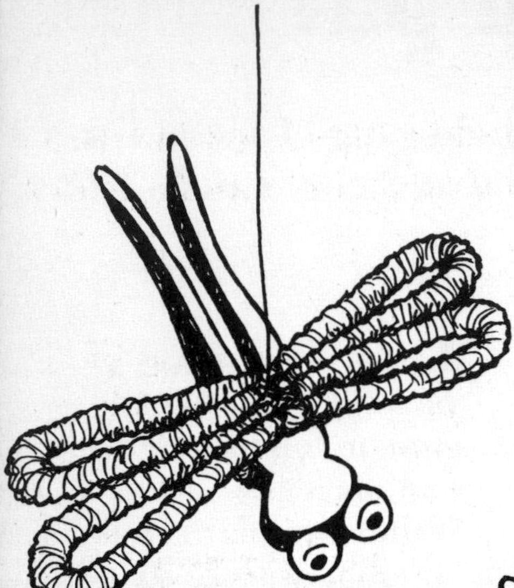

Use bold colors to decorate this neat dragonfly.

1. Color the clothespin with paint or markers. Or leave it the original color and just draw on markings.

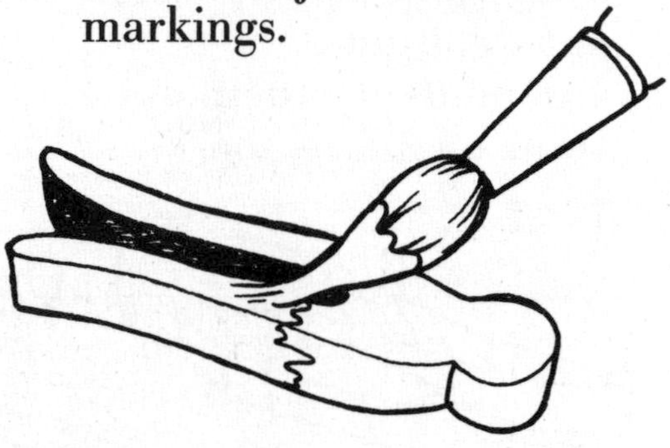

2. To make wings, wrap one of the pipe cleaners around the middle of the clothespin and twist it twice. Shape each half of the pipe cleaner into a long, narrow wing and fasten its end to the center area. Repeat this with the other pipe cleaner.

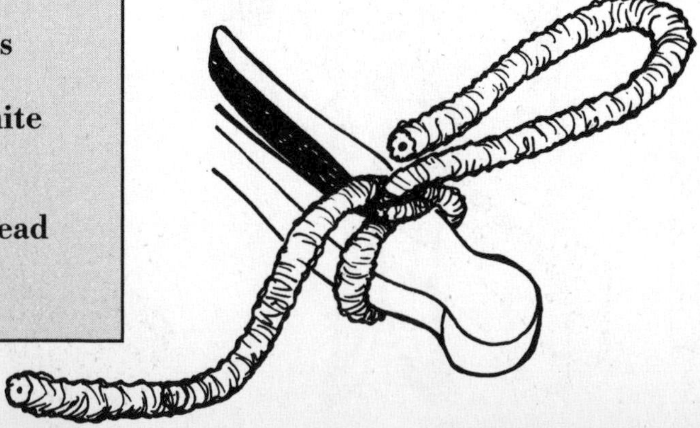

3. Glue the beads to the head for eyes. Allow them to dry.

4. Cut a length of fishing line and tie it around the dragonfly. Hold the dragonfly up to see if it is balanced. Adjust the line, if necessary, and knot it in place. Hang up your dragonfly.

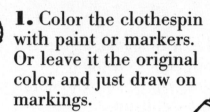

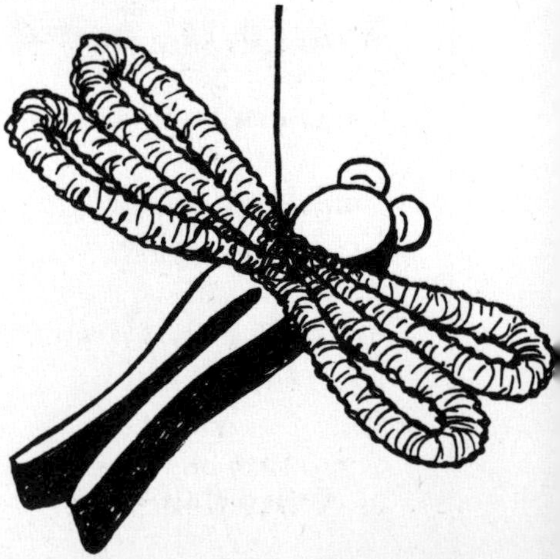

You will need

- a flat craft clothespin
- markers or acrylic craft paint and a brush
- 2 pipe cleaners
- 2 round beads
- scissors and white craft glue
- fishing line, thread or yarn

Gazelle

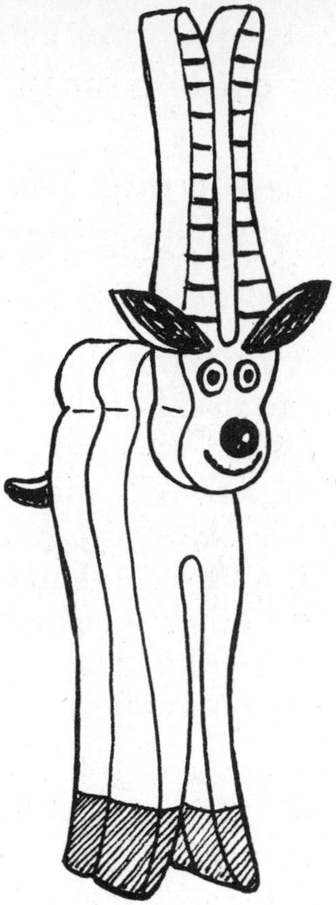

Some gazelles have long, straight, ringed horns. This makes it easy to create a model gazelle from clothespins.

1. On one of the clothespins, draw fine lines across the two ends to create horns.

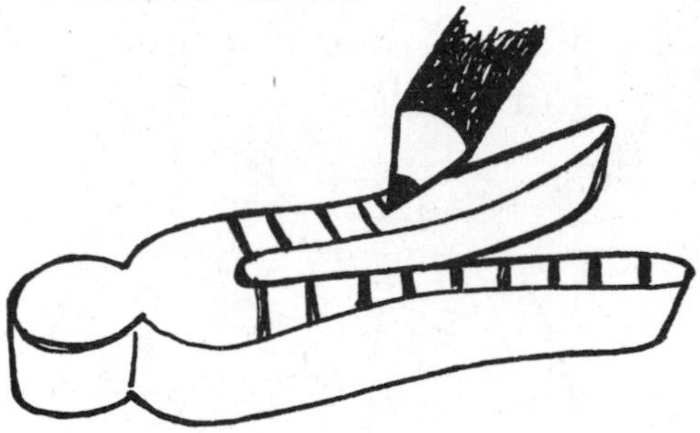

2. Glue together the other two clothespins. Now glue the head to the legs as shown.

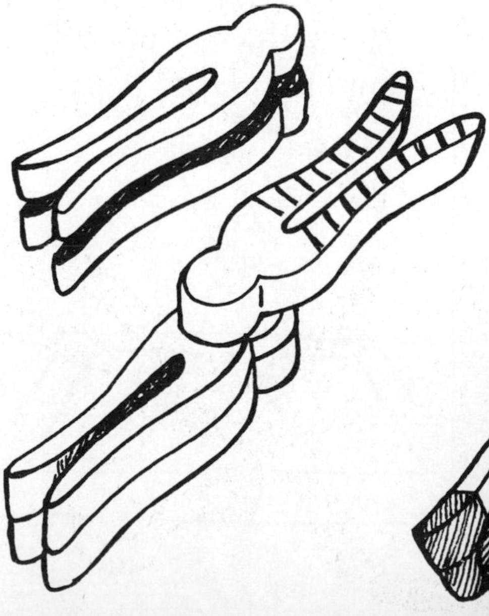

3. Cut out ears and a short tail from the felt or construction paper. Glue them in place.

4. Use roly eyes, beads or markers for the face. Draw on hooves.

You will need

3 flat craft clothespins

◎

markers

◎

scissors and white craft glue

◎

beads or roly eyes (optional)

◎

a scrap of felt or construction paper

Sparkly paper chain

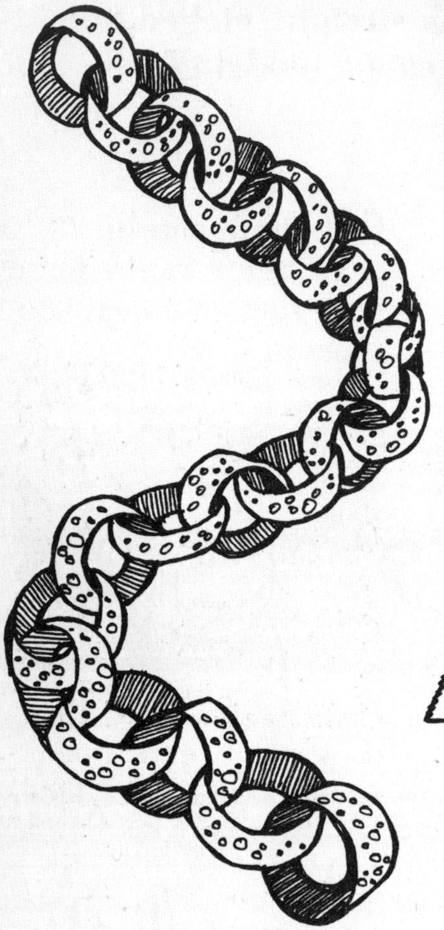

Make your paper chain as long as you like. You can make a plain chain if you don't have glitter.

1. Place a sheet of construction paper on the waxed paper. Squirt glue all over it in lines and swirls.

2. Sprinkle glitter over the glue. Shake the sheet a little to make sure all the glue is covered. Shake the extra glitter onto the waxed paper.

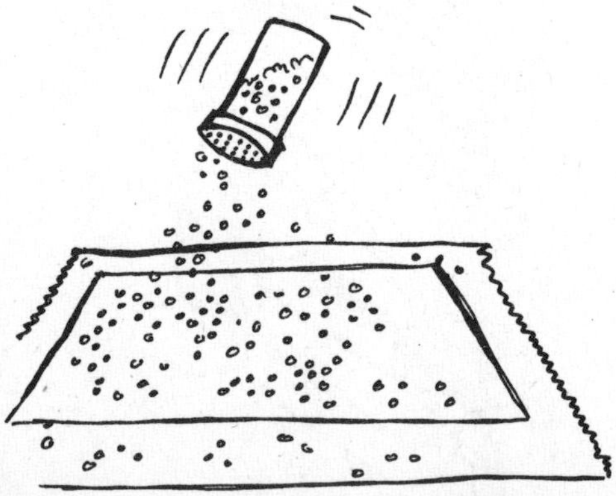

3. Set aside the glittery paper to dry. Lift the sides of the waxed paper to form a trough and pour the extra glitter back into the container. Prepare other sheets of different-colored construction paper.

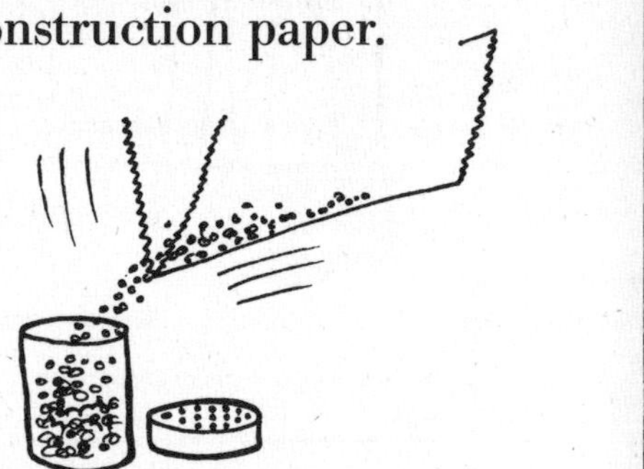

4. When the sheets are dry, cut them into narrow strips. Glue one strip into a circle. Slip another strip through the circle, and glue that strip into a circle, too. Keep going until you've used all the strips.

You will need

a sheet of waxed paper
construction paper
white craft glue
glitter
scissors

Paper cutouts

Try different color combinations for this neat craft. Make miniatures for gift tags and decorations.

1. Fold one sheet of paper in half, then in half again. Or fold it any way you like.

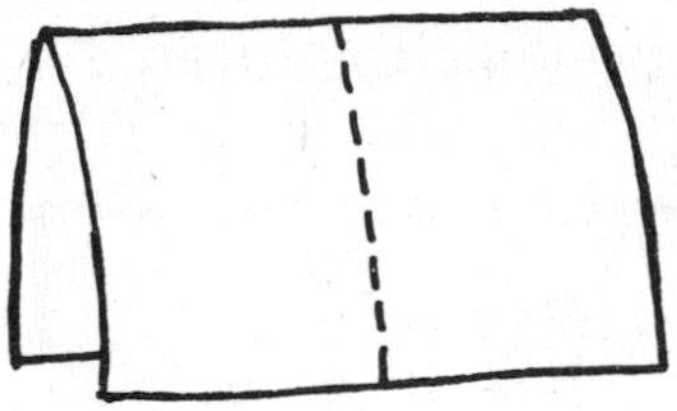

2. Cut away pieces of the folded paper. Open it.

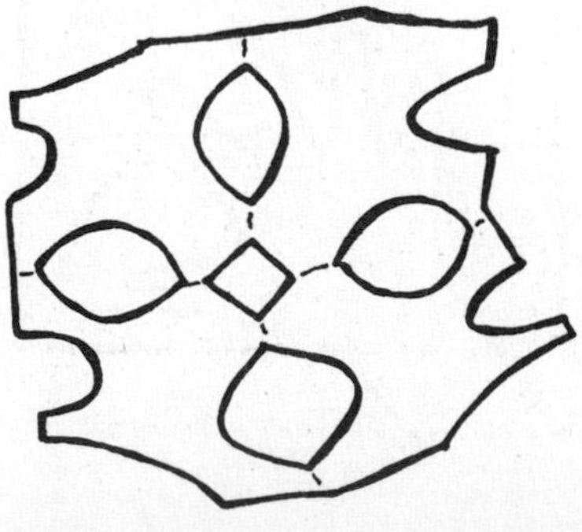

3. Glue it onto the other sheet of construction paper.

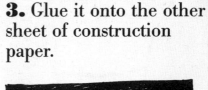

You will need

2 different-colored sheets of construction paper

◎

scissors

◎

white craft glue or a glue stick

Hand art

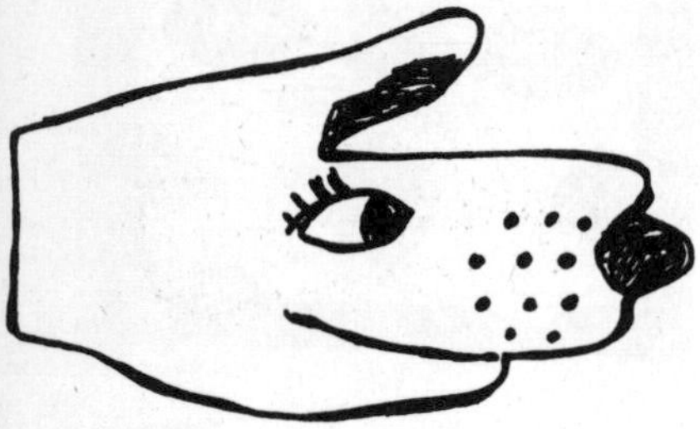

Do some hand art every year to keep track of how much your hands are growing! Send some hand art to Grandma and Grandpa so they can see how you've grown, too.

1. Place one hand on the paper. You can spread out your fingers a little or a lot or hold them close together.

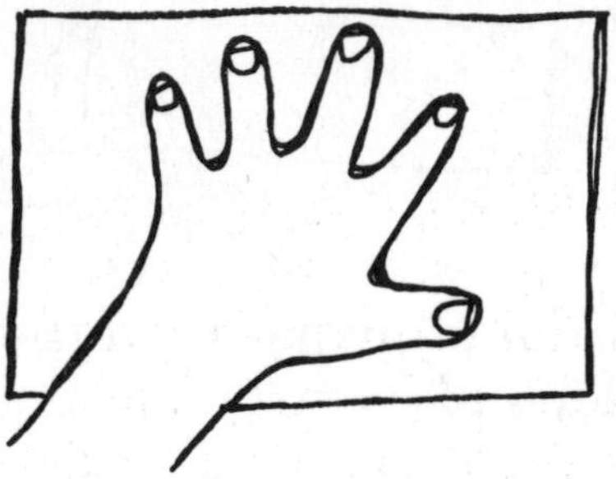

2. Trace around your hand and cut the shape out.

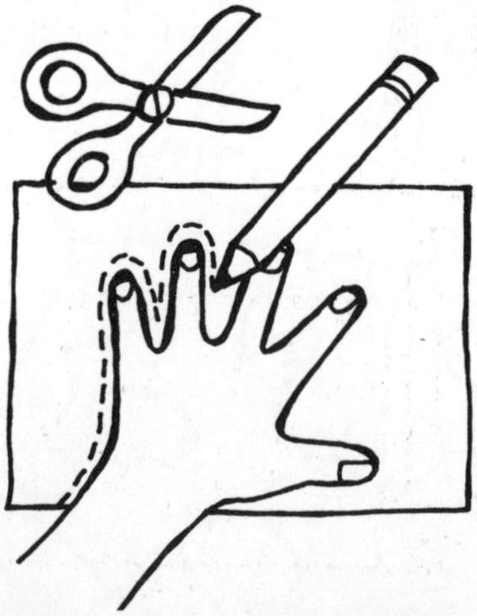

3. Look at your cutout from all angles. Does it look like an animal? Could two hands together be butterfly wings? Antlers for a reindeer? Decide what to make. Draw on details with the markers. Write your name and the date on the back.

4. Try more hand positions for different pictures. You may want to decorate your hand by drawing on pretty jewelry and nail polish. Or make your hand scary!

You will need

construction paper

◎

a pencil, scissors and markers or crayons

Fancy fans

Keep cool with this pretty fan. You can decorate the construction paper before you begin folding it.

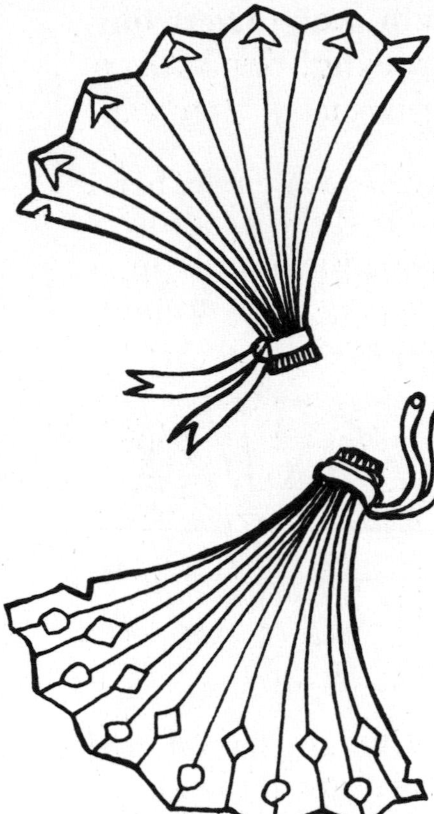

1. Place the short end of a sheet of construction paper on the table in front of you. Fold over the end.

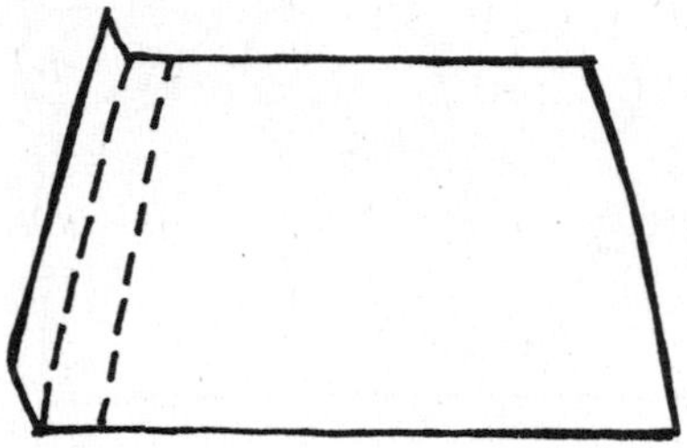

2. Flip the paper over and fold over the end again, making the fold the same width as the first fold.

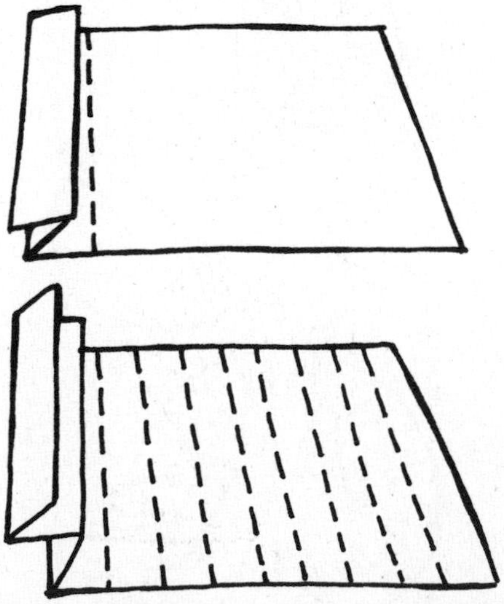

3. Flip the paper back and fold it again. Keep folding until you reach the other end. Staple or tape the bottom to hold the folds.

4. Close the fan. Cut out small pieces of the folds. Open the fan and admire!

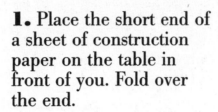

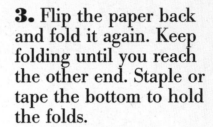

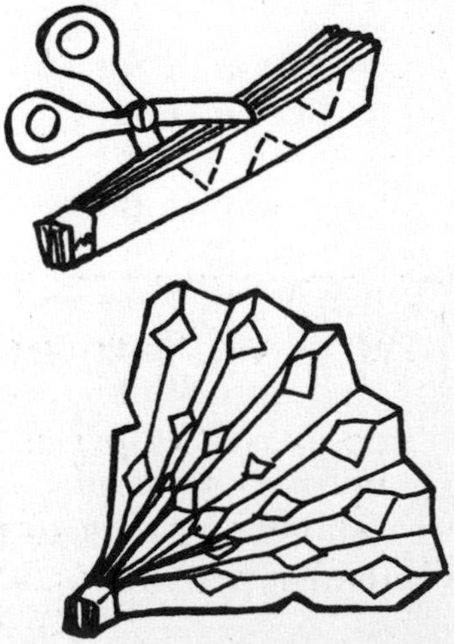

You will need

construction paper
◎
a stapler or tape
◎
scissors

Blooming paper

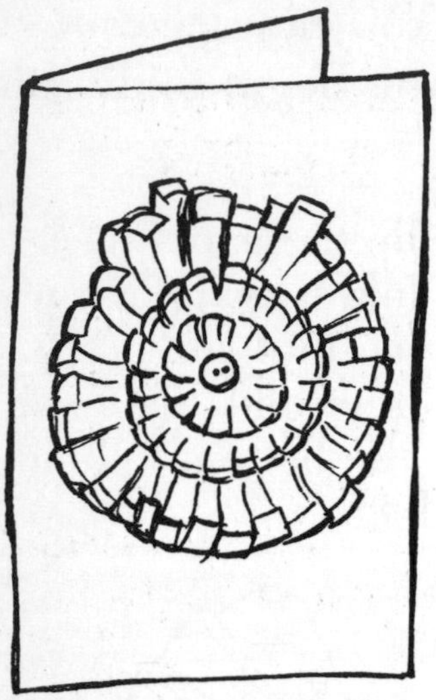

Glue this pretty paper flower in a picture or on the front of a card.

1. Trace three different-sized circles onto the construction paper and cut them out.

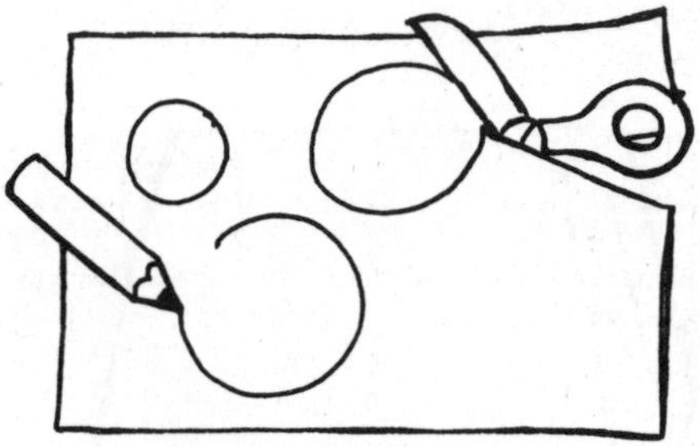

2. Make cuts part way into each circle, all the way around to form petals.

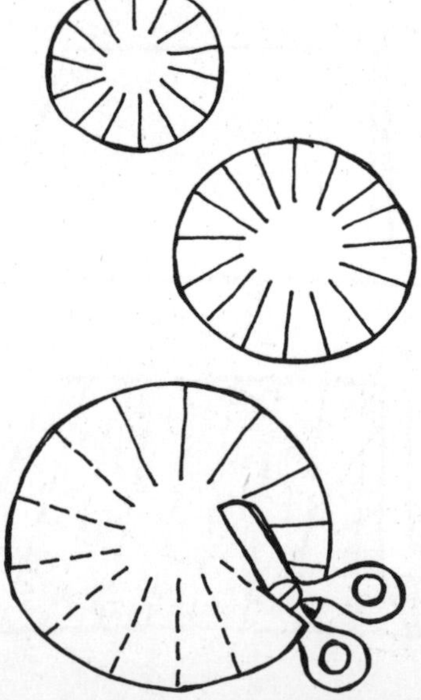

3. On each circle, bend and curl the petals by rolling them up or by wrapping them around your pencil.

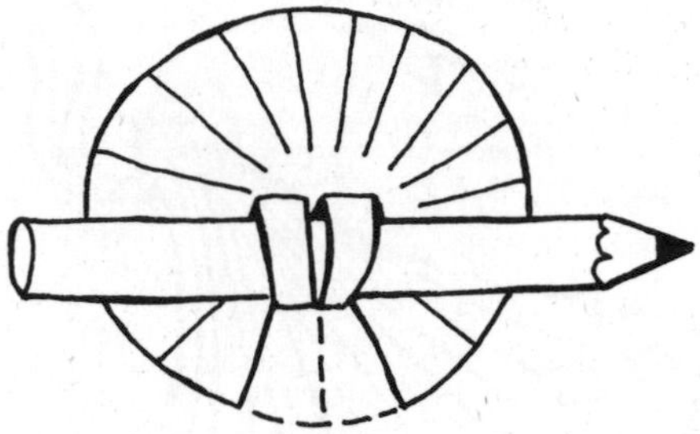

4. Glue the largest circle in place first, then the middle one and then the smallest. Draw a center in the flower or glue on a button or bead. Draw a stem and leaves or cut them out of construction paper.

You will need

cups, plastic tubs and lids to trace

◎

construction paper

◎

a pencil, scissors and white craft glue or a glue stick

◎

markers, crayons, a button or a bead (optional)

Folded frog puppet

Once you've made this funny frog, fold sheets of different-colored paper into different characters. Can you make a dragon? A dog? A rabbit?

1. Fold the sheet of paper lengthwise into thirds. Now fold it in half so the open ends are together.

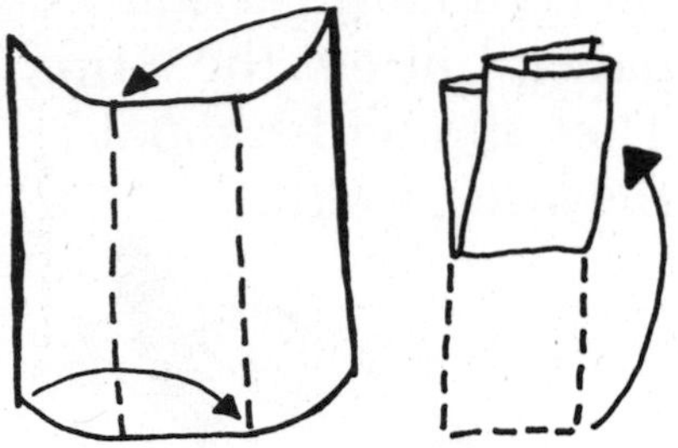

2. Undo this last fold, and then fold each open end to the center fold. Fold the paper in half again so the open ends are now on the top and bottom, facing outwards, and the paper zigzags.

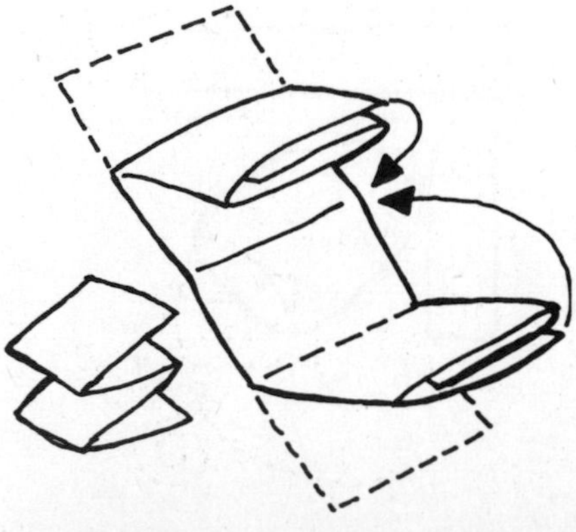

3. Glue the cotton balls on the top. Glue the roly eyes to the front of the cotton balls or draw on eyes. Cut out a red tongue and glue it in place.

4. To make your puppet talk, slip your fingers in the top open end and your thumb in the bottom open end.

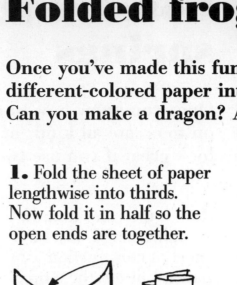

You will need

a sheet of green construction paper

2 cotton balls

white craft glue

2 large roly eyes or a marker

scissors

scraps of fabric or construction paper

Construction-paper springs

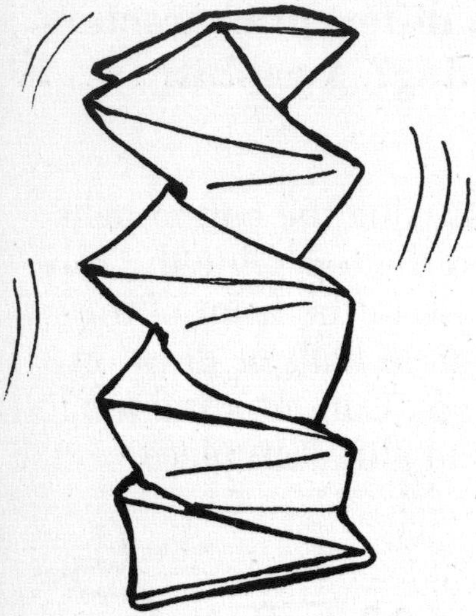

Once you know how to make these springs, read on to create all kinds of neat stuff. The springs look great if you use two different-colored strips.

1. Use the ruler to draw two lines lengthwise on a sheet of construction paper. Cut out the strips. They should be about the same width.

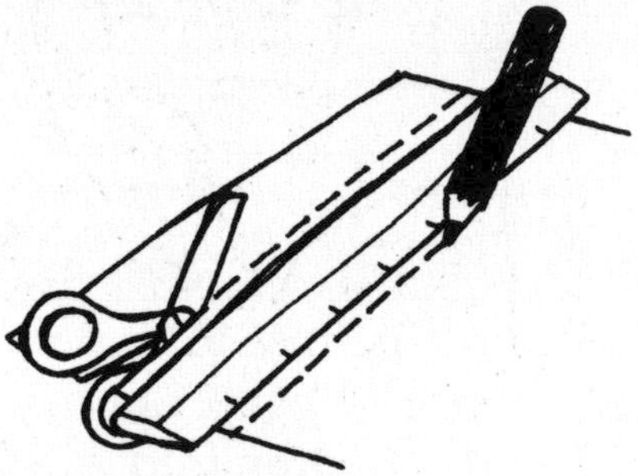

2. Glue the strips together to form a squared corner, as shown.

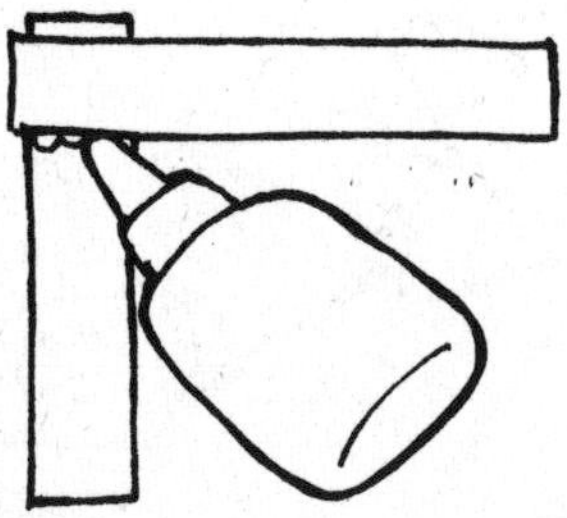

3. Fold the vertical strip upward. Fold the horizontal strip over to the left.

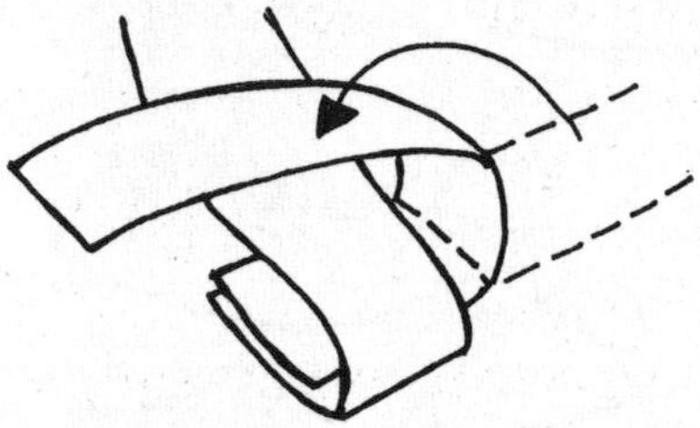

4. Now fold the vertical strip down and the horizontal one to the right. Keep folding the strips together this way.

5. When you reach the end, glue the two ends together. Trim them if needed. Read on for fun projects to make with your springs.

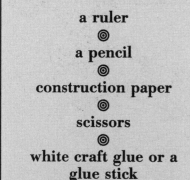

You will need

a ruler

a pencil

construction paper

scissors

white craft glue or a glue stick

Greeting card surprise

Fold two wide strips together. Glue one end of the spring inside a card you're making. Glue a heart, flower or message to the other end so it will jump out when someone opens the card.

More spring-loaded stuff

You can use these springs for legs on animals, for bug-eyed paper monsters or to make a dress-up necklace and bracelet set.

"Spring" flower

Fold two different-colored strips together. When you finish, bring the two ends around to form a circle. Glue them together. Dab a little glue on the end of a pipe cleaner and poke it into one of the folds. Add pipe-cleaner or construction-paper leaves if you wish.

Caterpillar

Make an extra-long spring by taping strips together, end to end, before you begin folding. When your spring is finished, draw a face on one end. Add pipe-cleaner or construction-paper antennae.

Paper weaving

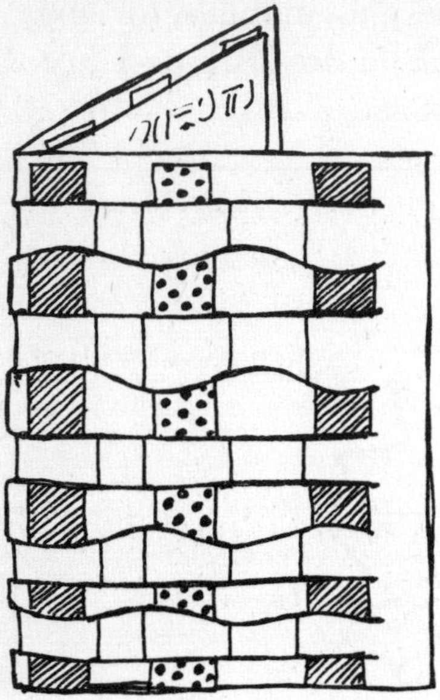

Once you've tried weaving, you'll want to do it often. Make the crafts listed on the next page by following these instructions.

1. Fold one sheet of construction paper in half.

2. Starting at the folded edge, make cuts that end about two finger widths from the open edge. You can make the cuts wavy, straight or zigzag, and they can be different widths.

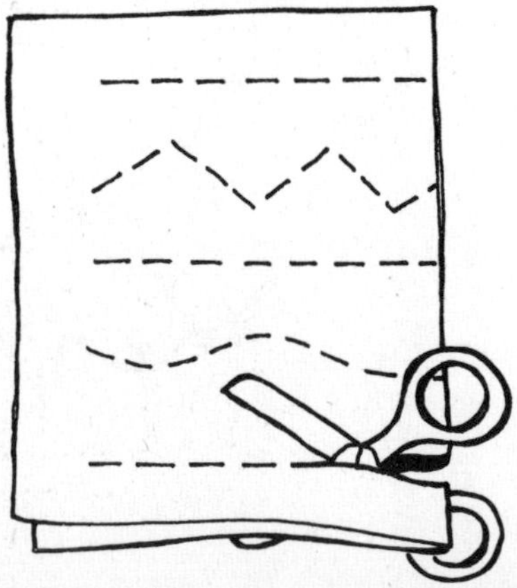

3. Cut 10 to 15 strips along the width of the second sheet. The strips don't need to be straight or even.

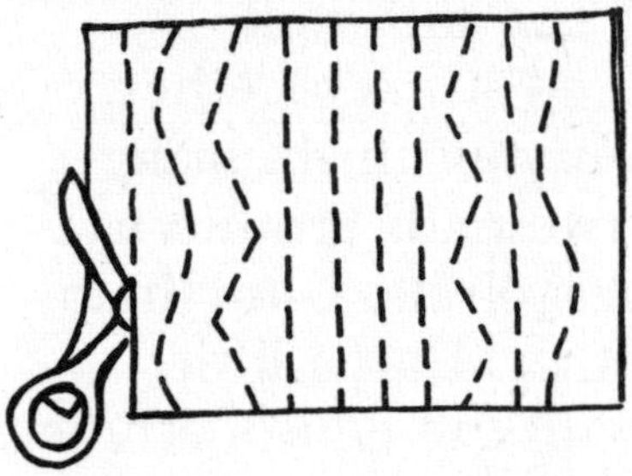

4. Open the first sheet of construction paper. Starting at one side, weave a strip of paper under and over the cuts in the construction paper. Slide the strip as far to one end as you can.

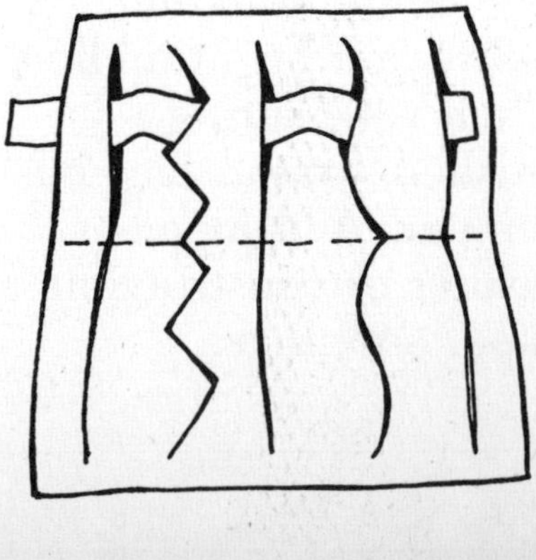

You will need

2 different-colored sheets of construction paper

◎

scissors and white craft glue

5. Weave in the second strip, with an over and under pattern opposite to that of the first strip. Push the second strip close to the first.

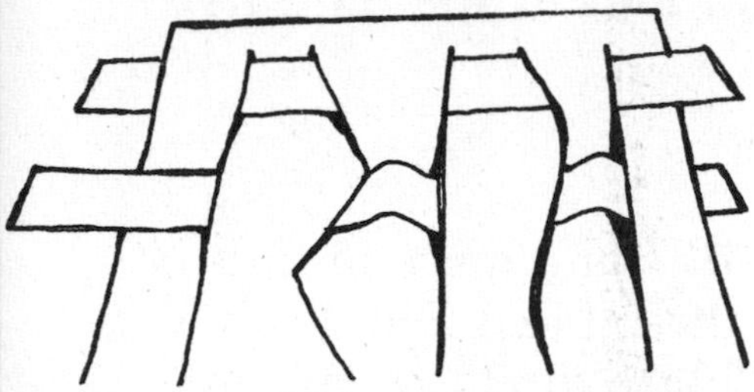

6. Continue weaving in strips until you run out of space. Glue down all the strip ends on both sides of the sheet.

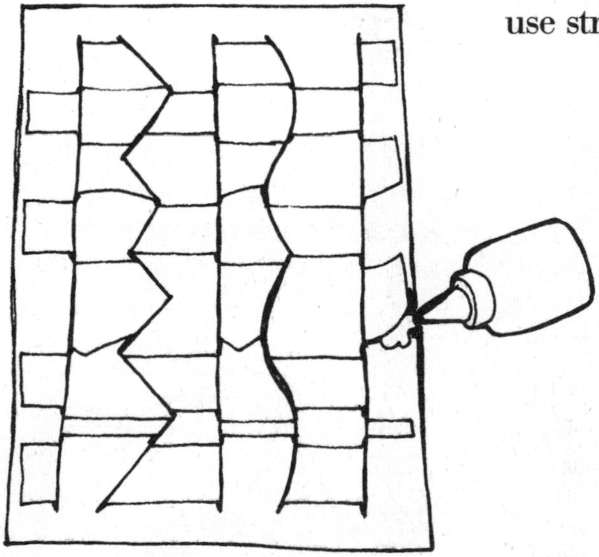

Placemat

Cover your weaving with clear self-adhesive vinyl (available at hardware stores). Cut two pieces of vinyl a little larger than the weaving. Remove the paper backing from one piece and place it sticky side up on your table. Carefully set the weaving onto the vinyl. After removing the paper backing, place the second sheet of vinyl on the weaving and smooth both sides. Trim the vinyl all around if necessary.

Greeting card

Fold the weaving in half. Glue a sheet of paper inside to write on your greetings.

Rainbow weaving

Instead of using just one color for the strips, cut strips from many sheets of construction paper. You'll have rainbow weaving! Or, instead of construction-paper strips, use strips cut from wrapping paper or leftover wallpaper.

Cookie-cutter decorations

Use markers, crayons, fabric and paper scraps, buttons, beads, yarn, ribbon and other trim to decorate your cutout.

1. Trace a cookie cutter twice onto the construction paper. Cut out both shapes.

2. Spread glue all over one side of one of the shapes.

3. Cut a piece of floss or thread and fold it in half. Place the floss ends in the glue and place the other cookie-cutter shape over top.

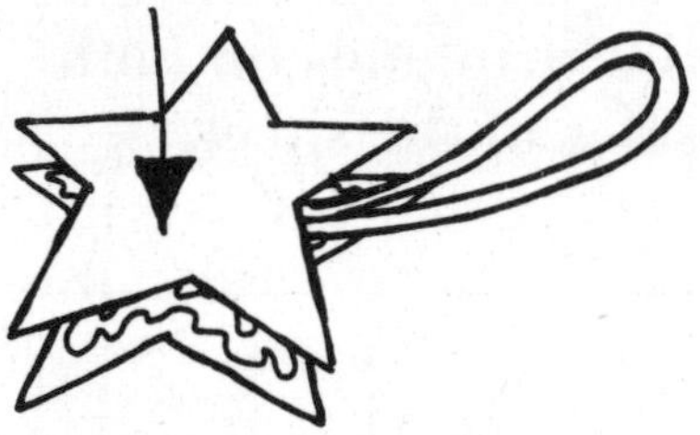

4. Decorate one or both sides. Use your cutout for a decoration or gift tag. Make lots more!

You will need

cookie cutters
construction paper
a pencil, scissors and white craft glue
embroidery floss or thread
supplies for decorating

Gift tags

These small, shaped cards are perfect for gift tags. Make them large and use them for greeting cards, too.

1. Fold a piece of construction paper in half. It does not need to be a full sheet.

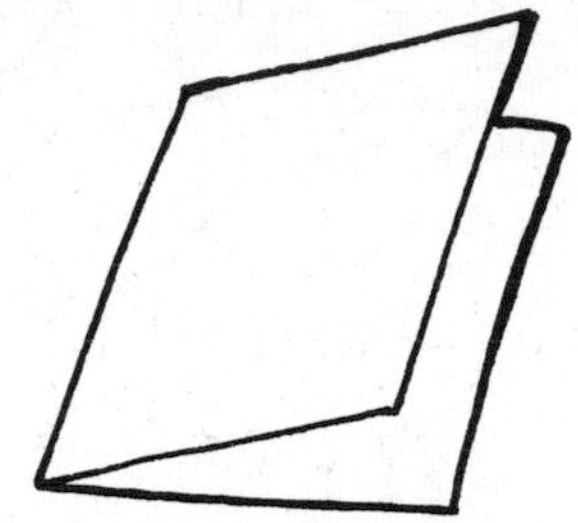

2. Draw a cookie-cutter shape on the paper, with part of the shape against the folded edge.

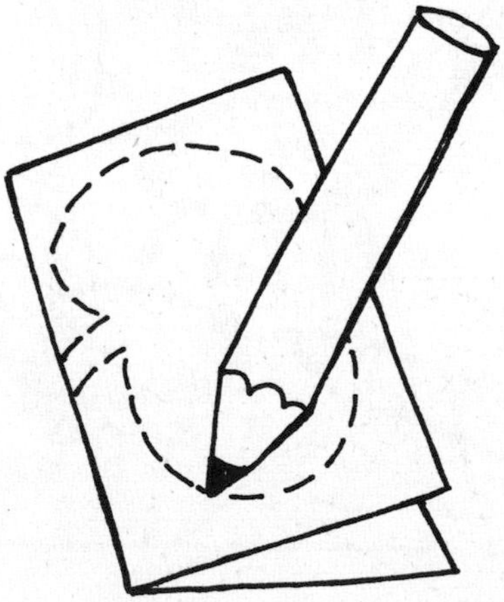

3. Cut it out, leaving the folded edge, and decorate it with crayons or markers. Write your message inside.

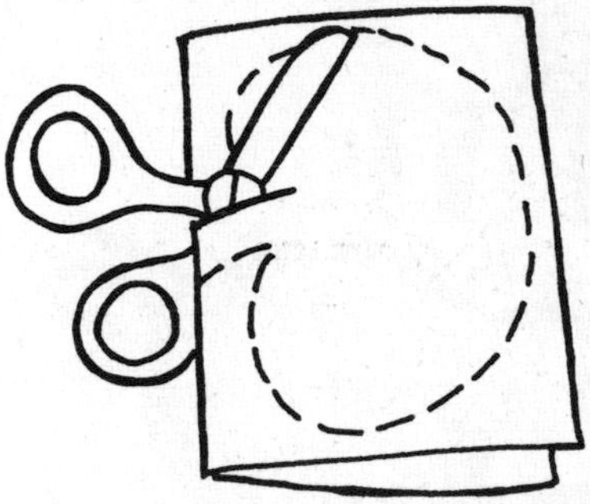

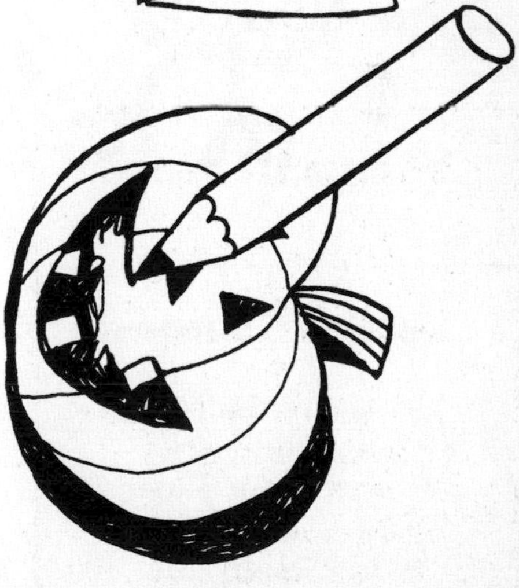

You will need

construction paper
◎
cookie cutters
◎
a pencil and scissors
◎
markers or crayons

Cotton-ball sheep

Try this method to make other animals, too – such as bunnies or chicks.

1. Slightly stretch out a cotton ball. You'll find it stretches out easier one way than the other. Glue it on the paper.

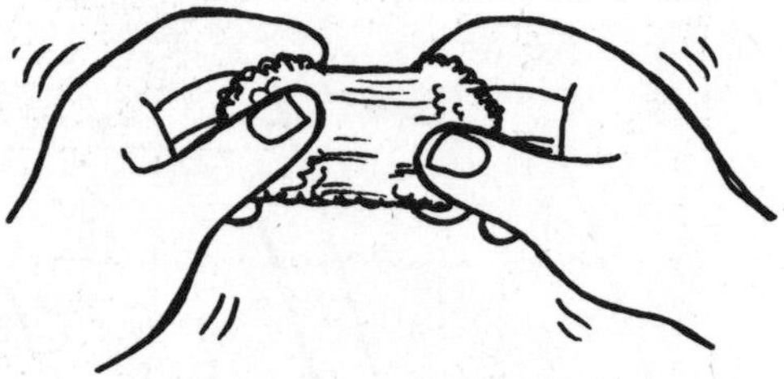

2. Draw on legs, a tail and a head. Make more sheep.

3. If you like, you can create a whole scene. Add cotton-ball clouds and draw on more details, such as shrubs and grass.

You will need

cotton balls
◎
construction paper
◎
white craft glue
◎
markers or crayons

More cotton-ball fun

Snow scene

Create a snowy landscape. Use two or more cotton balls to make a snowman. Draw on details. Pull apart cotton balls to look like snow on the ground. Roll up bits of cotton for snowflakes falling from cotton-ball clouds.

Cotton-ball trim

Draw a picture of a person. Glue on cotton-ball hair or a cotton-ball mustache and beard. Also, draw a hat and glue on fluffy, white trim. Use cotton balls on masks and costumes, too.

Mustache

Stretch out a cotton ball. Loop a piece of masking tape on the back and try on your tickly mustache!

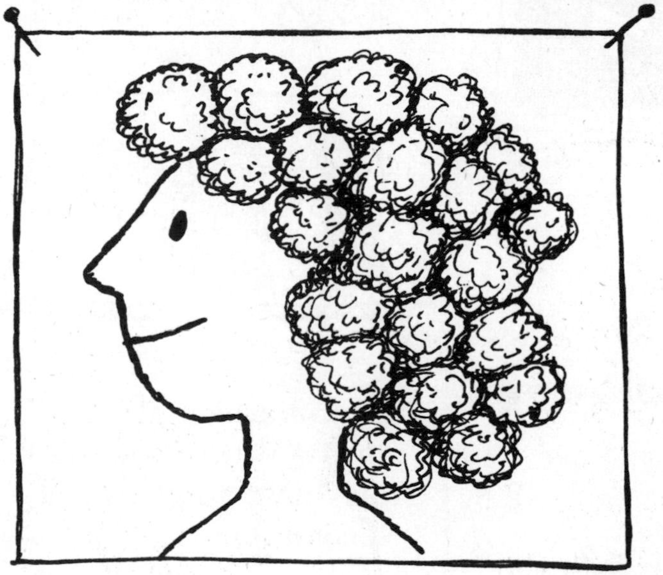

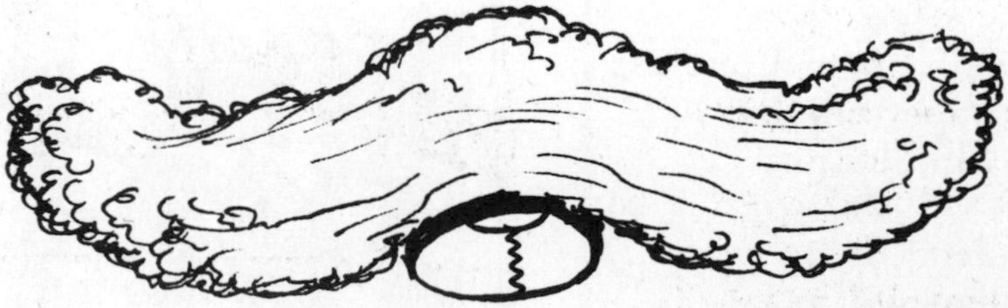

Scratch pictures

Have fun with this surprise scratch picture. Cover your work surface with newspaper to catch the bits of crayon that are rubbed or scratched off your picture.

1. Cover the cardboard with crayon stripes of color in any direction. (Instead of doing this, you can use the colorful printed side of the cardboard and go to step 2.)

2. Color over all the stripes with black. You may need to go over it a second time.

3. Use the nail to scratch a picture in the crayon.

4. Wipe over the picture with a tissue.

You will need

thin cardboard (from a cereal box)

crayons, including a black one

a nail, opened-out paper clip or bobby pin

facial tissue or a small rag

Crayon magic pictures

Use watercolor paints, such as the type you find in a paint box, for this neat project.

1. Use the white crayon to draw a picture on the paper.

2. Paint over it. The picture will appear like magic!

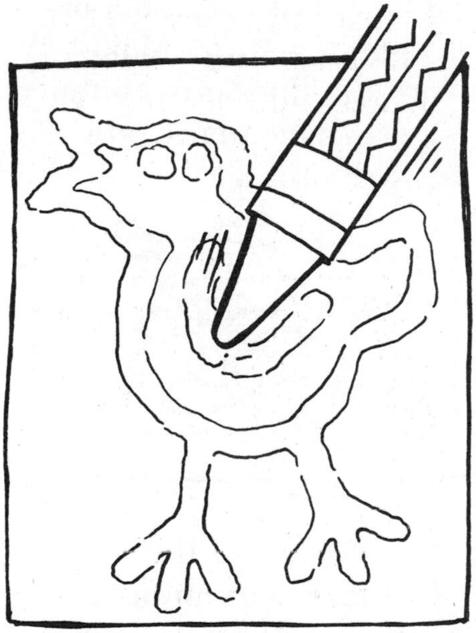

You will need

white paper
◎
a white crayon
◎
watercolor paint
◎
a paint brush and water

More ideas

Leave someone a mystery message by using a white crayon on white paper. He or she will have to paint the paper to get the message!

◎

Instead of painting over paper with one color of paint, use a rainbow of colors.

Crayon stained glass

Use crayon scribbles to make a stained-glass window!

1. Place the sheet of paper on the scrap paper. Use the black crayon to draw a loopy scribble or a simple picture. Make sure the lines cross often so you have many odd-shaped areas.

2. Color in all the areas with different colored crayons. When you are finished, turn the picture over.

3. Dip a couple of cotton balls into the oil. Rub oil into the back of the picture, but not to the edges of the page. (Tape will not stick to oil so the picture would be difficult to hang up.)

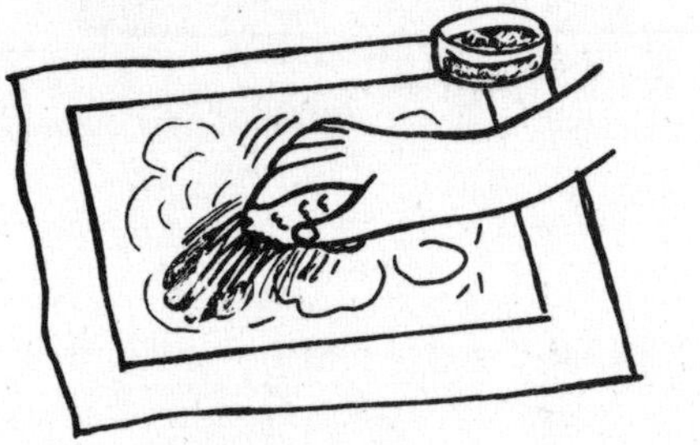

4. Hang your crayon stained-glass picture in a bright window.

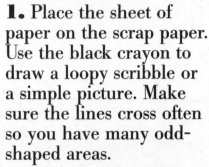

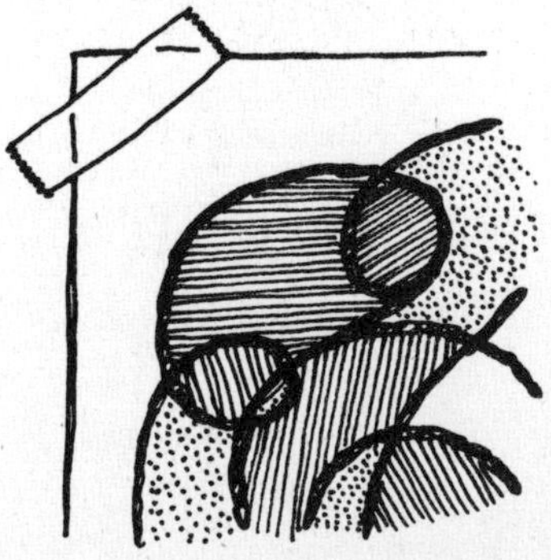

You will need

- scrap paper
- a sheet of paper
- crayons, including a black crayon
- cooking oil
- cotton balls

Rubbings

Look for textured surfaces and objects to rub. Try puzzle pieces, keys, coins, buttons, bark, leaves, shells and the bottom of your shoe.

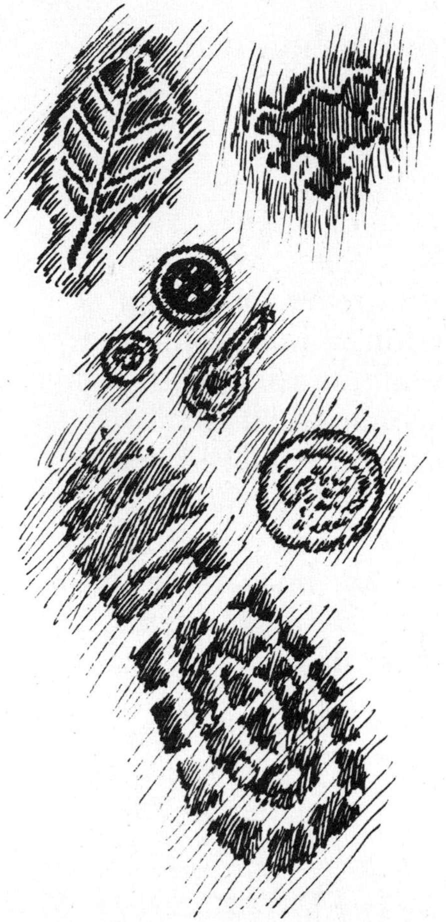

1. Hold the paper over the surface or object you wish to rub.

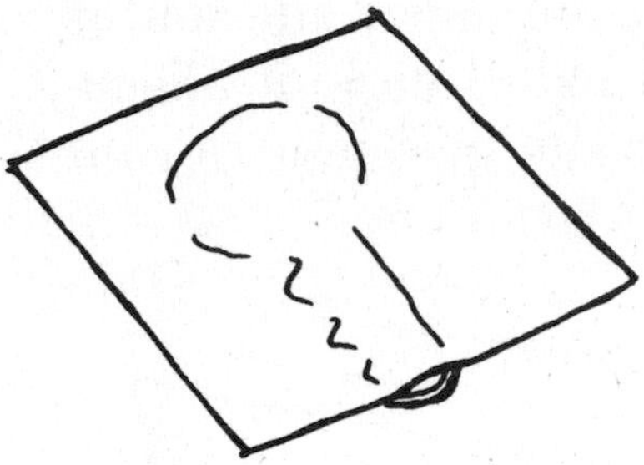

2. If the object is small, such as a coin, key or button, it's a good idea to hold it in place with a loop of tape on the back.

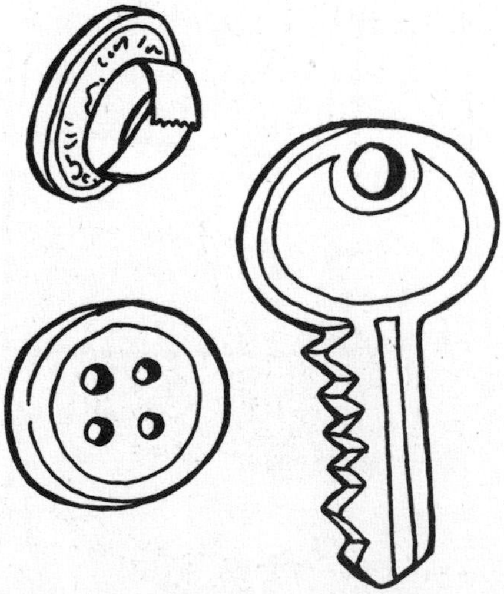

3. Rub the crayon over the paper and watch the design appear.

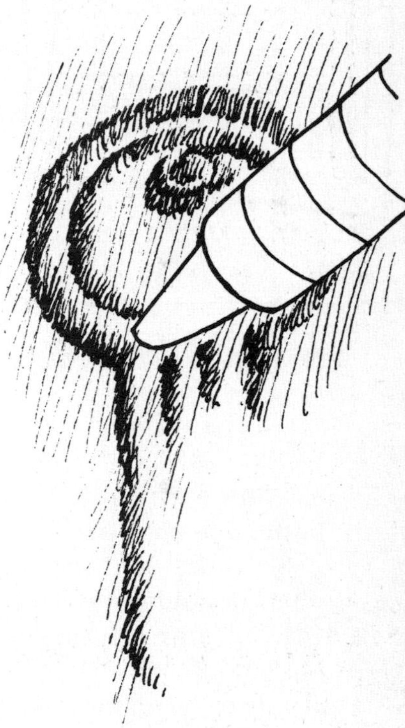

You will need

a sheet of paper
◎
objects to rub
◎
tape (optional)
◎
crayons

Melted-crayon designs

It is best not to use your ironing board for this craft just in case some bits of crayon get left on it.

You will need

waxed paper

crayons with their papers peeled off

a crayon sharpener or a dull knife or scissors

a pile of newspaper or clean rags

an iron

scissors

construction paper and white craft glue (optional)

1. Tear off a sheet of waxed paper and fold it in half. Unfold it. Place it on the newspaper or on a rag.

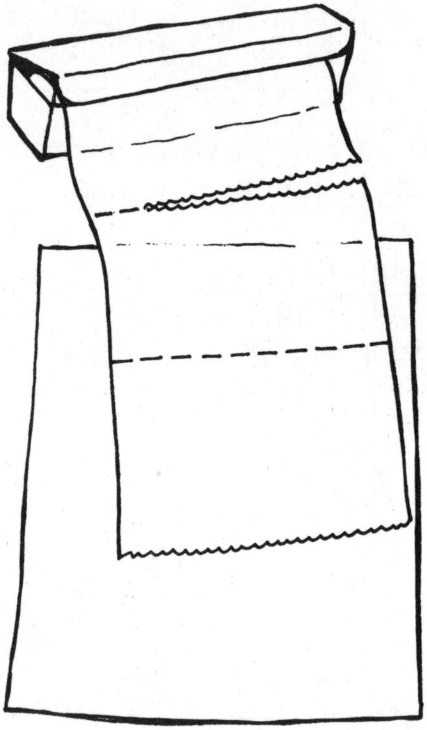

2. Use a crayon sharpener (or ask an adult to help you use a knife or scissors) to scrape off bits of different-colored crayons onto half of the waxed paper. You can arrange the crayon shavings into separate areas or mix them up.

3. Fold the other half of the waxed paper over the shavings.

4. Place a smooth rag or a couple of sheets of newspaper on top of the folded waxed paper.

5. Ask an adult to iron over it. Check to see if the crayon shavings have melted. If the crayon needs to melt more, cover it again. Be careful you don't iron it too much or you'll end up with a dull brown color.

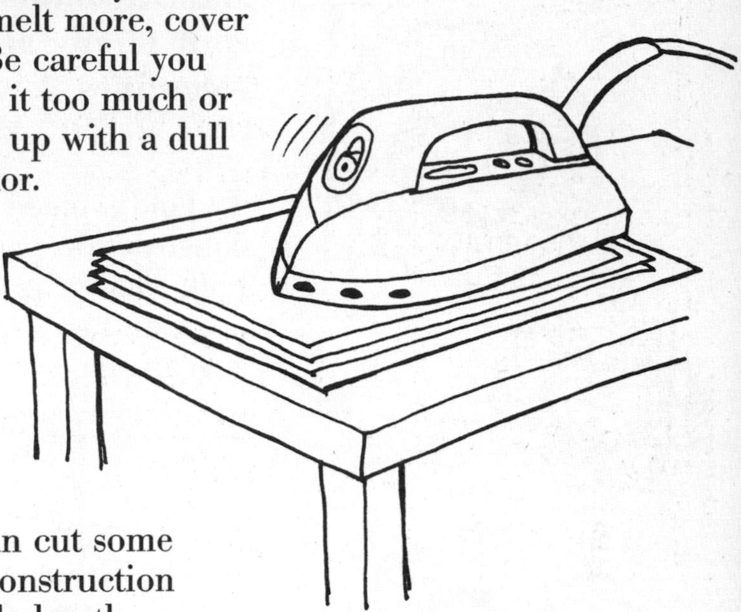

6. You can cut some strips of construction paper and glue them around your artwork for a frame, or simply trim away some of the waxed paper. Framed or not, your melted-crayon creation will look great in the window.

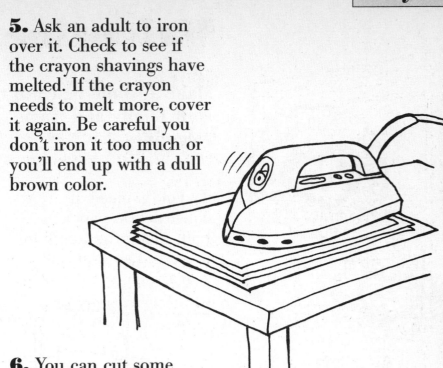

Valentine doily

Make a whole batch of these so you can give your family and friends pretty handmade valentines.

1. Fold a piece of construction paper in half. Along the fold line, draw and cut out half a heart.

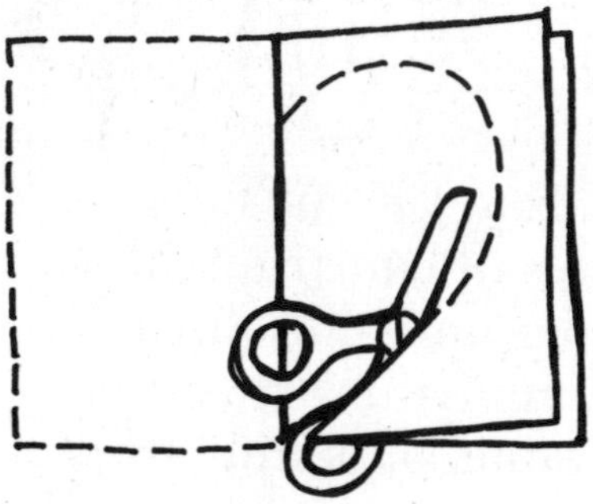

2. Open the heart and place it on the doily.

3. Use markers or crayons to decorate the valentine or to write on a message.

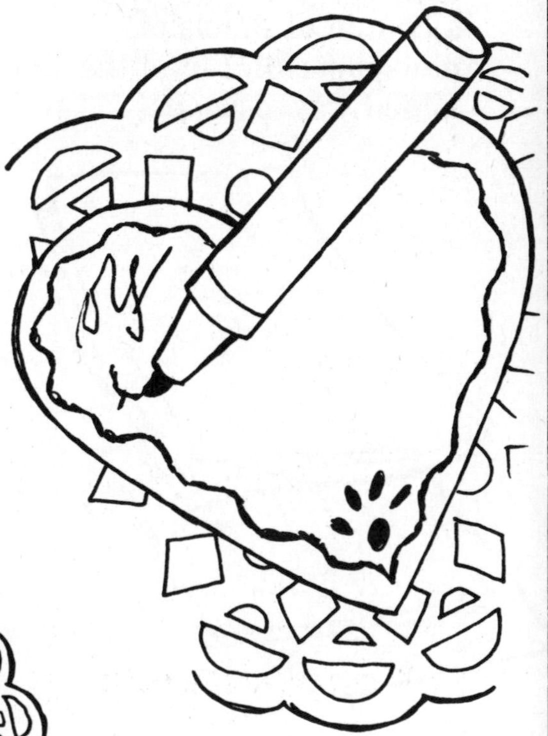

You will need

red or pink construction paper

scissors and white craft glue or a glue stick

a paper doily

markers or crayons

Paper cones

Make a bunch of these and fill them with small treats. You can also make them in seasonal colors and hang them from a Christmas tree.

1. Glue the paper doily onto the construction paper. Allow it to dry, then cut it out.

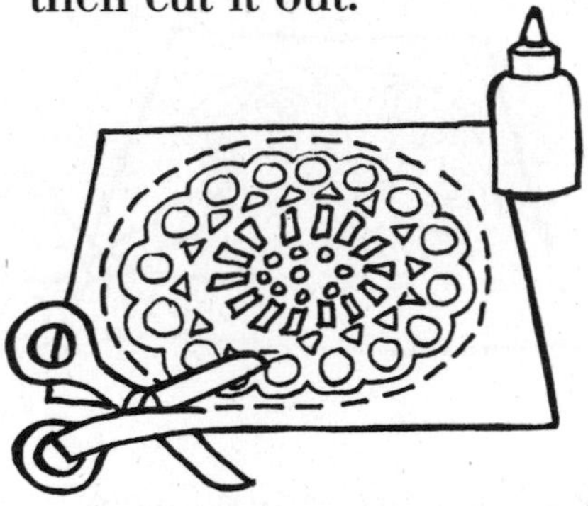

2. Fold the circle in half, open it and cut it in half along the fold line. Set aside one half to make into a cone when you finish the first one.

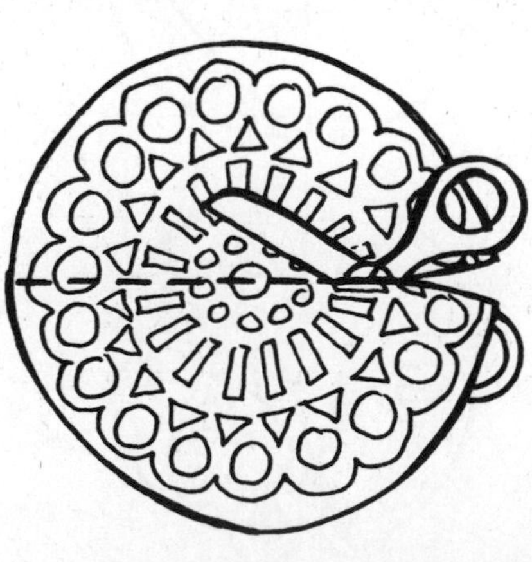

3. Glue or staple the half-circle into a cone shape.

4. Cut a strip of construction paper for a handle and glue or staple it in place.

You will need

a round paper doily

scissors and white craft glue or a glue stick

construction paper

a stapler (optional)

Doily angel

This angel can stand on its own or be hung up if you tie fishing line or yarn from the halo.

1. Glue the paper doily onto the construction paper. Allow it to dry, then cut it out.

2. Fold the doily circle in half, open it and cut it along the fold line.

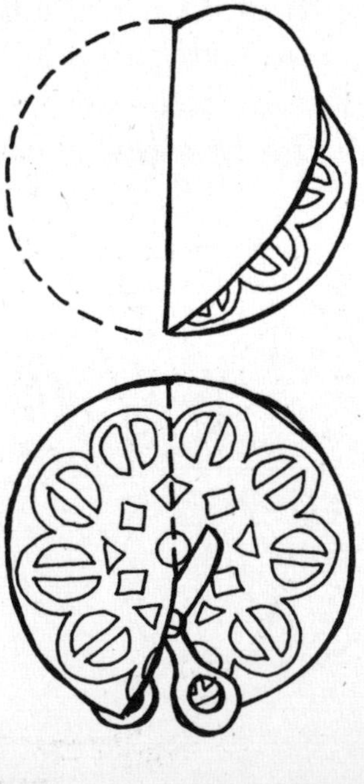

3. Staple one of the halves into a cone shape. Set aside the other half for the angel wings.

4. Make a small circle halo in the center of the pipe cleaner as shown. Thread the bead onto the pipe-cleaner ends. Bend the halo so it sits on the bead head.

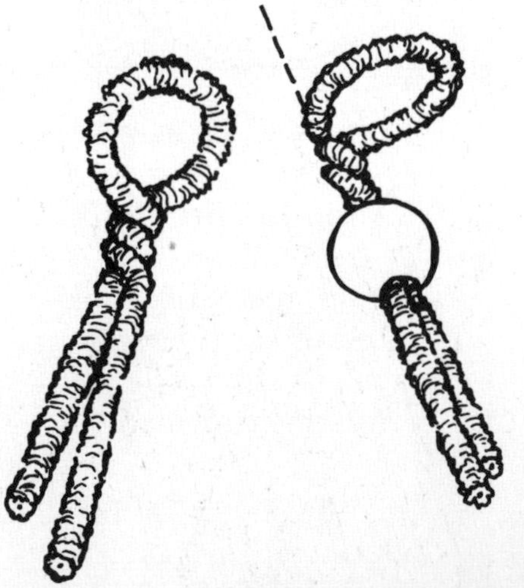

You will need

a paper doily about 13 cm (5 in.) in diameter

construction paper

scissors and a glue stick or white craft glue

a stapler

a tinsel or regular pipe cleaner

a wooden bead

paint and a brush or markers

yarn or fishing line (optional)

5. Poke the pipe-cleaner ends into the small hole in the pointed end of the cone. Staple one or both pipe-cleaner ends to the inside of the cone. Trim the ends if they stick out past the bottom of your angel's dress.

6. Trim off a little of the straight edge of the doily wings. Glue or staple them to the back of the angel.

7. Draw or paint on an angel face.

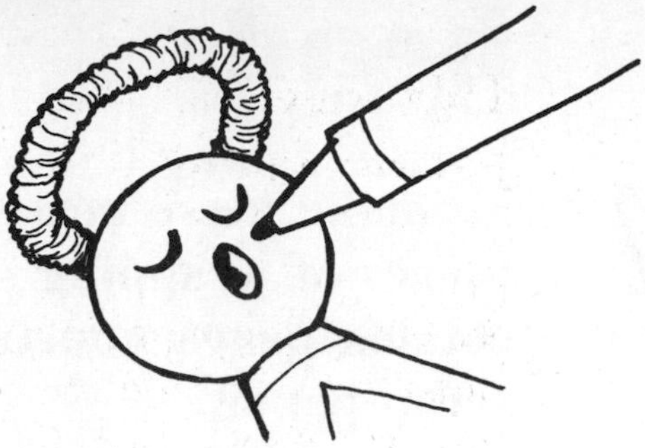

8. If you'd like your angel to have hair, cut a few strands of yarn and tie them loosely around the base of the halo. Style the hair if you wish.

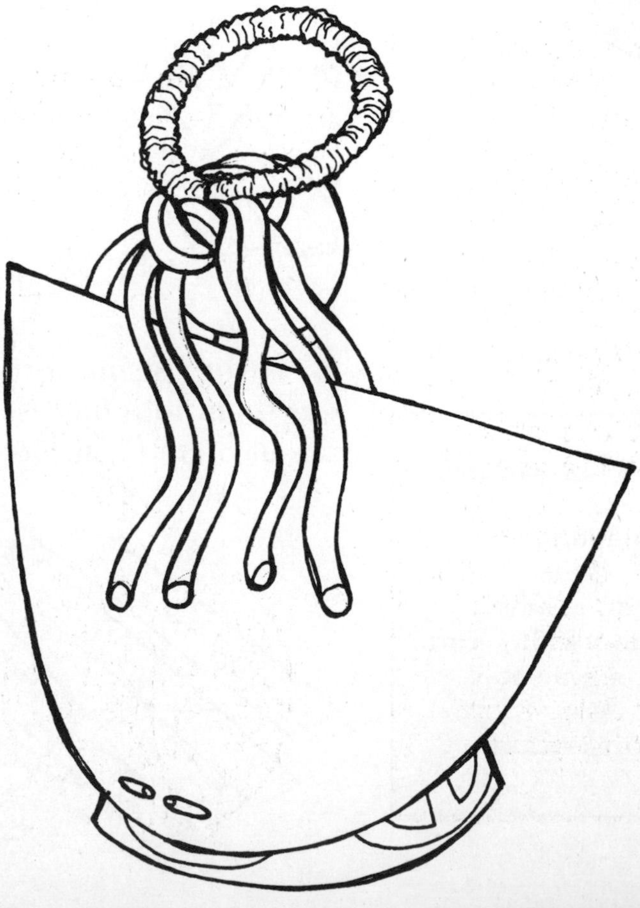

Drinking-straw beads

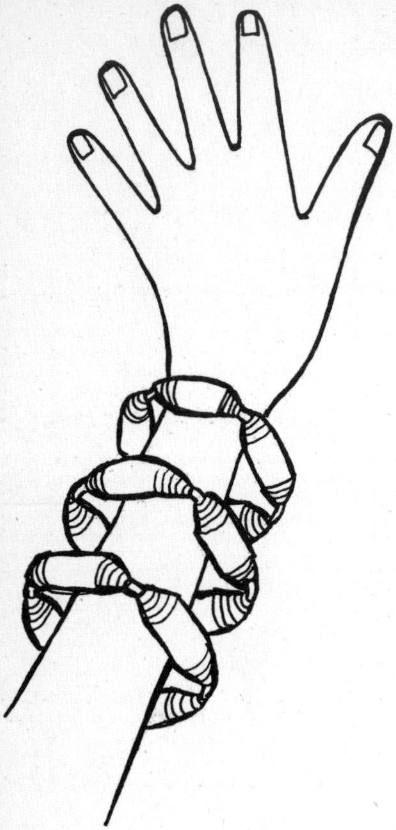

To make these beads, you can use leftover pieces of wrapping paper, colorful magazine and catalog pages, construction paper or any other scrap paper.

1. You can use a pencil and ruler to mark straight lines for cutting, or simply cut strips of paper. The strips can be as wide or narrow as you'd like your beads to be.

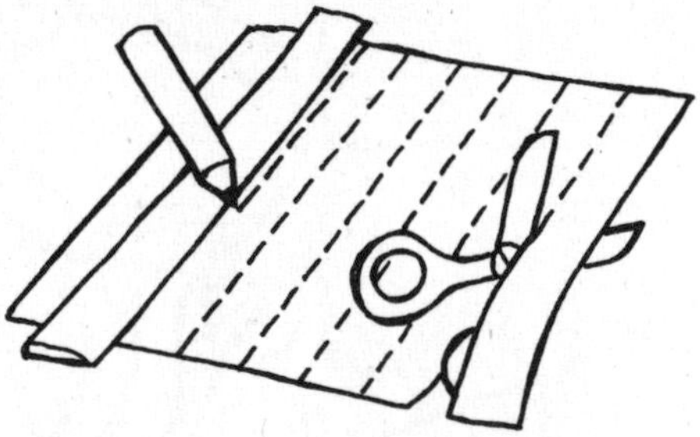

2. If your strips are long, cut them into pieces about 8 cm (3 in.) long.

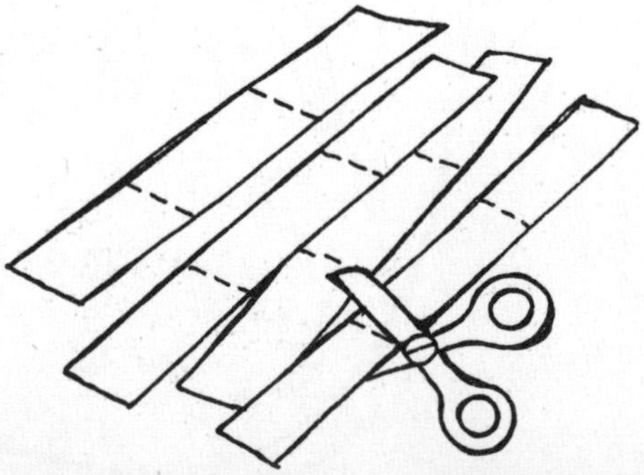

3. Begin winding one end of a strip of paper onto a straw. Spread a little glue on the paper as you go.

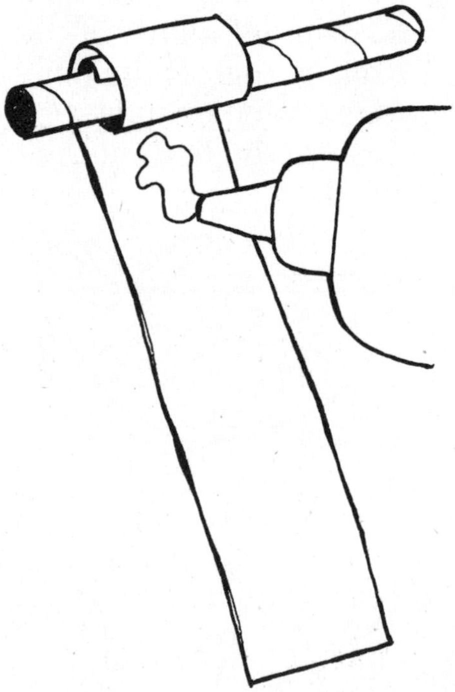

You will need

paper
◎
scissors, a ruler,
a pencil and white craft glue or a glue stick
◎
drinking straws

4. When you are near the end, spread a little more glue on the strip, then finish rolling it. Hold the paper for a moment while the glue dries.

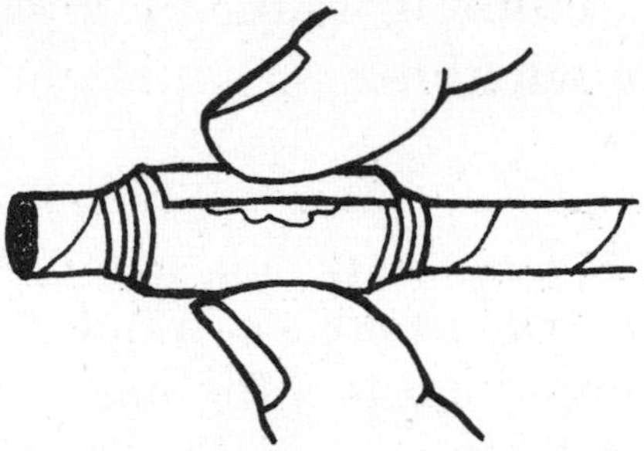

5. Slide the bead off the straw, or cut off the straw on each side of the bead. Make lots more beads!

More ideas

Wind more than one color of paper to make a bead. Begin with a wide strip. When you finish rolling it onto a straw, dab a bit of glue on it and wind a narrower strip around it. Add a third or fourth layer if you wish.

Cut long triangles of paper. To make the beads, wind the wide end of a triangle around the straw. Guide the paper as you roll so the point of the triangle ends up in the middle of the bead.

If you'd like shiny beads, coat them with acrylic varnish or a sealer product, such as Podgy or Mod Podge, while they're still on the straws.

Thread your beads onto elastic cord, plastic lace or yarn to make a necklace or a bracelet.

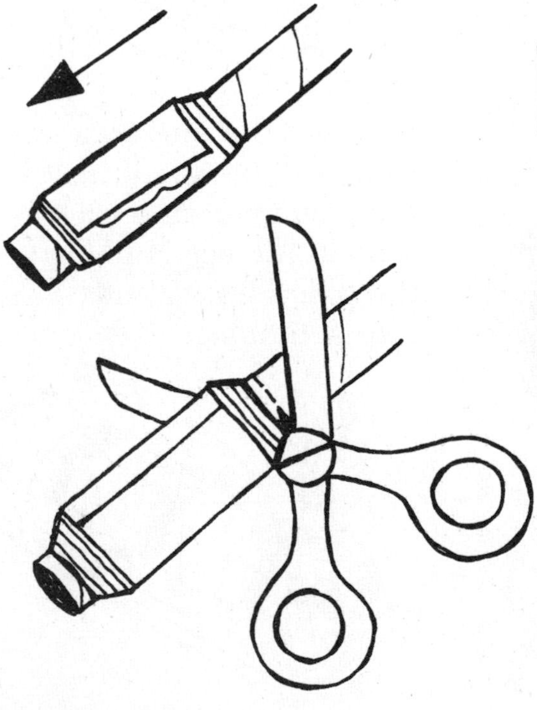

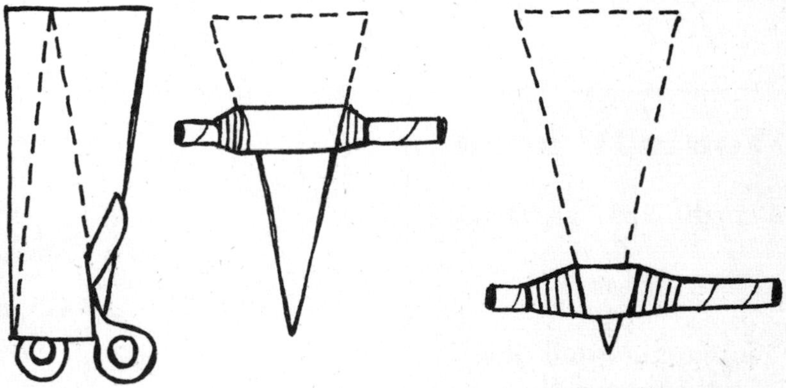

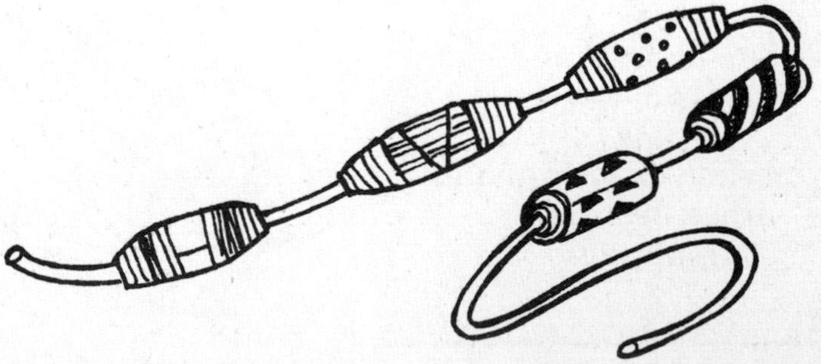

Egg-carton caterpillar

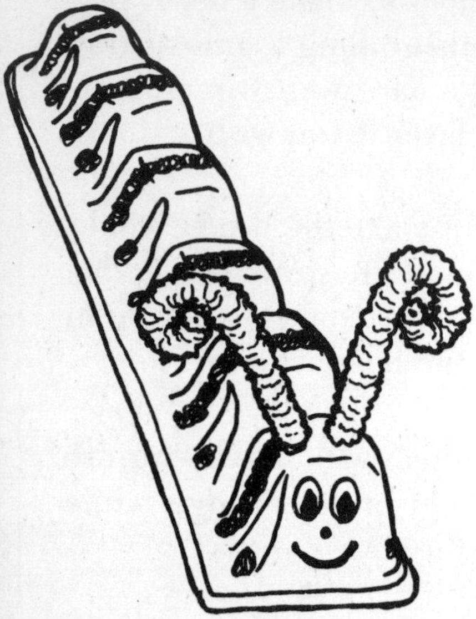

There are many ways to decorate this cheerful caterpillar. You can paint it, color it with markers and crayons or use stickers.

You will need

a cardboard egg carton

scissors

a pencil, a nail or a blunt needle

a 15 cm (6 in.) pipe cleaner

a marker or crayon and other decorating supplies

1. Cut out one of the rows of egg cups from the carton.

2. Decorate the caterpillar any way you'd like. Draw on a face.

3. Use the pencil, nail or needle to poke two holes into the top of the head egg cup.

4. Bend the pipe cleaner in half. From underneath, poke one end into each hole in the egg cup. Curl the pipe-cleaner ends into antennae.

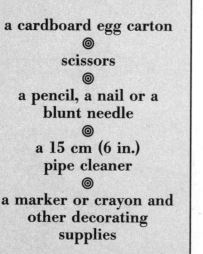

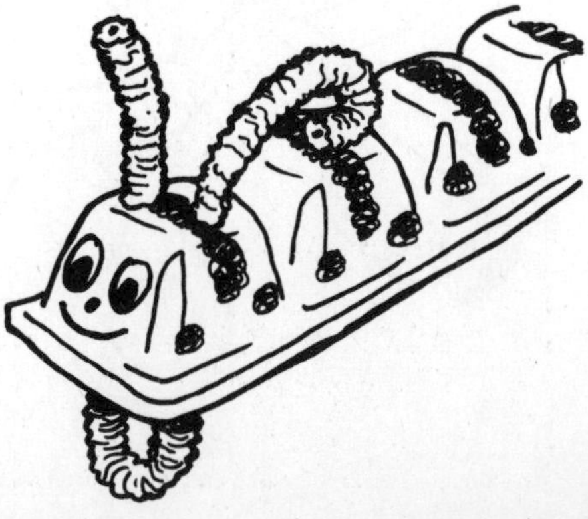

Egg-carton raccoon

This raccoon is a funny little character with his black mask and ringed tail.

1. Cut an egg cup out of the center area of the carton rather than one of the corners.

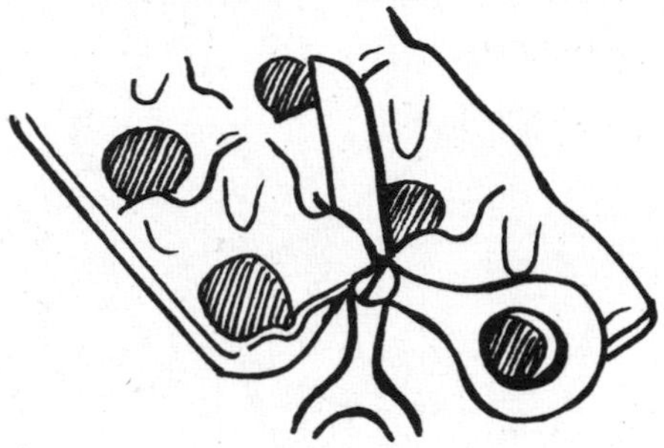

2. Trim off any ragged edges, but otherwise leave the cup as it is. It should have three scooped-out sides and one straight one. The straight side will be the raccoon's backside.

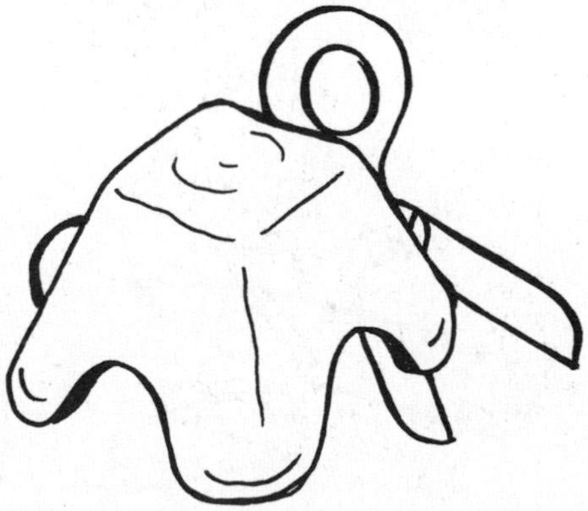

3. On the front, draw ears, a nose, whiskers and a black mask-like area where the eyes will go. Draw lines on the paws. Glue the beads in place for eyes.

4. Cut a tail from the egg-carton lid. Draw stripes on it and glue it to the raccoon's backside.

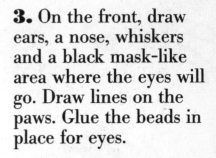

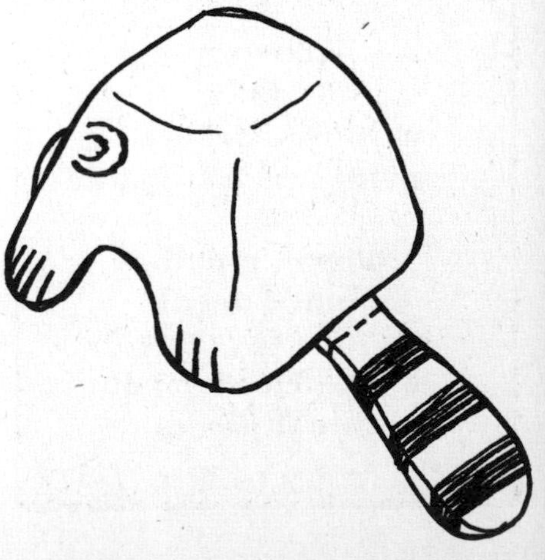

You will need

a cardboard egg carton

scissors

a black marker

beads or roly eyes

white craft glue or a glue stick

Ladybug

After you've made this charming bug, try making lots of other colorful critters. You could make a spider with eight black pipe-cleaner legs.

1. Cut an egg cup out of the carton. Trim it so it is smooth and straight all around.

2. Color or paint the egg cup red.

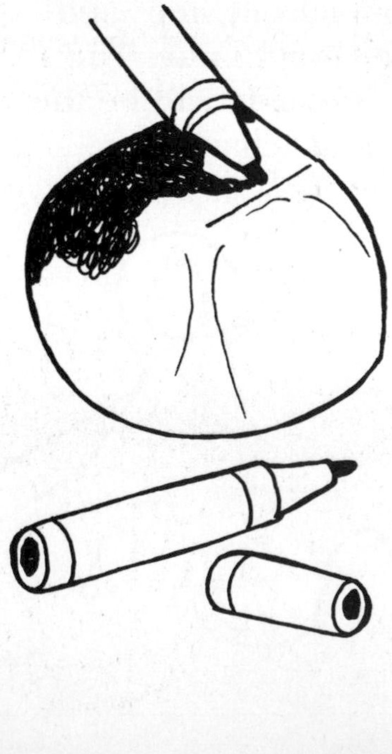

3. Draw or paint on a face, black spots and a line down the center of the ladybug's back.

4. Make three small holes on each side of the cup. Poke a piece of pipe cleaner into a hole on one side and out the hole straight across on the other side. Make the other legs the same way.

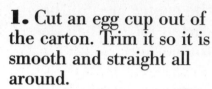

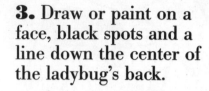

You will need

a cardboard egg carton

scissors

crayons, markers or paint and a brush

a pencil, a nail or a blunt needle

a pipe cleaner cut into 3 pieces

Blossoms

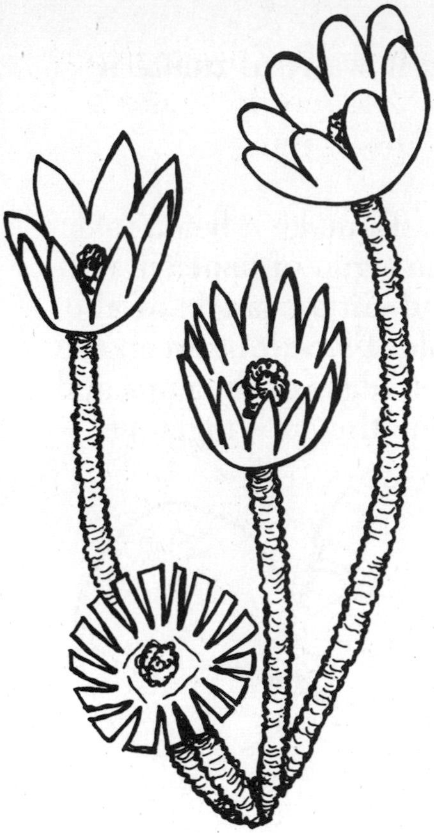

You can color these blossoms with crayons, markers or just about any kind of paint. Make many so you can add them to your button bouquet (see page 33).

1. Cut an egg cup out of the carton. Trim it so it is smooth and straight all around.

2. There are many ways to cut petals. You can cut them large and round, small and pointy, or small and smooth or simply make many small cuts to make fringe-like petals.

3. Color your flower or leave it the color it is and draw on dots, circles or stripes.

4. Poke a small hole in the center of the flower with the pencil, nail or needle. Thread on a pipe cleaner. Bend a little curl into the end of the pipe cleaner to keep it in place.

You will need

a cardboard egg carton

scissors

crayons, markers or paint and a brush

a pencil, a nail or a blunt needle

pipe cleaners

Egg-cup chick

These chicks are so cute, you'll want to make a dozen of them!

1. Cut two egg cups out of the carton. Trim them so they are smooth and straight all around.

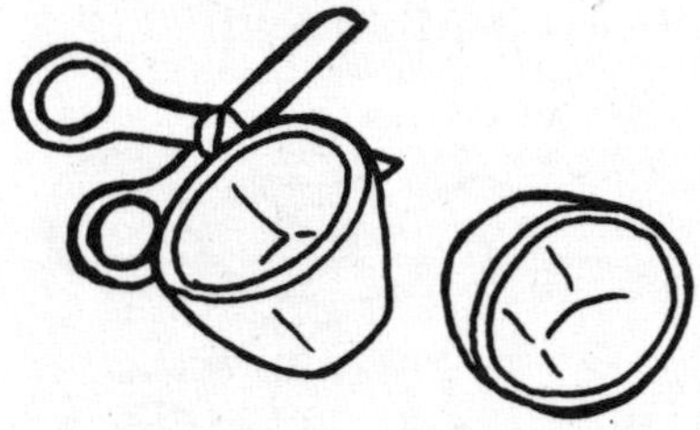

2. Color or paint them both yellow or any color you like.

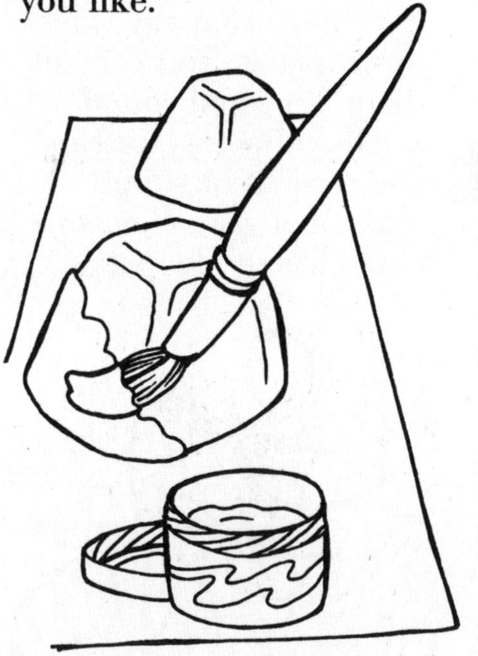

3. To make a beak, fold the scrap of paper in half and cut a triangle on the fold. Place it between the cut edges of the cups and glue the cups together.

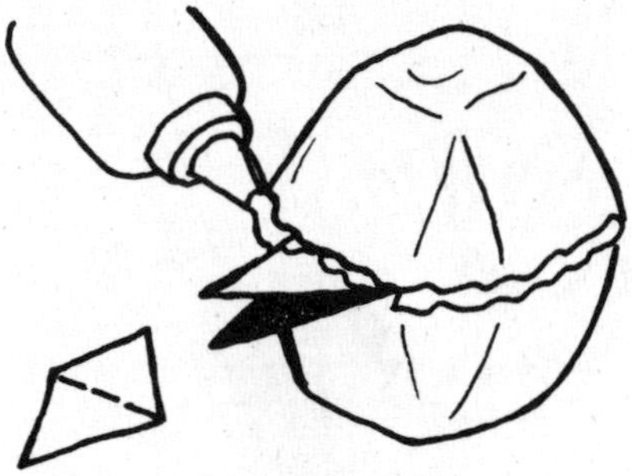

4. Draw on eyes. Make a hole in the back of the top cup. Poke in the tail feather.

You will need

a cardboard egg carton

scissors and white craft glue

crayons, markers or paint and a brush

a scrap of construction paper

a pencil, a nail or a blunt needle

a colored craft feather

Egg-cup piggy nose

This little piggy nose looks great with the piggy ears on page 96.

1. Cut an egg cup from the center area of the carton rather than one of the corners. Trim off any ragged edges, but otherwise leave the cup as it is. The straight edge will be at the bridge of your nose.

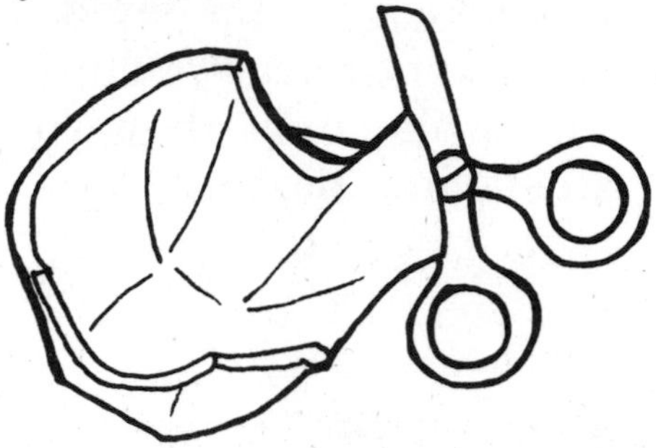

2. Color or paint the egg cup.

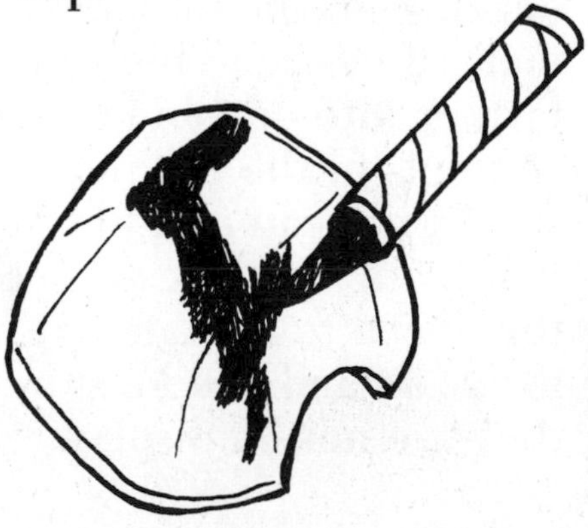

3. Glue the two buttons on the cup so they look like nostrils. Allow the glue to dry.

4. Punch a hole on each side of the cup except for the straight side. Tie yarn into each side hole to hold your piggy nose in place and try it on!

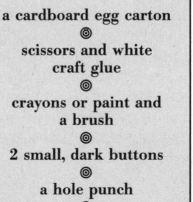

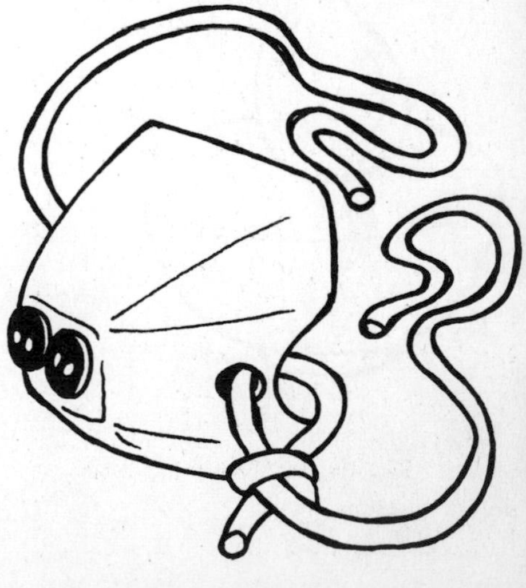

You will need

a cardboard egg carton

scissors and white craft glue

crayons or paint and a brush

2 small, dark buttons

a hole punch

yarn

Decorating eggs

You can decorate eggs that are hard-boiled or blown out. Here's how to prepare each type of egg. See the next page for lots of decorating ideas.

Hard-boiled eggs

Place the eggs in a pot and cover them completely with water. Put the lid on the pot. Ask an adult to bring the eggs to a boil, remove the pot from the heat and let it stand for 20 minutes. When the time is up, cool the eggs thoroughly in cold water. Dry them off and decorate them. Decorated hard-boiled eggs can be eaten in a day or two as long as they have been kept refrigerated. If you wish to keep the eggs for display only, they will be fine for a couple of weeks in a basket.

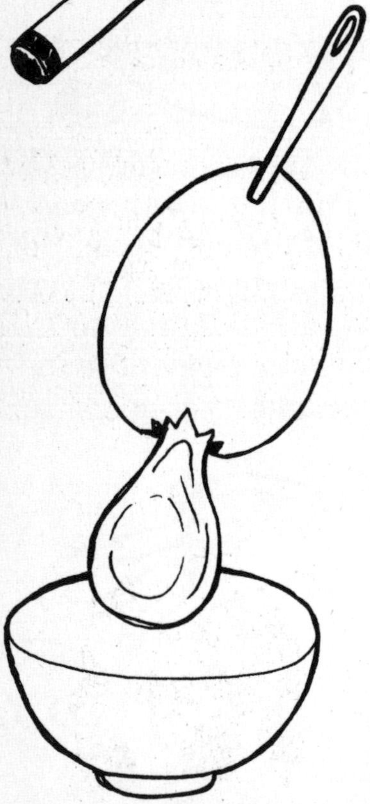

Blown-out eggs

Eggs will need to be blown out by an adult. Thoroughly wash and dry each egg. Use a long darning needle to poke a small hole in each end. To make it easier to blow out the yolk, poke the needle farther into one end to break the yolk. Blow the contents of the egg into a small bowl. Rinse out the shell with water and blow it out. Dry off the egg and it is ready to be decorated. These eggs are fragile so they need to be handled very gently. They will keep for years and can be stored in an egg carton when they are not on display.

Decorating ideas

You can display your fancy eggs in egg cups or a basket or on small bottle lids. You can make stands by cutting sections off a toilet-paper roll or taping a strip of construction paper into a small circle.

Dyed eggs: To get nice pastel colors, stir food coloring into a mixture of equal amounts of water and vinegar. Dip white eggs into the mixture and set them in a cup or carton or on a paper towel to dry.

Drawn on and dyed eggs: Draw a design or message on a white egg with a white crayon. Dye the egg as described above.

Painted eggs: You can paint eggs with watercolor paint, acrylic craft paint or dimensional fabric paint. Allow the egg to dry on a stand or in a cup. Instead of using paint, you can draw on eggs with markers.

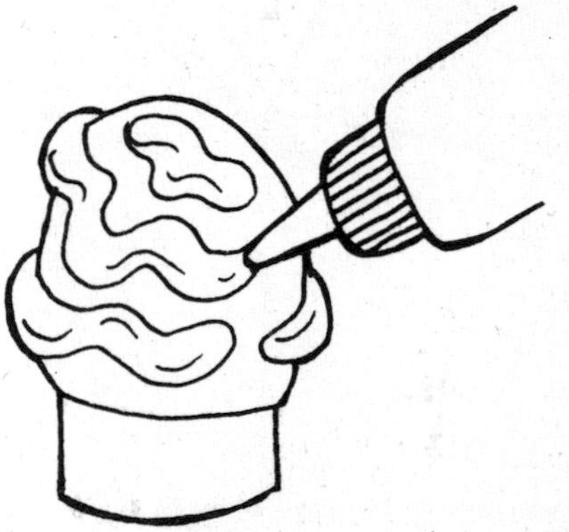

Sponge-painted eggs: Use a small piece of a sponge to dab acrylic craft paint all over an egg. Allow it to dry, then sponge another color over top. Or, cut a small square or rectangle of sponge, dip it in paint and create designs on an egg.

Envelope bookmark

Here's a great way to recycle used greeting-card and junk-mail envelopes.

1. Fold the scrap paper in half. Along the fold line, draw and cut out half a medium-sized heart.

2. Open the heart and place it so its point is in one of the bottom corners of the envelope. If the heart is too large for the envelope, fold the heart again and trim it.

3. Trace the curved parts of heart (lobes) onto the envelope. Hold the envelope sideways as shown, and decorate it. Write on a message, such as "I love reading," "Hold my spot" or "I was here."

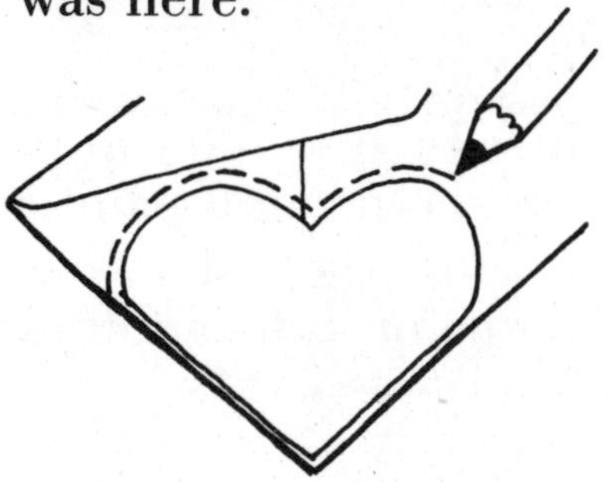

4. Cut out the heart. To use it, open it and slide it over the top right-hand corner of the page you'd like to mark.

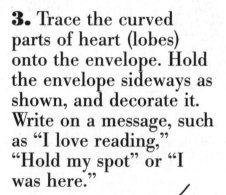

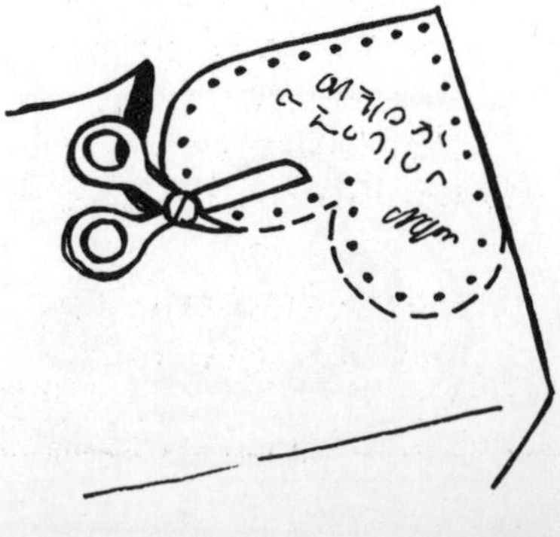

You will need

scrap paper
◎
a pencil and scissors
◎
a used envelope
◎
markers or crayons

Penguin

Your penguin will look like it is waddling if you stand it up and gently rock it.

1. Trace part of a cup in one of the bottom corners of the envelope.

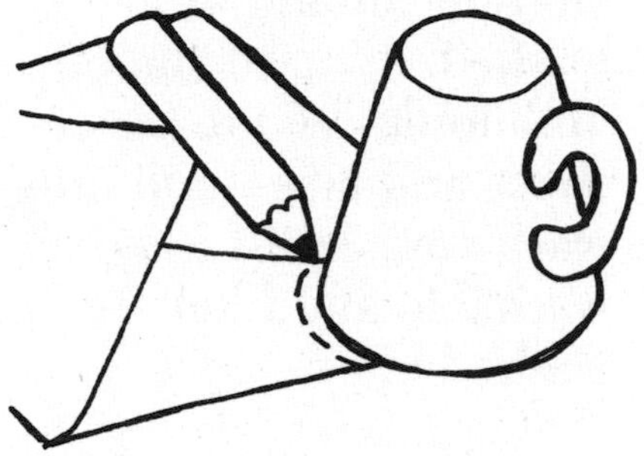

2. Fold over the tip of the corner to make the penguin's head. Draw on eyes and a beak.

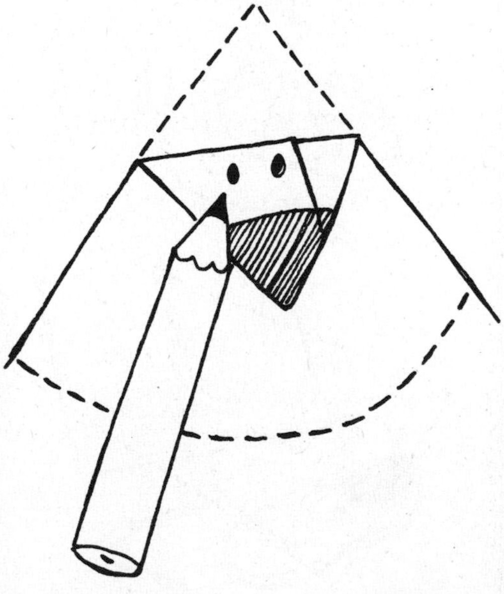

3. Use a black crayon or marker to draw wings. Cut out the penguin.

4. Cut out a pair of rounded orange feet. Bend up the straight end and glue the feet in place.

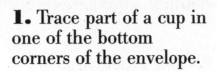

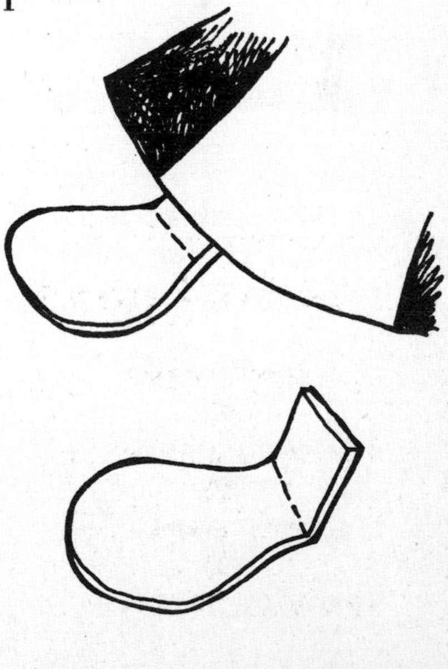

You will need

a white or light-colored used envelope

◎

a cup

◎

a pencil, scissors and white craft glue

◎

crayons or markers including a black one

◎

orange construction paper

Fabric-paint fun

When you decorate clothing, use fabric paint. Try some of the printmaking ideas from pages 138 and 139 or use dimensional fabric paint (it comes in small, squeezable bottles) to draw on designs.

1. Your article of clothing should be washed, dry and smooth. You don't need to wash shoes and laces, and only wash your hat if it is washable and likely to be washed often.

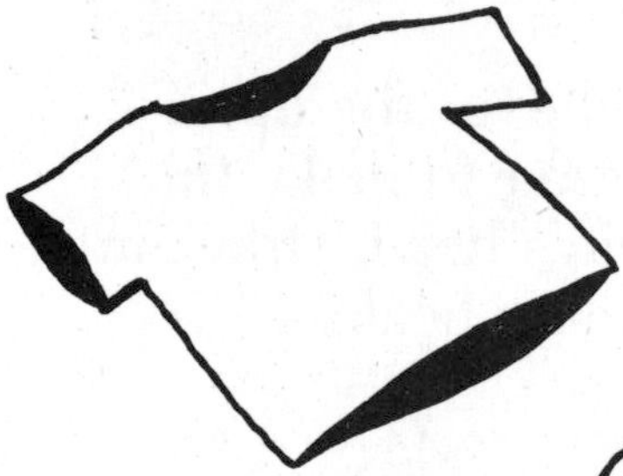

2. Here's how to prepare different articles of clothing for printing.

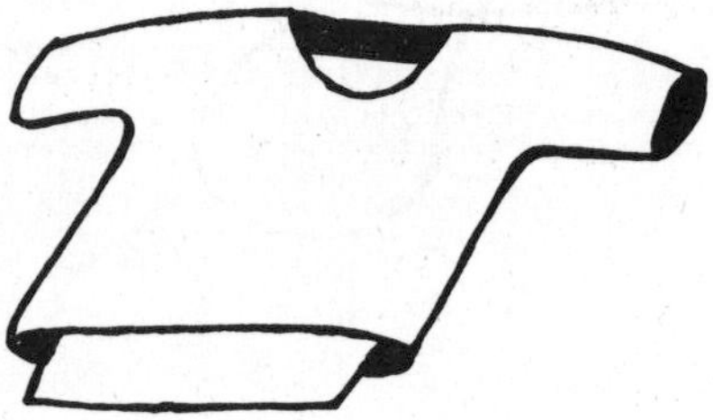

- Put cardboard in between the two layers of fabric for a shirt, shorts, a jacket, socks or gloves.

- Remove the laces from shoes and fill the toes with crumpled paper.

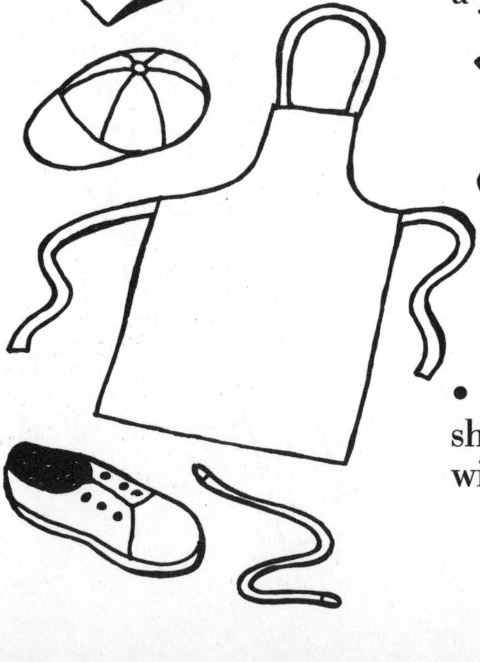

You will need

an article of clothing such as a T-shirt, a hat, gloves, socks or shoes and laces

◎

cardboard

◎

fabric paint

◎

scrap paper

◎

printing supplies

• Tape the ends of shoelaces to your work surface.

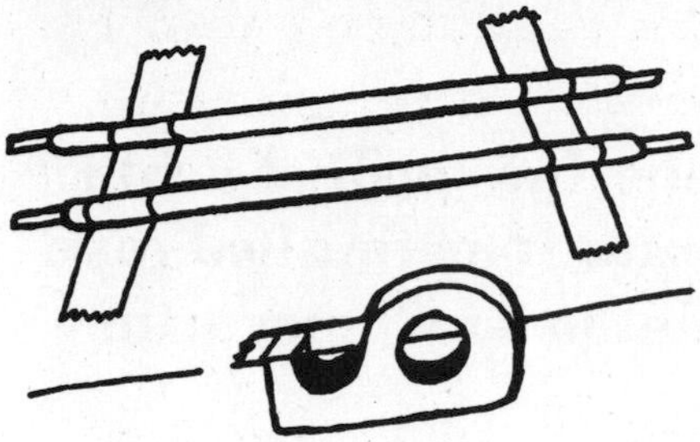

• Stuff a hat with crumpled paper or place it over an upside-down bowl.

3. Test your designs on scrap paper first, then print or draw designs on your article of clothing.

4. When your article of clothing is dry, you need to set the paint. Cover the printed area with a clean cloth and have an adult iron it on a hot setting for two minutes (or follow the paint manufacturer's instructions). You do not need to set the paint for items that will not be washed or if you used dimensional fabric paint.

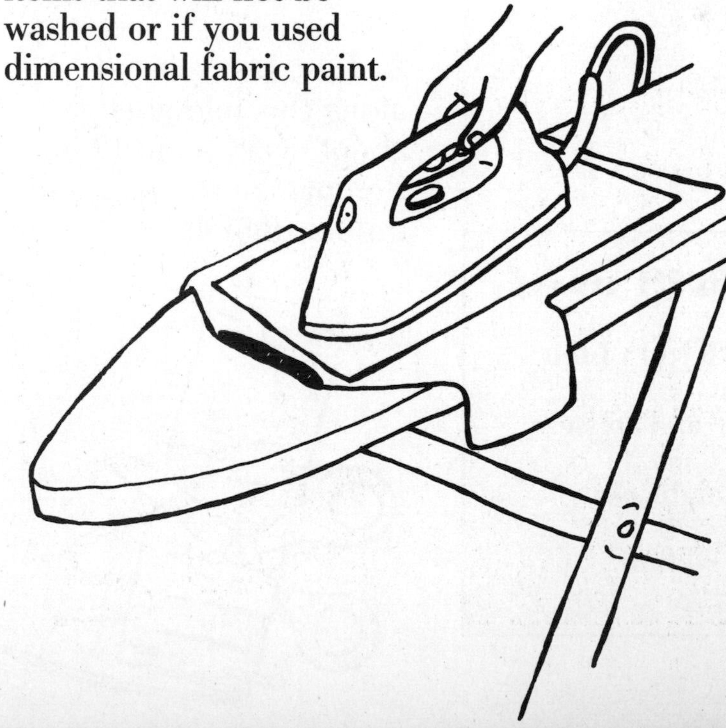

No-sew dress-up cape

You can buy felt by the meter (or yard) at a fabric or craft-supply store. Decorate your finished cape with dimensional fabric paint or any fancy trim.

1. Fold over and pin about 5 cm (2 in.) of the felt along one of the long sides.

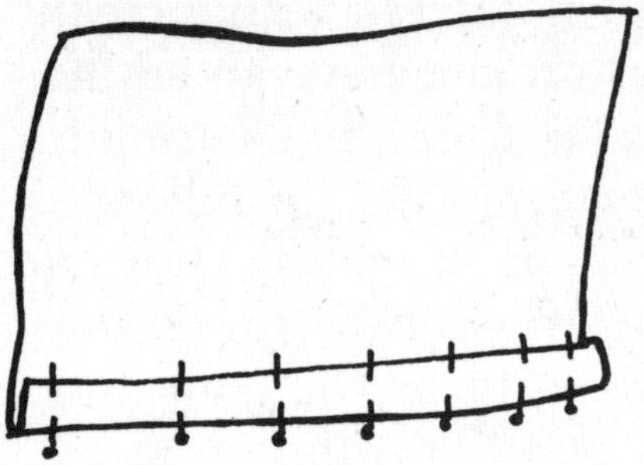

2. Cut short slits all along this folded edge about every 5 cm (2 in.). Remove all the pins and unfold the felt.

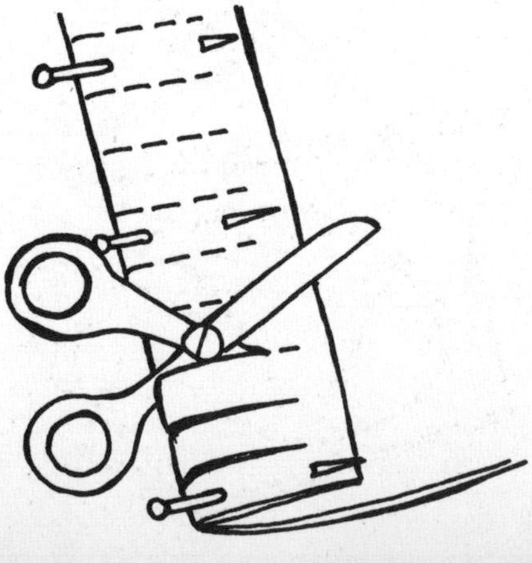

3. Weave a length of ribbon in and out of the slits and gather the felt to look like a cape. Knot a ribbon end into the first slit on each side of the cape to keep the ribbon from being pulled out.

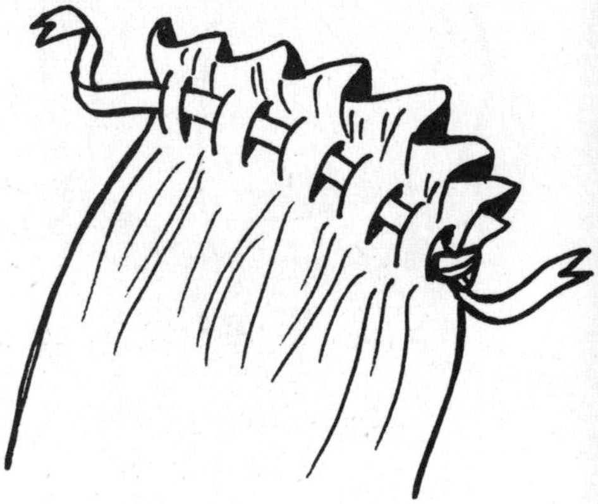

4. Try on the cape. Trim the bottom edge so you don't trip on it. Make it jagged for a witch's cape, wavy for a princess or straight for a superhero.

You will need

1 m (1 yd.) of felt
◎
a ruler and scissors
◎
straight pins
◎
ribbon

Felt funny faces

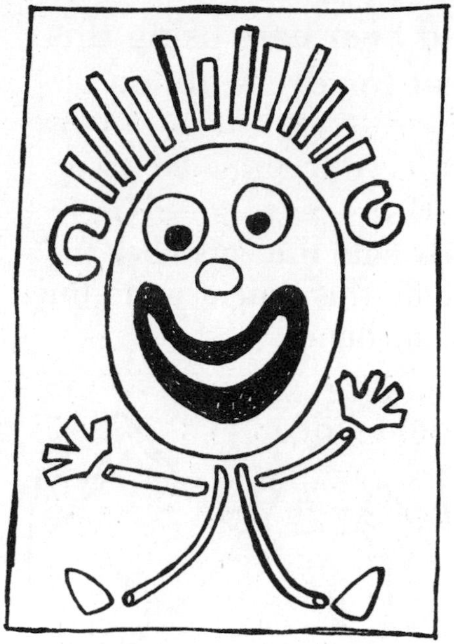

Begin with a piece of cardboard large enough to have a good-sized face glued onto it.

1. Spread glue on the cardboard and cover it with felt.

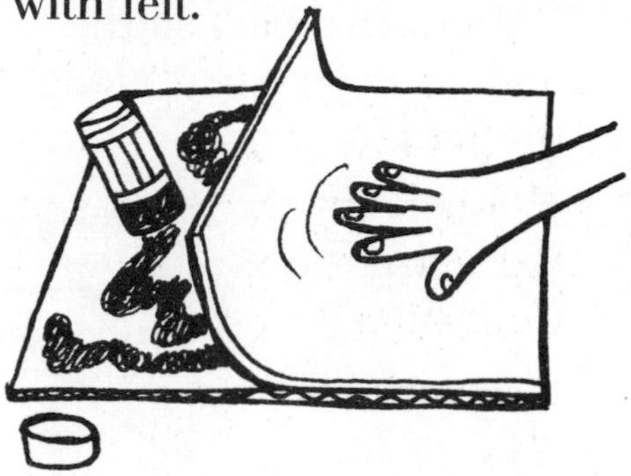

2. From another piece of felt, cut out a circle for a face. Glue it onto the felt-covered cardboard.

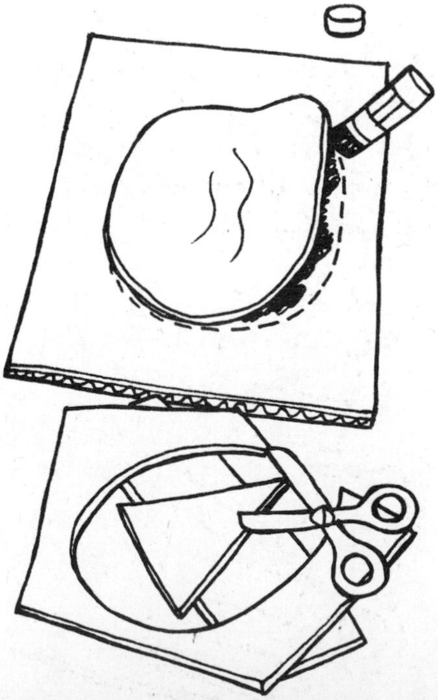

3. Cut out many different sizes and shapes of eyes, ears, noses, mouths and eyebrows. For hair, cut out felt styles or cut lengths of yarn. You can also make funny features, such as clown lips or animal ears.

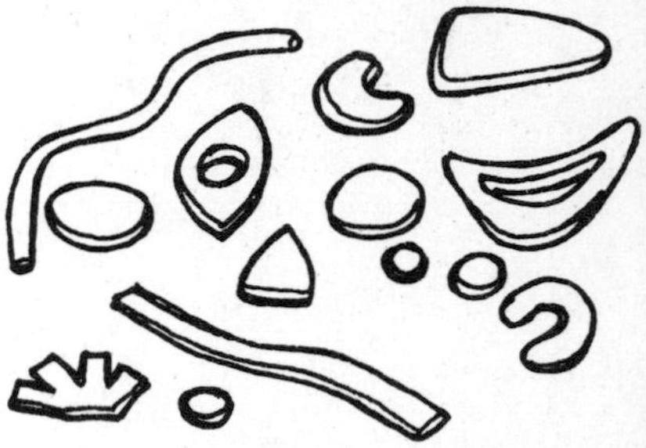

4. Mix and match the parts of the face to make all types of new faces.

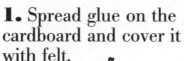

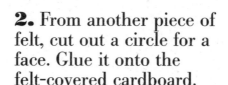

You will need

white craft glue or a glue stick

◎

corrugated or thin cardboard

◎

felt squares and scraps

◎

scissors

◎

yarn (optional)

Animal ears

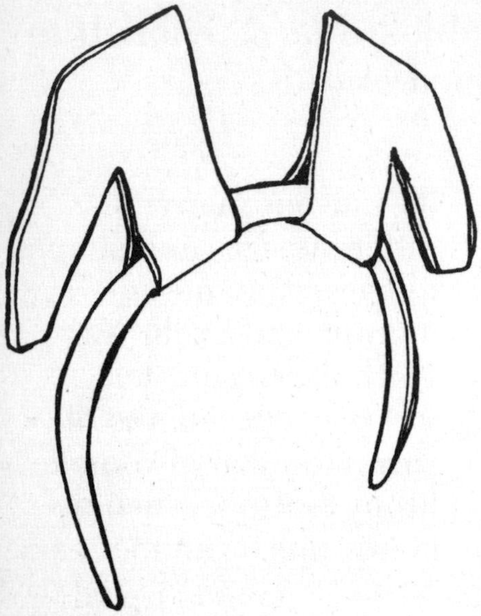

Try making pig, cat, dog and bear ears using this simple method. They're great for dress-up, or plays or just for fun.

1. Fold the felt in half. Cut out two ears so the base of each ear is along the fold.

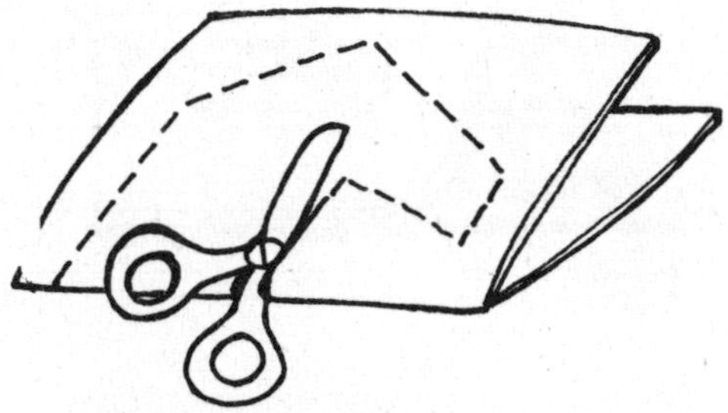

2. Unfold the ears and spread glue over the inside of each.

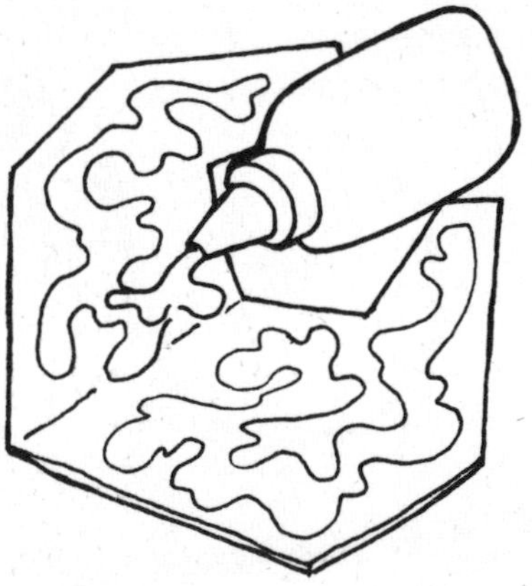

3. Fold the ears back in half, this time around the hair band.

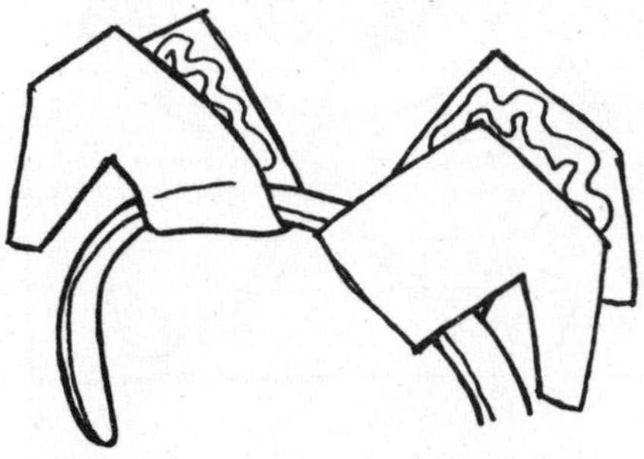

4. Use the paper clips to hold the ears together close to the hair band. Remove the paper clips when the glue is dry.

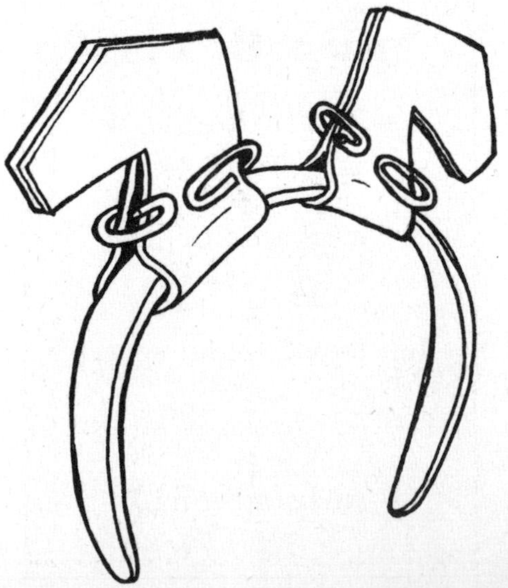

You will need

a square of felt

scissors and white craft glue

a hair band

paper clips

Weather chart

You can also use this felt board for other felt figures and shapes that you have made or bought. Large pieces of felt are available at fabric and craft-supply stores.

1. Glue together two pieces of cardboard, each about the size of a cookie sheet. (You may need to put heavy books on top to keep them flat.)

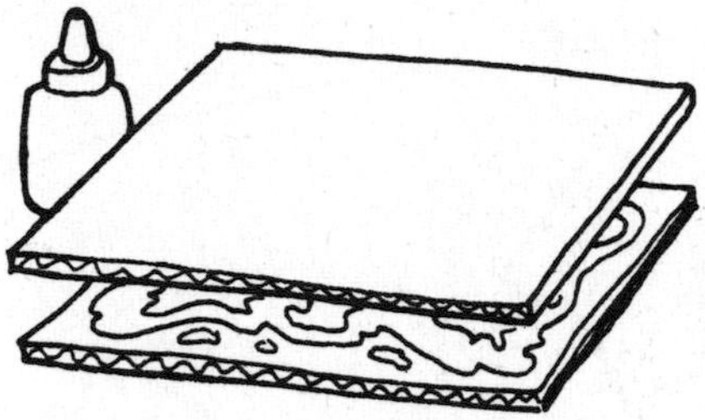

2. Spread glue over one side of the cardboard and smooth a piece of felt over it.

3. Cut out felt weather symbols, such as clouds, a bolt of lightning, raindrops, an umbrella, a sun, snowflakes and a bent-over tree or wavy grass for wind. You can use permanent markers to add detail if you like.

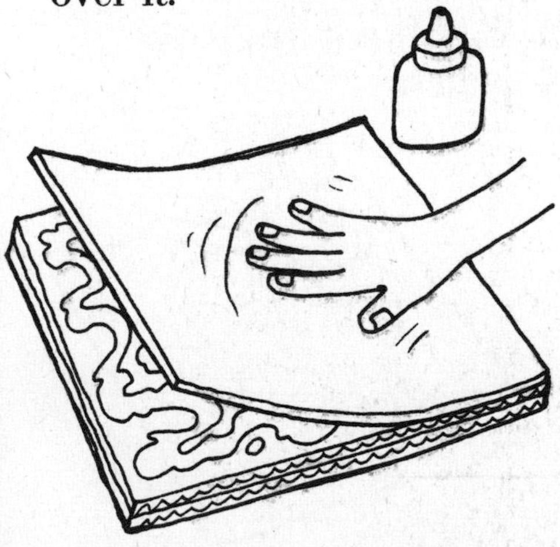

4. Check the weather and place the proper symbols on your weather chart.

You will need

corrugated cardboard

white craft glue and scissors

felt

non-toxic permanent markers (optional)

Glue-together puppet

Use thick, white craft glue for this puppet. It is also helpful if the felt is real rather than acrylic. Use the pattern you create to make many puppets and put on a play.

1. Place your hand on the paper and draw a wide outline around your hand and wrist. Make sure the bottom is very wide.

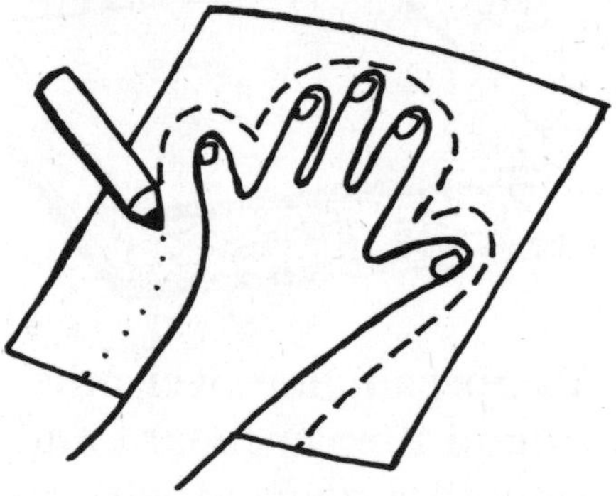

2. Cut out this paper pattern.

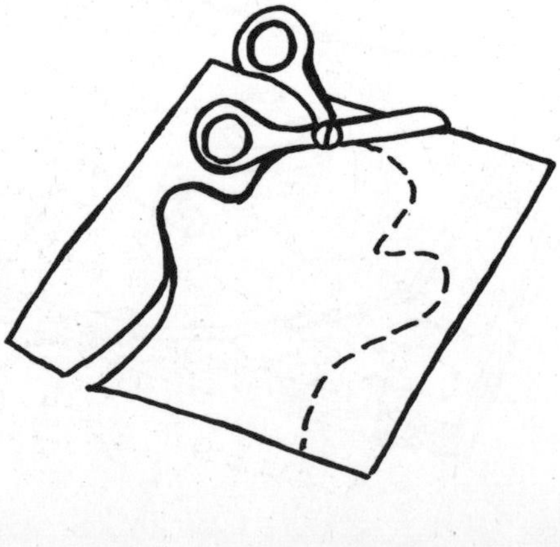

3. Trace your pattern twice onto the felt with a pencil. (Use chalk or a dried sliver of soap if your felt is a dark color.)

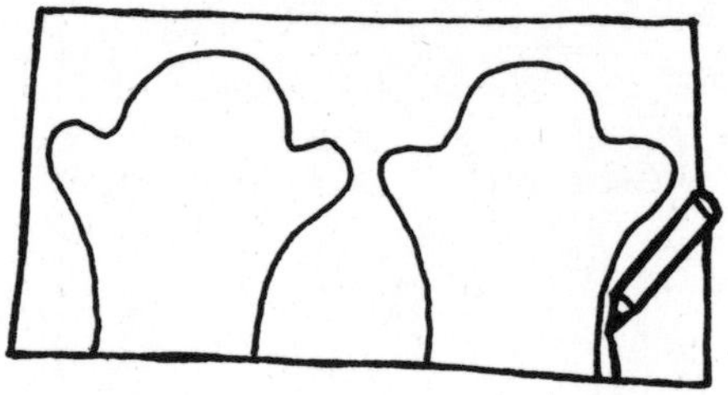

4. Cut out the two felt shapes.

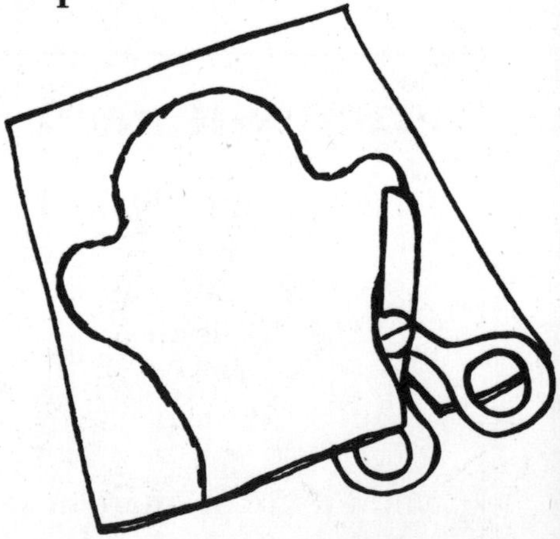

You will need

paper, a pencil, scissors and white craft glue

felt

buttons and other materials for a face (see step 7)

5. If your puppet needs ears or eyes that stick out above the head, cut them out and glue them to one of the puppet shapes.

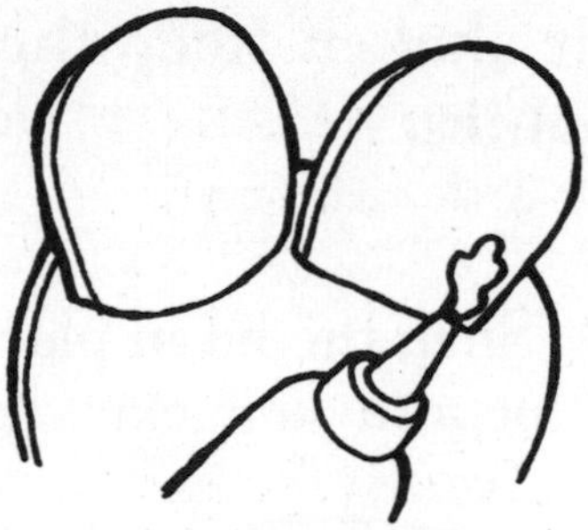

6. Glue the puppet shapes together around the edges.

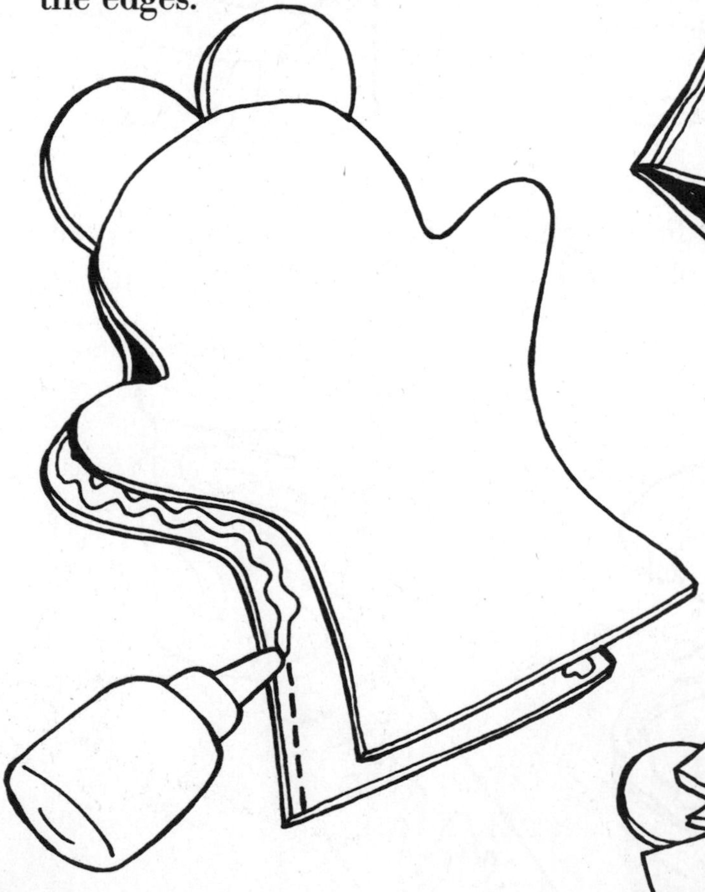

7. Glue on items, such as roly eyes, buttons, beads, yarn and other colors of felt, to create the face and other features.

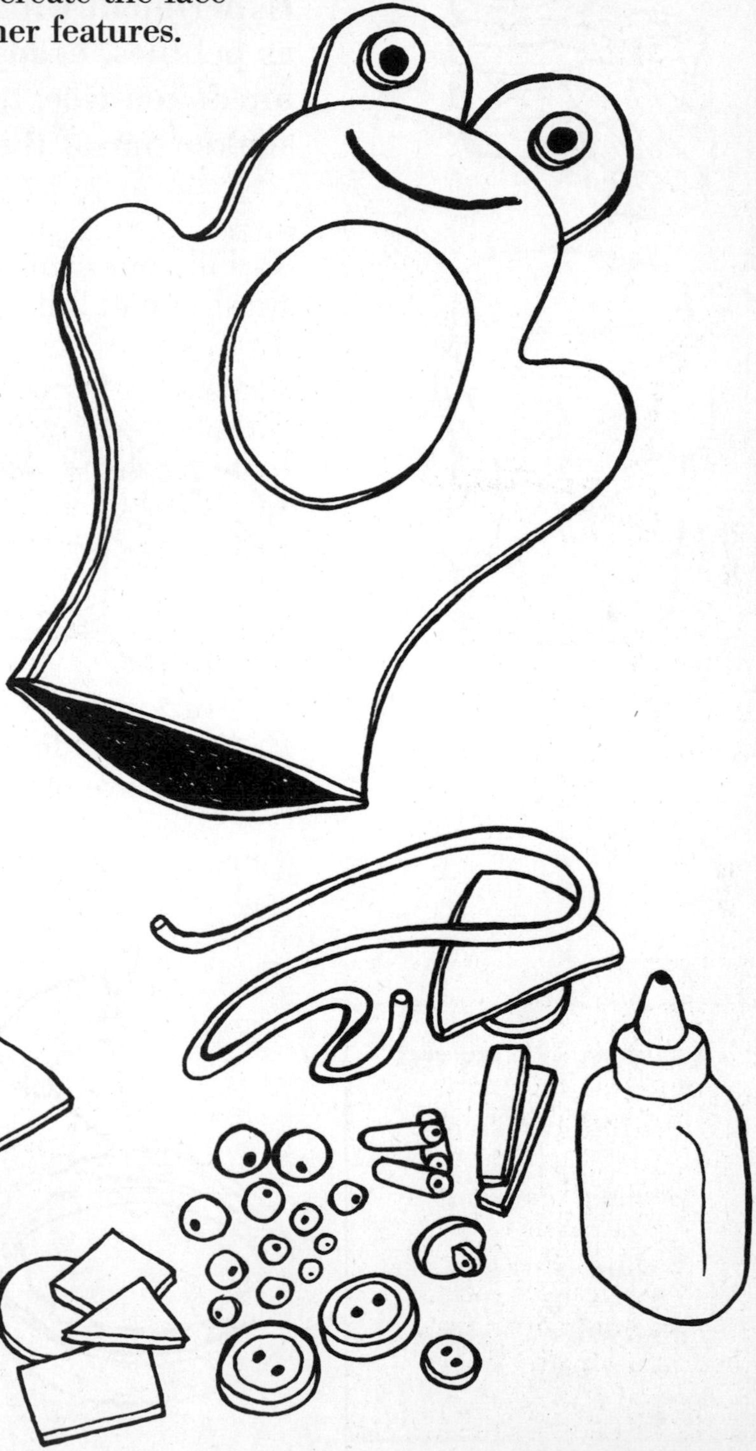

Mini shakers

Experiment with different materials, such as pebbles, beads, beans, buttons, sand and uncooked rice, to put in your shaker. Keep the shaker out of the reach of babies.

1. Fill your canister one-third to half full.

2. Run a thin line of glue in the groove of the lid.

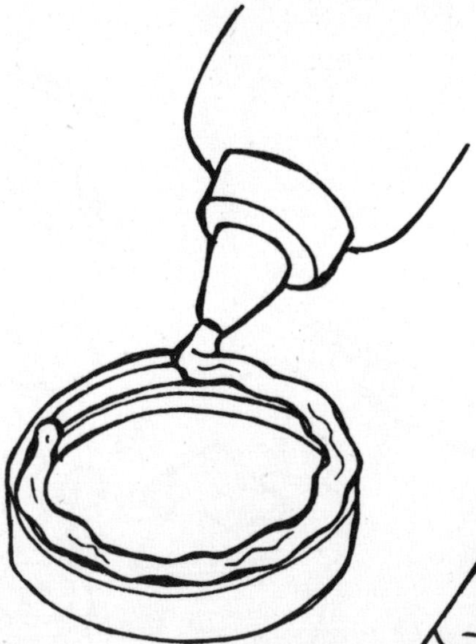

3. Snap the lid in place. Wipe away any extra glue.

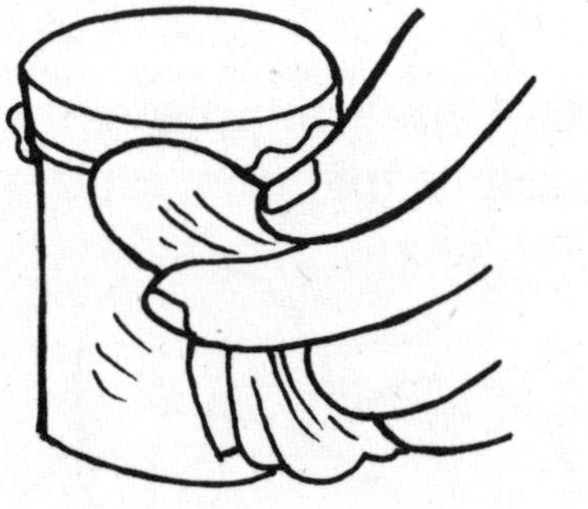

4. Decorate your shaker with paint.

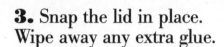

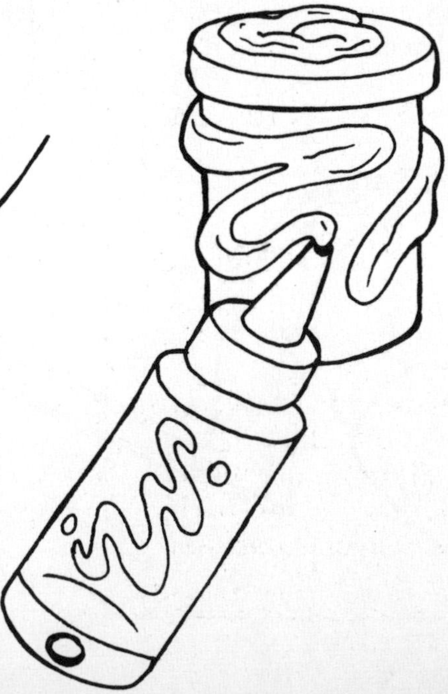

You will need

a film canister
◎
shaker materials
◎
white craft glue
◎
dimensional fabric paint

Tooth or treasure keeper

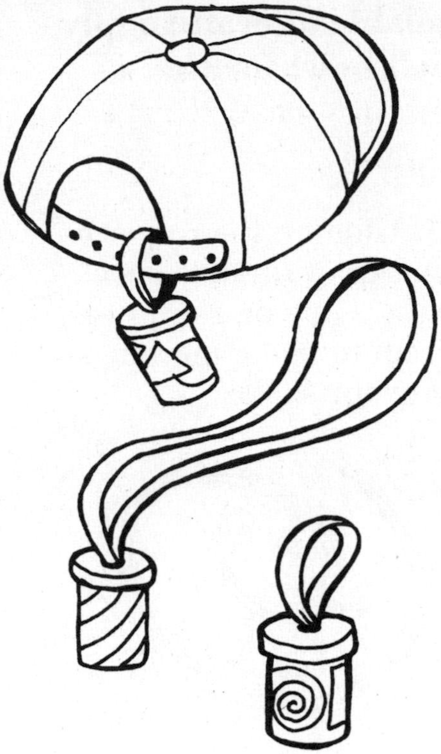

When you lose a tooth, here's a handy spot to keep it until bedtime. You can also use the keeper for other small treasures or coins.

1. With the lid still on the container, use the nail to poke a hole in its center.

2. Cut a piece of ribbon or yarn long enough to go around your neck, wrist or to use to fasten your keeper to a zipper or hat. Remove the lid, thread both ribbon ends through the hole and knot them together.

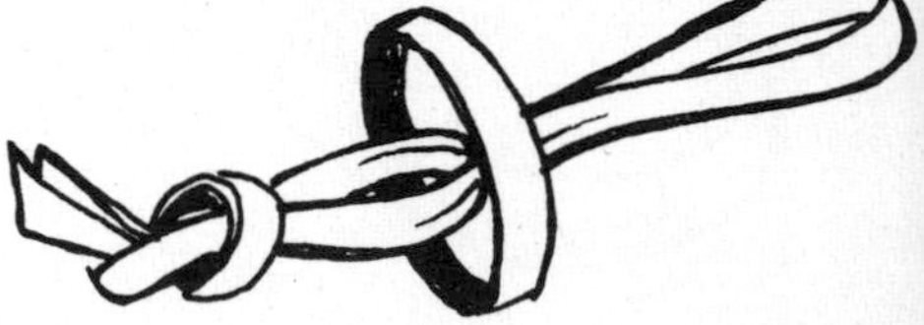

3. Decorate the keeper any way you'd like.

You will need

a nail
◎
a film canister
◎
scissors
◎
narrow ribbon or yarn
◎
paint and a brush, stickers or non-toxic permanent markers

Coiled snake

Sheets of craft foam are available at craft-supply stores. Trace a saucer or small bowl for the outline of your coiled snake.

1. Use a pen to trace your object onto a foam sheet. Cut it out.

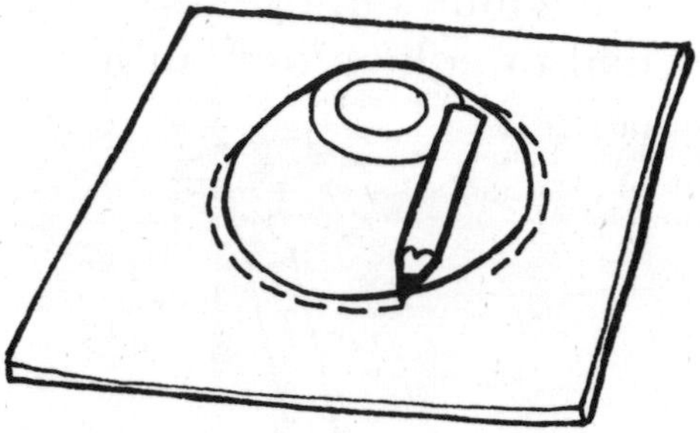

2. Cut out a coiled snake by cutting in a swirl as shown. Leave enough uncut foam in the center for the snake's head.

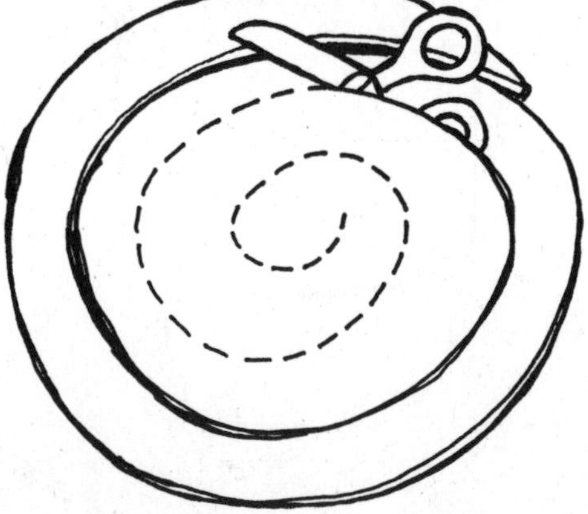

3. Glue on the roly eyes and draw on dots for a nose. Glue on scraps of foam to make markings on your snake.

4. Bring the needle and knotted thread up through the snake's head. Remove the needle and hang up the snake.

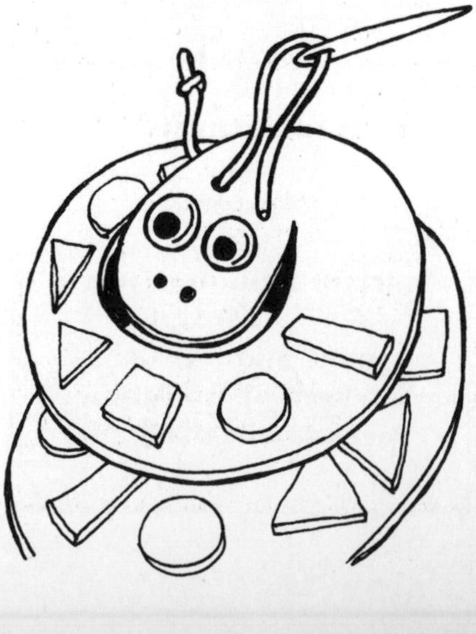

You will need

a round object to trace
◎
a pen, scissors and white craft glue
◎
craft foam
◎
roly eyes
◎
a needle and thread or fishing line

Fridge magnets

Make lots of magnets using many colors and shapes of foam.

1. Draw a shape on a foam sheet. Try a flower, a heart or sports equipment.

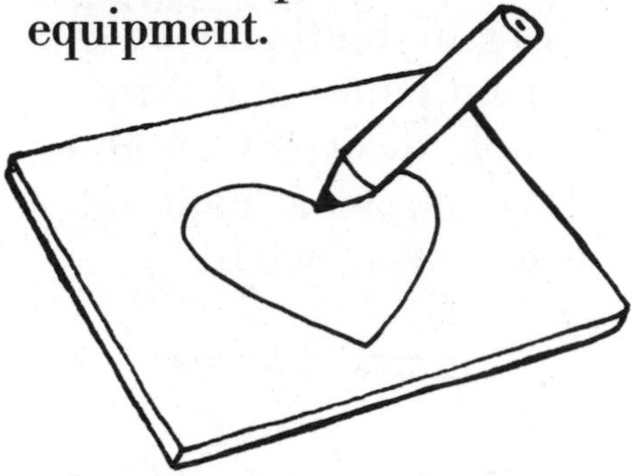

2. Cut out the shape. If you have another color of foam, glue the shape onto it. Cut out the shape a little larger so both colors show.

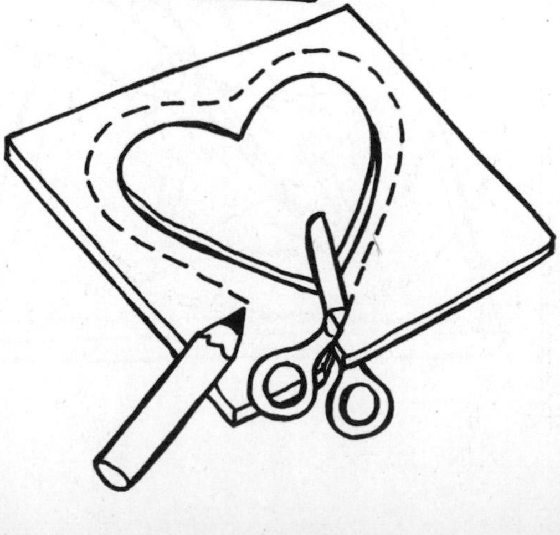

3. If you wish, you can write a message on the foam with a pen.

4. Cut a piece of magnetic strip, peel off the paper backing and press the magnet onto the back of the foam shape. Stick your finished magnet on the fridge.

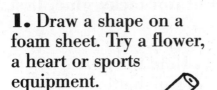

You will need

craft foam
◎
a pen, scissors and white craft glue
◎
self-adhesive magnetic strip

Glitter and glue ornaments

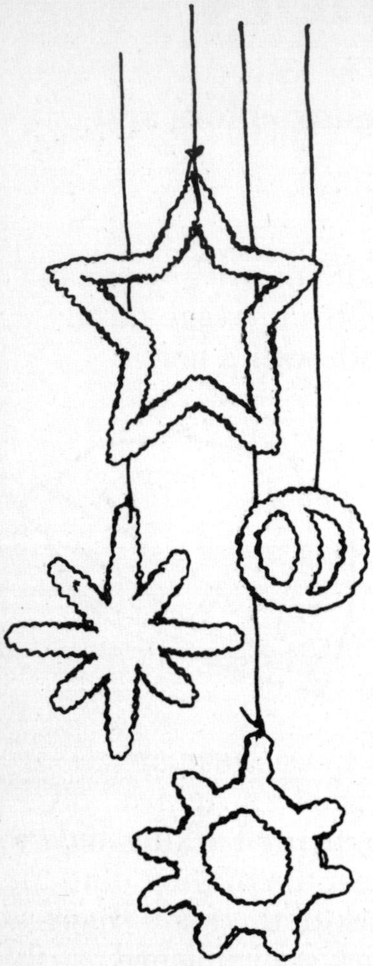

Use thick white craft glue for these ornaments, but not tacky glue. It stays too soft.

1. Hold the nozzle of the glue bottle above the waxed paper and draw simple designs with glue. Try a circle, a diamond, a star or an icicle.

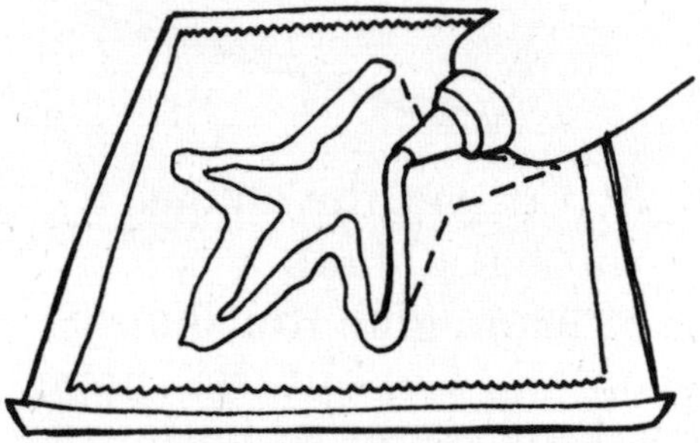

2. If the glue is uneven, smooth it out a little with a toothpick.

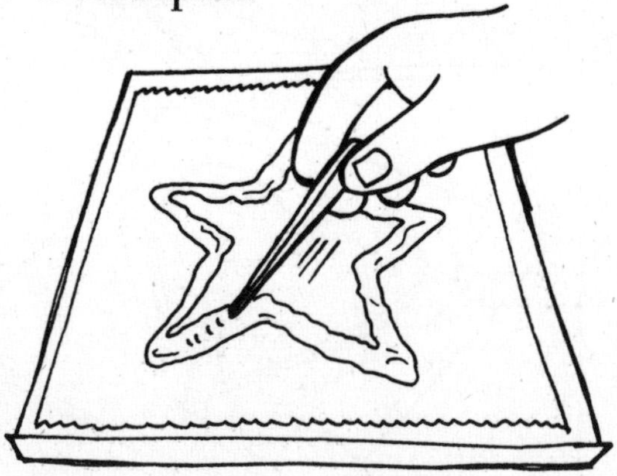

3. Sprinkle glitter all over the designs so you cannot see any glue. Leave the extra glitter on the design.

You will need

a waxed-paper lined cookie sheet

white craft glue

glitter

a toothpick or pencil

a needle and thread or fishing line

4. Set the tray in a warm spot to dry overnight.

5. If the ornaments are dry, they should lift easily off the waxed paper. If the ornaments are still stuck, allow more drying time.

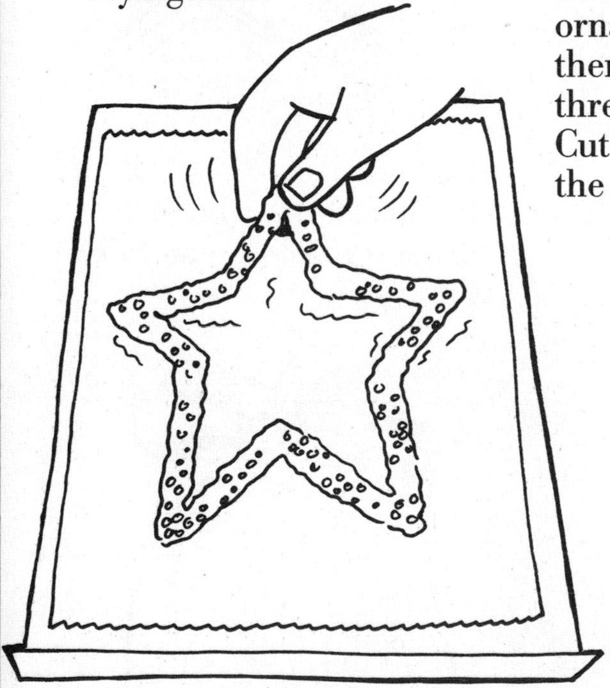

6. When your ornaments are dry, it is optional to spread a thin layer of glue on the back of each one and sprinkle on a little more glitter. Allow them to dry again.

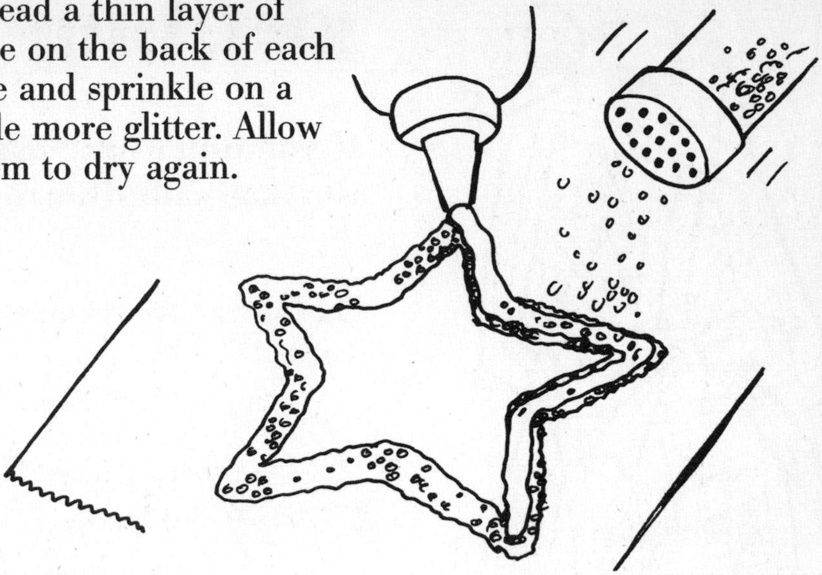

7. To hang up your ornaments, poke through them with a needle and thread or fishing line. Cut the thread and tie the ends into a knot.

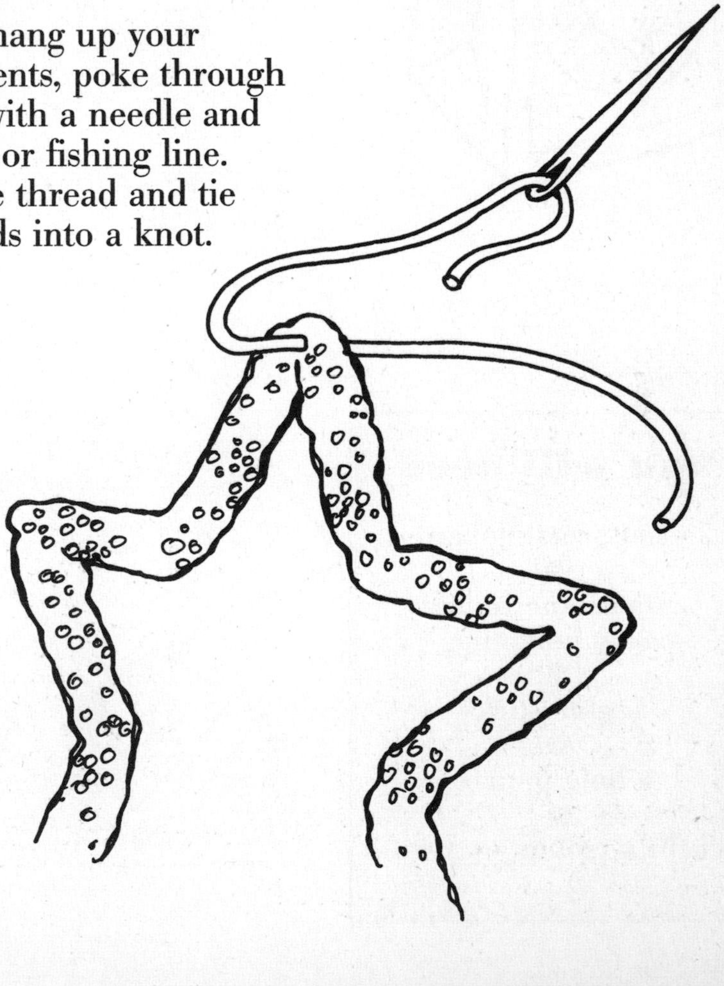

Greeting-card gift bag

If you don't have used greeting cards, decorate the bag with drawings or stickers.

1. Cut the fronts off the cards.

2. Glue a card to each side of the bag.

3. Place the gift inside and fold down the top of the bag. Punch two holes in the folded area.

4. Thread the ribbon through the holes and tie it in a bow.

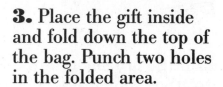

You will need

2 used greeting cards

a square-bottomed paper lunch bag

a glue stick

a hole punch

curling ribbon or yarn

Lantern

Put some crumpled yellow tissue paper in the lantern to make it look like candlelight.

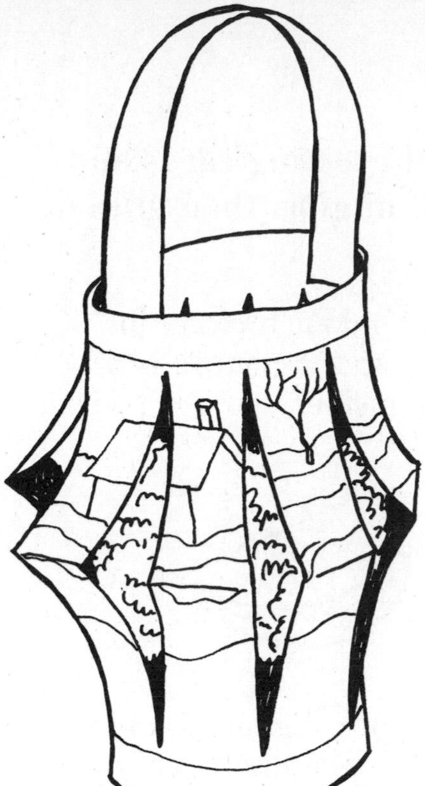

1. Cut off the front of the card. Fold it in half lengthwise so that the picture shows.

2. Make cuts that start at the folded edge but stop before the opposite edge.

3. Unfold the card and glue the ends together. Hold the glued area for a moment while it dries.

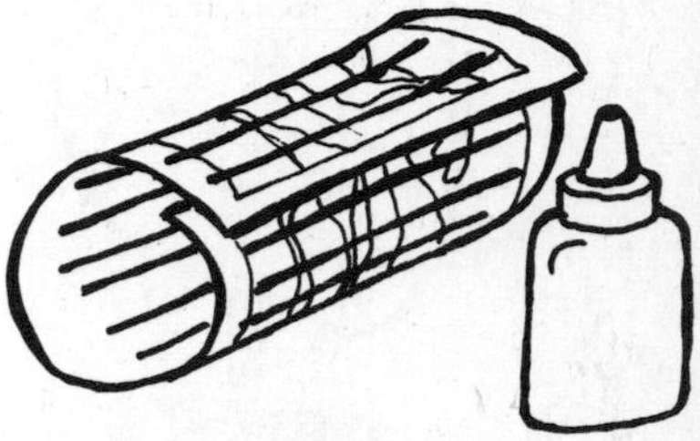

4. For a handle, cut a strip from the back of the card or from another card front. Glue the ends across the inside of the top of the lantern.

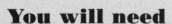

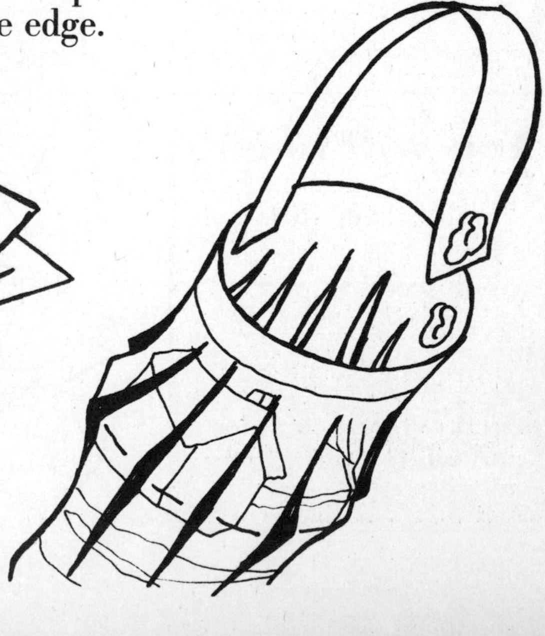

You will need

a used greeting card

scissors and white craft glue or a glue stick

Greeting-card ornament

For a festive look, use seasonal greeting cards and dip the edges of the ornament in glue, then glitter.

1. Fold a length of embroidery floss about 40 cm (16 in.) long in half and set it aside.

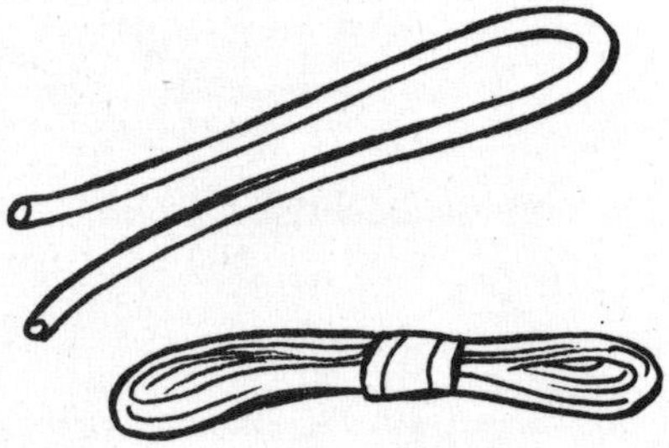

2. Use the cup to trace five circles onto colorful areas of the cards. Cut them out.

3. Fold each circle in half so the picture is on the inside.

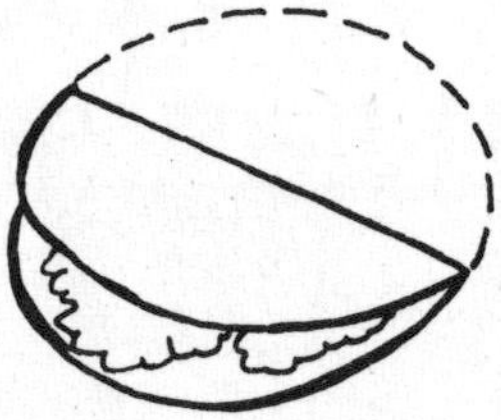

4. Spread glue on one of the plain halves of one of the folded circles. Press half of another folded circle onto the glued area.

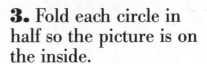

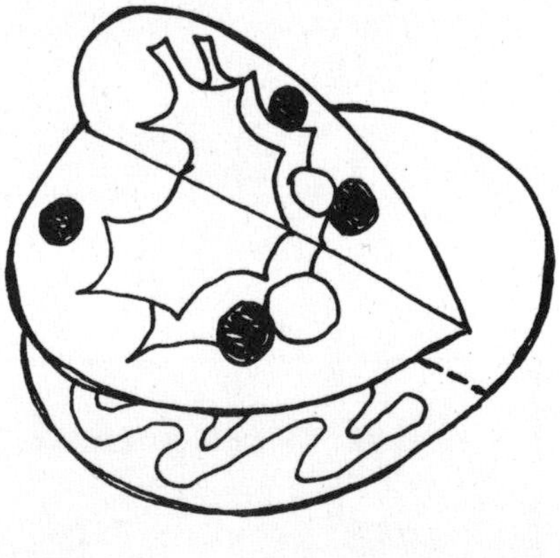

You will need

embroidery floss

used greeting cards

a cup

pencil, scissors, a ruler and white craft glue

5. Apply glue to the other half of the second circle and press on a third circle. Then glue on the fourth circle.

6. Run a line of glue down the center area. Place the folded floss in it so the ends are in the glue and the looped end is free.

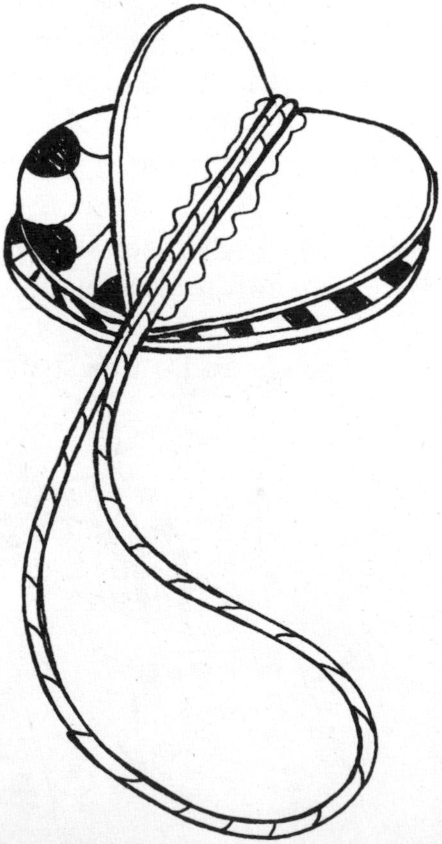

7. Glue the last folded circle in place to close the ornament. Allow the glue to dry before you hang up the ornament.

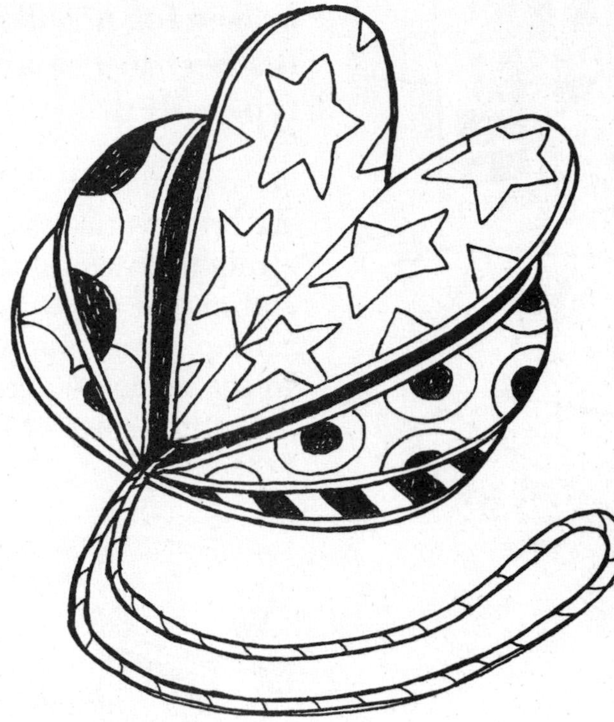

Eraser prints

Use an art gum or white vinyl eraser for this project. Also try stamping with a new pencil eraser for a polka-dot design. For easy clean-up, it's best to use a washable ink stamp pad, but any type will do.

1. Press your eraser straight down on the ink stamp pad a few times. Stamp it on scrap paper to see what it looks like. Try other sides of the eraser, too.

2. Stamp on your good paper. Try to make interesting designs.

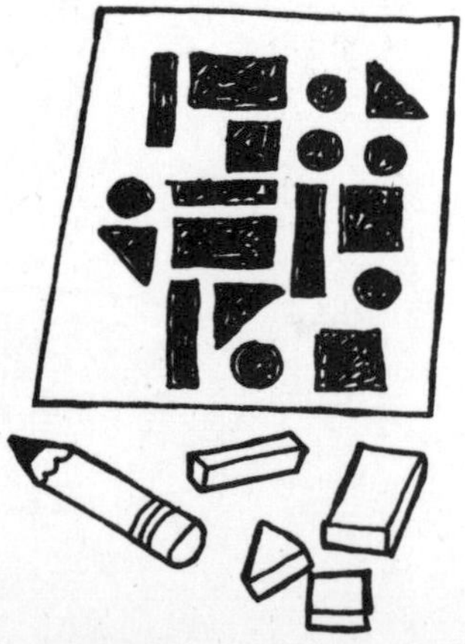

3. Before you use another color of ink on your eraser stamp, stamp it over and over on scrap paper to get rid of all the ink.

4. Use eraser stamps to decorate note paper, envelopes, posters, gift bags and other stuff.

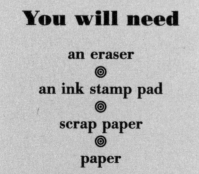

You will need

an eraser
◎
an ink stamp pad
◎
scrap paper
◎
paper

Thumbuddies

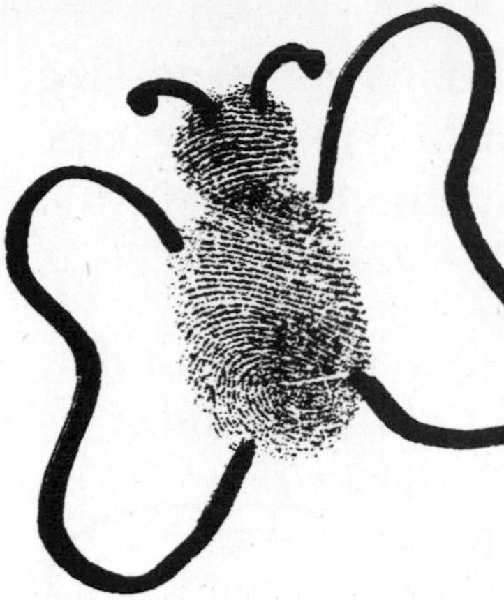

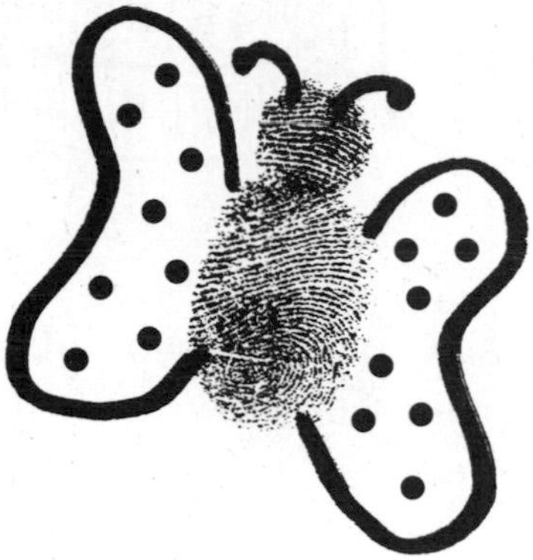

Use a stamp pad with non-toxic, washable ink so your hands don't get stained.

1. Press the pad of your thumb onto the stamp pad.

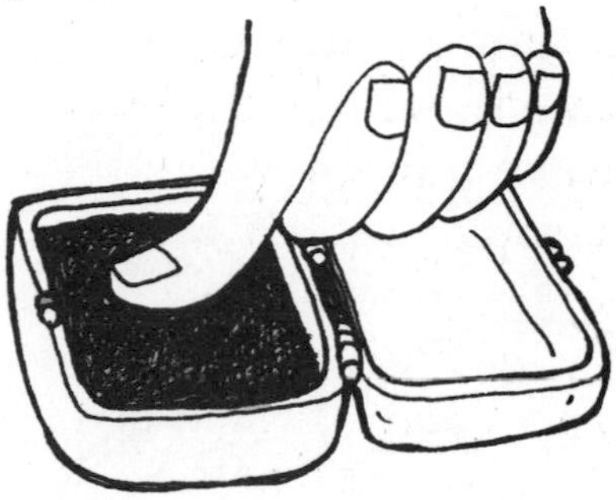

2. Press your thumb onto paper. Use a pen or marker to draw a face, arms and legs. You can add other features, too, such as a hat or a cane.

3. What other characters can you make? How about a row of fingerprints to make a caterpillar? Or a thumbprint and fingerprint for a butterfly body and you add the wings?

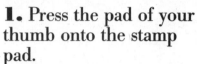

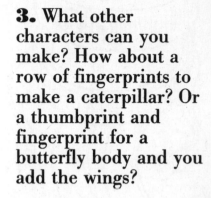

You will need

an ink stamp pad
◎
paper
◎
markers or a pen

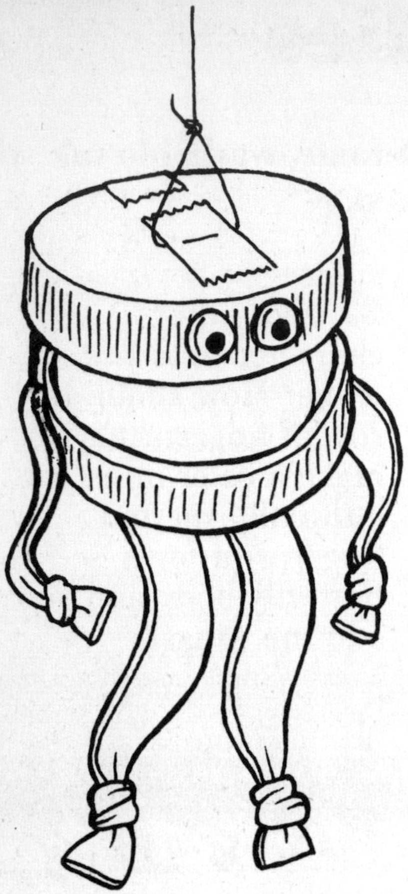

Jar-lid marionette

Peanut butter or mayonnaise lids are a good size to use for this funny character. Use masking tape or cloth tape rather than clear tape.

1. Place the two lids upside down on the table so they are touching. Tape them together to create a hinge.

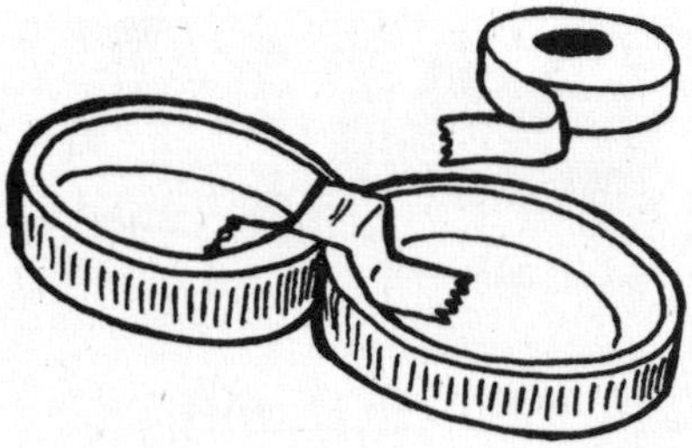

2. Flip one lid over the other one so the lids now look closed. Tape the lids together in the same spot, this time on the outside. The hinge is at the back of the marionette.

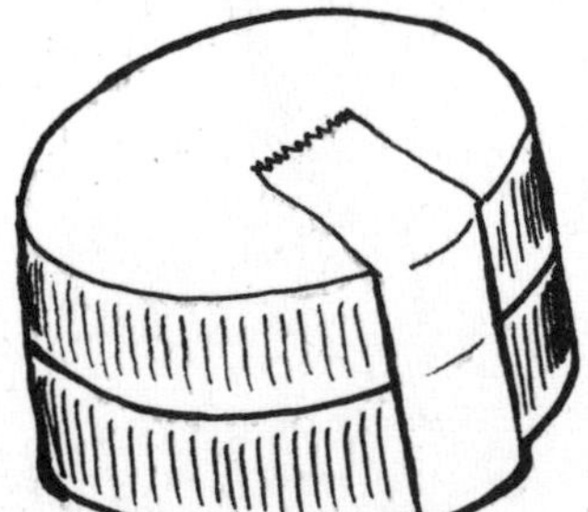

3. Glue the eyes to the front of the top lid.

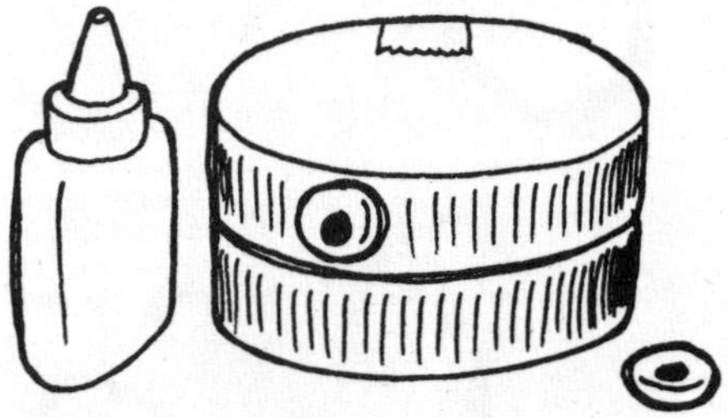

4. Cut four strips of felt from the square.

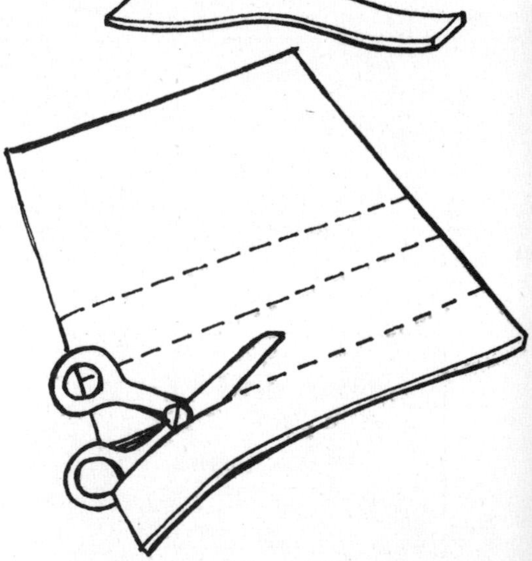

You will need

2 plastic jar lids the same size
◎
masking tape
◎
large roly eyes
◎
white craft glue and scissors
◎
a square of felt
◎
thread or fishing line

5. Tape or glue two strips to the underside of the bottom lid for legs. Tape or glue a strip on each side of the same lid to make arms.

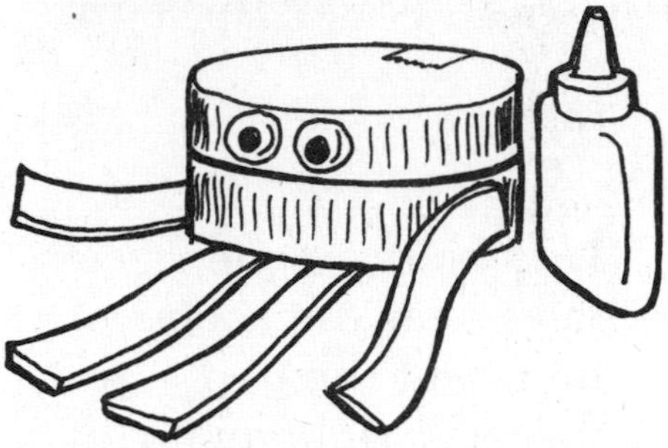

6. Make a knot near the end of each strip to make hands and feet. Trim the ends if they're too long.

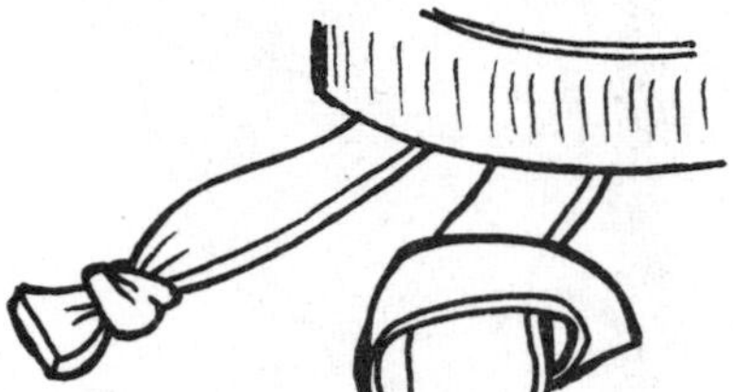

7. Cut a piece of fishing line. Knot a loop into each end. Tape one loop to the top of the top lid. Put your finger in the other loop to make your marionette talk.

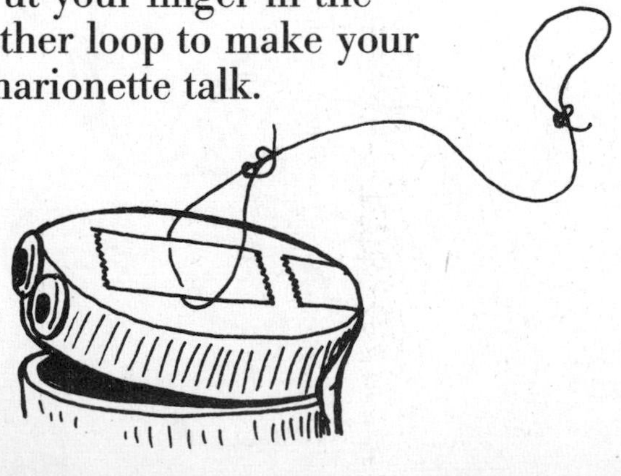

More ideas

Make a lid frame. Use the lid to trace the area of a photograph or drawing you wish to frame for someone. Cut out the picture and glue it inside the lid. Leave the lid plain or tie ribbon around it. Press on a piece of magnetic strip and place your picture on the fridge or glue on a cardboard stand.

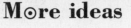

Jingle bell

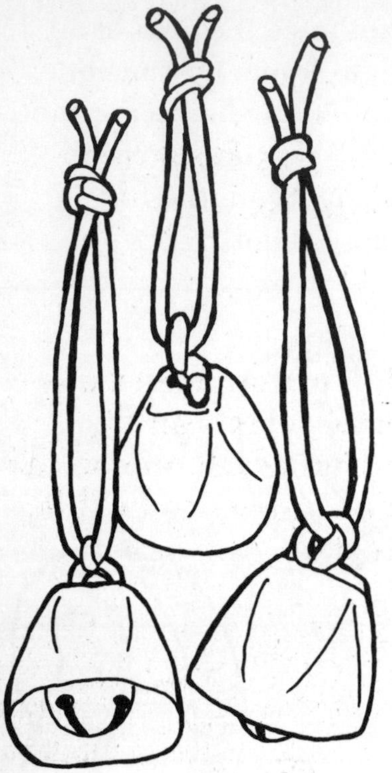

This bell makes a lovely ornament. For a festive look, you can glue on glitter or decorate the bell with glitter glue. For a shiny bell, cover the cup with aluminum foil.

1. Cut an egg cup from the carton. Trim the cup so it is smooth and straight all around. Color or paint it.

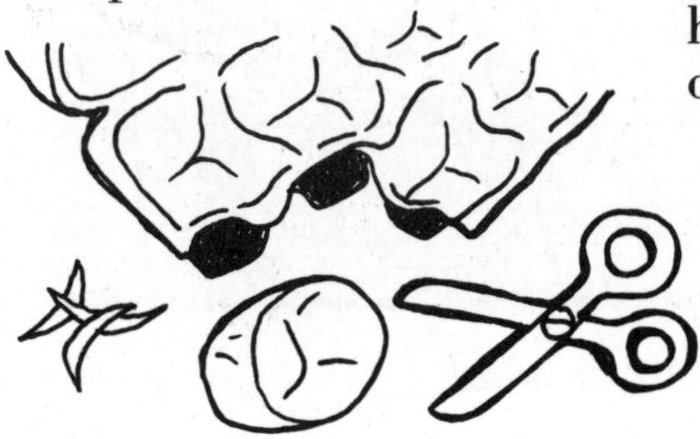

2. Tie the bell in the center of the yarn or ribbon.

3. Poke two good-sized holes near the center of the top of the cup. Thread a ribbon end through each of the holes. Knot the ribbon on top of the bell cup.

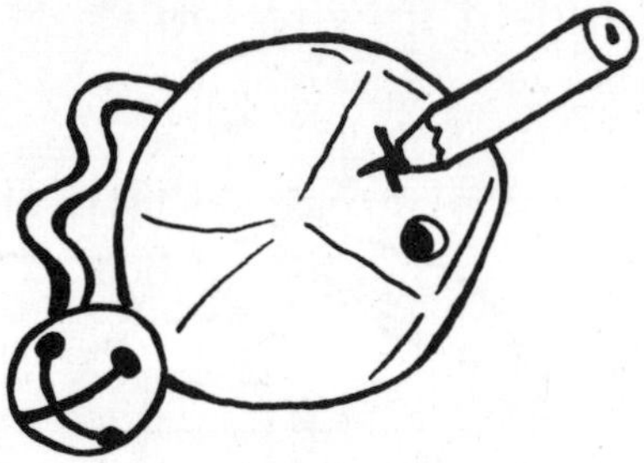

4. Use an overhand knot, as shown, to fasten the ends of the ribbon together.

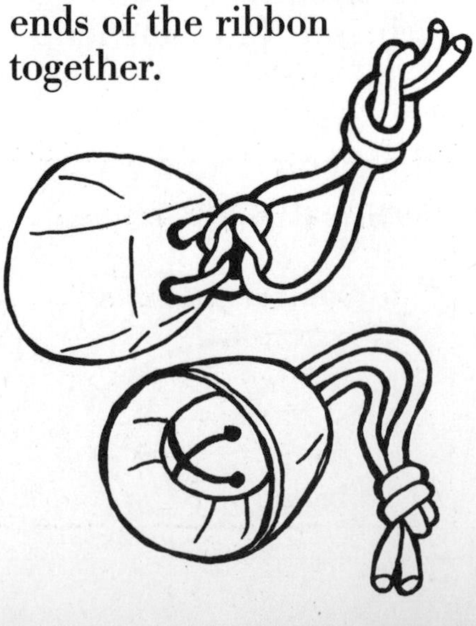

You will need

an egg carton

scissors

crayons, markers or paint and a brush

a piece of yarn or narrow ribbon about 30 cm (12 in.) long

a jingle bell

a pencil or nail

Jingle-bell instrument

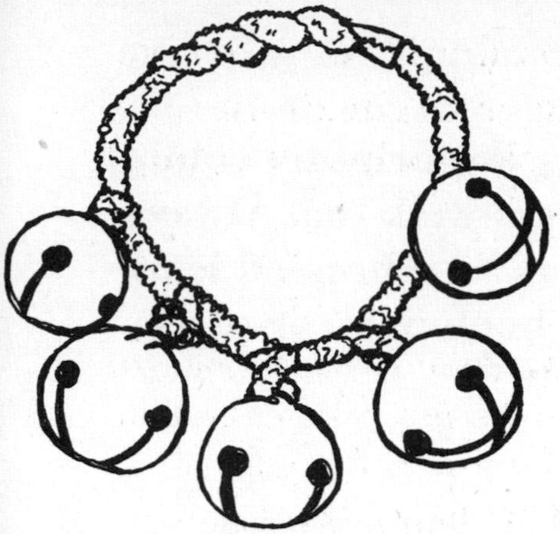

Check the index at the back of this book for more musical instruments to make.

1. Thread a bell onto the pipe cleaner so it is near the end.

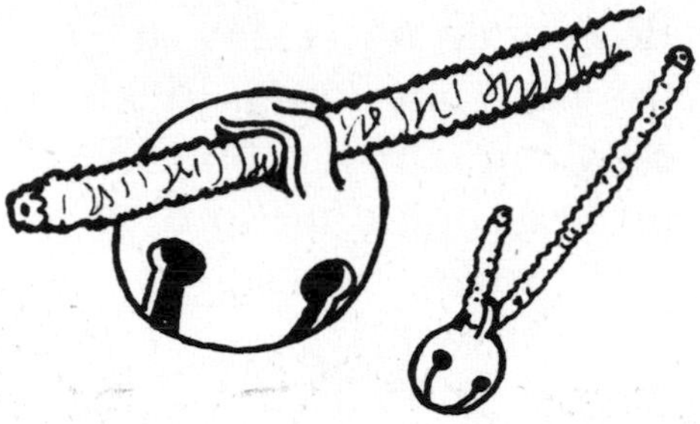

2. Bend the pipe cleaner and twist the bell twice. Straighten the pipe cleaner.

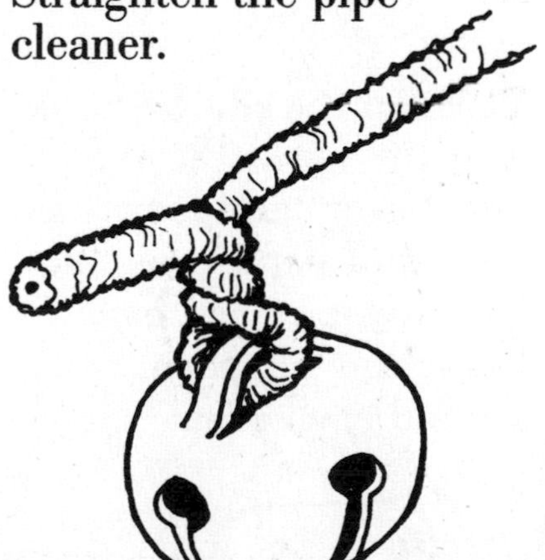

3. Thread on as many bells as you can fit, twisting each one on the pipe cleaner to hold it in place.

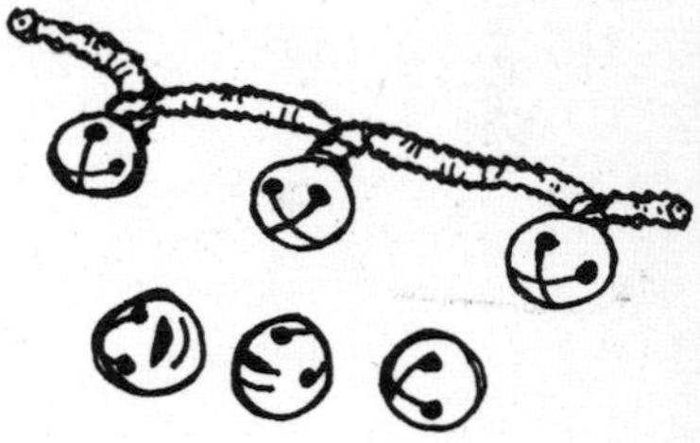

4. Twist the ends of the pipe cleaner together to make a circle. If the pipe-cleaner ends feel sharp, wind some tape around them.

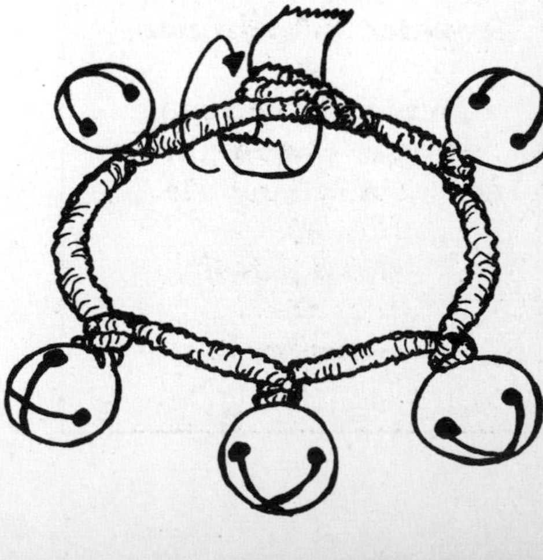

You will need

5 or more jingle bells

a pipe cleaner

tape (optional)

Pressing leaves and flowers

The best flowers for pressing are brightly colored and not too thick. Leaves press well, too. Always get permission to pick flowers. Use pressed leaves and flowers to make a card, bookmark or place mat (see page 118).

1. Pick or cut the flowers on a dry day so they are not damp. Pick only as many as you can press at one time so they don't wilt.

2. Open the phone book near the back. Place a few flowers and leaves as open and flat as possible face down on the page. Leave lots of space around each one.

3. If you are using newspaper and a catalog instead of a phone book, place at least two layers of newspaper in the open catalog. Lay the plants on it and carefully place two layers of newspaper on top.

4. Use scraps of paper to mark where in the book you've pressed flowers.

You will need

fresh leaves and flowers
an old phone book, or newspaper and a catalog
scrap paper
heavy books

5. Gently roll some of the phone book or catalog pages closed over the plants. Place more plants in the book for pressing, marking the pages as you go.

6. Lay the book or catalog flat in a warm, dry place where it is not likely to be disturbed. Place a few heavy books on top.

7. Wait at least one week before you check the plants. If they are stuck to the paper or feel damp, they are not ready. Check them again in a week.

8. Remove some plants to make crafts and press more. Keep adding to your collection. Pressed flowers can be stored in a book for months or years.

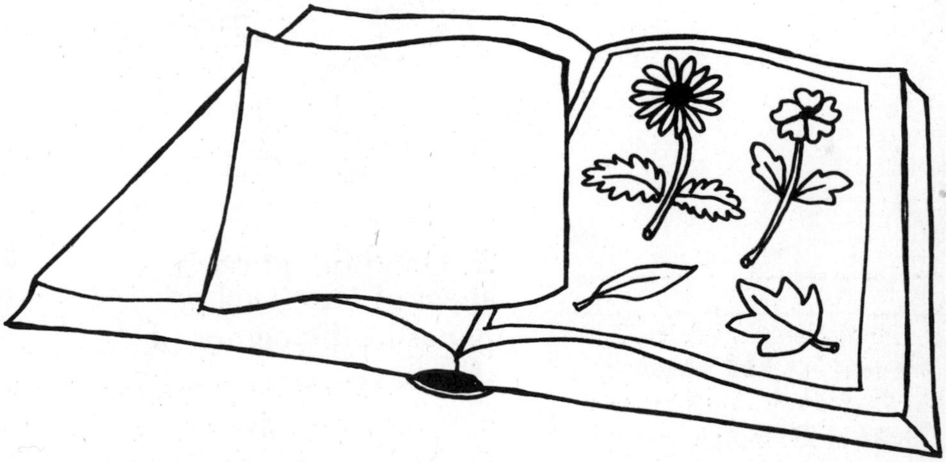

More ideas

Since thick flowers, such as roses, do not press well, you can remove the petals and press them separately. Use them as you would use other pressed plants.

Pressed-flower place mat

Use pressed flowers and leaves (see pages 116 and 117) for this place mat. If you don't have any, trace some real leaves onto colorful construction paper and cut them out along with some paper flowers.

1. Cut two pieces of vinyl a little larger than a sheet of construction paper. Peel off the paper backing from one and place it sticky side up on the table.

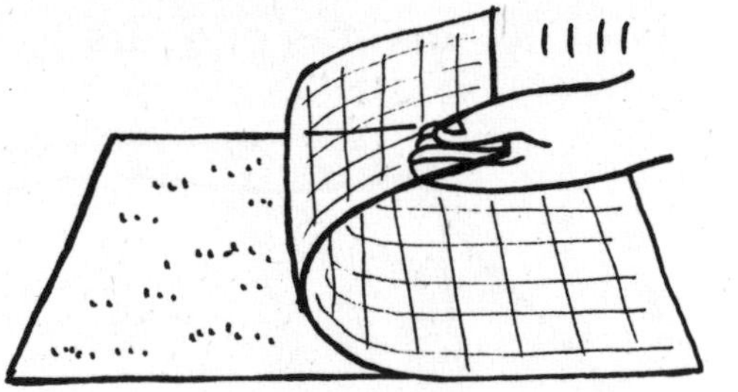

2. Carefully place a sheet of construction paper in the center of the vinyl.

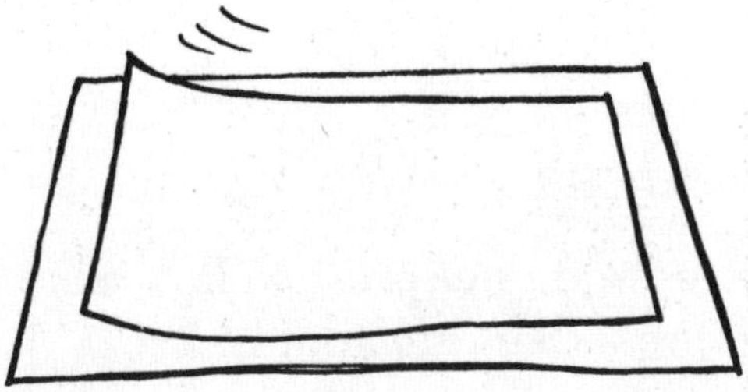

3. Arrange some pressed flowers and leaves on the construction paper. When you are pleased with how they look, cover the display with the other piece of vinyl.

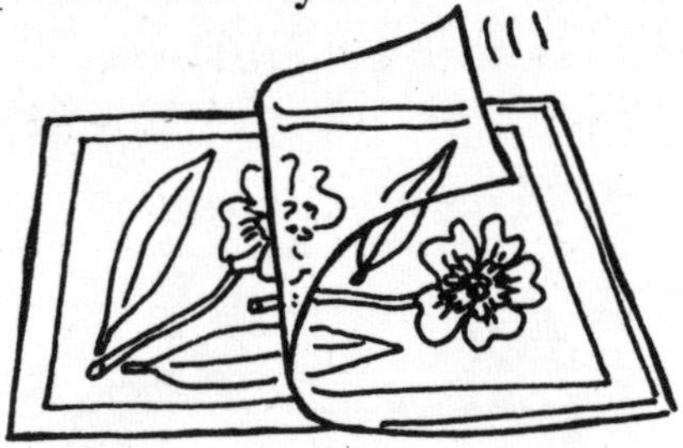

4. Trim the vinyl around the edges of your place mat.

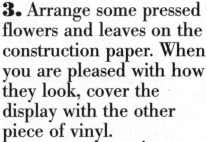

You will need

clear self-sticking vinyl
◎
scissors
◎
construction paper
◎
pressed flowers and leaves

Leaf and flower pictures

Use pressed flowers and leaves (see pages 116 and 117) or fresh plants to create these lively figures.

1. On a sheet of construction paper, arrange flowers and leaves to make different shapes. Perhaps a leaf is a fancy dress, a flower is a hat and maple keys are shoes.

2. Use small amounts of glue to hold everything in place.

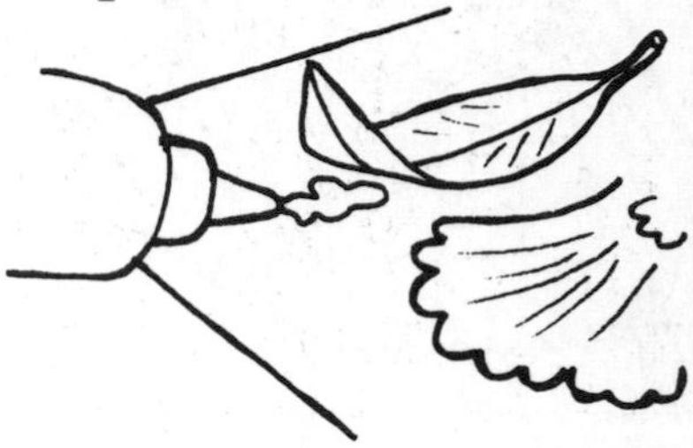

3. Use crayons or markers to add details, such as faces and hands, to your pictures.

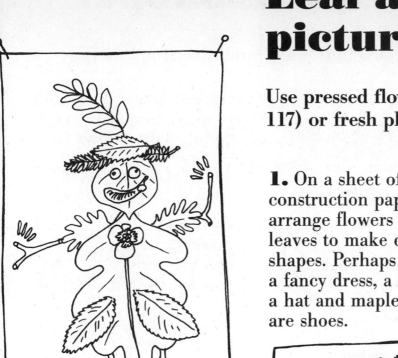

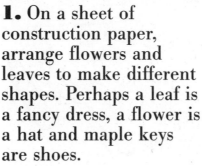

You will need

construction paper
◎
leaves and flowers
◎
white craft glue
◎
crayons or markers

Lunch-bag puppet

Use a square-bottomed lunch bag for this fun puppet.

You will need

a paper lunch bag

crayons or markers

2 sheets of scrap paper

ribbon (optional)

yarn

scissors and white craft glue

1. Draw a face on the bag in the area shown.

2. Open the bag and stuff the head with two crumpled sheets of paper. Tie a piece of ribbon or yarn loosely around the neck.

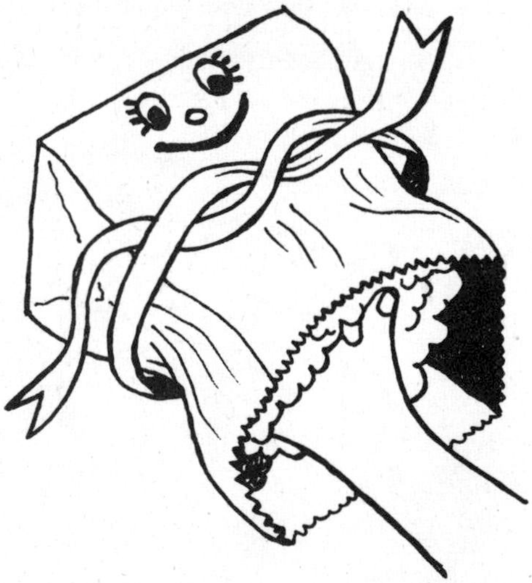

3. Cut some strands of yarn and glue them to the head for hair. Add other details if you wish.

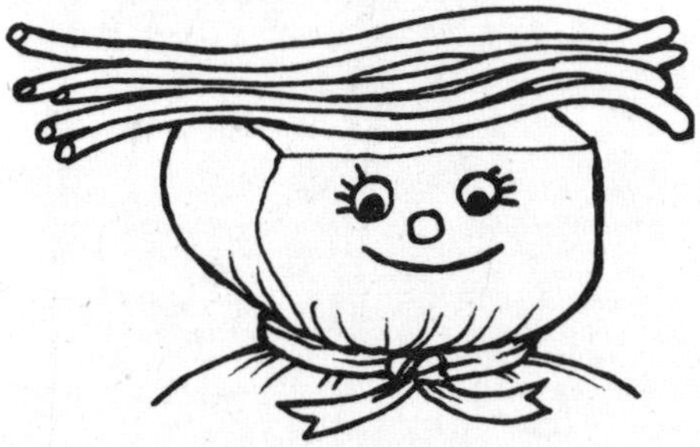

4. Tear or cut a hole on each side of the puppet, just under the neck. Put your thumb and baby finger in these holes to make puppet arms. Your other three fingers should fit in the head so you can make your puppet move.

Animal puppets

Dog

Draw a face on the folded-over bottom of the bag. The fold will be the mouth. Cut out a pink or red construction-paper tongue. Glue it under the fold so it looks like a panting dog. Cut out ears, a collar and a dog tag and glue them in place. Draw on eyes and a nose. Put in your hand and position it so you can open and close the dog's mouth.

Funny bunny

From the inside, use a pencil to poke out two holes in the bottom of the bag. From the outside, cut or tear these holes so they are each large enough to fit your fingers. Draw a bunny face on the front of the bag and draw or glue on other features. Put your hand inside and poke two fingers through the holes. Make your funny bunny's ears wiggle! Try making an elephant puppet with your finger as the trunk or a giraffe with your fingers as the horns.

Paper-bag basket

Use a square-bottomed paper bag, any size, for this project. Instead of a twisted paper handle, you can punch a hole in each side and fasten on a pipe cleaner.

You will need

a paper bag
◎
scissors
◎
a stapler
◎
supplies for decorating (see step 4)

1. Cut about one-third off the top of the bag. Twist the strip to make a basket handle.

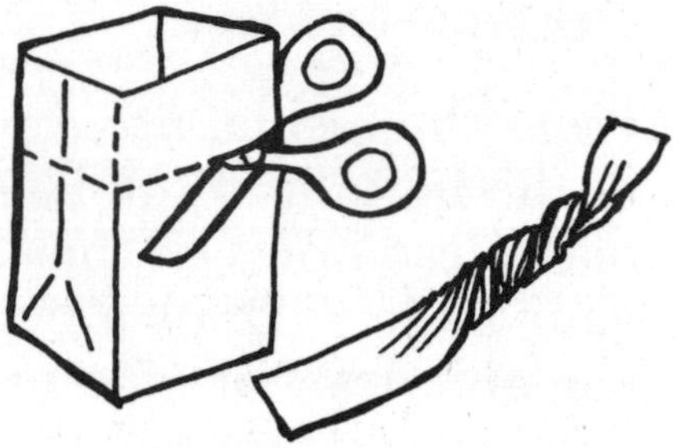

2. Fold down the top of the bag all around. Smooth it and fold it down again. If there is writing on the bag, you may wish to keep folding down the top until none of the writing shows.

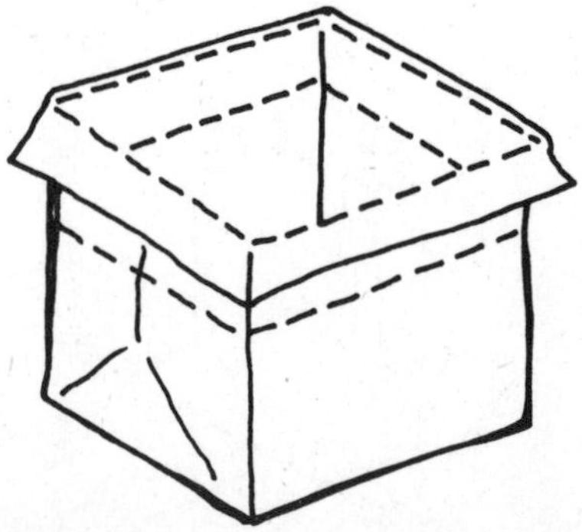

3. Hold the handle in place and trim it if it is too long. Untwist just the ends of the handle so you can staple them to the sides of the bag.

4. Decorate the basket with crayons, markers, eraser stamps (see page 110) or stickers. You could also glue on buttons, beads, ribbon, lace or magazine pictures. Use your basket to hold a craft project, some treasures or your picnic lunch.

Wind sock

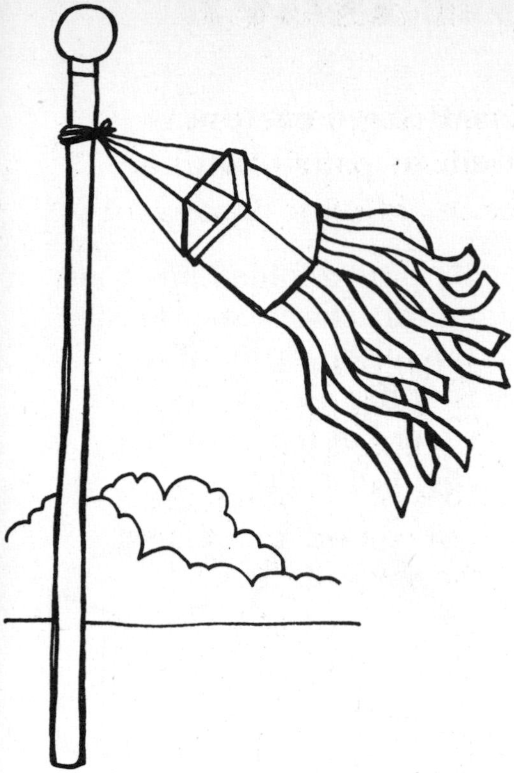

You can hang up this pretty wind sock or have fun running around outside with it.

1. Cut out the bottom of the bag.

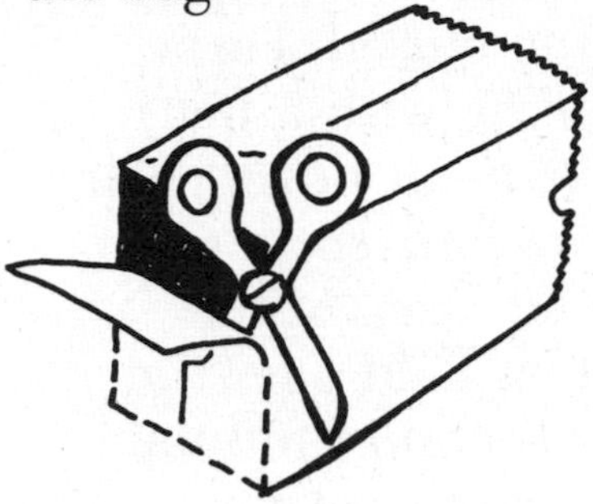

2. Fold down the top of the bag all around. Punch a hole at each of the four corners.

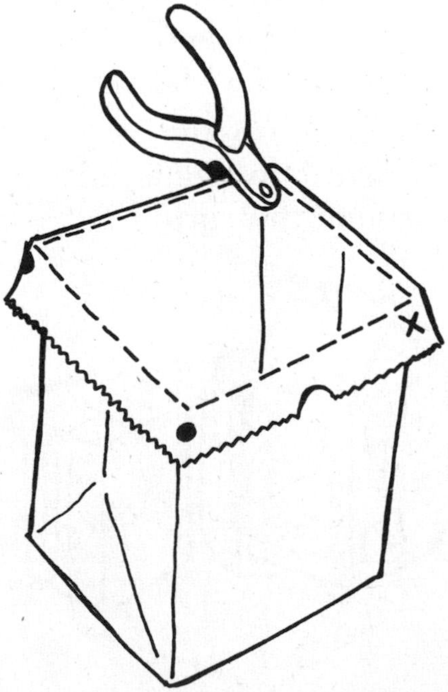

3. Cut a piece of yarn about two adult arm lengths. Cut three more the same length. Thread one into each hole and knot all eight ends together.

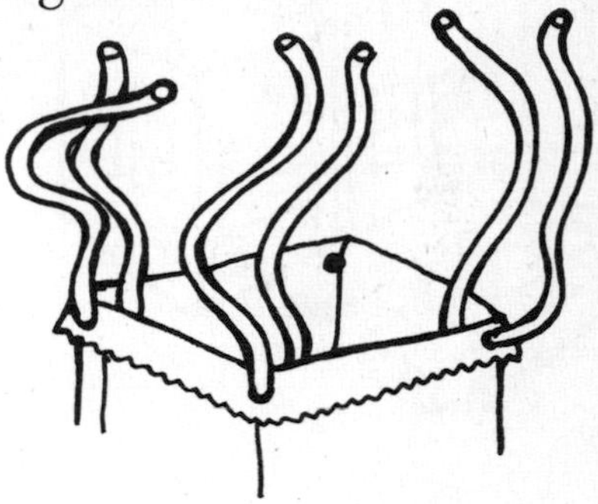

4. Glue streamers or tissue strips to the end of the wind sock. Decorate the sock with glitter, drawings or whatever you like.

You will need

a square-bottomed paper lunch bag

◎

scissors and white craft glue or a glue stick

◎

a hole punch

◎

string or yarn

◎

streamers or strings of colorful tissue paper

◎

supplies for decorating (see step 4)

Milk-carton town

As you collect many different-sized cartons, decorate them and add them to your town.

1. For a building with a peaked roof, tape the carton closed. For a building with a flat roof, make a cut down each of the four corners on the top area of the carton. Fold over the four sections and tape the top closed flat.

2. Tape or glue construction paper all around the carton.

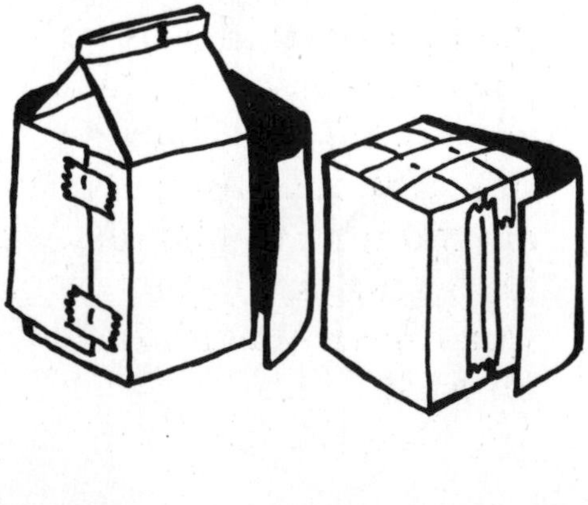

3. Glue a folded piece of construction paper to the top of the carton if the roof has a peak. Glue a square of paper to the roof if it is flat.

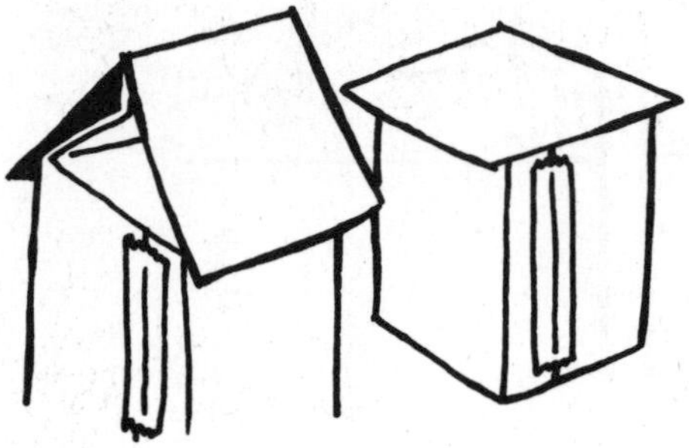

4. Draw on windows, doors, stairs and other features with the crayons or markers.

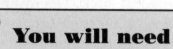

You will need

clean, dry milk or juice cartons

masking tape

construction paper

scissors and white craft glue or a glue stick

crayons or markers

Bird feeder

Fill the base of this feeder with oiled sunflower seeds or other birdseed.

1. Hold the carton closed. Use the pencil to poke a hole on each side near the top of the carton. Also poke a hole in the center area of each of the four sides of the carton. Finally, poke a hole on two opposite sides of the carton, near the bottom edge.

2. Using the holes poked in the center of each of the four sides to start your cutting, cut out a window on each long side of the carton. Don't cut too near the bottom of the carton or you won't have enough space for seeds.

3. Thread some string through the holes in the top of the carton. Knot the carton closed leaving long ends on the string so you can hang up the feeder.

4. Poke the stick through the two bottom holes so the birds will have a perch.

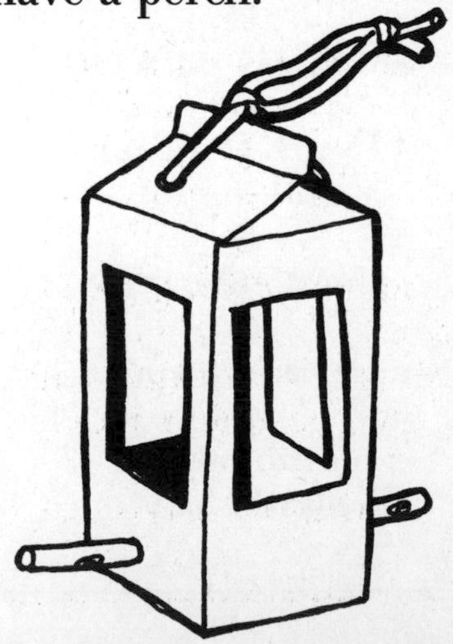

You will need

a clean, dry milk or juice carton
◎
a pencil and scissors
◎
string
◎
a stick

Cooked play dough

This recipe makes a dough that you can play with over and over again. It can be rolled, sliced and molded into shapes, such as people, animals, food and flowers. Ask an adult to help you cook the dough.

You will need

250 mL (1 c.) flour
◎
125 mL (1/2 c.) salt
◎
30 mL (2 tbsp.) cream of tartar
◎
250 mL (1 c.) water
◎
15 mL (1 tbsp.) cooking oil
◎
food coloring
◎
a pot and a spoon
◎
plastic tubs or plastic bags

1. In the pot, mix together the flour, salt and cream of tartar. Stir in the water and oil.

2. Cook the mixture over medium-low heat, stirring constantly. When the mixture is thick and smooth, turn off the stove and remove the pot.

3. Spoon the play dough out onto a counter that's dusted with flour. Allow it to cool for a few minutes.

4. Divide the dough into two or three balls. Knead a different food coloring into each ball until the color is even. (Or you can make all the dough the same color.) If the dough gets sticky, mix in a bit more flour.

5. Store each color of dough in a separate plastic bag or tub when you aren't playing with it, and it will keep for months.

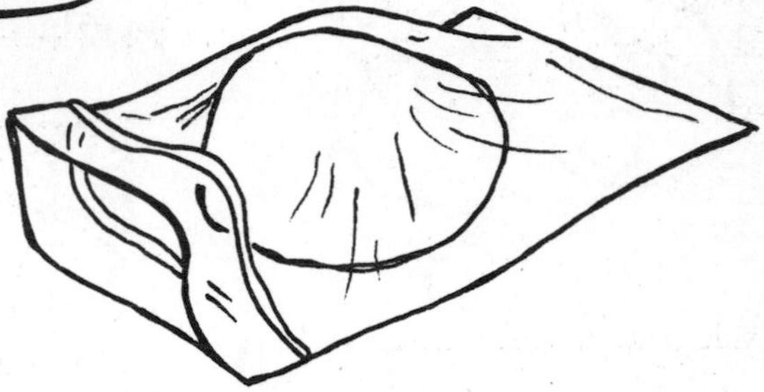

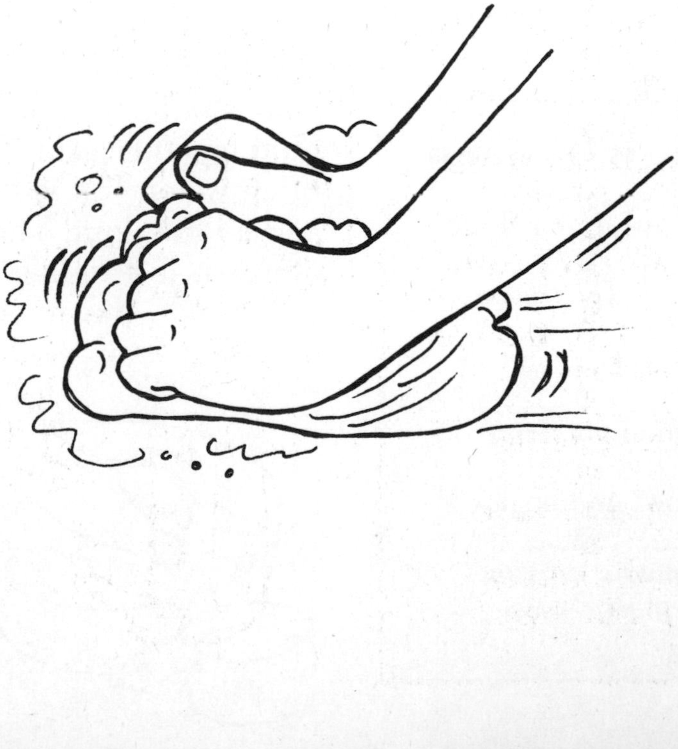

Uncooked dough

This dough is fast and easy to make because it doesn't need to be cooked. It is best to use this dough for making stuff you want to harden and keep rather than for playing with over and over again.

1. In the bowl, stir together the flour and salt and then add the water.

2. Mix the dough with your hands. If it does not hold together, add a little more water. If it is sticky, add a little flour. The dough is just right when it does not stick to your hands.

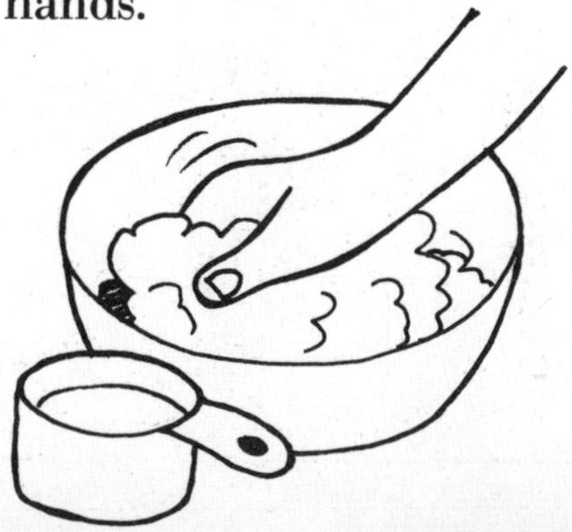

3. Divide the dough into two or more balls. Mix a few drops of food coloring into each ball. For a marbled look, just mix the coloring in a little.

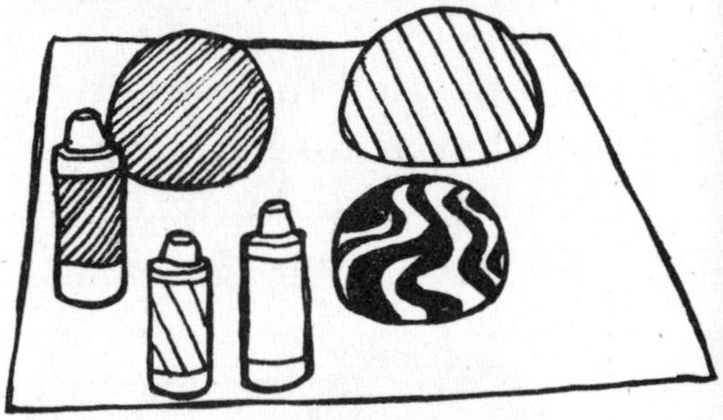

4. If you are not going to use the dough right away, store it in separate plastic bags or tubs. It will last in the fridge for one to two weeks.

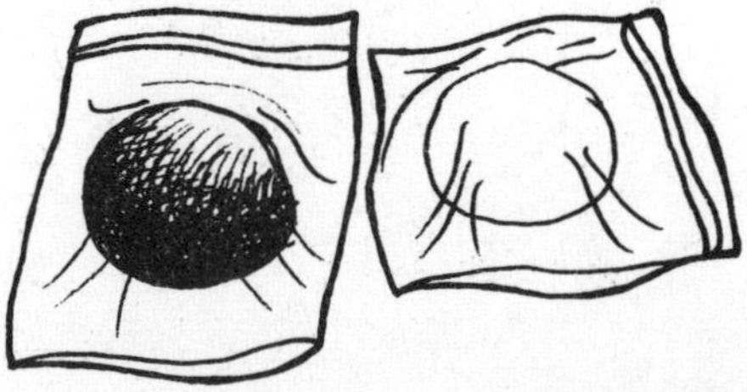

You will need

250 mL (1 c.) flour

50 mL (1/4 c.) salt

125 mL (1/2 c.) water

food coloring

a bowl and a spoon

plastic tubs or plastic bags

Stuff to make

Beads

Make beads by rolling some dough between your palms. Roll little beads between your index finger and thumb. Make holes in the beads with a straw, a pencil or a toothpick. (If you are going to bake your beads, make a large hole. The heat will puff up the beads and cause a small hole to close.) See below for how to finish your beads.

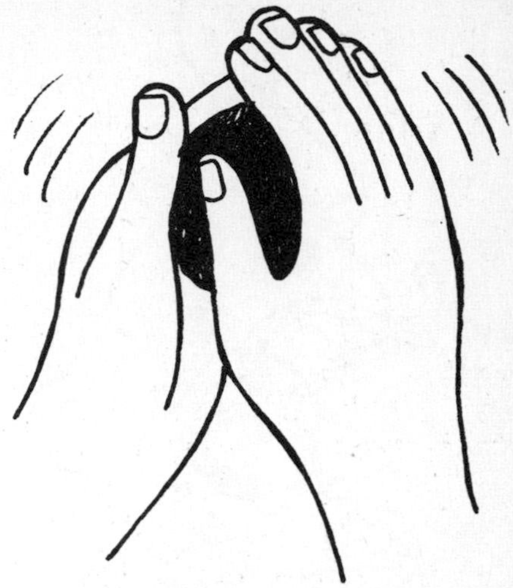

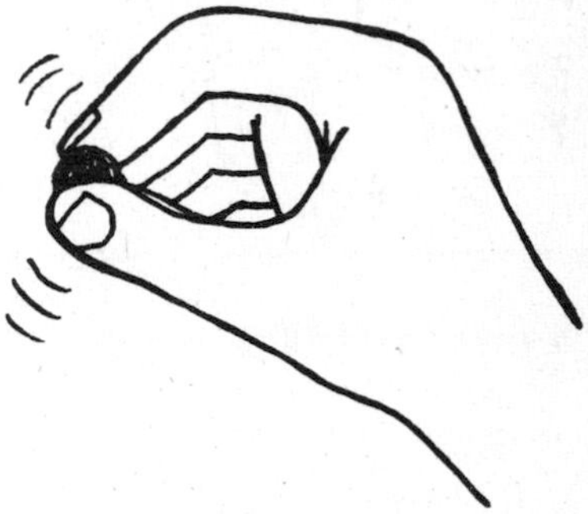

Fridge magnets

Pat some dough flat on a sheet of waxed paper. Press a cookie cutter into the dough and carefully lift off the cutout. See below for how to finish your magnet.

Finishing

To harden your beads or cutouts, place them on waxed paper to air-dry for a few days. Or place the beads and cutouts on a foil-lined cookie sheet and bake them in the oven at 120°C (250°F) for two to four hours. When the beads are dry, you may want to coat them with acrylic varnish or a Podgy-type product. To make the cutouts into fridge magnets, stick a magnet on the back of each one.

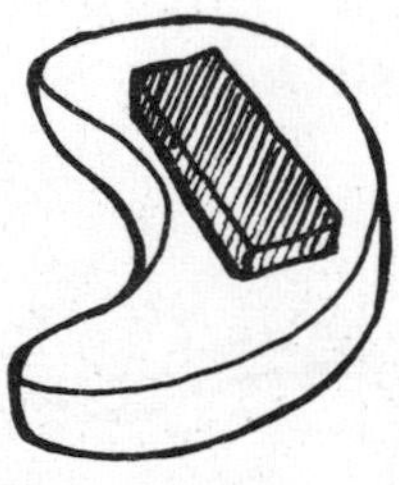

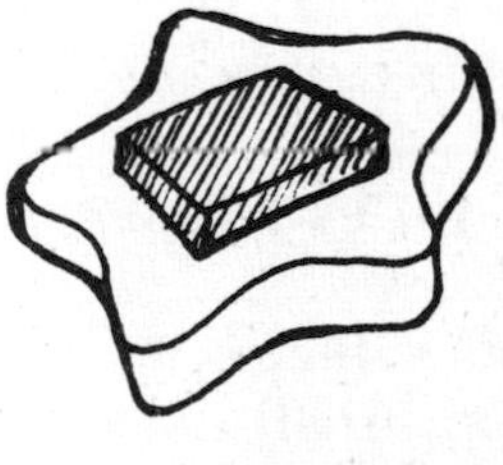

Cooked creative clay

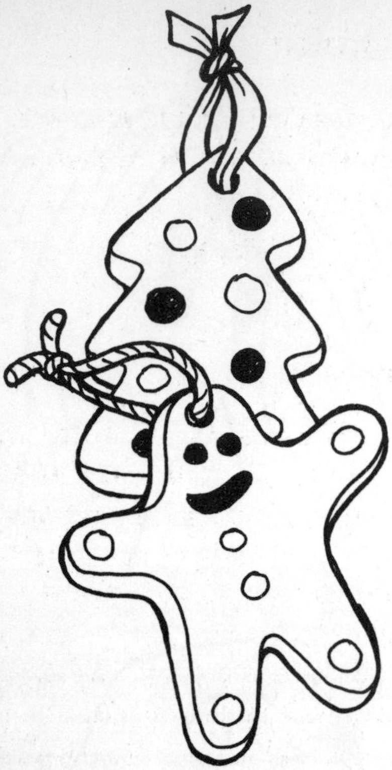

The things you make with this dough will be hard, smooth and easy to paint. Ask an adult to help you cook the dough. If you'd like colored clay without painting it, add food coloring to the water before you mix it with the cornstarch and baking soda.

You will need

125 mL (1/2 c.) cornstarch

250 mL (1 c.) baking soda

175 mL (3/4 c.) water

food coloring (optional)

a small pot, a spoon and a bowl

a damp kitchen cloth

a plastic tub or a plastic bag

1. In the pot, mix together the cornstarch and baking soda and then add the water. Stir the mixture until it is smooth and no longer feels stuck to the bottom of the pot.

2. Cook the mixture over medium-low heat, stirring constantly. After a few minutes, it will start to thicken. When it looks like smooth, thick mashed potatoes, turn off the stove and remove the pot.

3. Spoon the ball of clay into a bowl. Cover the bowl with the damp cloth to cool.

4. When the clay is cool, knead it on a surface dusted with cornstarch. Knead in a little more cornstarch if the clay feels sticky.

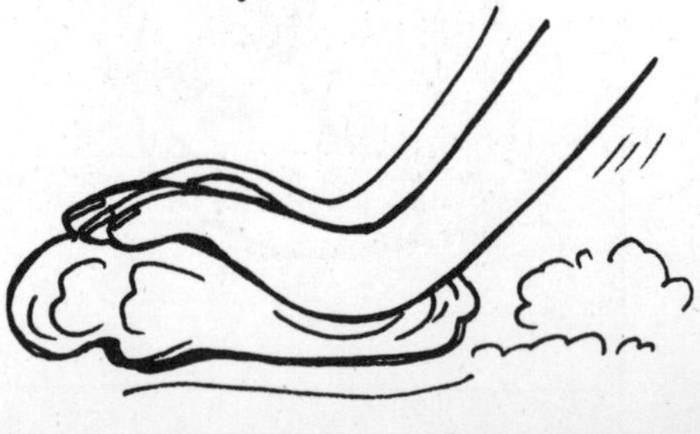

5. Store the creative clay in a plastic tub or bag. It will keep for a couple of weeks in the fridge. Read on for what to make and how to finish your projects.

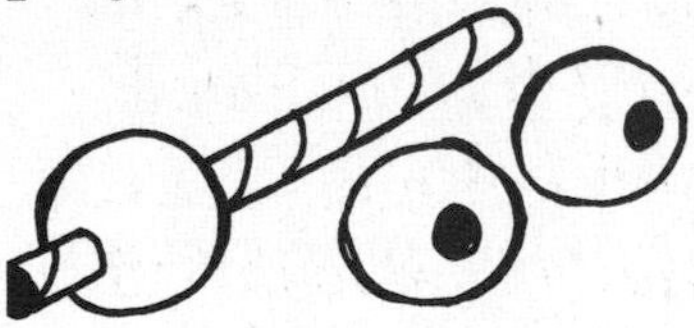

Stuff to make

See page 129 for how to make beads and fridge magnets. When they are dry, paint them with acrylic craft paint. Also, try the following ideas.

Ornaments

Roll out some clay on a sheet of waxed paper. If the dough sticks to the rolling pin, rub on a bit of cornstarch. Use cookie cutters to cut out shapes. Use a straw to poke a hole in the center top of each ornament. Leave the ornaments in a warm place to dry for a day or two, or bake them on a foil-lined sheet at 120°C (250°F) for a couple of hours. When the ornaments are hard and dry, paint them with acrylic craft paint. Thread a ribbon through each hole and hang up the ornaments. Or thread yarn or a long ribbon through the hole and wear an ornament around your neck.

Mobile

You could make a mobile by tying ornaments to criss-crossed sticks.

Frame

Make a mini frame by cutting out a large shape with a small shape cut out of the center. Paint and decorate the frame with buttons, beads or sequins. Tape or glue a photograph to the back.

Acorn-head doll

For the stuffing, use crumpled paper, felt scraps or a part of a clean rag. If you include some potpourri with the stuffing, your doll will be sweet-smelling.

1. Trace the plate onto the felt and cut it out.

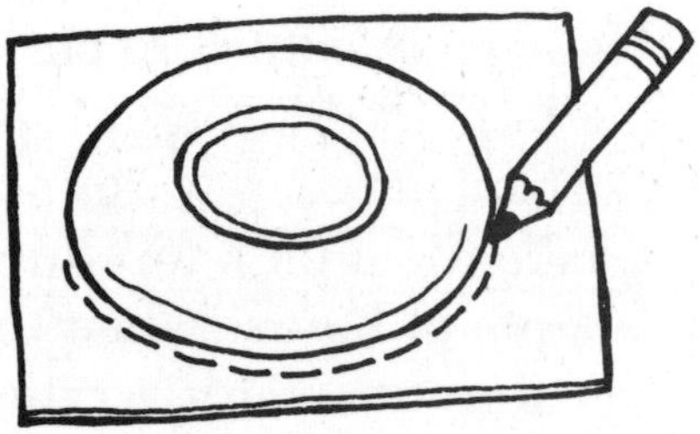

2. Gather the felt circle around the stuffing. Twist it closed with the pipe cleaner.

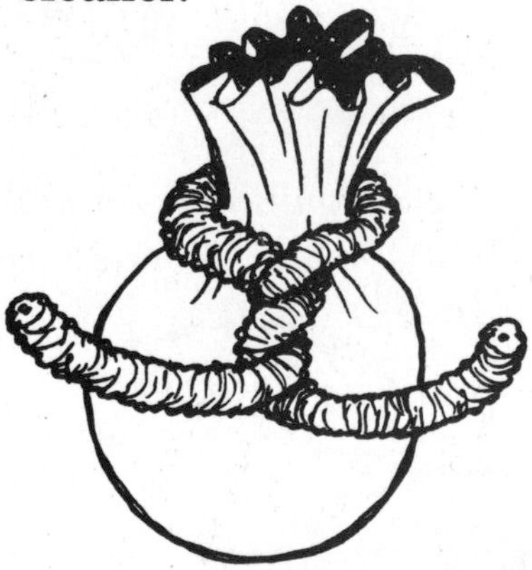

3. Trim the pipe cleaner and bend the ends to look like arms and hands.

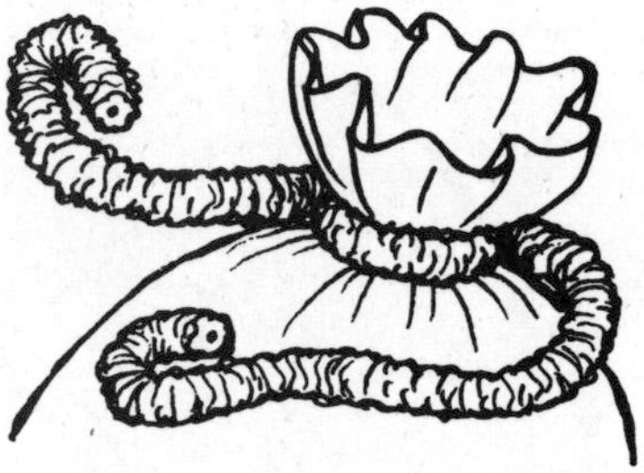

4. Squirt glue into the center of your doll's gathered neck and sit the acorn on it. Let it dry, then give your doll a face. If you like, remove the cap from the acorn, glue on some yarn hair and glue the cap back in place.

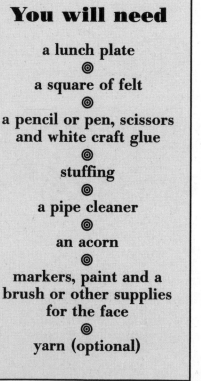

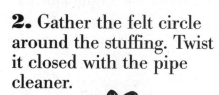

You will need

a lunch plate

a square of felt

a pencil or pen, scissors and white craft glue

stuffing

a pipe cleaner

an acorn

markers, paint and a brush or other supplies for the face

yarn (optional)

Walnut strawberry

A strawberry out of a walnut? It makes a great ornament.

1. Paint or color the walnut red.

2. Draw or paint on green spots for seeds. If you are using paint, try dotting on the seeds with the wrong end of the paint brush.

3. Cut out a felt star shape for the leaves.

4. Knot a piece of embroidery floss into a circle. Glue the leaves over the knot on top of the strawberry. Allow the glue to dry before hanging up the walnut strawberry.

You will need

a walnut
◎
red and green paint and a brush or markers
◎
green felt
◎
scissors and white craft glue
◎
embroidery floss or thread

Walnut roller

Get your friends to make a mouse roller, too, so you can have races! If you don't have a nut cracker, try splitting open the walnut by wedging in a dull knife and turning it.

1. On the pointed end of the walnut shell, draw on a nose and eyes (or glue on roly eyes).

2. For ears, tie a piece of yarn into a bow. Trim off the ends so only the two loops are left. Glue the loops onto your mouse's head.

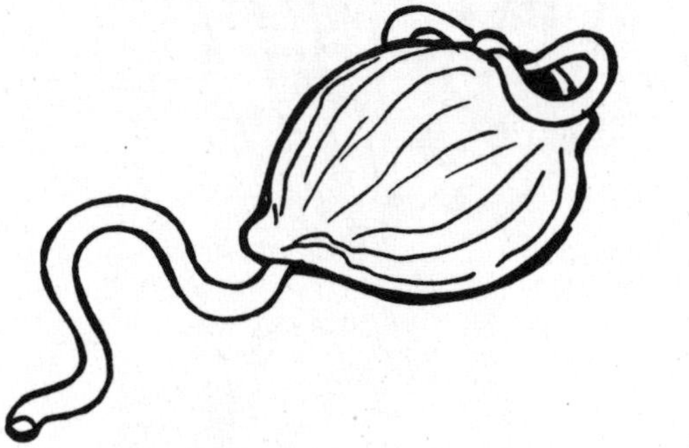

3. Cut a piece of yarn for the tail and glue it under the shell at the back. Let the glue dry.

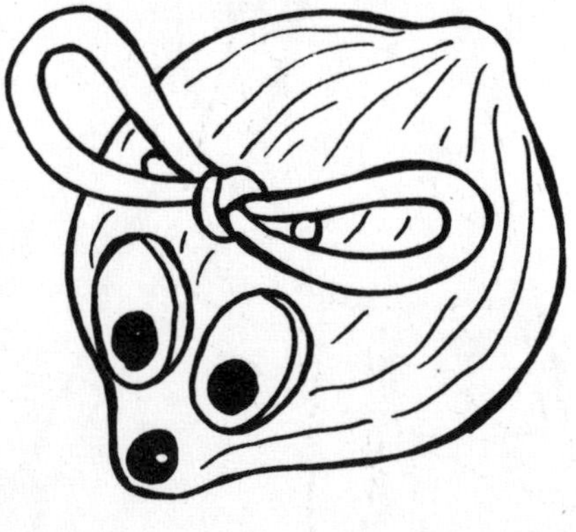

4. Place the mouse on a marble. Use a couple of books to make a ramp and watch your mouse roll!

You will need

half a walnut shell
◎
a black marker
◎
white craft glue
◎
roly eyes (optional)
◎
yarn
◎
scissors
◎
a marble

Mini sailboat

This is likely the smallest boat you'll ever see, but it really sails! Make a whole fleet of them.

1. Cut a small triangle from the paper. If you like, decorate it using crayons or markers.

2. Attach the sail to the toothpick by poking in small holes.

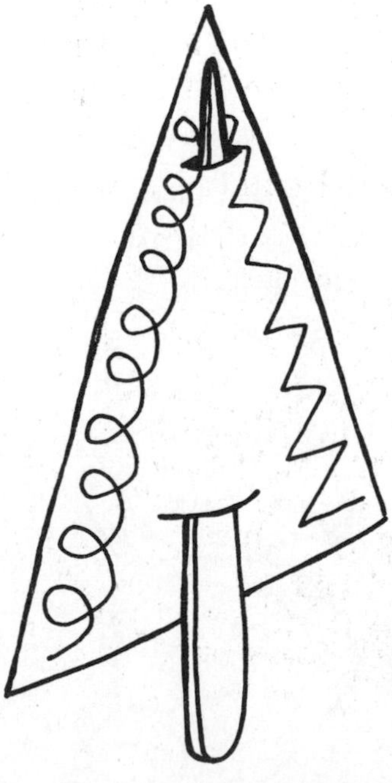

3. Put a small lump of Plasticine into the bottom of the walnut boat. Poke in the sail.

4. Try out your boat in a puddle or sink of water. Gently blow on it to make it sail.

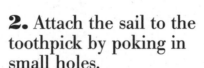

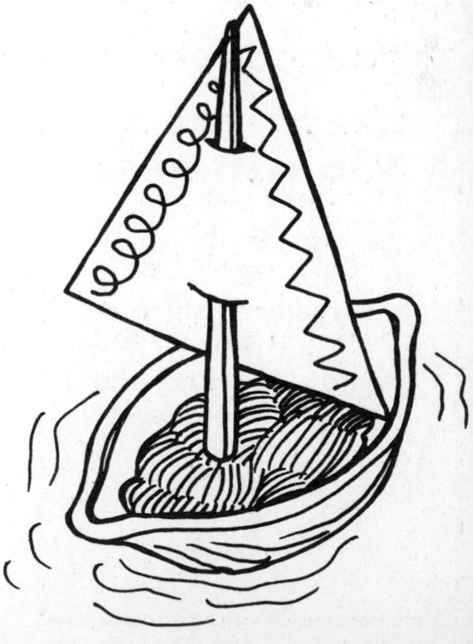

You will need

paper
◎
scissors
◎
crayons or markers
◎
a toothpick
◎
half a walnut shell
◎
Plasticine or modeling clay

Peanut buddies

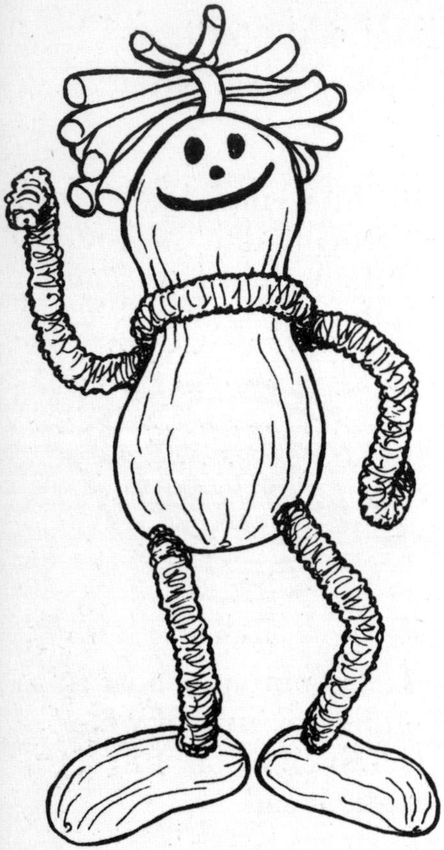

If you have a small acorn cap, try using it for a peanut-buddy hat! Can you make buddies that look like the members of your family?

1. Wrap a piece of pipe cleaner around the peanut, twist it at the back once and bring the ends forward to make arms. Trim them to arm length and fold over the tips to make hands.

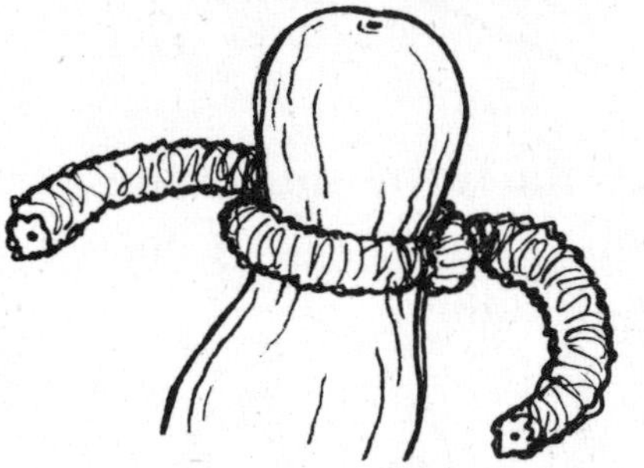

2. Use the push pin to carefully poke two small holes in the peanut where the legs will go. Cut two short pieces of pipe cleaner and poke them into the holes.

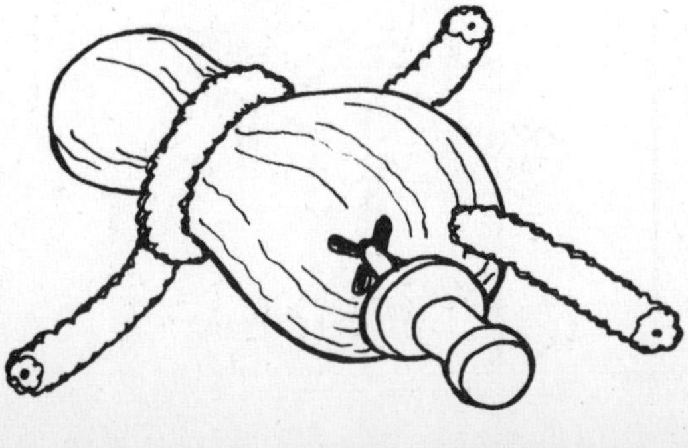

3. If you have a small peanut, open it and use the shells for shoes. Poke a tiny hole in each with the push pin and poke in the legs.

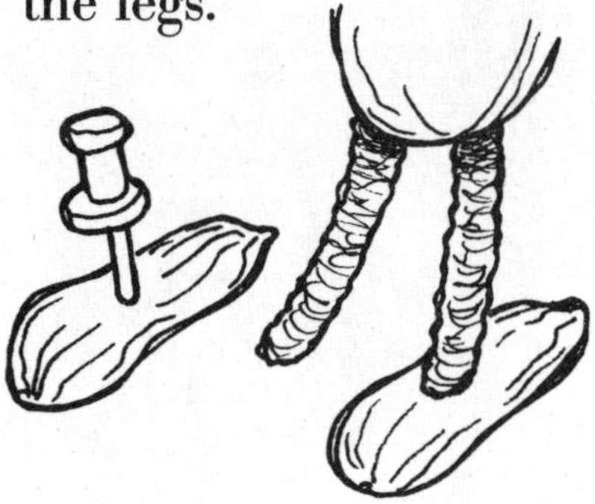

4. Draw a face and glue on yarn hair.

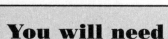

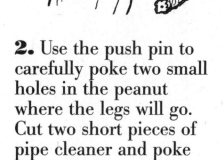

You will need

- peanuts in the shell
- a pipe cleaner
- scissors, markers and white craft glue
- a push pin
- yarn

Peanutasaurus Rex

Here's a nutty, newly discovered dinosaur. Can you invent some of your own?

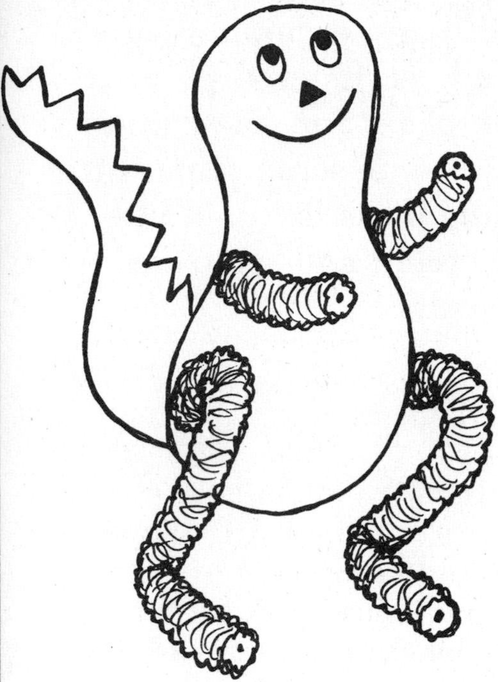

1. Cut a long, thin triangle tail. Split open the peanut shell, remove the peanuts and glue the shell back together with the tail in between.

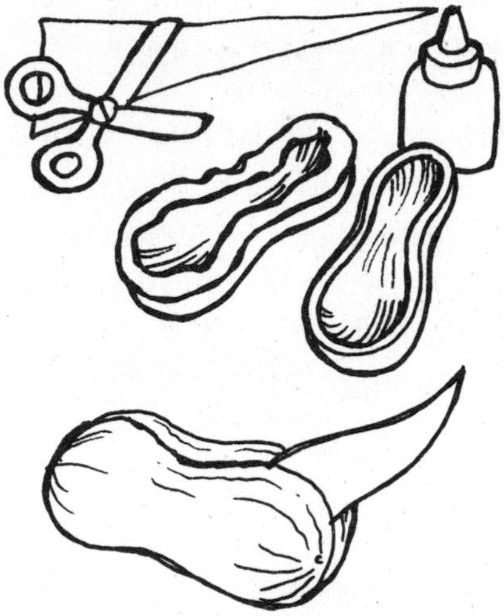

2. Cut two short pieces of pipe cleaner for arms. Use the push pin to poke two tiny holes in the peanut. Push in the arms.

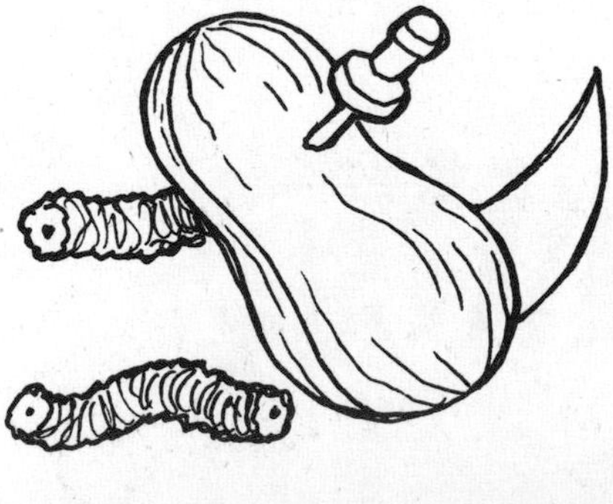

3. Shape two dinosaur legs out of pieces of pipe cleaner. Poke two tiny holes in the shell and push in the legs. Your dinosaur should be able to stand on its legs with its tail for balance.

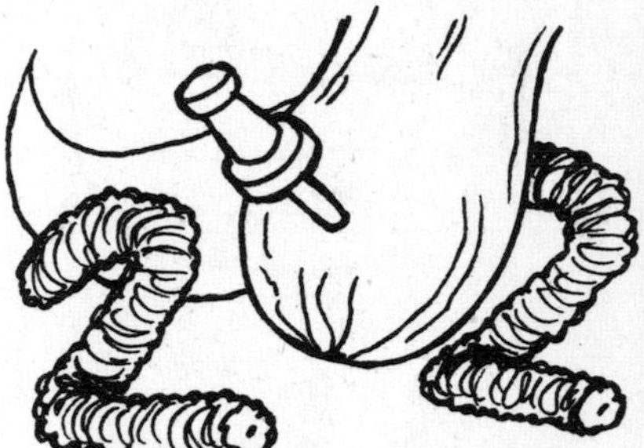

4. Draw on a face and spots if you like.

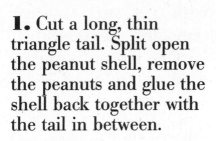

You will need

construction paper

scissors, white craft glue and markers

a peanut in the shell

a pipe cleaner

a push pin

Printmaking

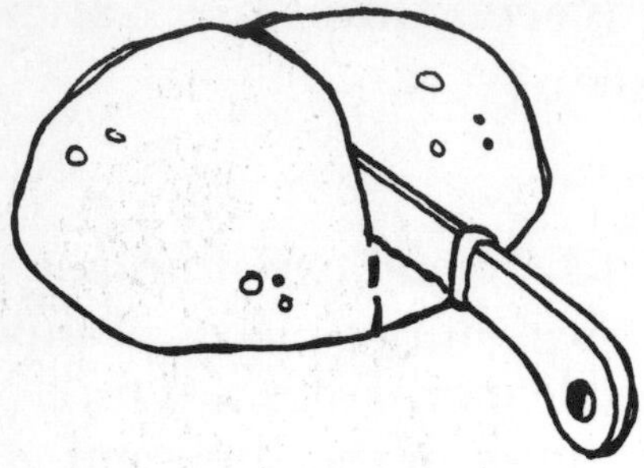

Here are many great ideas for decorating posters, pictures, greeting cards, gift bags, wrapping paper and lots more. You will need acrylic craft paint, a paint tray, such as a foil pie plate, and a few more items described below. Have some scrap paper on hand to try out your printing ideas. If you'd like to print clothing, use fabric paint and see pages 92 and 93 for how to get ready.

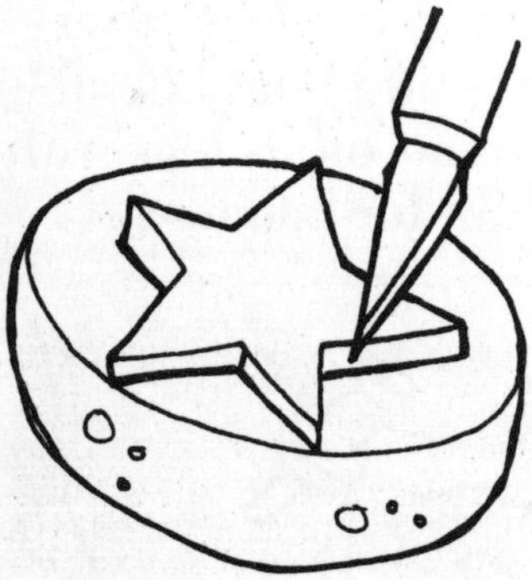

Potato printing

Ask an adult to slice a potato in half and cut in a design such as a flower, star, heart or geometric shape. Dip the potato in paint, test it and decorate your item. If you wish to change paint colors, rinse and dry the potato and dip it in the new color. You can cut and dip other vegetables and fruits too.

Handprints and footprints

You can place your open hand in paint and print it. Or try making a hand-footprint by printing the little-finger side of your fist. Make the toes by dipping your fingertips in paint and printing them. You can also dip an old running shoe into paint and "walk" it across your paper.

Dip, drizzle and splatter

Dip a Popsicle stick into paint and let it drizzle and drip onto your paper. Or dip the bristles of an old toothbrush into paint and, holding the bristles downwards, flick them with a Popsicle stick. Use lots of colors of paint.

More printing possibilities

Dip any of the following items into paint and print with them: crumpled waxed paper, sponge shapes, pipe cleaners bent into designs or string glued onto a small block of wood.

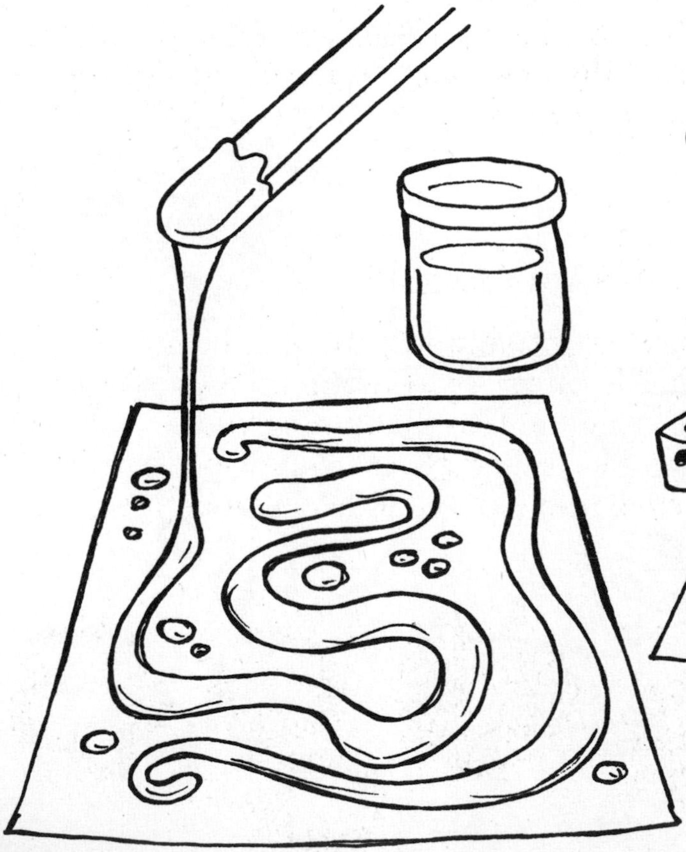

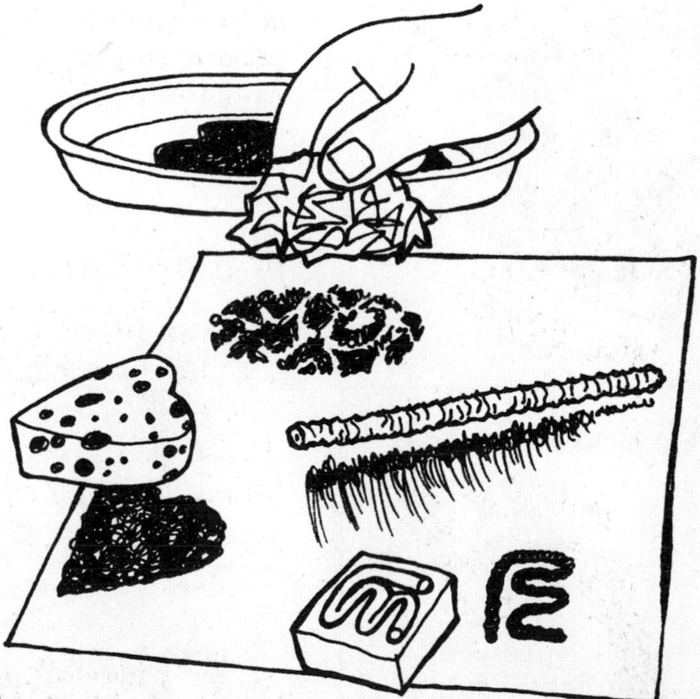

Squashed-paint pictures

Every time you make one of these pictures, it will be a one-of-a-kind work of art. Use a separate spoon or Popsicle stick for each color of paint you use.

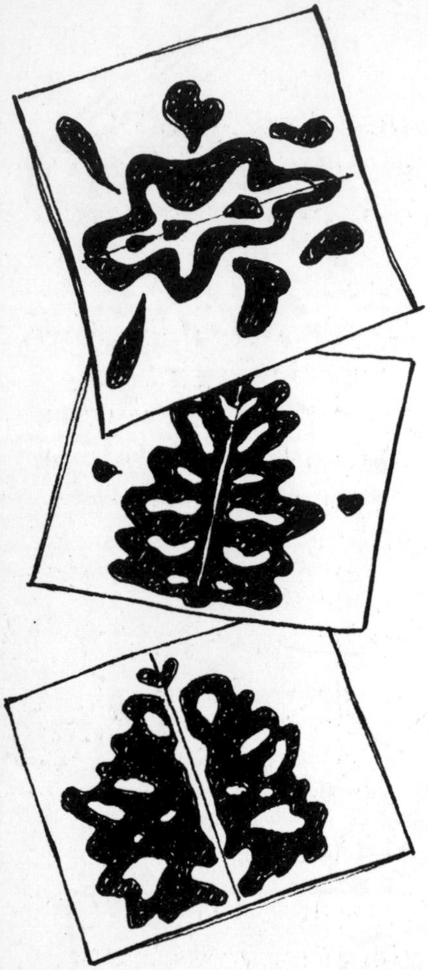

1. Cover your work surface with newspaper.

2. Fold a sheet of paper in half; open it again. Use a spoon or stick to dribble paint just along the fold, on one side only, or all over the paper.

3. Fold the paper in half and smooth it with your hands. Open it and look at your masterpiece!

You will need

newspaper
◎
paper
◎
plastic spoons or Popsicle sticks
◎
paint

Dipped-string pictures

You can dip string directly into a small jar of paint or pour some paint out onto a pie plate. Use a separate string for each color of paint you use.

You will need

newspaper
a sheet of paper
scissors
string or yarn
paint

1. Cover your work surface with newspaper.

2. Fold a sheet of paper in half; unfold it. Cut three lengths of string.

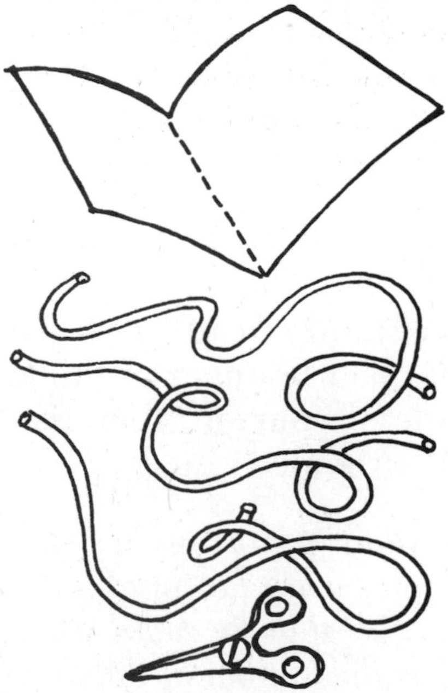

3. Dip each of the three strings into paint and place them any way you like on the right side of the paper. Refold the paper.

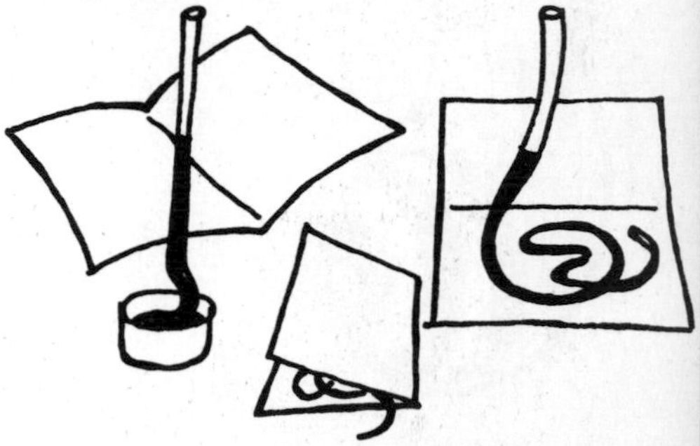

4. Press gently on the top of the folded paper and pull out the strings one at a time. Open your paper to see the designs you've created.

Pantyhose ball bouncer

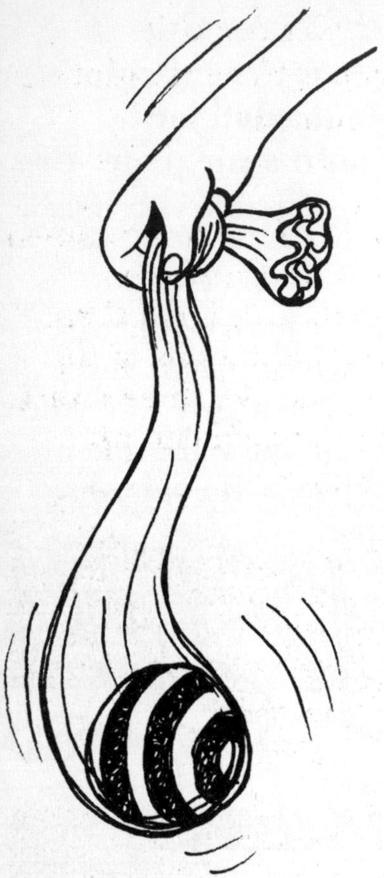

This craft and game is a terrific way to use an old, holey pair of tights or pantyhose.

1. Pull one of the legs of the tights inside out. Push that leg into the other to double it.

2. Cut the doubled leg off the tights. Push the ball into the toe area. Knot the top of the leg.

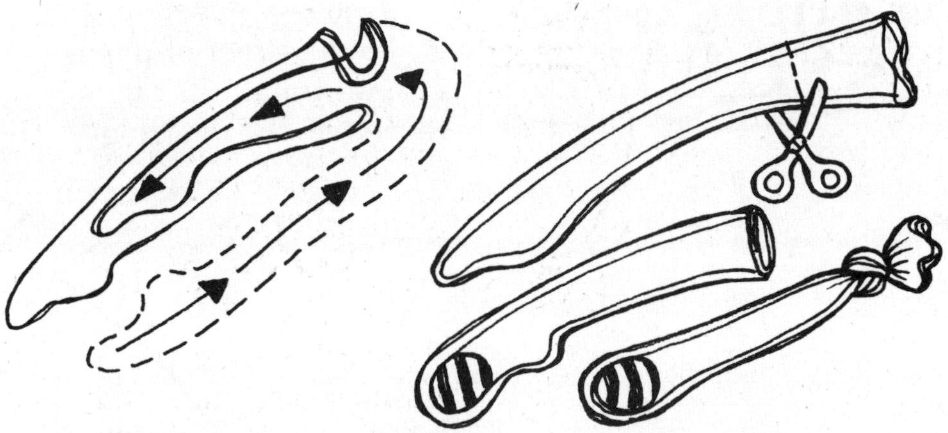

3. Stand outside with your back against a wall. Hold the ball bouncer at the knot and hit the wall on one side of yourself, then back and forth as you chant this rhyme:

A sailor went to sea, sea, sea
To see what he could see, see, see
But all that he could see, see, see
Was the bottom of the deep blue sea, sea, sea.

Each time you come to the three "sea"s or "see"s, lift the leg opposite to the hand in which you are holding the bouncer, and bounce the bouncer under the lifted leg. When you get good at this chant, do it as fast as you can!

You will need

a clean pair of tights or pantyhose
◎
scissors
◎
a rubber ball

Dress-up braids

Use old, clean pantyhose or tights for this braided wig. You can use three different-colored pantyhose or three the same colour.

1. On one of the pairs of pantyhose, make a short cut on each side of the center seam in the crotch area.

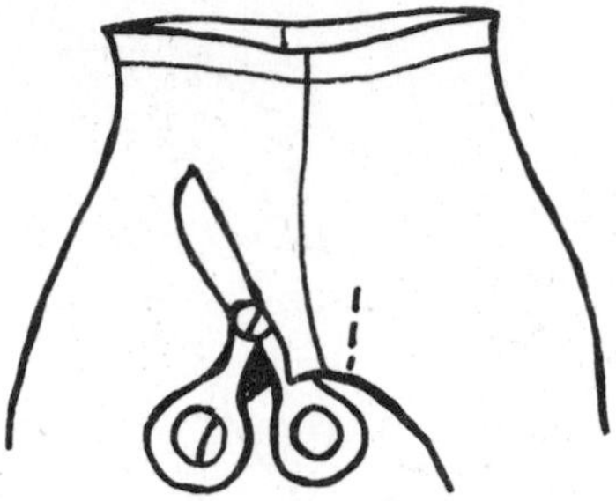

2. On the other two pairs of pantyhose, cut off the top part above the legs so the legs are still connected.

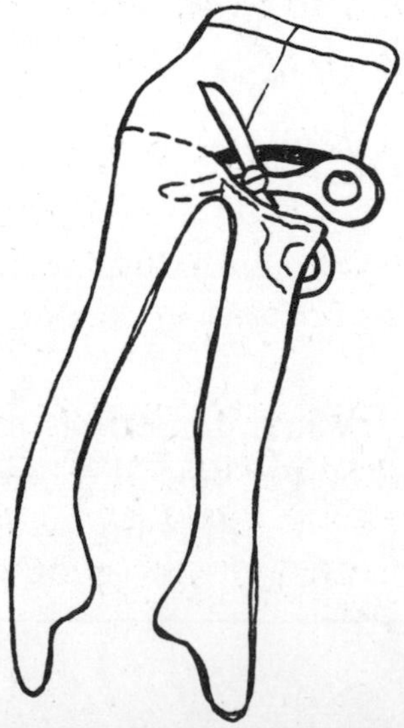

3. Hold the two trimmed pairs of pantyhose together and pull them through the slits in the first pair. All three crotch areas should end up together.

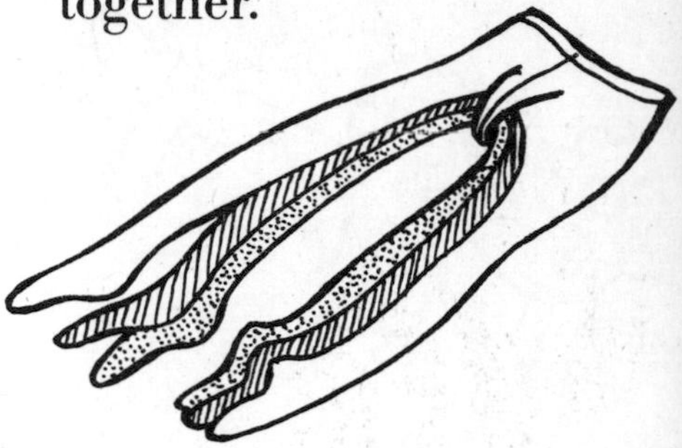

4. Braid each side. Fasten the ends with a rubber band and trim the ends if they are uneven. Tie bows over the bands if you like.

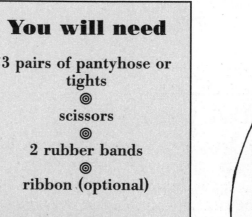

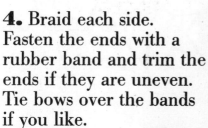

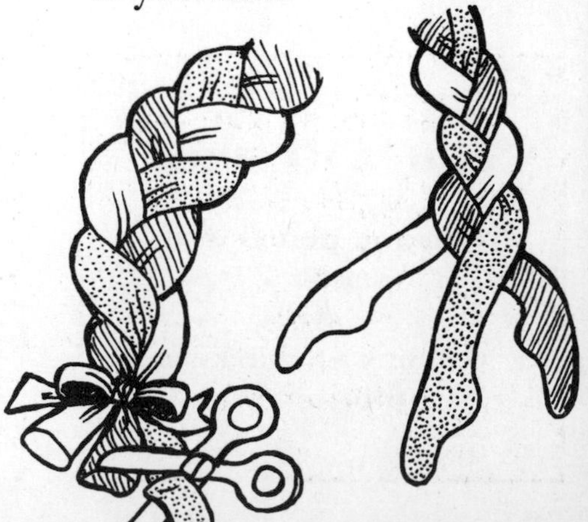

You will need

3 pairs of pantyhose or tights

scissors

2 rubber bands

ribbon (optional)

Paper-doll strings

Try this with a regular sheet of paper first. Then try it with wrapping paper or newsprint from a roll.

1. Fan-fold your paper as shown, wide enough to draw a doll on it.

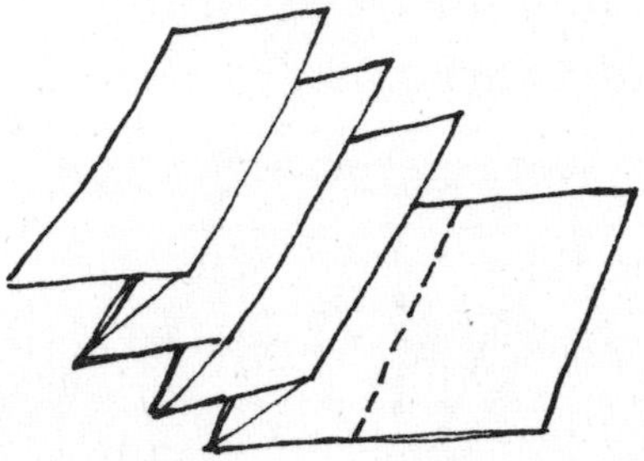

2. Draw on a doll shape making sure that at least the arms go off the edges of the folded paper.

3. With the paper still folded, cut out the doll shape. Unfold the string of dolls and color them in, if you like.

You will need

paper, a pencil and scissors

◎

crayons or markers (optional)

More ideas

Try making strings of trees, hearts, eggs, bears – whatever you like. Just make sure that parts of the drawing go off the folded edges.

Snowflakes

Make a variety of sizes of snowflakes by tracing cups, bowls, saucers and plastic tubs onto almost any type of paper.

1. Trace circles onto the paper and cut them out.

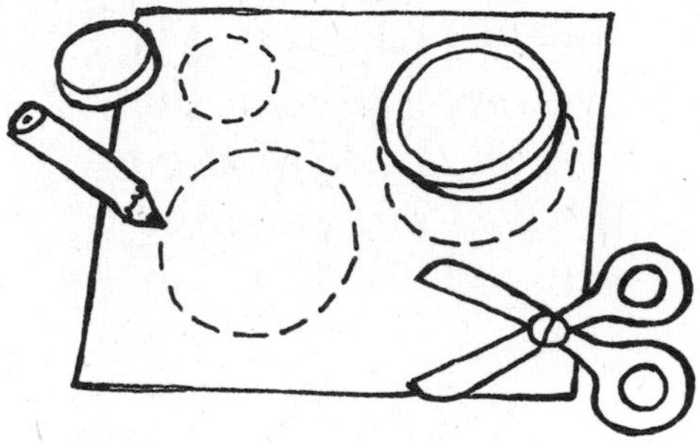

2. Fold each circle in half and then in thirds.

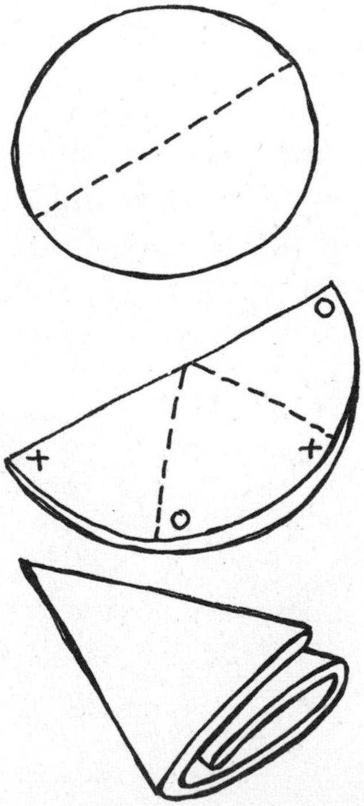

3. Cut out pieces from the folded circles as shown. Open them to find one-of-a-kind snowflakes.

4. If you like, you can spread a bit of glue on a snowflake and sprinkle on glitter. Tape the snowflakes to windows or walls or tie on thread and hang them on doorknobs, ceilings or archways.

You will need

paper

cups or bowls to trace

a pencil and scissors

white craft glue and glitter (optional)

Folded-paper puppy card

After making this puppy, try making a pig with a large two-hole button for the nose.

1. To make a square, fold the top end of the sheet of paper so it is even with the left side. Cut off the strip along the bottom. Keep the square folded diagonally.

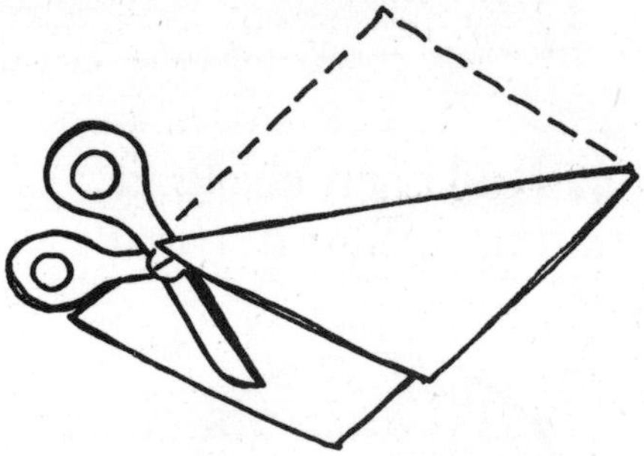

2. Position the triangle as shown. Fold up the bottom point, then fold it and glue it back down to make a nose. Color the nose.

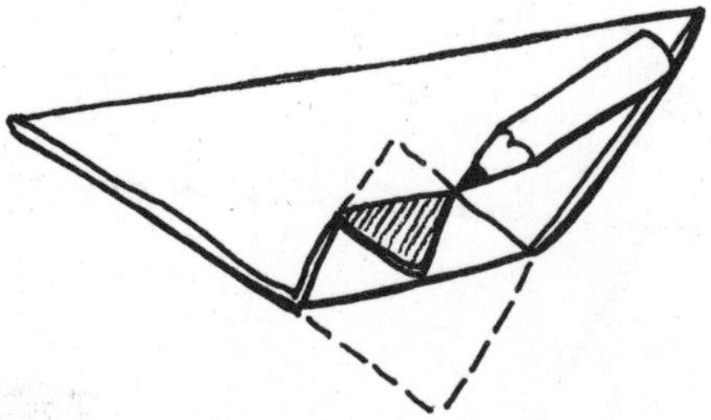

3. Fold down the other two points to make ears. Draw or glue on eyes. Color in other markings.

4. Fold a sheet of construction paper in half and glue the puppy to it. Write a message inside, such as "Have a doggone good birthday."

You will need

a sheet of paper

crayons or markers, scissors and white craft glue or a glue stick

roly eyes (optional)

construction paper

Folded-paper tiger card

You can make a mini tiger by using a small square of paper. Glue it onto a Popsicle stick to make a puppet.

1. To make a square, follow step 1 on page 146. Keep the square folded diagonally.

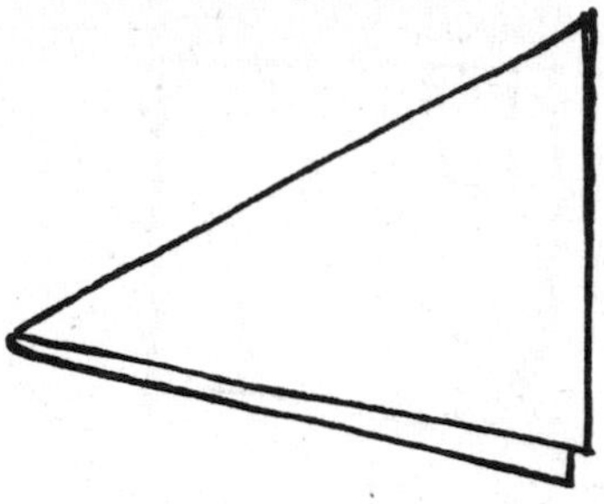

2. Bend down the top of the triangle so the tip ends up about halfway down the triangle.

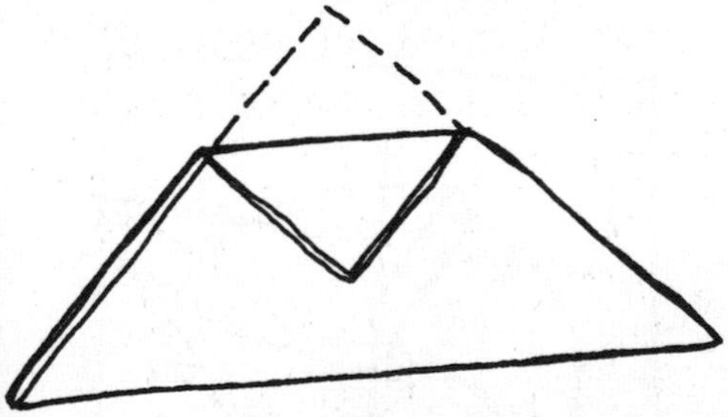

3. Bend up the other two corners to make ears. Flip the shape over and adjust the ears until they look just right.

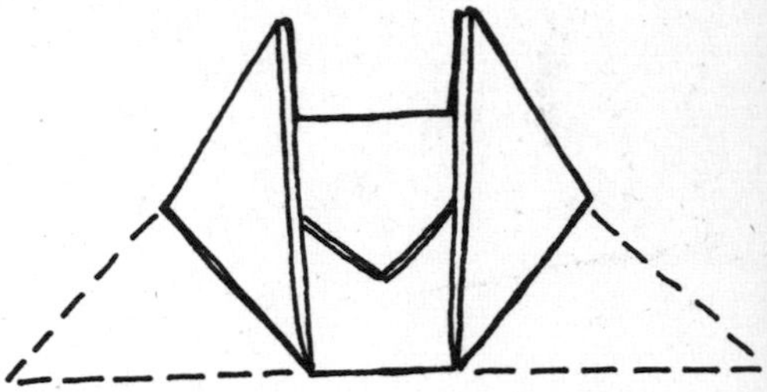

4. Draw on a face and tiger stripes. Fold the construction paper in half and glue the tiger to the front of it. Glue half a sheet of white paper inside so you can write on a message, such as "Go wild on your birthday."

You will need

paper

crayons or markers, scissors and white craft glue or a glue stick

a sheet of black construction paper

Fly-away ladybug

Make this ladybug any two colors you like. If you use black for the head, use a white crayon, acrylic paint, beads or roly eyes to make the face.

1. For the bug's body, trace a circle onto black construction paper. Draw a round bump on it for the head. Cut out the head and body.

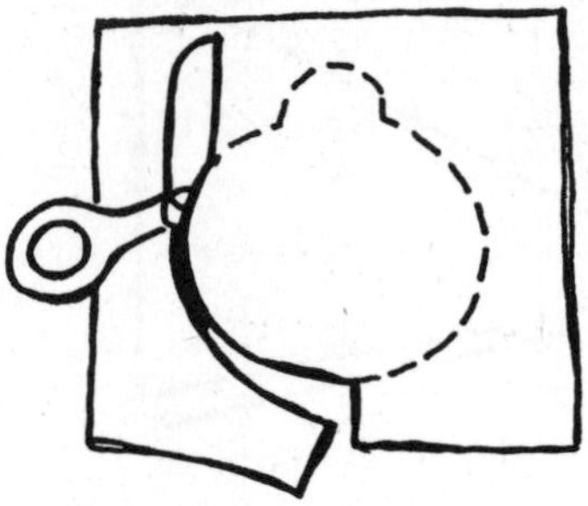

2. For the wings, trace a larger circle onto red paper and cut it out. Fold it in half and cut it along the fold line.

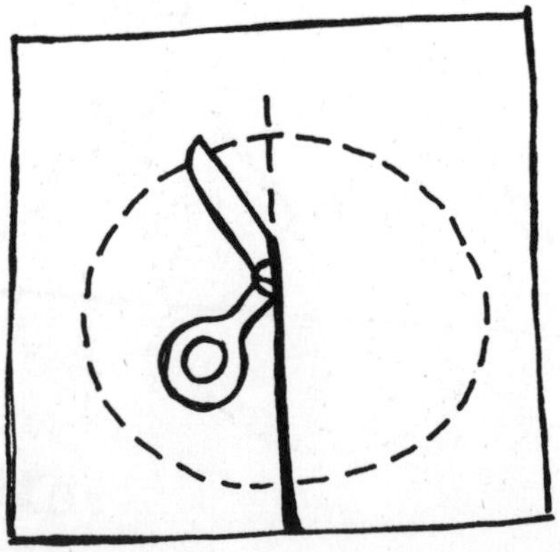

3. Draw ladybug spots on the wings or cut out black construction-paper dots and glue them on.

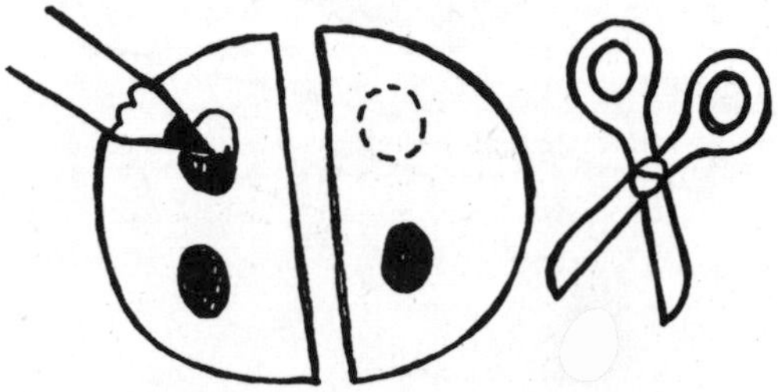

4. Slightly overlap the top of the wings and poke the paper fastener through them. (You may need to poke in a pencil hole first.) Fasten the wings to the neck area. Draw on a face and antennae.

You will need

black and red construction paper

cups or lids to trace

a pencil, scissors and white craft glue or a glue stick

a paper fastener

crayons or markers

Hatching-egg surprise

See if your family or friends can guess what will hatch from this big egg!

1. Draw a large egg on a sheet of construction paper. Cut it out.

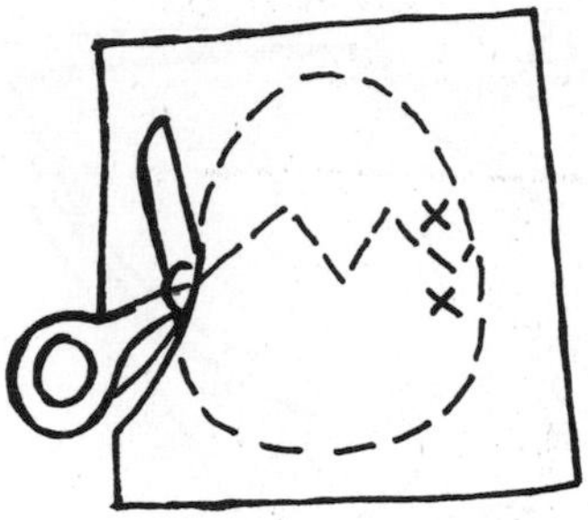

2. Cut the egg in half by making a jagged line. Poke a hole in a corner of each half of the shell and hold the halves together with a paper fastener.

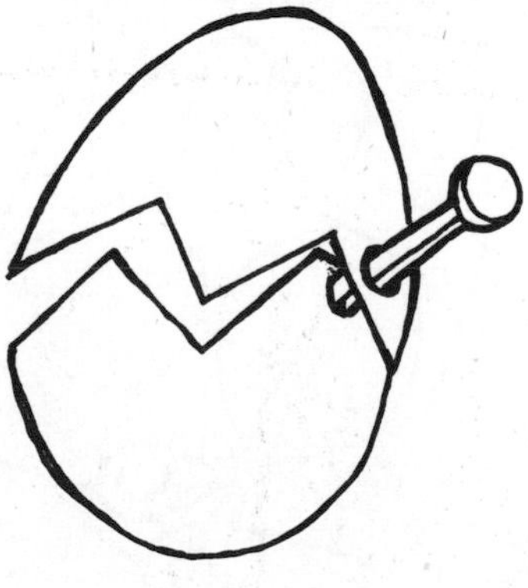

3. On a different color of paper, draw the top half of a chick, bird, lizard, snake, turtle or dinosaur. Draw on a face and cut it out.

4. Glue the creature to the bottom half of the shell so its head and neck are showing. When you close the shell, you should not be able to see what's inside.

You will need

a pencil, scissors and white craft glue or a glue stick

◎

construction paper

◎

crayons or markers

◎

a paper fastener

Movable fuzzy bear

After you've made this fuzzy bear, try making a bunny with long, movable ears or a dog with a waggy tail.

1. Glue the felt to the sheet of paper.

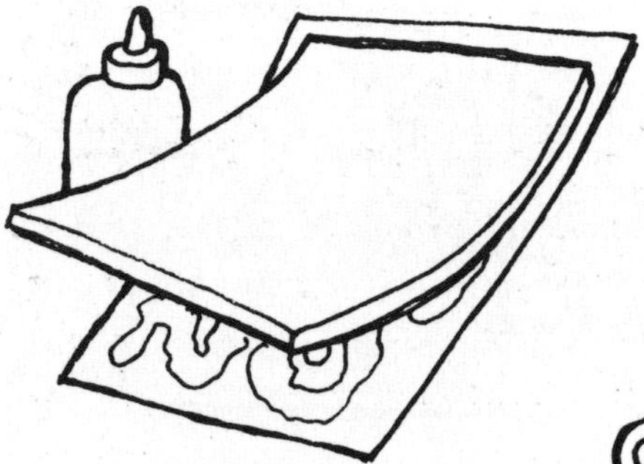

2. On the paper side, draw four chubby legs, an oval body and a round head with ears. Cut out all six parts.

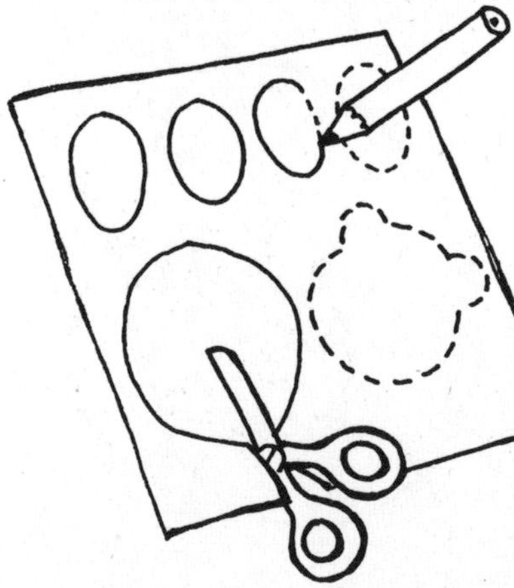

3. Use the scissors to carefully cut or poke small holes into one end of each leg and the chin area of the head. Poke holes in the body and attach the head and legs with the paper fasteners.

4. Draw on a face and claws.

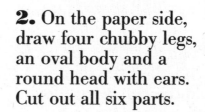

You will need

paper, a pencil, scissors and white craft glue

a square of felt

5 paper fasteners

markers

Wiggling caterpillar

You can use one color or many colors of construction paper for this cheerful caterpillar.

1. Trace four circles onto the construction paper. Cut them out.

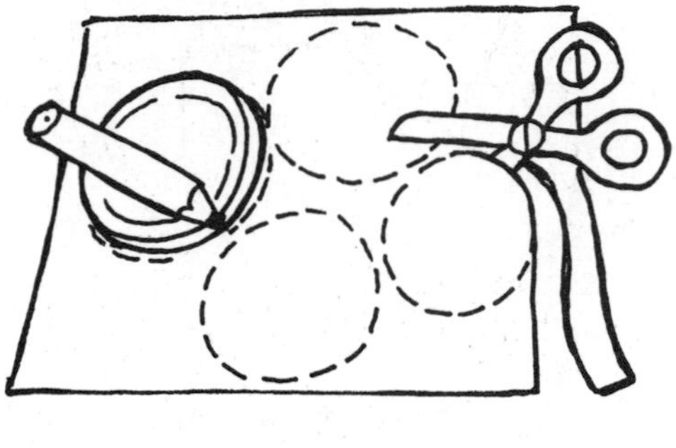

2. Fasten the circles together in a row with the paper fasteners.

3. Draw a face on one end of the caterpillar. To make antennae, poke in the pipe cleaner ends from the back to the front and curl the ends.

4. Tape a Popsicle stick to the back of the head and tail circles. Push the sticks together, then pull them apart to make the caterpillar move and wiggle.

You will need

a cup or lid to trace

construction paper

a pencil, scissors and tape or white craft glue or a glue stick

paper fasteners

crayons or markers

a short pipe cleaner

2 Popsicle sticks

Paper-plate clock

Here's a great way to practice telling time.

1. Flip over the paper plate. Draw the numbers on the clock, beginning with "12" and "6," then "3" and "9."

2. Use the scissors to poke a hole in the center of the clock.

3. For the hands, cut two strips of cardboard, one shorter than the other. Round off one end of each and cut the other end into a point. Punch a hole in each rounded end.

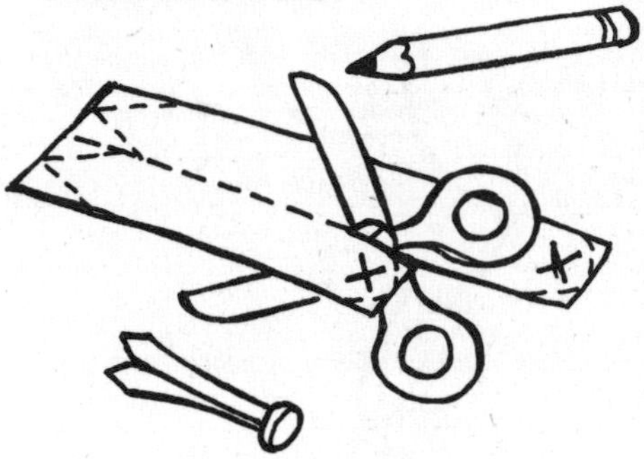

4. Use the paper fastener to tightly attach the hands to the clock face. What time is it now?

You will need

a paper plate
crayons or markers
thin cardboard (from a cereal box)
scissors
a hole punch
a paper fastener

Dancing marionette

For a stick, use a new, unsharpened pencil, a twig, a piece of narrow dowel or any other stick you have around.

1. Flip over the paper plate and draw on a face.

2. See page 62 for how to make construction-paper springs. Make four springs and glue them on for arms and legs.

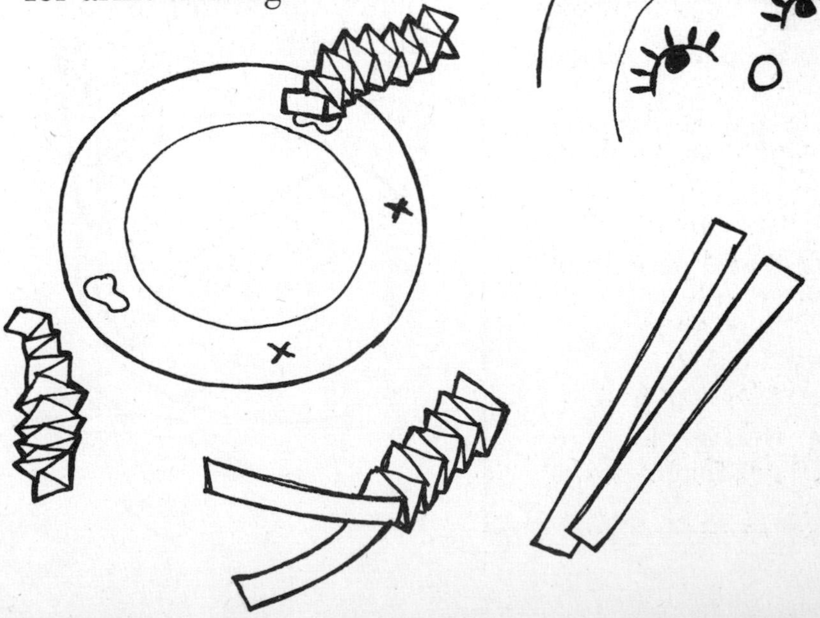

3. Punch two holes near the top of the plate. Tie a piece of yarn from each hole to the stick and make your marionette dance!

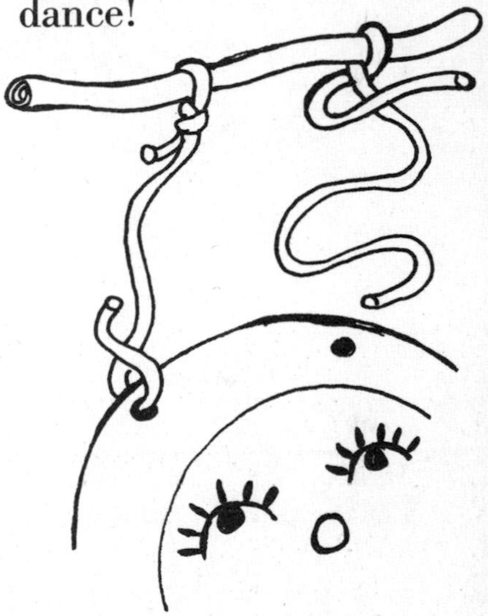

You will need

a paper plate
crayons or markers
construction paper
scissors and white craft glue or a glue stick
a hole punch
yarn
a stick

Paper-plate pouch

Use this handy pouch for postcards and greeting cards or fill it with flowers you've made from the instructions in this book.

1. Cut one of the paper plates in half. Punch about 12 holes evenly around its outside edge.

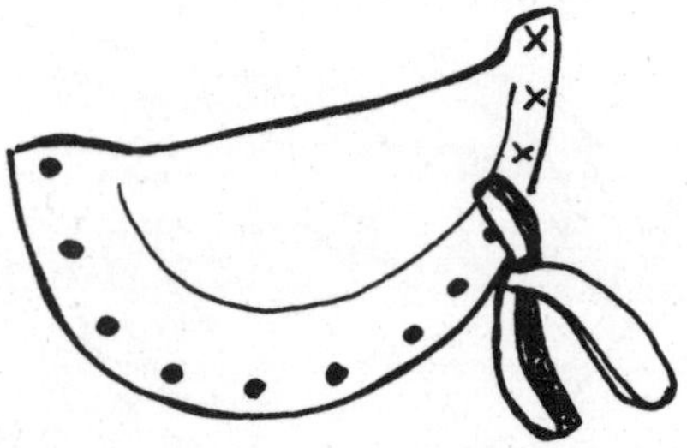

2. Place the half plate on the whole plate and use the pencil to mark where each hole should be made on the whole plate. Punch in the marked holes.

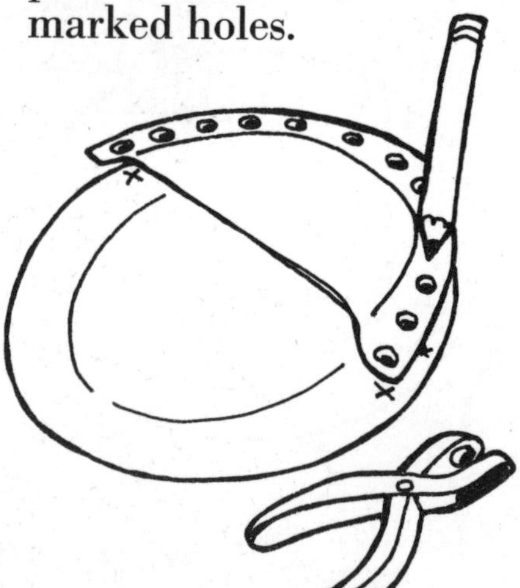

3. Cut a piece of yarn twice the length of an adult's arm. Wrap a little tape around one end.

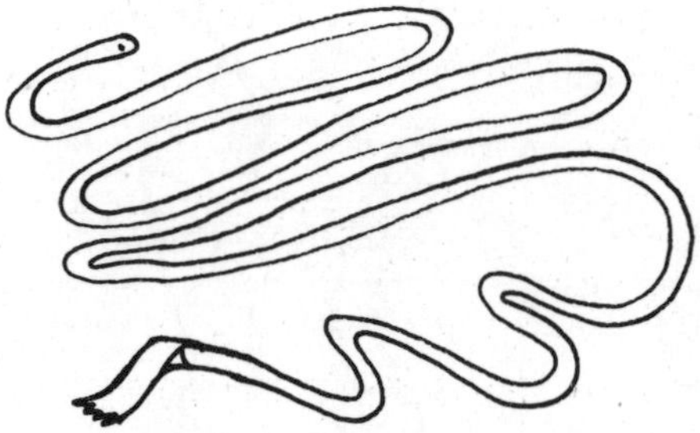

4. Place the half plate on the whole plate again and line up the holes. Thread the taped end of the yarn through the first set of holes. Tie the untaped end in this hole. Leave a tail on the knot.

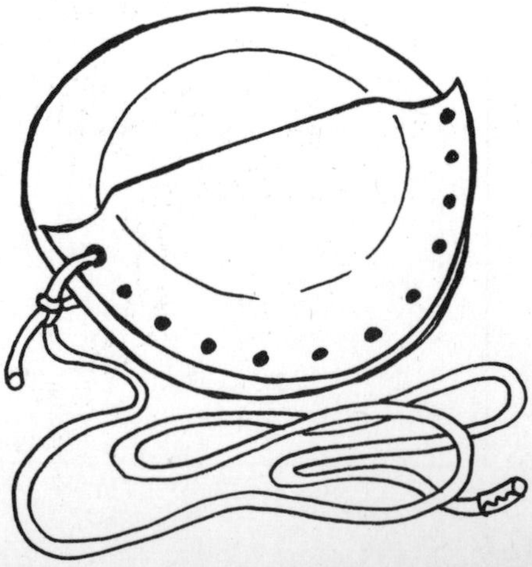

You will need

2 paper plates

a hole punch

scissors, a pencil and tape

yarn

crayon, markers or stickers

5. "Sew" the plates together using the taped end of the yarn as a needle.

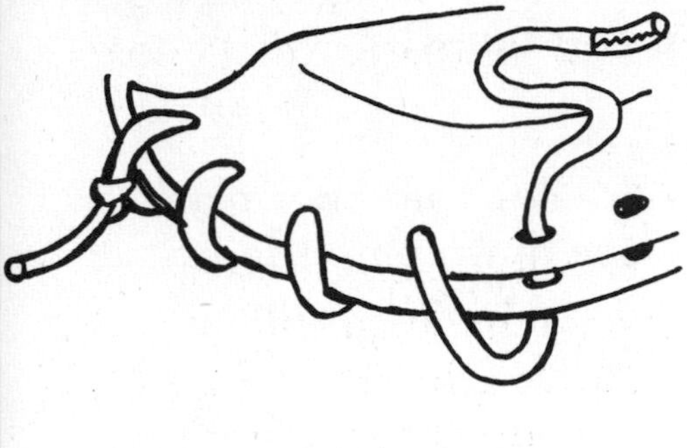

6. When you reach the end of the holes, sew back again to where you first started. Tie the yarn to the tail you left on the knot at the beginning. Cut the yarn and tuck the ends inside the pouch.

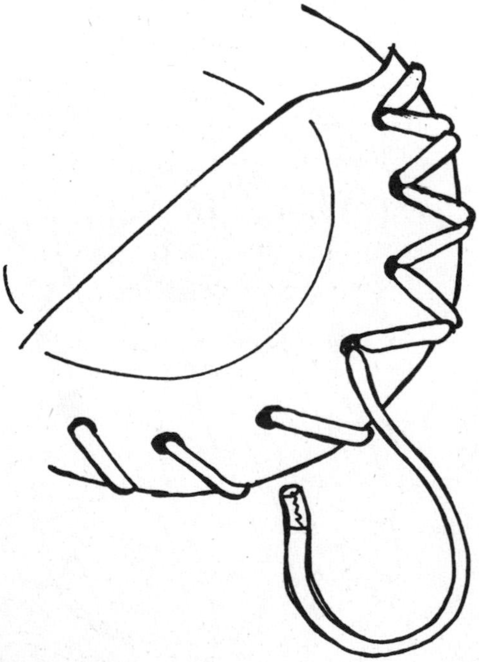

7. Punch two holes at the top of the whole plate. Thread a piece of yarn through them and knot the yarn ends together.

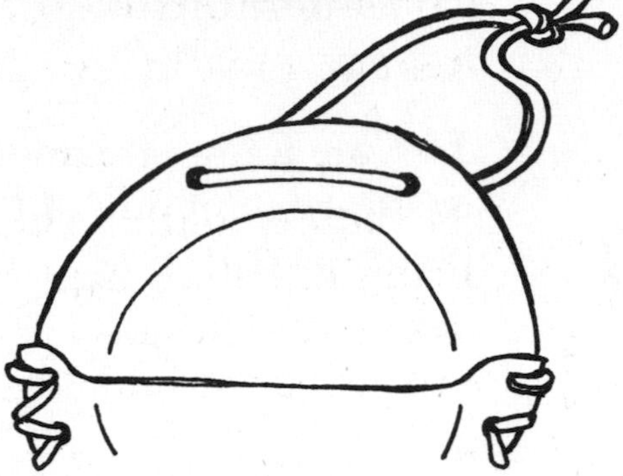

8. Decorate your pouch. Hang it on a nail, bulletin board or your doorknob.

Paper-plate shaker

This instrument is part shaker, part drum and part tambourine. Strike up the band!

1. Glue a few streamers to the edge of one of the paper plates.

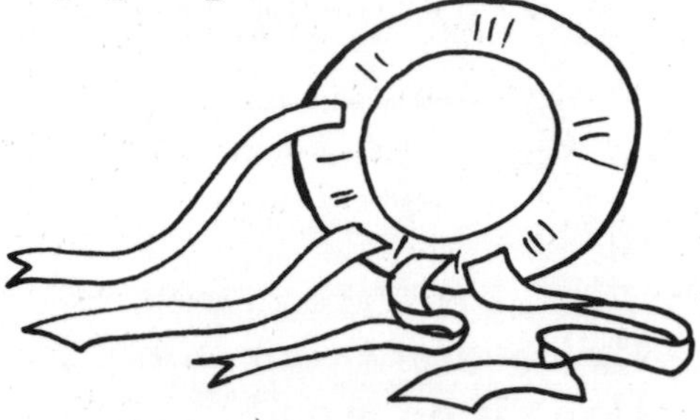

2. In this same plate, place the beans and the bells (if you are using bells).

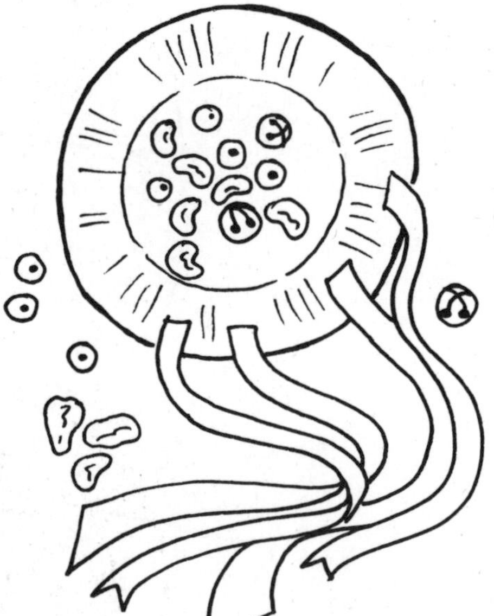

3. Glue the other plate face down onto the first one. Allow the glue to dry.

4. Decorate both sides of the shaker using markers, crayons, stickers, tissue paper or other items.

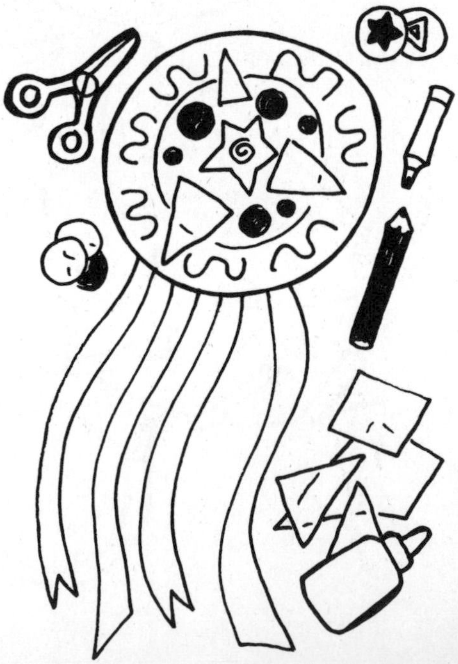

You will need

streamers, ribbon or strips of tissue paper

2 paper plates

white craft glue

beans, beads or pebbles

2 or more jingle bells (optional)

supplies for decorating (see step 4)

M◎re paper-plate ideas

Make a paper-plate painted turtle. Flip over the plate and decorate it with patches of color. Cut out a long, tapered tail, four rounded paws and a head. Glue them all to the underside. Draw on toes and a face.

◎

Use a paper plate for an animal head. Try a lion. Flip over the paper plate and draw on a lion face. Poke in holes around the nose and thread in pipe-cleaner whiskers. Cut bits of yarn and glue them all around the edge of the plate to make the mane. Glue on rounded construction-paper ears. What other animals can you make? They'll look great hanging on the wall.

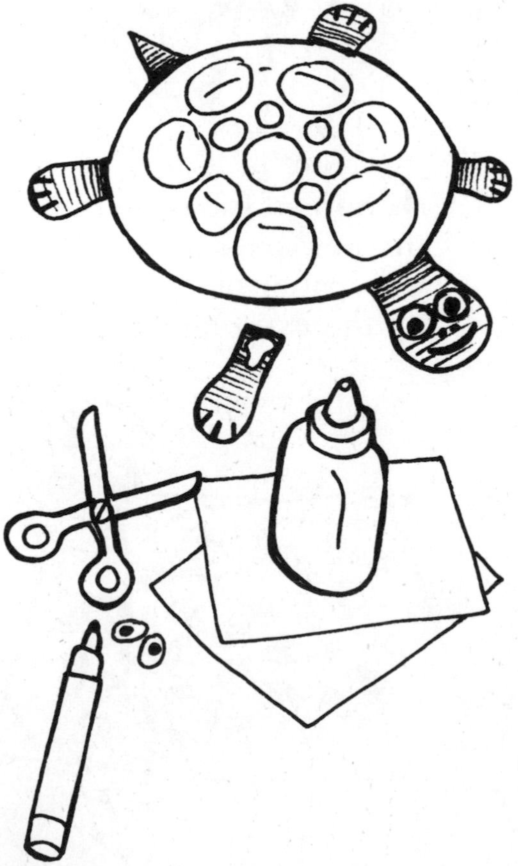

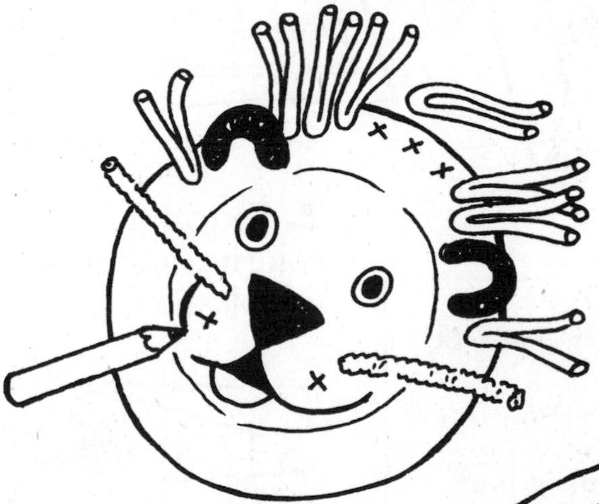

Colored pasta

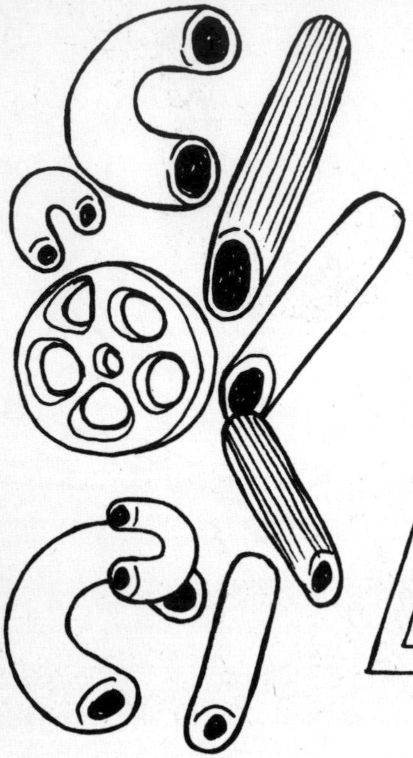

Try coloring many different types of pasta, such as macaroni, wagon wheels, rigatoni, tubetti and tubettini. Turn the page for ideas for what to do with the pasta.

You will need

newspaper

a small plastic bag

5 mL (1 tsp.) liquid food coloring

125 mL (1/2 c.) pasta

a spoon

waxed paper

plastic bags or tubs

1. Spread a double thickness of newspaper over your work area.

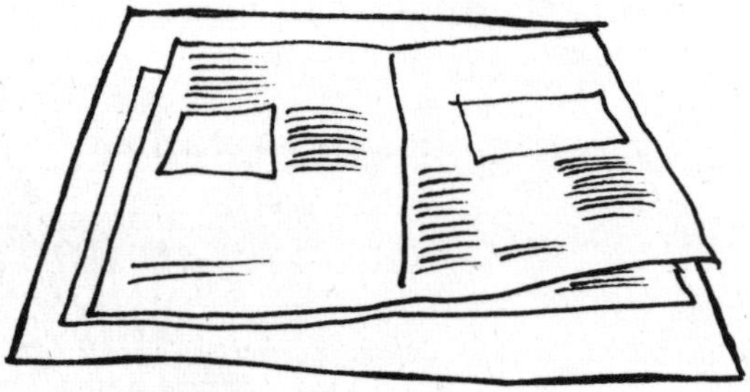

2. Pour the food coloring and pasta into the plastic bag.

3. Twist the bag and hold it closed while you shake it.

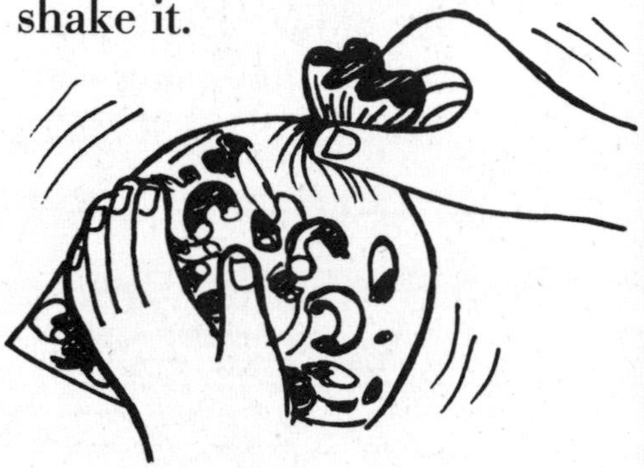

4. Spread the pasta onto the newspaper. The newspaper helps to soak up the extra liquid.

5. Before the pasta begins to dry and stick to the newspaper, slide it onto a sheet of waxed paper. Use the spoon to spread out the pasta so none of the pieces are touching.

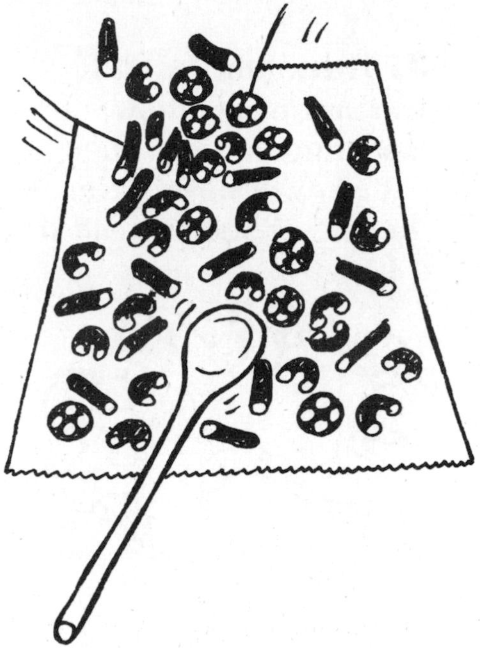

6. Let the pasta dry for about half an hour. This pasta is not for eating. Also, be careful not to get the pasta wet or the color may run.

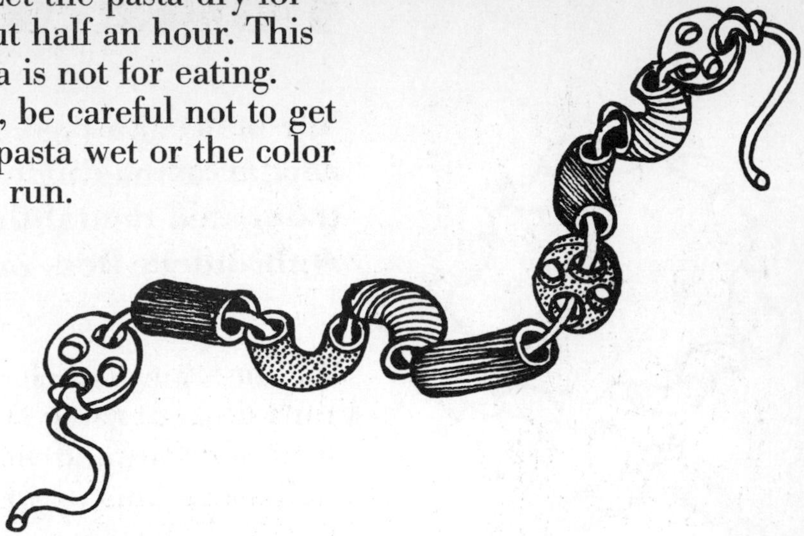

7. Store colored pasta in plastic bags or tubs.

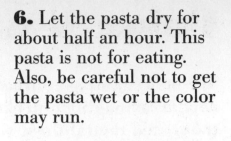

Pasta jewelry

For making a pasta bracelet, use elastic thread or cord. For making a necklace, garland or mobile, try waxed dental floss, waxed linen, fishing line, embroidery floss or heavy thread.

1. Cut a piece of elastic thread about three times the length around your wrist or as long as you'd like for a necklace.

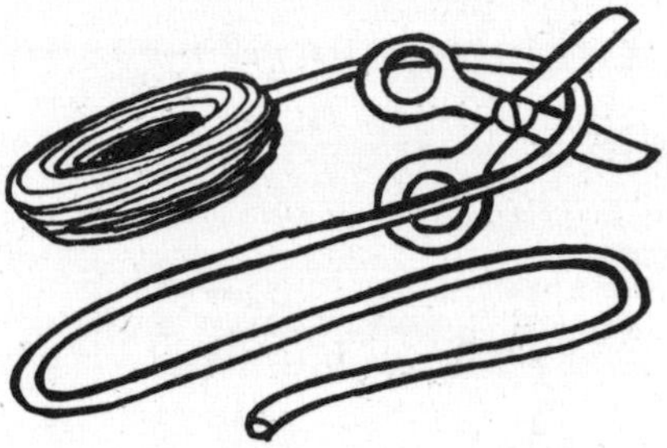

2. Tie a piece of small pasta near one end of your thread so the others won't fall off. (You may want to remove it when your jewelry is finished.)

3. Thread on pasta. If you are using elbow macaroni, a neat squiggly pattern will form. Trim the end of your thread if it frays.

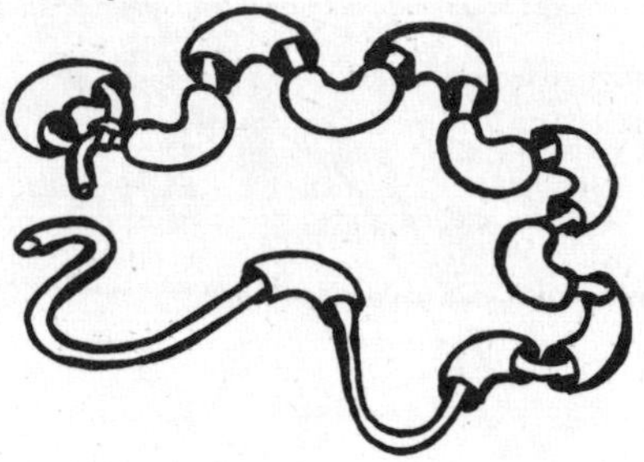

4. When your jewelry fits, triple knot the ends together.

You will need

colored pasta
(see pages 158 and 159)

elastic thread or cord

Pasta fun

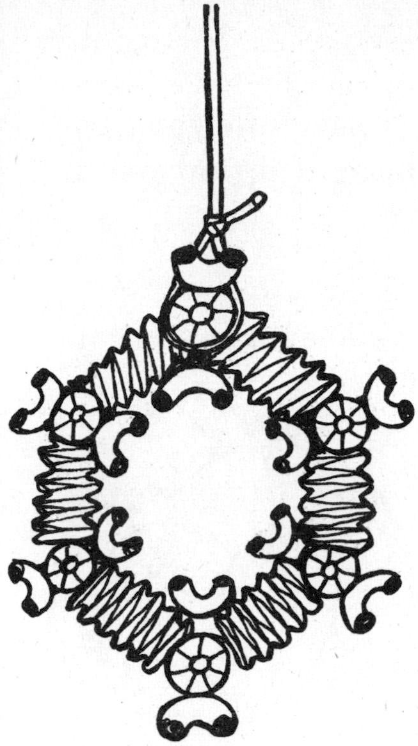

Have lots of colored pasta shapes on hand so you can make many one-of-a-kind designs.

1. Place the waxed paper on your work surface.

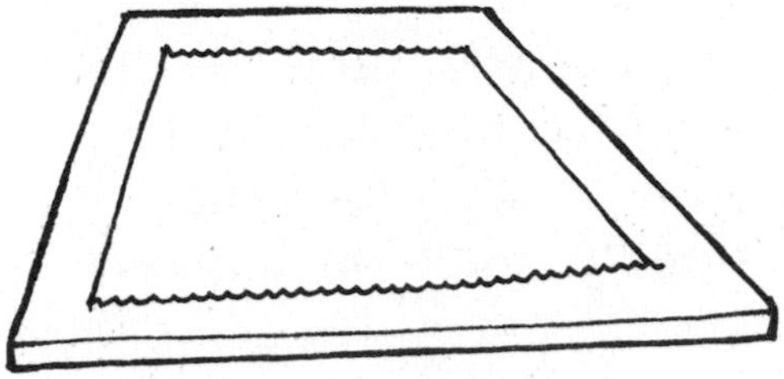

2. Play around with the pasta until you're happy with your design.

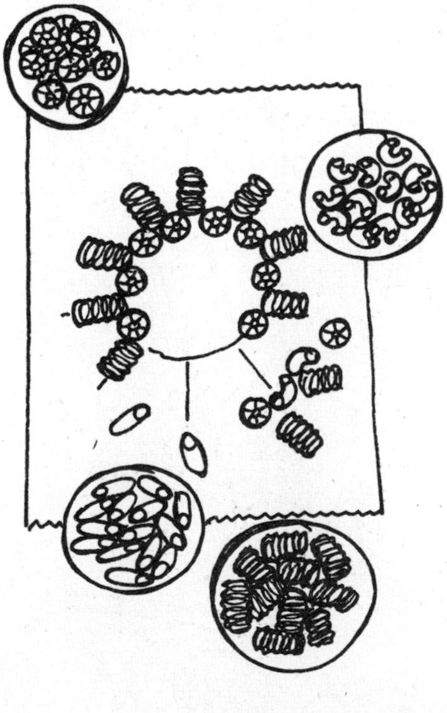

3. Glue the pasta pieces together. Allow the glue to dry.

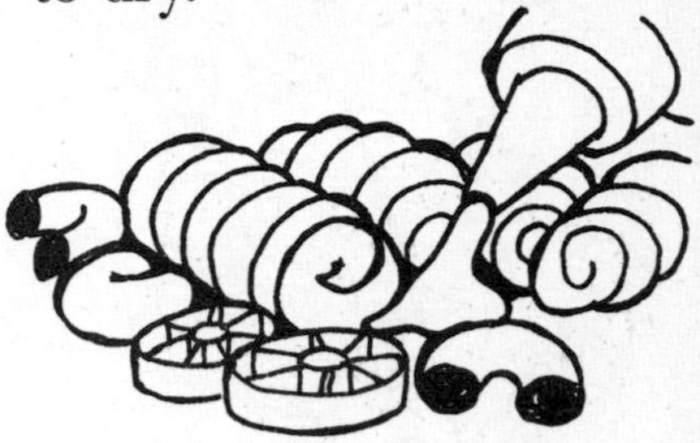

4. Peel your pasta design off the waxed paper. Tie a loop of fishing line or thread to it so you can hang it up.

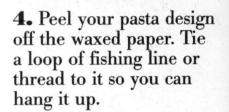

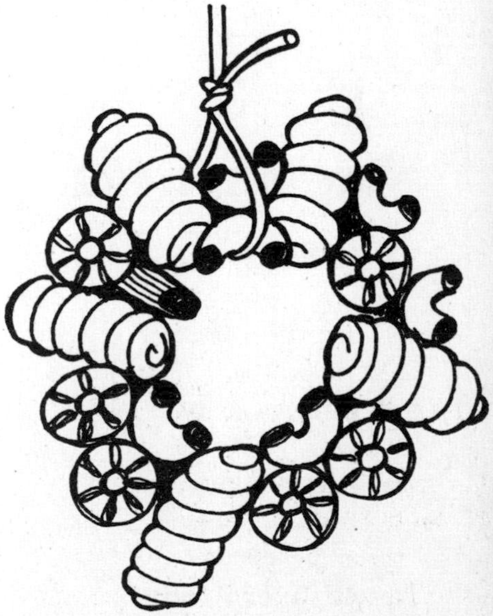

You will need

a sheet of waxed paper

◎

colored pasta (see pages 158 and 159)

◎

white craft glue and scissors

◎

fishing line or thread

Candy-cane reindeer

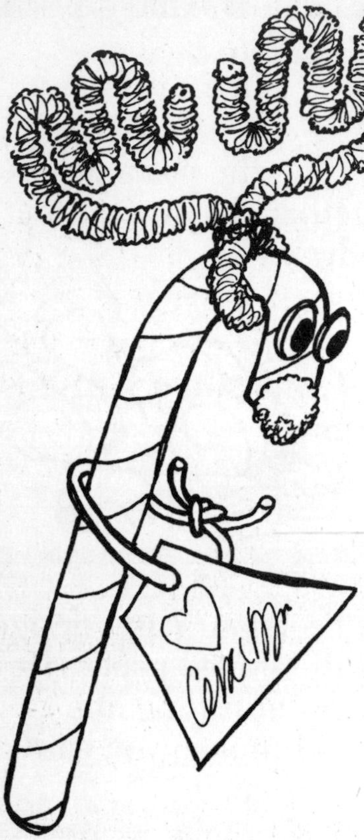

Don't eat all the candy canes – save one for this whimsical reindeer. You can hang it up or give it as a gift.

1. Twist the pipe cleaner around the crook of the candy cane. Bend the ends to look like antlers.

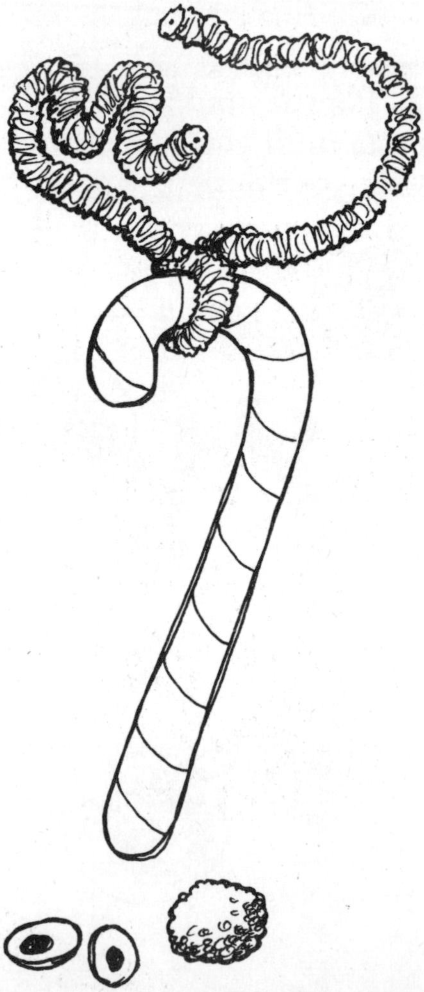

2. Glue on a pair of roly eyes.

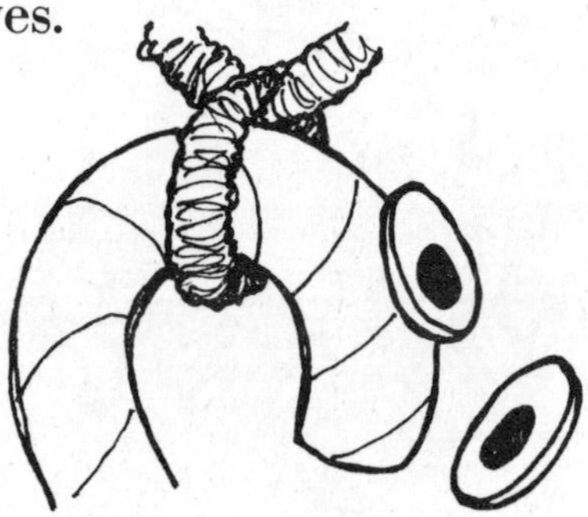

3. Glue on a pom-pom nose. Allow the glue to dry.

You will need

a candy cane
◎
a pipe cleaner
◎
a pair of roly eyes
◎
a tiny red pom-pom or bead
◎
white craft glue

Fuzzy flowers

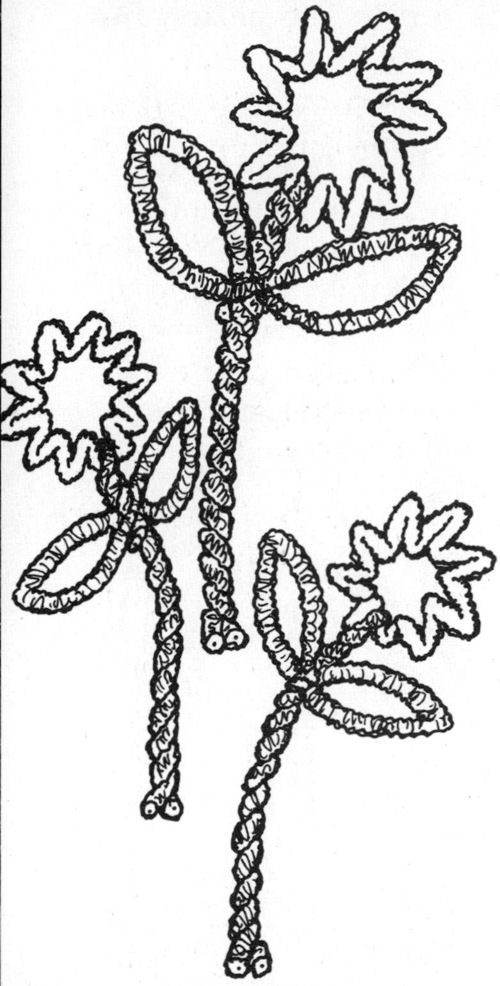

These instructions are for making one flower, but once you've made one, you'll want to make a whole bouquet!

1. Wind a pipe cleaner around the pencil so it looks like a spring.

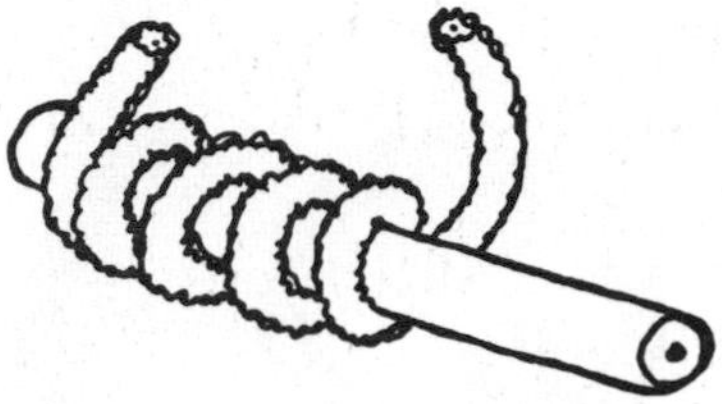

2. Slide the pipe cleaner off the pencil and stretch it out a little. Hook and twist the ends together to form a coiled circle.

3. Bend the second pipe cleaner in half. Hook it through the flower. Tightly twist it down its entire length to form the stem.

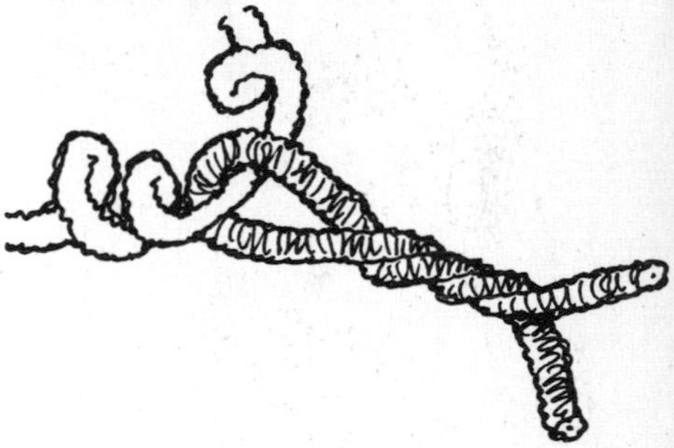

4. For the leaves, twist the third pipe cleaner around the stem as if you were fastening on a twist tie. Shape the ends into leaves.

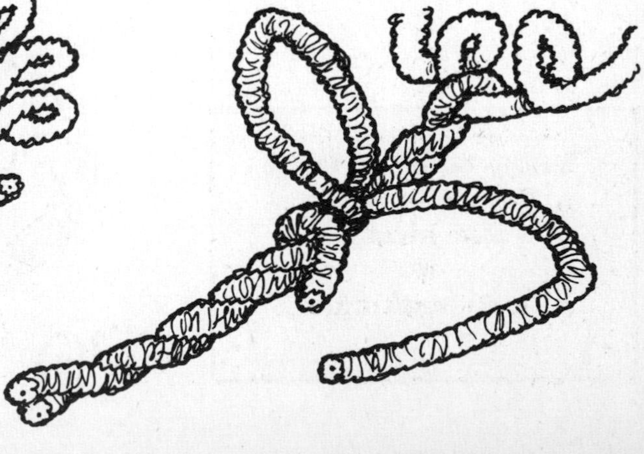

You will need

3 pipe cleaners
◎
an unsharpened pencil or a pen with a lid

Goofy glasses

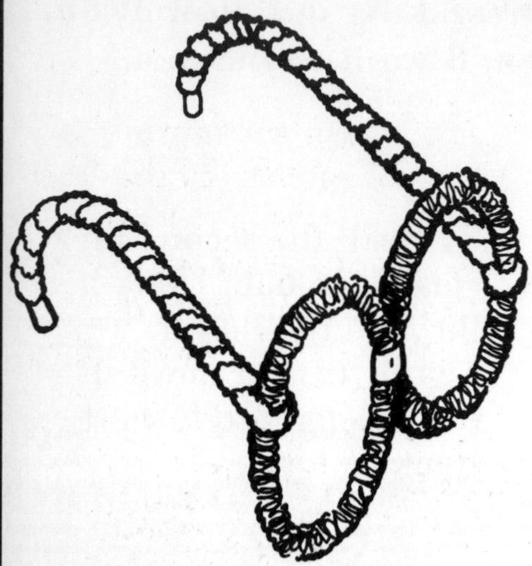

These glasses may not help you to see better, but they're a fun dress-up accessory.

1. Shape two of the pipe cleaners into big circles by twisting their ends together. Wrap the fastened area with tape so there are no sharp ends.

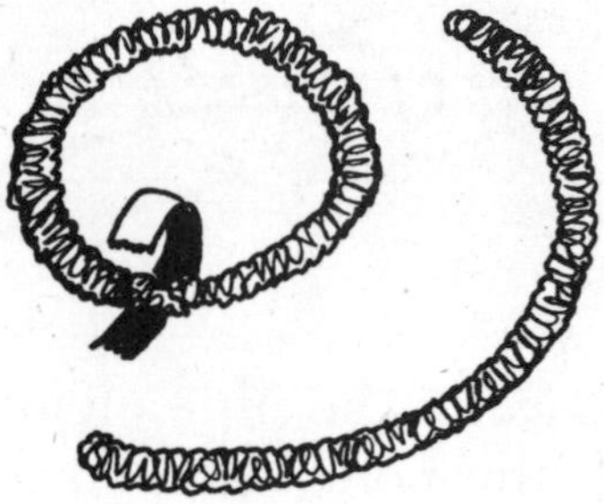

2. Place the circles side by side and tape them together as shown.

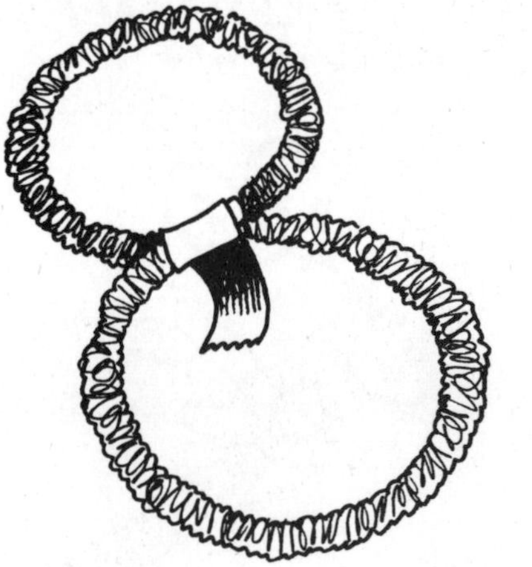

3. Bend the other two pipe cleaners in half. Fasten one on the side of each circle. Twist the arms and curve the ends to fit around your ears. Wind tape around the ends and try on your glasses.

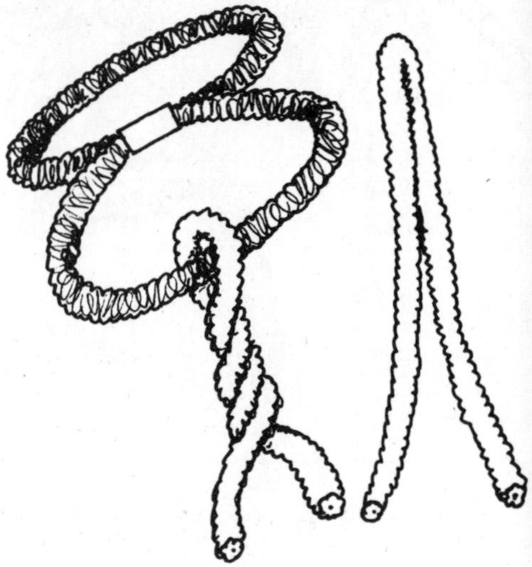

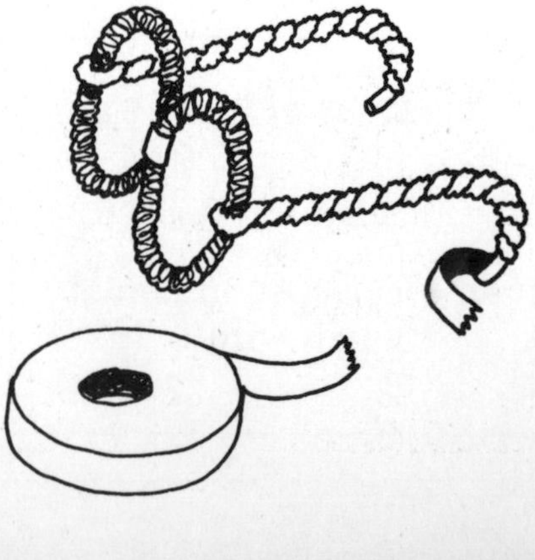

You will need

4 pipe cleaners

cloth or masking tape

Rainbow caterpillar

1. Begin wrapping a pipe cleaner around one spot on the pencil. When a little over half of the pipe cleaner is on the pencil, slide it off.

2. Do the same for the second pipe cleaner, then thread it onto the straight part of the first pipe cleaner. Position both ends so they are together and the same length. (You may need to wind the second one around itself a little more.)

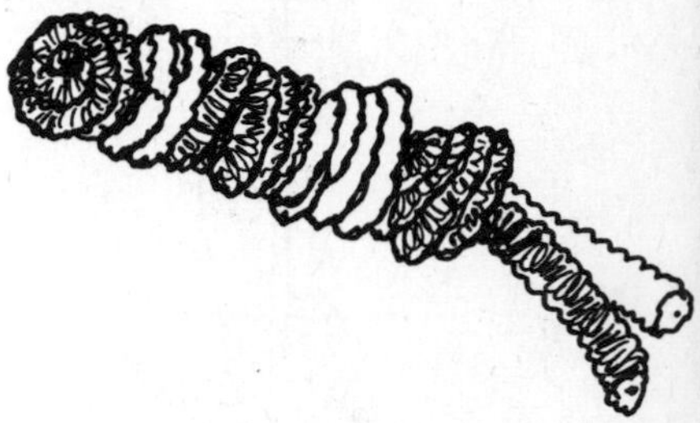

3. Wrap the entire length of each of the four remaining pipe cleaners into bundles around the pencil. Slide three of them onto the caterpillar.

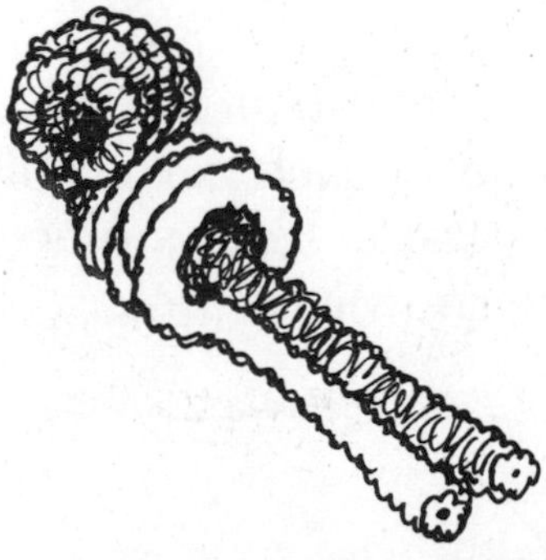

4. To put on the last bundle (which is the head) separate its coils a little. Thread part of the bundle onto the caterpillar. Bend the leftover pipe-cleaner ends straight up to make antennae. Curl the antennae around the pencil. Glue on the beads or roly eyes.

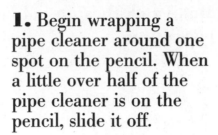

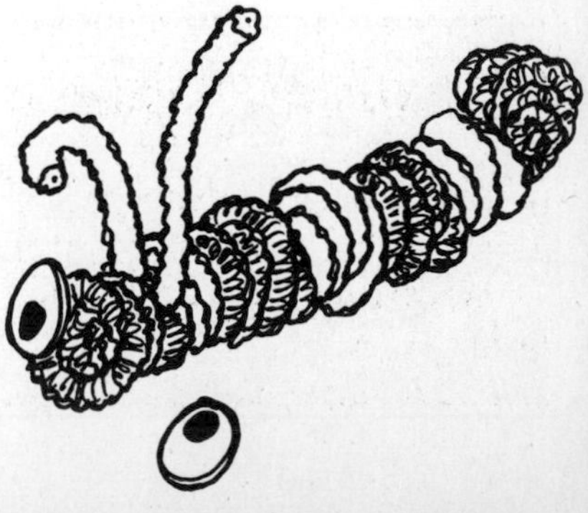

You will need

6 different-colored pipe cleaners

◎

an unsharpened pencil or a pen with a lid

◎

white craft glue

◎

2 small beads or roly eyes

Plastic-bag parachute

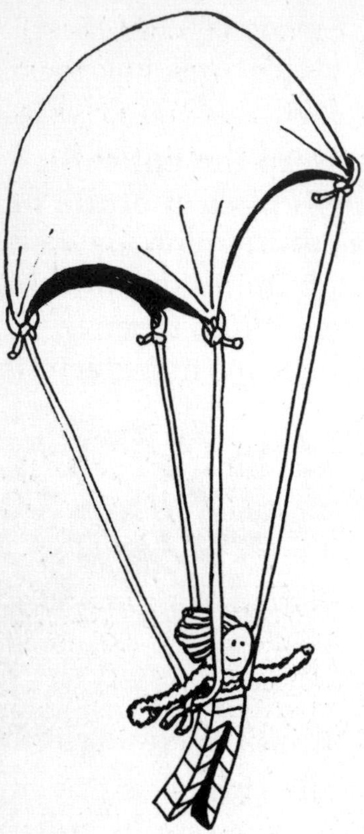

Make a clothespin pal (see page 53) to tie to this parachute.

1. From the grocery bag, cut a piece of plastic at least 35 cm (14 in.) square.

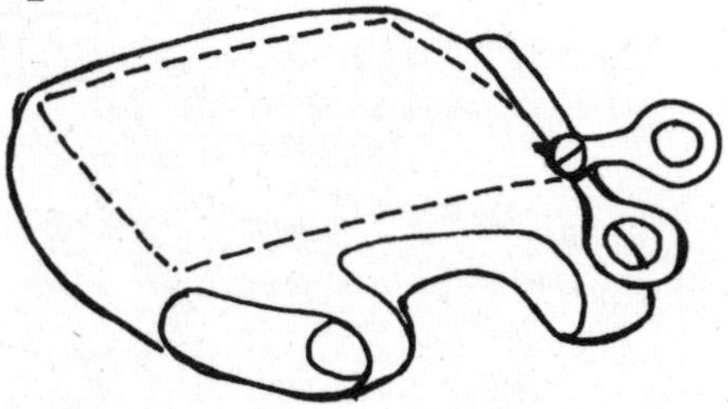

2. Cut four pieces of yarn, each 60 cm (24 in.) long.

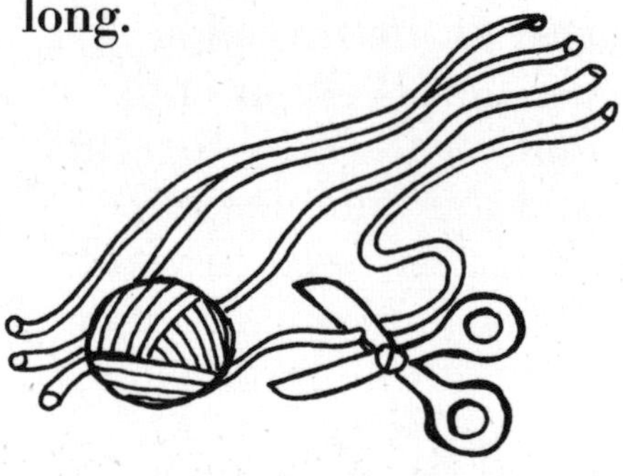

3. Use the pencil to poke a hole in each corner of the plastic. Knot a piece of yarn in each hole.

4. Hold the four yarn ends together and fasten them in an overhand knot as shown.

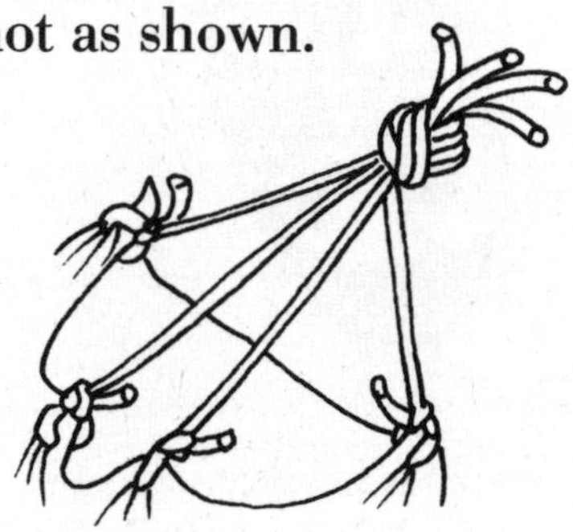

5. Loop the yarn around your clothespin pal's pipe-cleaner arms as shown (or fasten it to a plastic toy).

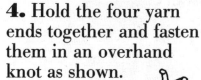

You will need

a plastic grocery bag

◎

scissors, a ruler and a pencil

◎

yarn

◎

a clothespin pal or small plastic toy

6. To prepare your parachute for sky diving, hold it by the center of the parachute so the strings and pal hang down. Fold over the parachute and loosely wind the strings and pal around it to make a small bundle.

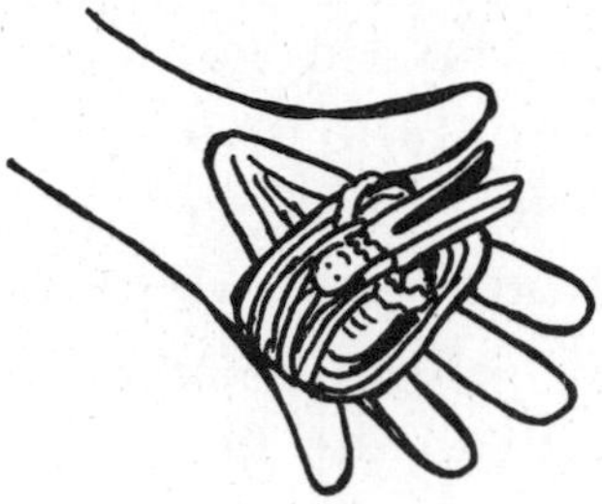

7. Toss up the parachute bundle as high as you can. It should float gently to the ground.

M◎re plastic-bag ideas

Make cheerleader pom-poms. Cut many 60 cm (24 in.) long strips from different-colored plastic bags. Pull them through a rubber band or hair holder. Fold the strips in half and fasten them with another rubber band or hair holder. Rah! Rah!

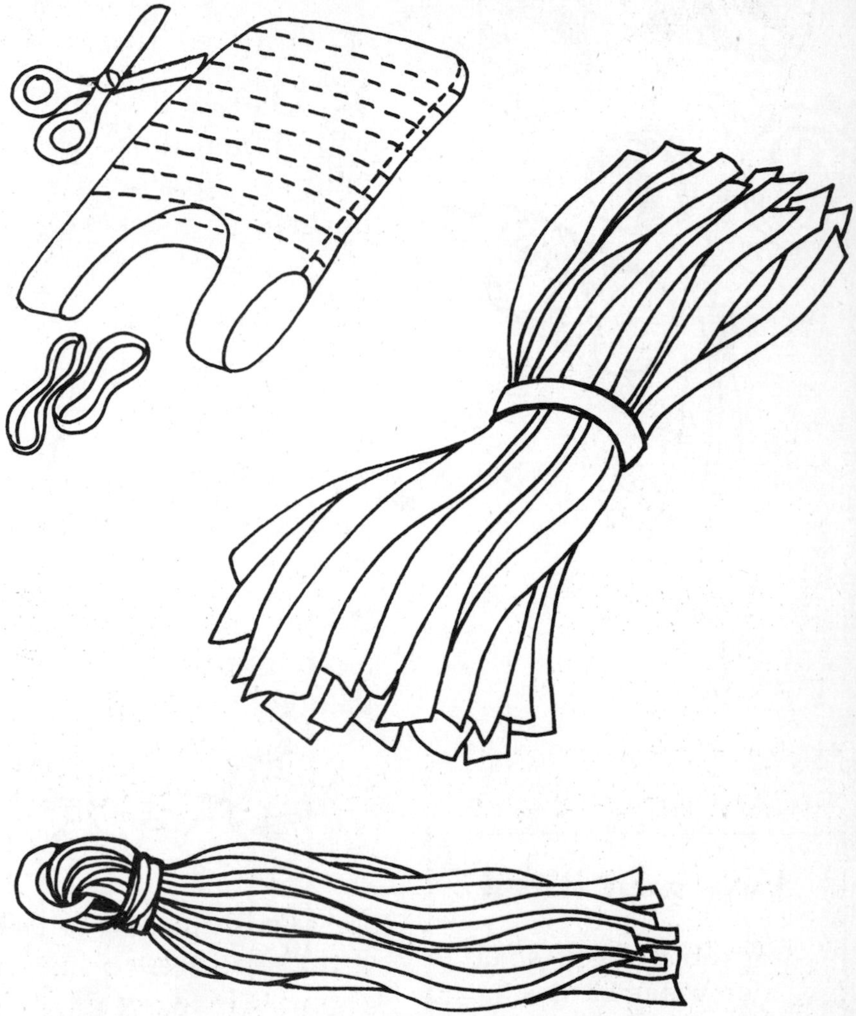

Plastic-bottle bowling game

If you find your plastic-bottle bowling pins fall over too easily, use stones, marbles or dried beans to put a little weight in them.

1. Decorate the bottles with dimensional fabric paint, stickers or permanent markers.

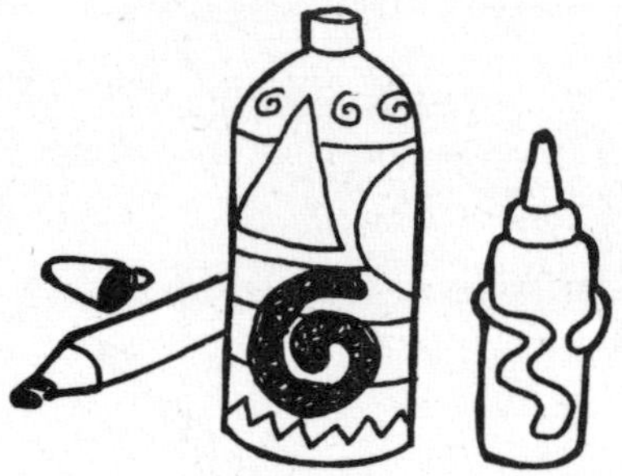

2. Set up the bottles in a straight line or in a triangular pattern.

3. To play the game, use masking tape or a length of yarn to make a line on the floor for bowlers to stand behind somewhere in front of the bowling pins. Each player gets three tries to knock over all the pins. Have fun!

You will need

3 or more plastic soda or water bottles

supplies for decorating (see step 1)

a ball

Plastic-jar puppy bank

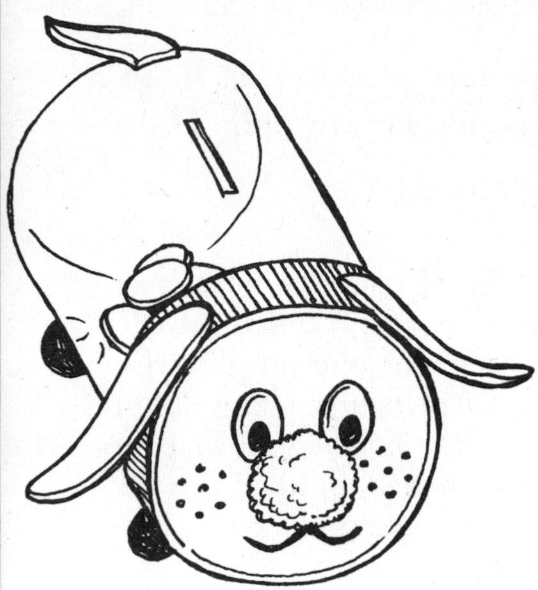

Use a plastic jar, such as a peanut butter jar. Before you begin, have an adult cut a slot into the side of the jar. The slot should be at the top when the puppy bank is finished.

1. Trace the lid onto felt. Cut out the circle, glue it to the outside of the lid and screw the lid on.

2. Glue on the roly eyes and pom-pom nose. Draw on freckles and a mouth.

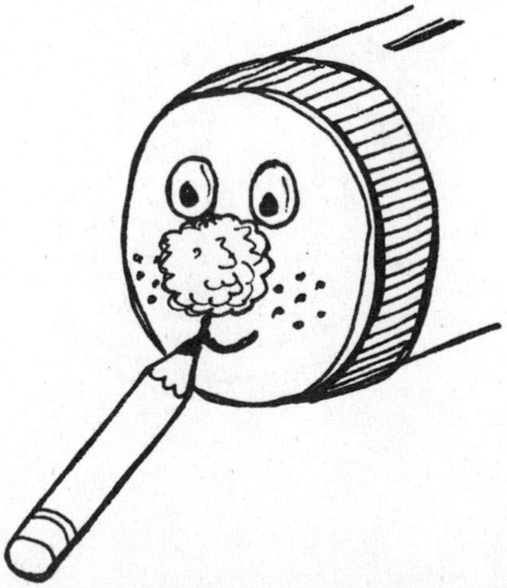

3. Cut out felt ears and a tail and glue them in place.

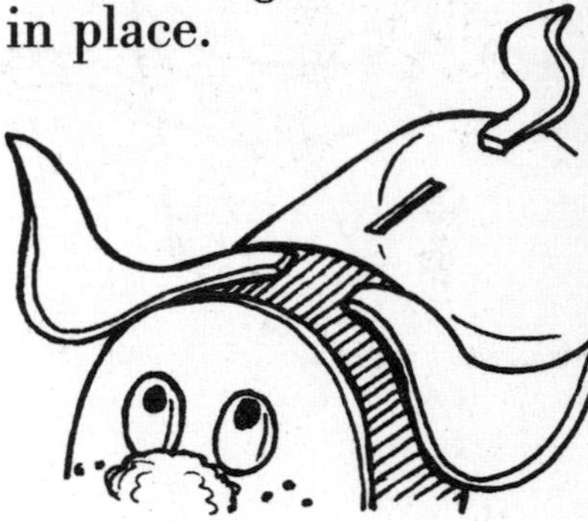

4. Glue the four beads onto the bottom of the jar. You may need to tape them in place until the glue dries.

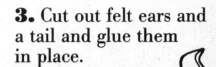

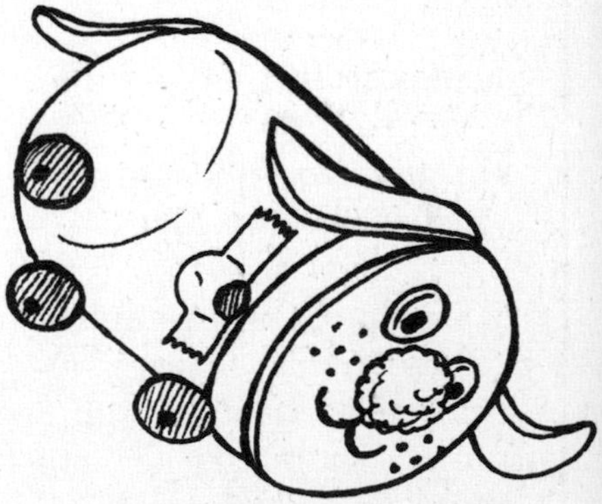

You will need

a plastic jar with a lid

◎

a pencil, a marker, scissors and white craft glue

◎

felt, roly eyes and a pom-pom

◎

4 large beads

◎

tape (optional)

Marching-band drum

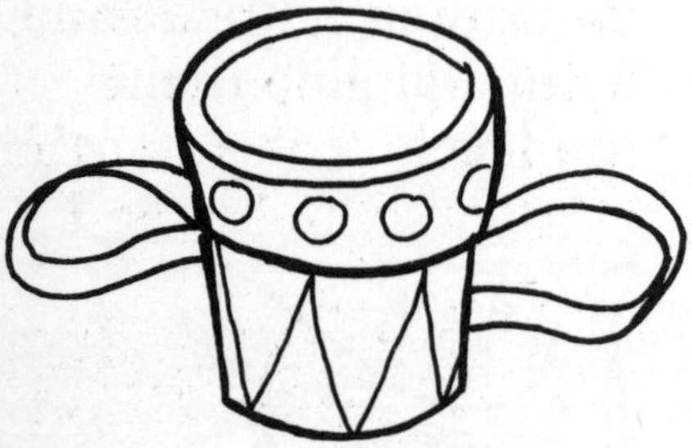

For this drum you can use any plastic tub, from a small yogurt cup to a large ice-cream pail. Then join the marching band.

1. Drape the ribbon around your neck. Cut it a little longer than where you'd like your drum to hang.

2. Make a knot in each end of the ribbon. Open the plastic tub and place the knotted ends inside, across from each other. Close the lid.

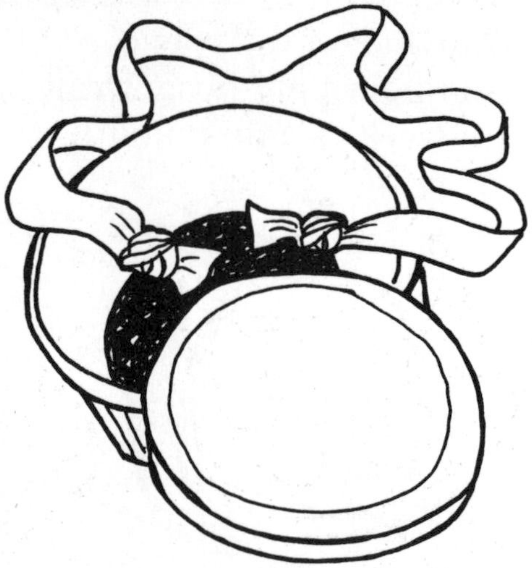

3. If you like, you can decorate the drum with stickers, cutout pictures or drawings using non-toxic permanent markers. It is best to keep the lid undecorated.

4. For drumsticks, use the eraser ends of the pencils. Or use other sticks with a ball of tape or a large bead on one end. Drum roll, please!

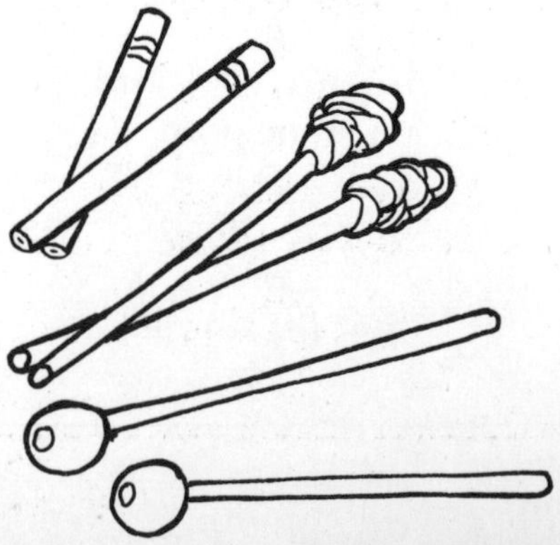

You will need

ribbon
◎
scissors
◎
a plastic tub with a lid
◎
supplies for decorating (see step 3)
◎
2 unsharpened pencils with erasers or other sticks and tape or beads

Bead-toss game

Use scraps of wrapping paper, construction paper or colorful magazine pictures to cover the writing on the yogurt cup.

1. Glue cut-up scraps of colorful paper on the yogurt cup to decorate it.

2. Turn the cup upside down and use the nail to poke a hole in the center of the bottom.

3. Thread a 50 cm (20 in.) ribbon or string through the hole from the bottom to the inside. Knot the ribbon so it can't come out. Knot the bead on the other end.

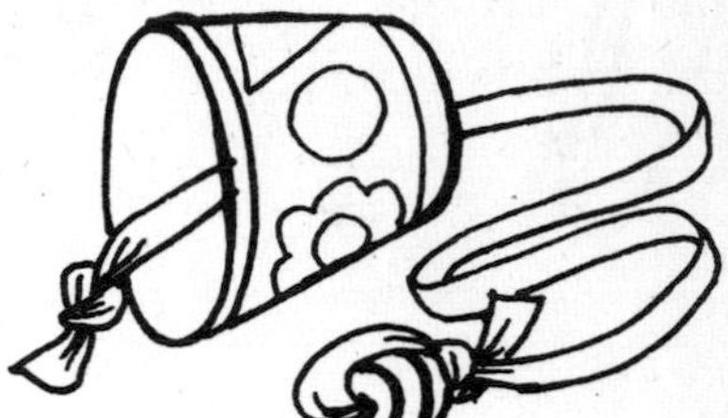

4. Toss the bead into the air and catch it in the cup. How many times in a row can you catch it?

You will need

scraps of colorful paper

◎

scissors, white craft glue and a ruler

◎

a small plastic yogurt cup

◎

a nail

◎

narrow ribbon or heavy string

◎

a large bead

Frog eyes

Use store-bought green pom-poms for this craft.

1. Glue the pom-poms a little way apart on the top of the hair band. It is helpful to place the hair band against a book (or something similar) while the glue dries.

2. Cut out two small circles from the cardboard. Draw on large black dots.

3. Glue the circles to the front of the pom-poms. Allow the glue to dry. Try on your frog eyes. Ribbet!

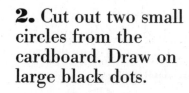

You will need

a hair band

2 large pom-poms

white craft glue and scissors

thin cardboard (from a cereal box)

markers or crayons

Antennae

Use any combination of colors for the hair band, pipe cleaners and pom-poms. If your hair band is smooth, you may need to add tape to hold the pipe cleaners in place.

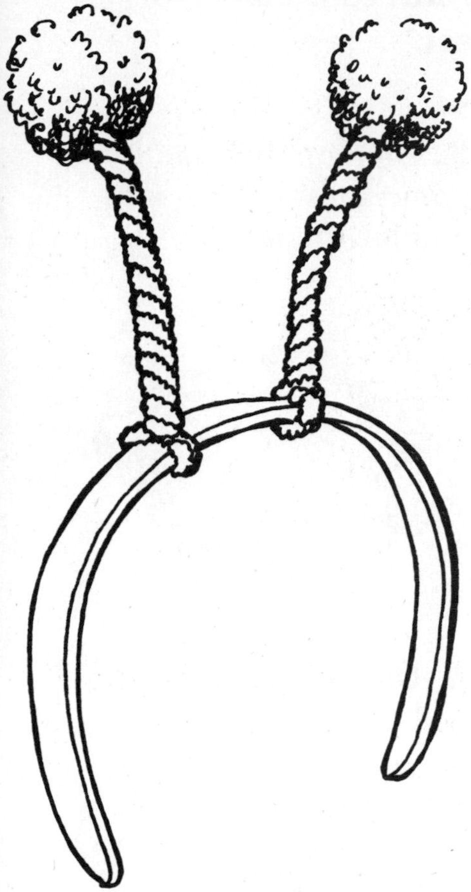

1. Twist the center of one pipe cleaner firmly around one of the pom-poms.

2. Twist the pipe-cleaner halves together almost to the ends. Fasten the ends to the hair band, making sure the tips of the pipe cleaners end up on top of the band so you don't get poked.

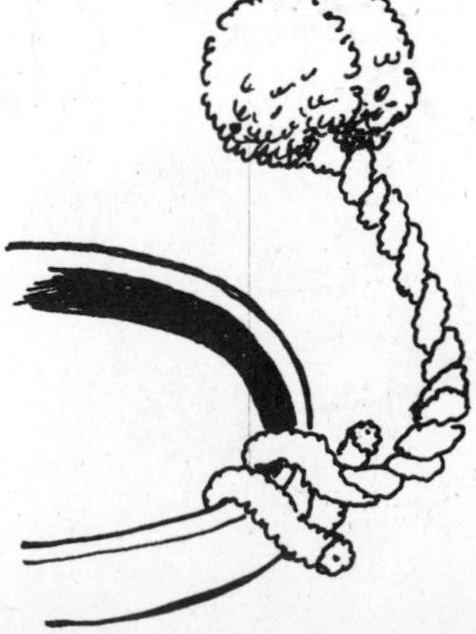

3. Follow steps 1 and 2 for the other antenna. Fluff the pom-poms so you can't see the pipe cleaners wound around them.

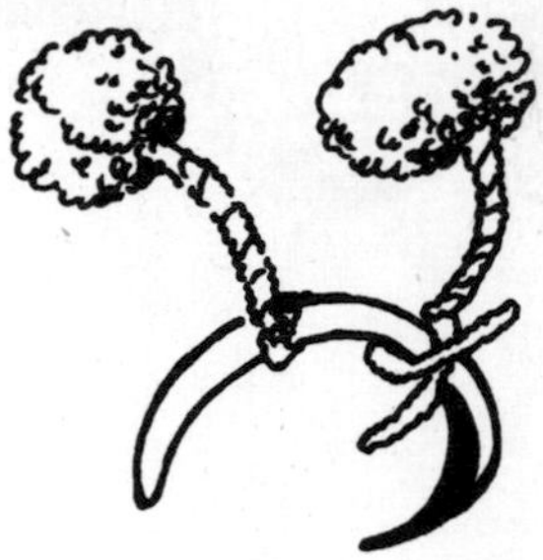

4. Curve the antennae (or zigzag them) and try them on.

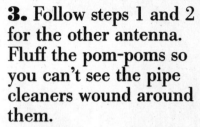

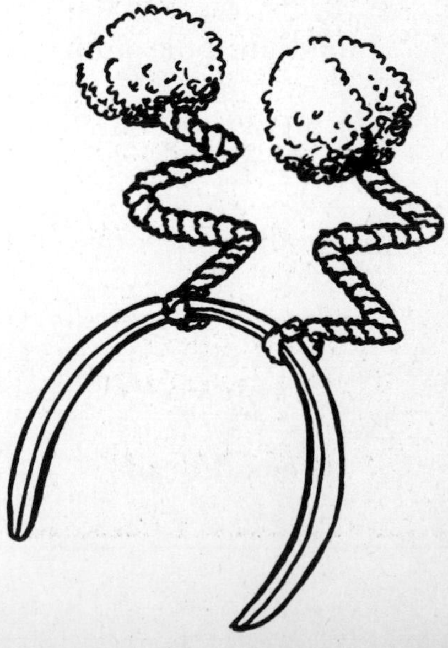

You will need

2 pipe cleaners

2 pom-poms

a hair band

Pom-pom bear

You may want to use a few different colors of pom-poms for this fuzzy bear.

1. For the head and body, glue the medium pom-pom to the large one.

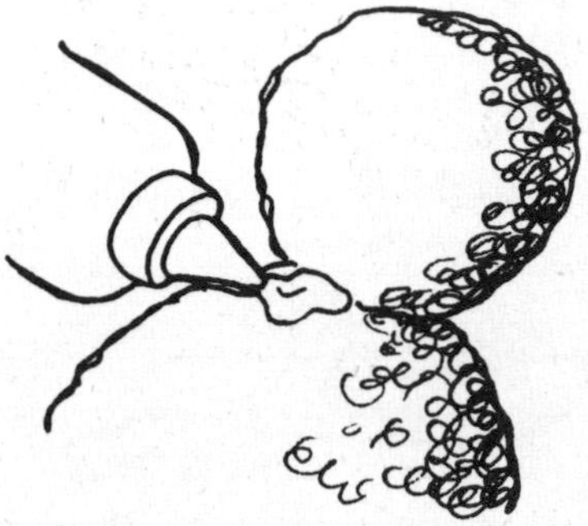

2. Glue a medium-small pom-pom to the face to make a muzzle. Glue on the other four medium-small pom-poms for legs.

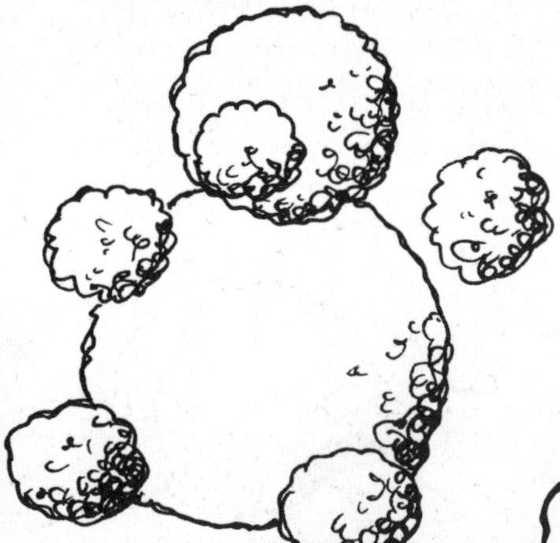

3. Glue on two small pom-poms for ears and one for the tail.

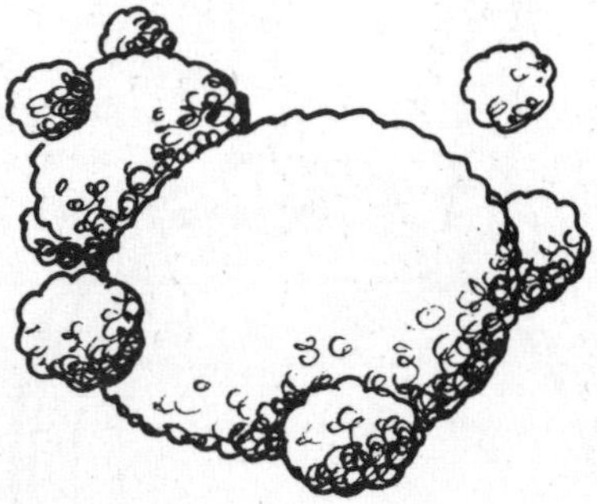

4. Glue on the roly eyes and a bead nose.

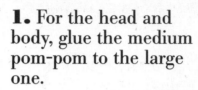

You will need

1 large pom-pom

1 medium pom-pom

5 medium-small pom-poms

3 small pom-poms

white craft glue

2 roly eyes

1 small bead

Hummingbird

Make a few of these in different colors, then make them into a mobile (see page 191).

1. Glue the pom-poms together.

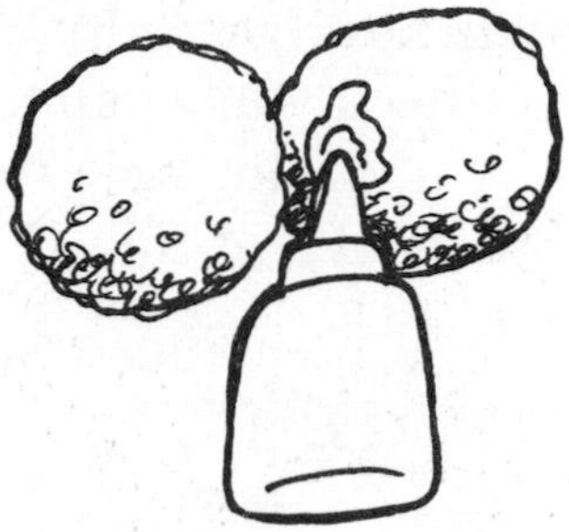

2. Spread glue on the end of a short feather and poke it into the pom-pom for a tail. Glue in longer feathers for the wings.

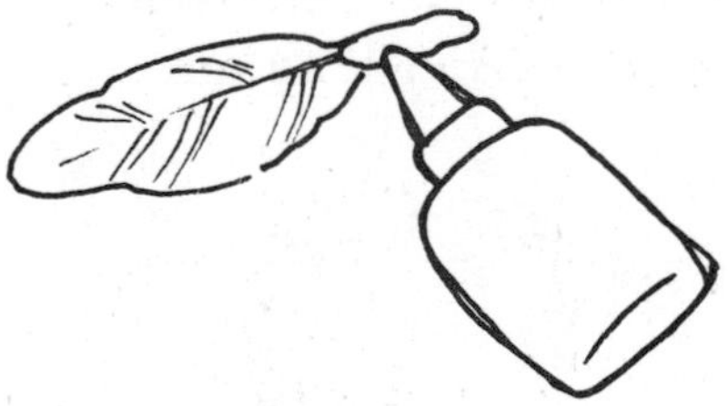

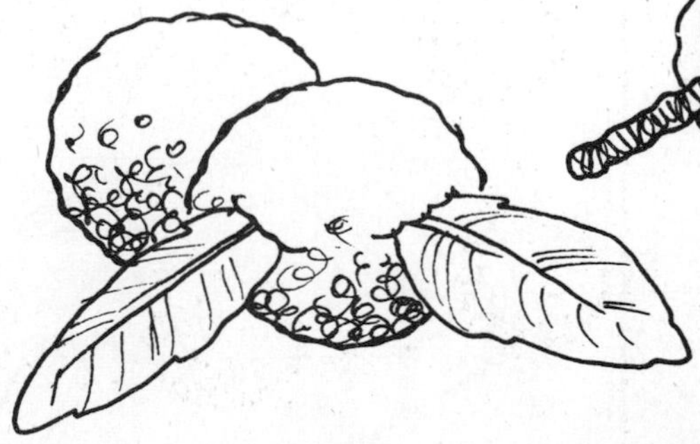

3. Cut a short piece of pipe cleaner and glue it in place for a beak. Glue on the roly eyes or beads.

4. When the glue is dry, tie fishing line around the hummingbird and hang it up.

You will need

2 medium pom-poms
white craft glue
craft feathers
a pipe cleaner
roly eyes or beads
fishing line or thread

Popsicle-stick star

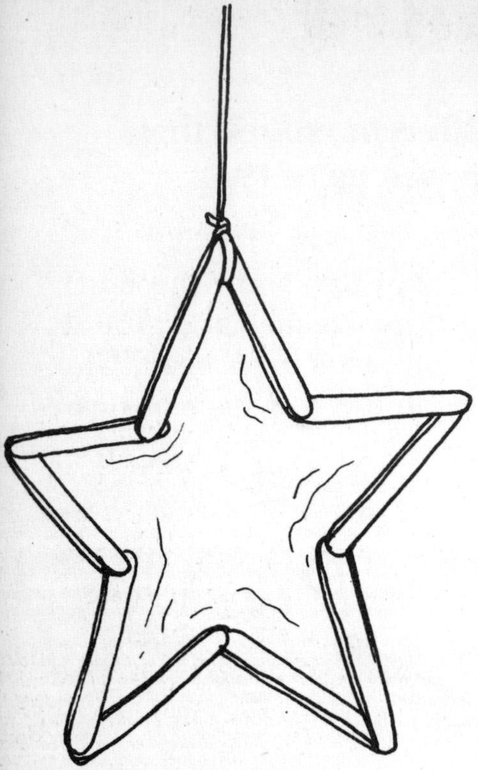

Hang or stand this star in the window. What other shapes can you make?

1. Spread waxed paper on your work surface. Arrange the Popsicle sticks into a star shape, as shown. Make sure the sticks overlap at all 10 corners.

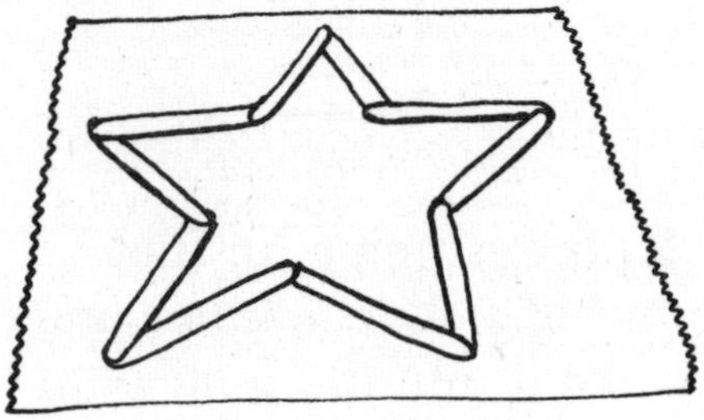

2. Glue the star together everywhere the sticks overlap. Let it dry.

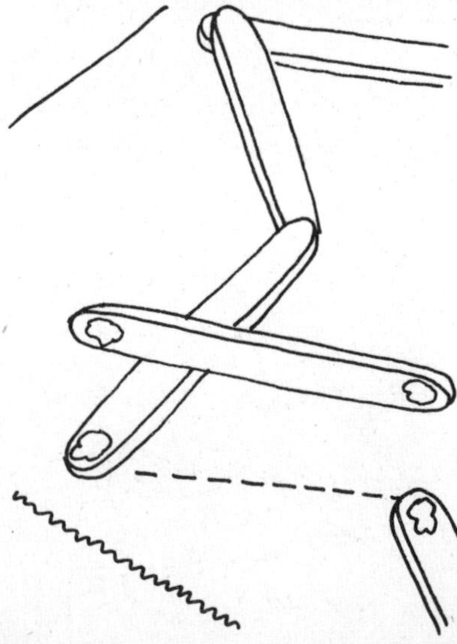

3. Spread a thin layer of glue on the Popsicle sticks all around the star. Smooth the sheet of tissue paper over the glue. Trim off the extra tissue paper.

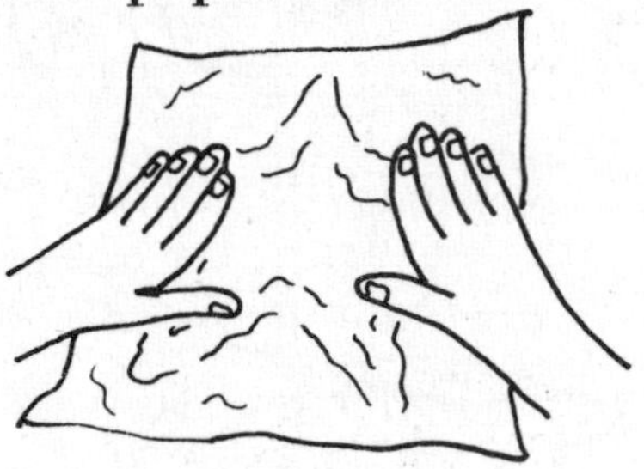

4. To hang up your star, poke a tiny hole in the tissue paper at one of the points. Thread through some fishing line. If the tissue ever tears, replace it as in step 3.

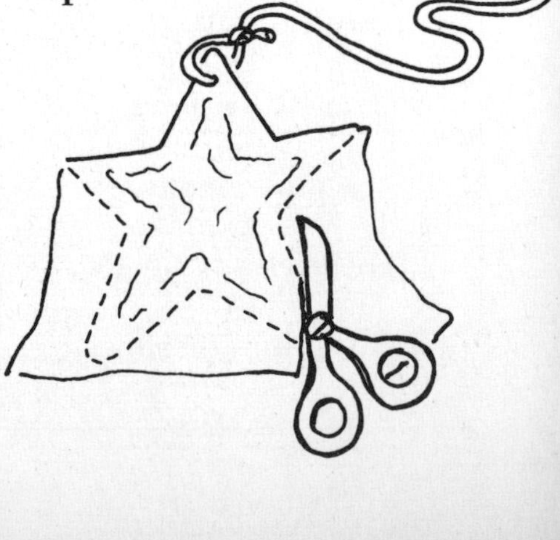

You will need

waxed paper

◎

10 Popsicle sticks, colored or plain

◎

white craft glue and scissors

◎

tissue paper

◎

fishing line or yarn

Popsicle-stick basket

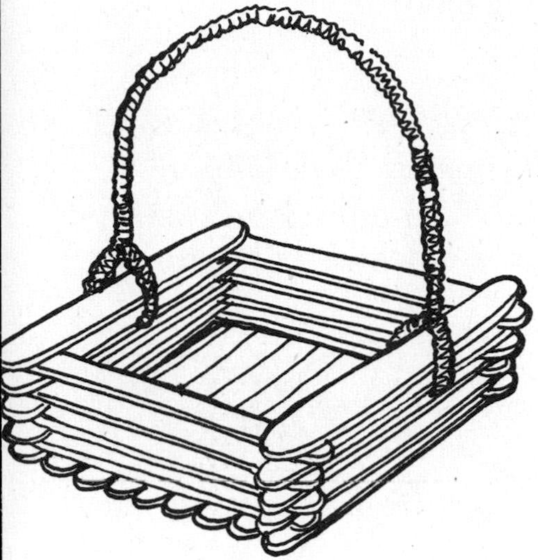

If you have colored sticks, you can use them. If you don't, you can color them with paint or markers or leave them plain.

1. On a sheet of waxed paper, line up about 10 sticks, side by side.

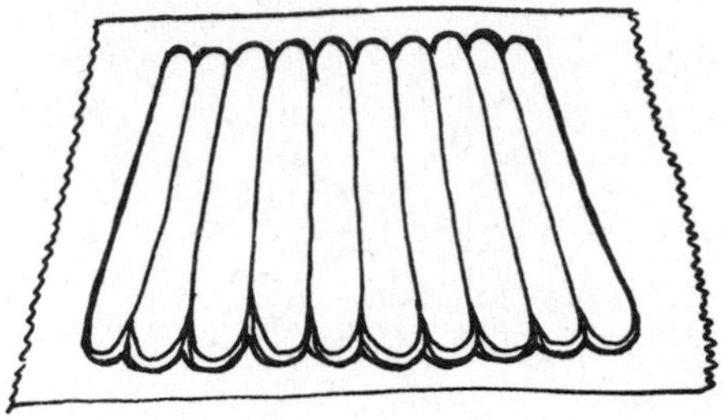

2. In the opposite direction and evenly spread apart, glue four sticks to the first layer. Make sure each stick is glued to all 10 sticks under it. After it dries, flip it over.

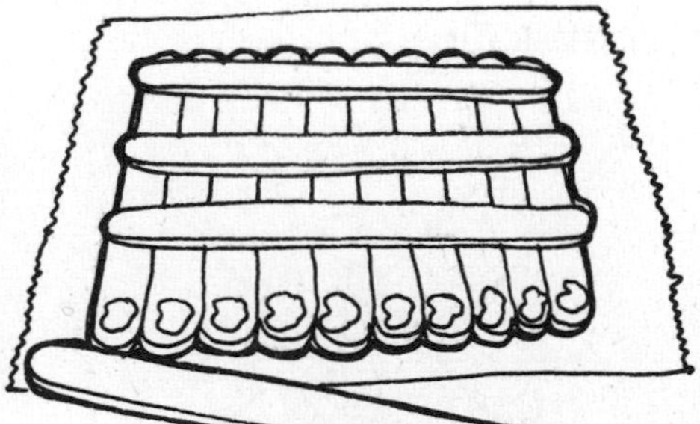

3. Now build the sides of the basket. First, glue a stick on each side, then on the top and bottom. Alternate between the sides and the top and bottom until the basket is as tall as you want. Let it dry.

4. For the handle, fasten on a pipe cleaner.

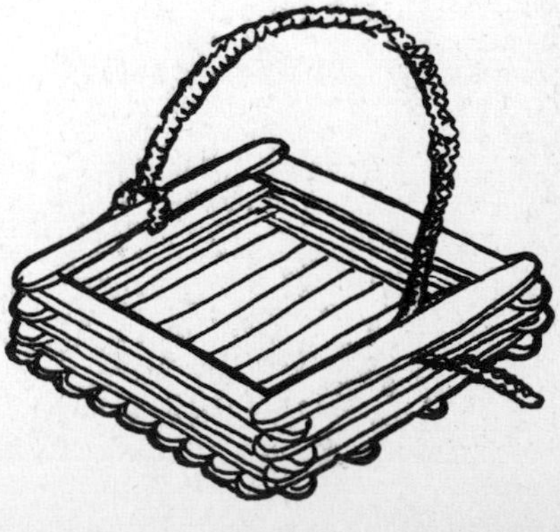

You will need

Popsicle sticks
◎
white craft glue
◎
a pipe cleaner
◎
waxed paper

God's eye weaving

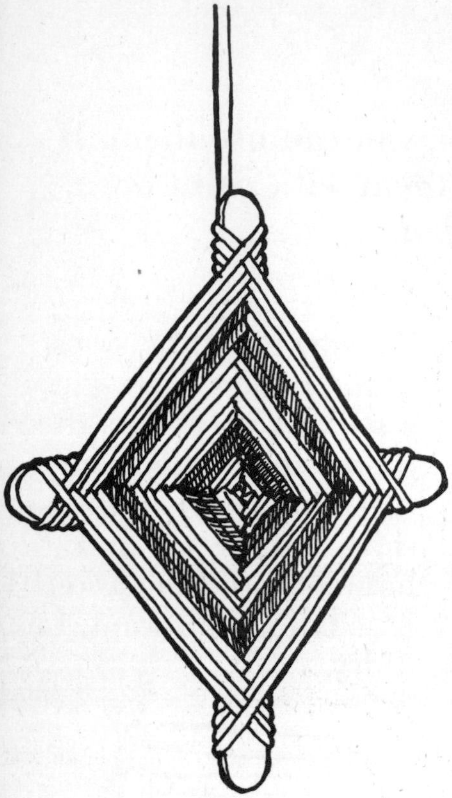

Variegated yarn has many colors on one ball. It works great for this type of weaving.

1. Cross the sticks and hold the end of the yarn in the center of the cross. Wind the yarn in both diagonal directions to cover the yarn end and hold the sticks together.

2. Position the cross so the yarn crosses on top of the center from the lower left corner to the upper right corner. Tightly wind the yarn once behind and around the stick on the right side.

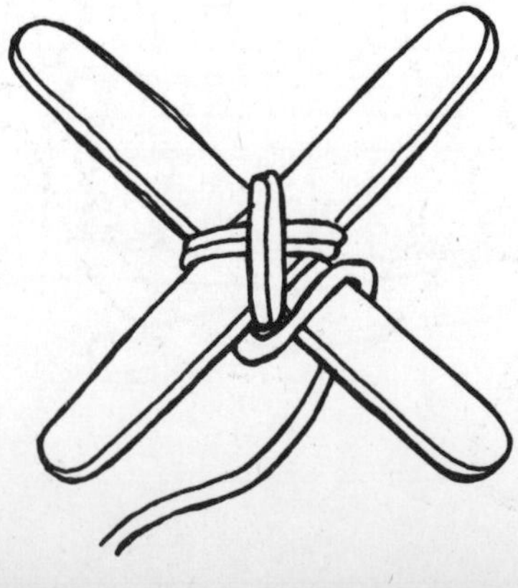

3. Turn the cross as you bring the yarn behind and around the next stick in a clockwise direction.

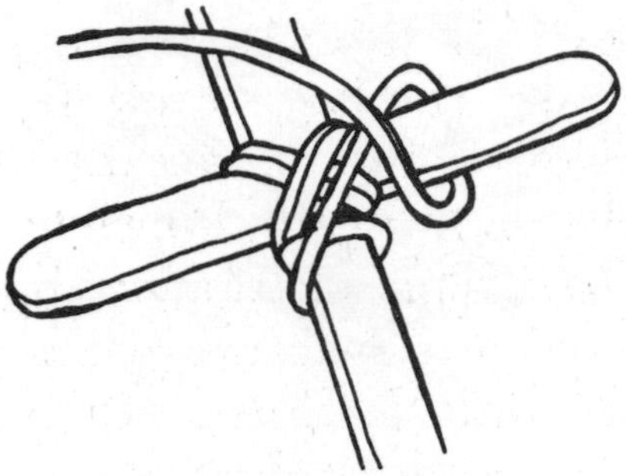

4. Keep turning the cross and tightly winding the yarn around each stick. Do not overlap the yarn.

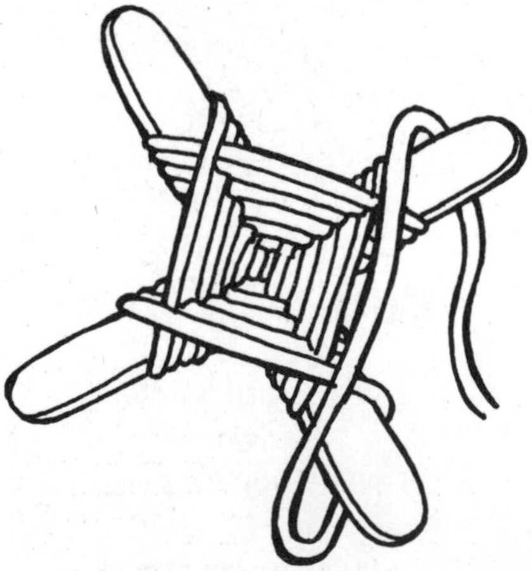

You will need

2 Popsicle sticks

variegated yarn

scissors

5. When you run out of space, cut the yarn leaving a long tail.

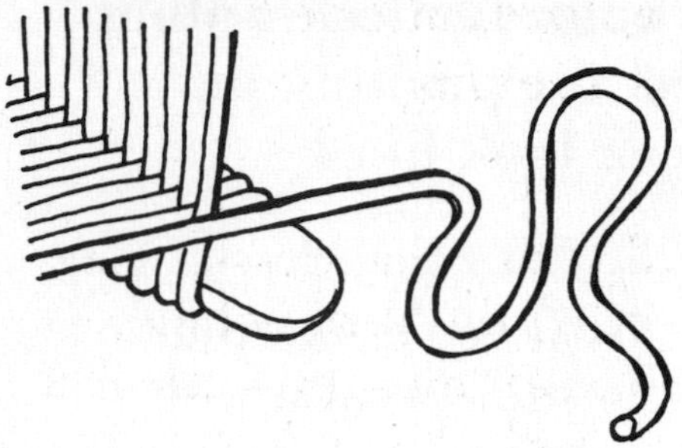

6. Tuck the yarn end under the last strand of yarn on the diamond to the right of the Popsicle stick. Thread it through the loop as shown. Pull the tail upwards so the knot ends up behind the stick.

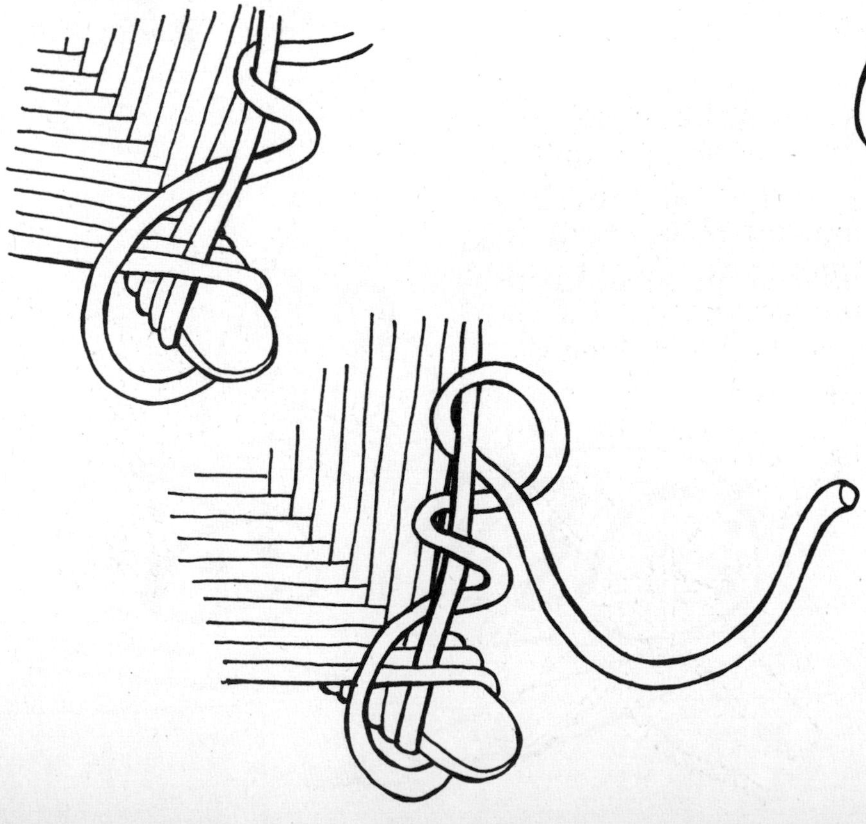

7. Repeat step 6. Use the yarn end to hang up your woven design. It will turn so you can see how beautiful the other side is, too.

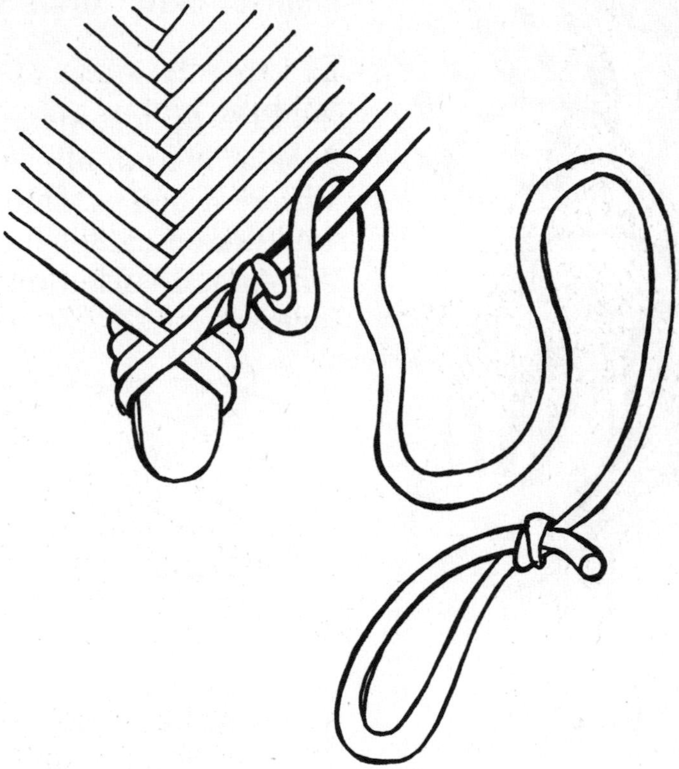

Rock painting

Many rocks look like ladybugs, turtles or other creatures. Some are perfect for painting on scenes. What does your rock look like?

1. Pick up a stone and look at it from all different angles. Does it look like a car? A bug? An animal curled up sleeping?

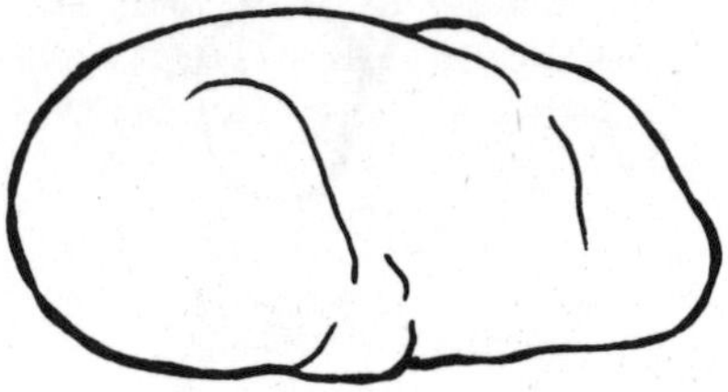

2. Paint the rock any way you like. You can even swirl different colors of paint together to give it a marbled look. Place it on waxed paper to dry.

3. If you'd like your rock to shine, coat it with varnish.

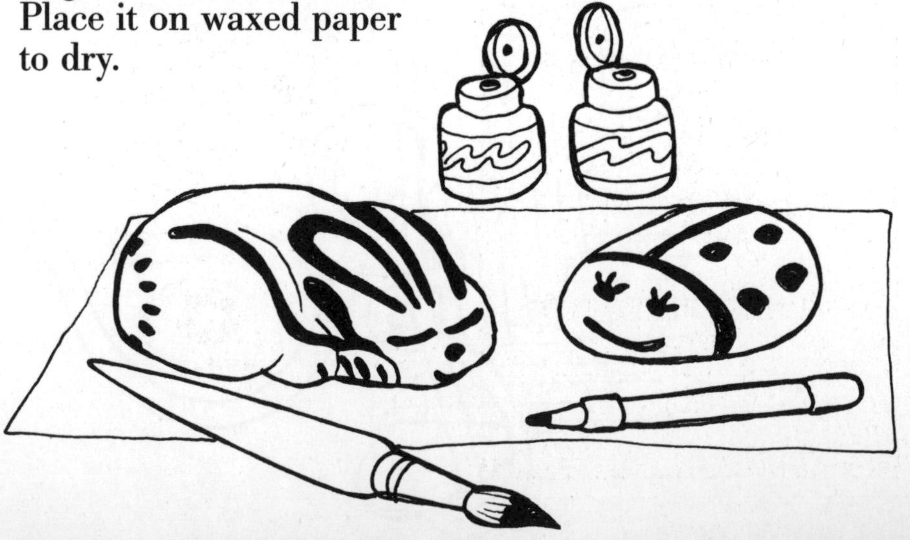

You will need

interesting rocks
◎
acrylic craft paint and a brush
◎
waxed paper
◎
acrylic varnish (optional)

Stone writing

When you're at the beach, look for many small, smooth, flat stones for these magnetic message rocks.

1. Write something on each stone. If you write a letter of the alphabet on each one, you can put them together to make words. If you write words, you can make sentences. Or write on numbers or the names of special people and places.

2. Cut pieces of the magnetic strip and press them to the backs of the stones.

3. Leave someone a message on the fridge.

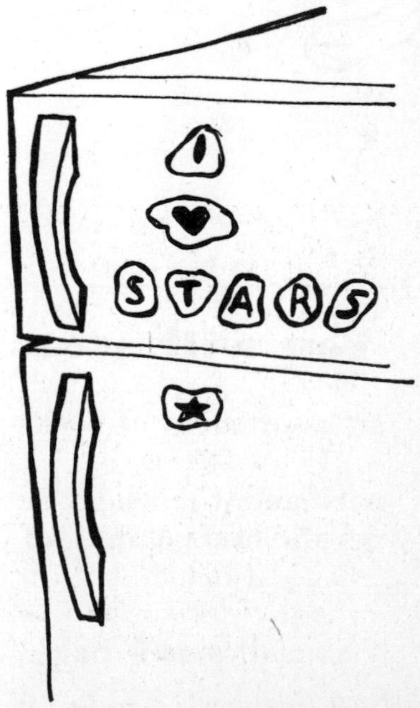

You will need

clean, flat stones

◎

non-toxic permanent markers

◎

self-sticking magnetic strip

◎

scissors

Rocky puzzle

Find a handful of rocks and pebbles to make a unique rock puzzle. These instructions are for a person, but you could make animals, a tiny town or a rock band!

1. Choose a round rock for the head and an oval rock for the body. Find narrow stones for the arms and legs and small round ones for the hands. See if you can find small, oval stones for the shoes. Can you find a stone for a hat?

2. Draw or paint on a face, hair, clothing and shoes.

3. Place all the rocky puzzle pieces into the plastic bag. See if your brother, sister or friend can put it together.

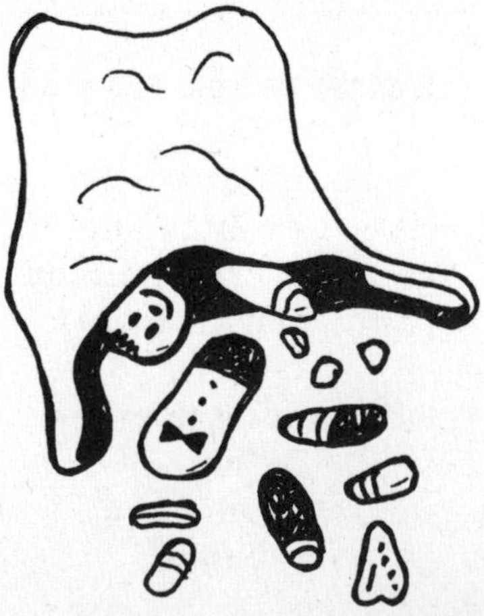

You will need

an assortment of rocks

permanent markers or acrylic craft paint and a brush

a small plastic bag

Rocky bee

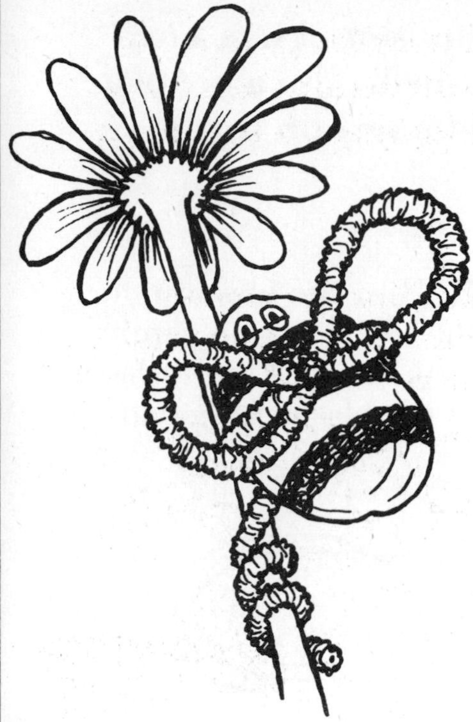

Place this bee in a bouquet of flowers you've made from page 33 or 163. Or place it in a bouquet of real flowers.

1. Color the stone yellow. Allow it to dry.

2. Paint or draw on black stripes and a face.

3. Wrap a pipe cleaner around the center of the stone and twist it twice on top. Shape each half into a wing and fasten them at the center.

4. Wrap a second pipe cleaner around the center, and twist it on the underside. Use these ends to hold up the bee in a vase of flowers. (If the pipe cleaners don't stay in position, you may need to apply some glue.)

You will need

a light-colored, oval stone

◎

yellow and black paint and a brush or permanent markers

◎

2 pipe cleaners

◎

white craft glue (optional)

Shell art

Do you have a shell collection stored in a box? Here's a way to display the shells. Use a pie plate if you have lots of shells and a tart tin if you have only a few.

1. Fill the pie plate almost half-full of water. Pour the water into the plastic tub.

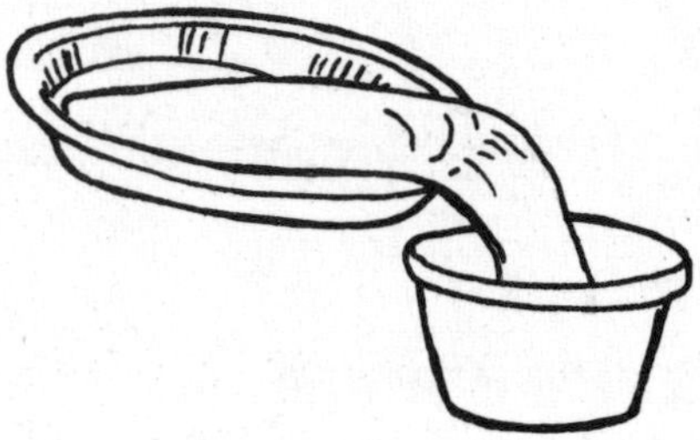

2. Spoon plaster into the water and stir it with the other spoon. Keep adding plaster and stirring until the mixture is thick and creamy with no lumps.

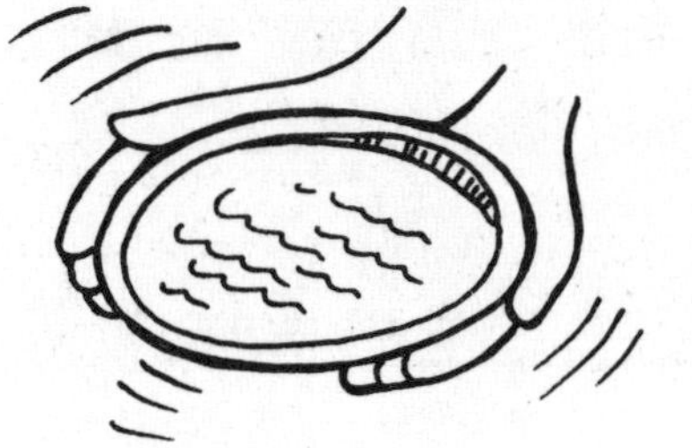

3. Pour the plaster into the pie plate and gently shake it until the surface of the plaster is smooth.

4. Push the shells slightly down into the plaster. Plaster dries quickly, so you'll need to work fast.

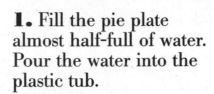

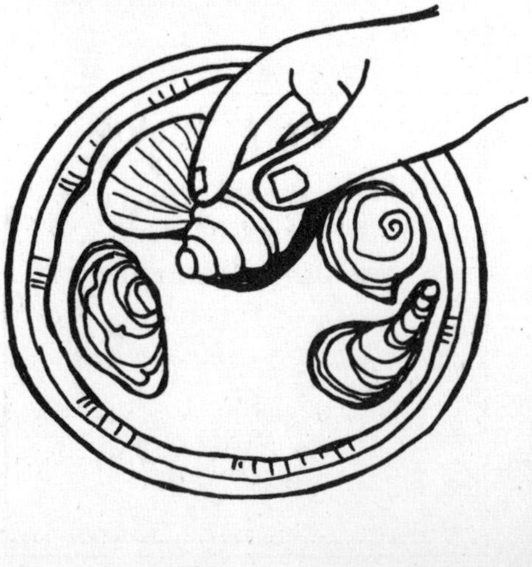

You will need

a foil pie plate

a plastic margarine or yogurt tub

casting plaster, such as plaster of Paris

2 old or plastic spoons

small and medium-sized shells

5. Allow the plaster to dry. Depending on the weather and the type of plaster you're using, this could take a few hours or a few days.

6. When the plaster feels hard, it will be easy to pop out of the pie plate. The bottom may need a little more time to dry, so place it on a cookie rack.

7. To display your shell art, place it on a plate stand or set it on a table. You could also hang it up using a store-bought plate hanger.

More ideas

Paint a design around the shells, or write on the plaster with a fine permanent marker to record where and when you found each shell.

Use this same method to display other found items, such as small, pretty stones, cones, acorns or nuts.

Painted seashells

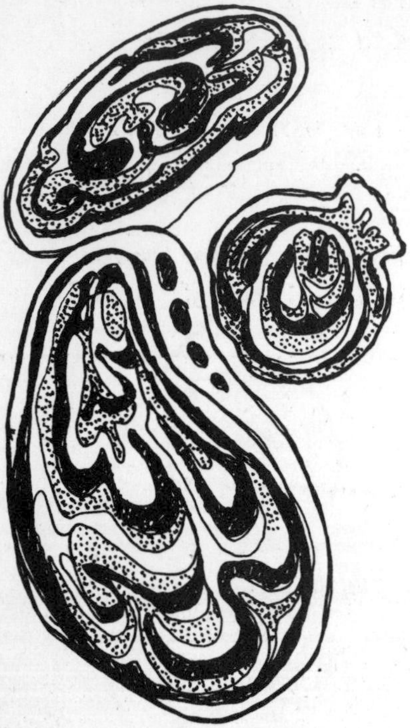

Use shallow, saucer-type shells for this craft. Place your painted shell where everyone can see it and wonder how you made it.

1. Cover your work surface with newspaper.

2. Squirt or pour a small puddle of each paint color near the center of the shell.

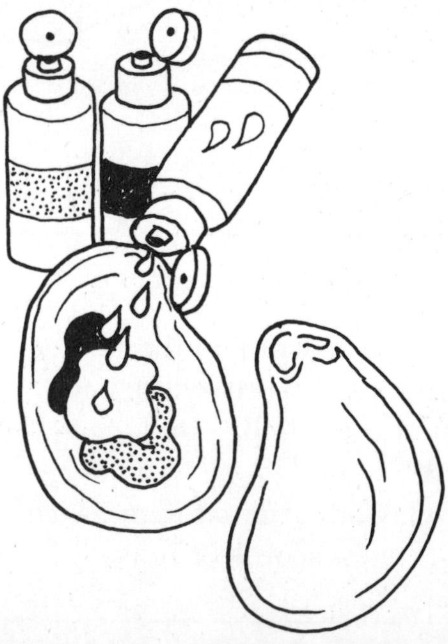

3. Hold the shell in your hands and slowly tilt it until the paint slides to the edge.

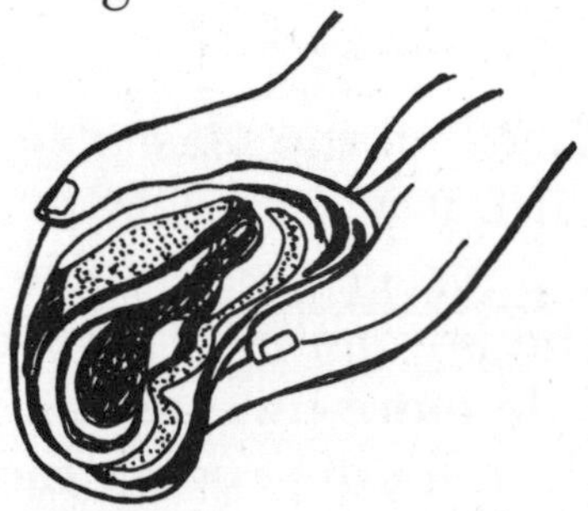

4. Keep tilting and turning the shell until the colors are all swirled together and the surface of the shell is covered.

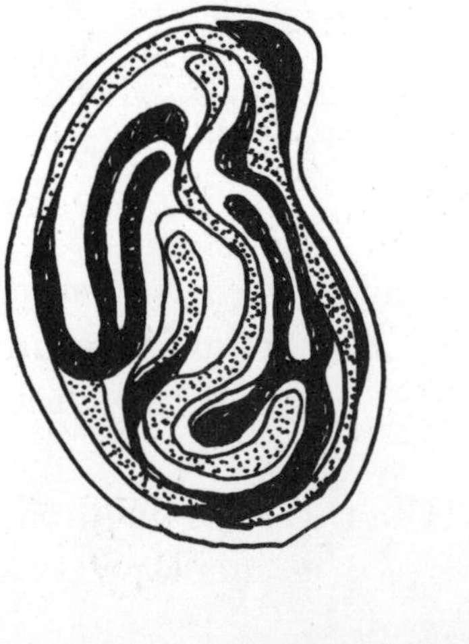

You will need

newspaper

3 or more colors of acrylic craft paint

a clean, dry shell

5. If there is too much paint left over, pour it out of the shell. Allow the paint to dry.

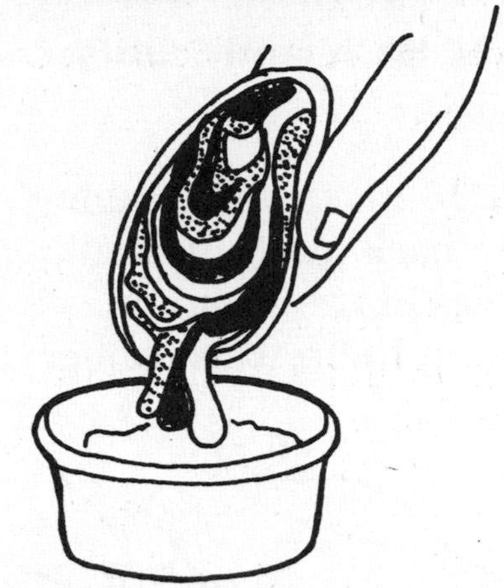

M◎re ideas

Use acrylic craft paint to paint a picture on a shell. Or use permanent markers to draw a scene.

◎

If you have a small shell with a flat area on it, stick on a piece of magnetic tape and make a fridge magnet.

◎

Shells are wonderful for gluing onto boxes, frames, bulletin boards and lots of other stuff.

Sock dragon

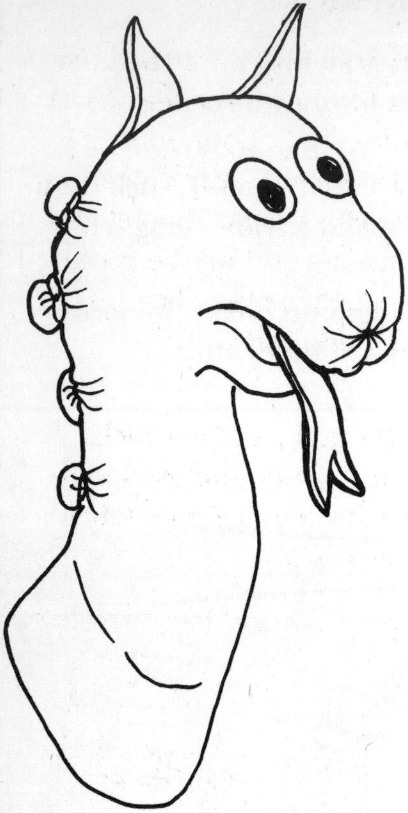

Try making other sock puppets, such as a horse, a cat or any other animal your sock looks like.

1. Turn the sock inside out. Fasten a rubber band around the toe area. Turn the sock right side out.

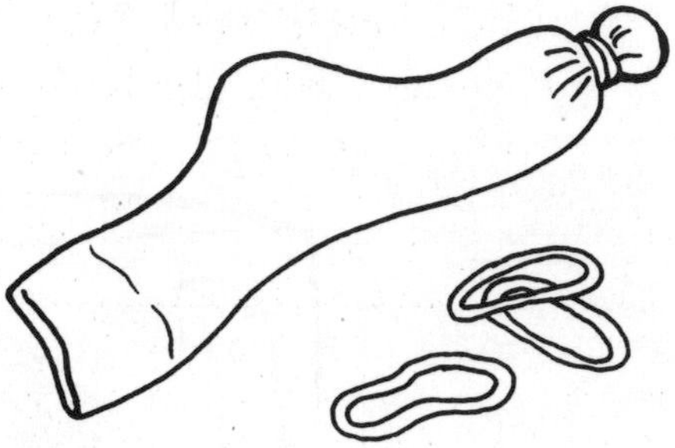

2. Put your hand inside the sock so your thumb goes in the heel and your fingers are in the foot area. This will create the mouth and give you an idea of where you'd like the eyes, ears and spikes to go. Remove your hand.

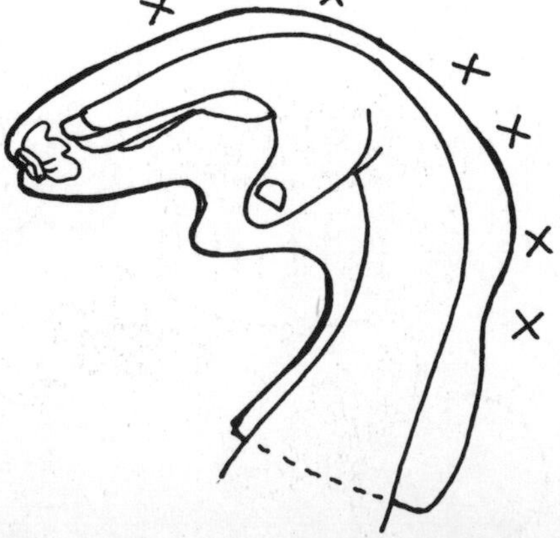

3. To make spikes along the back, pull up small areas of the sock and fasten them with rubber bands.

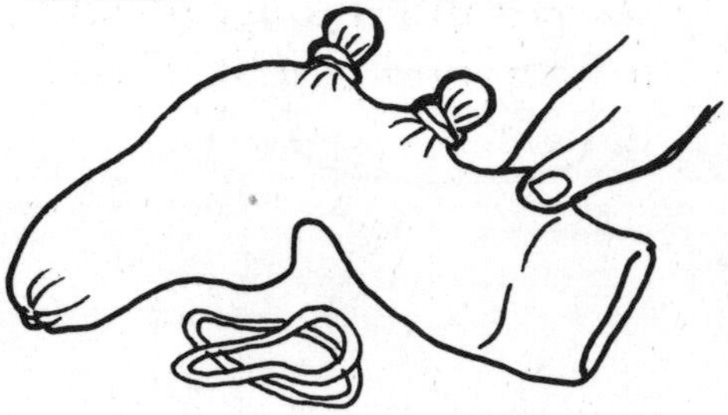

4. Glue on the roly eyes.

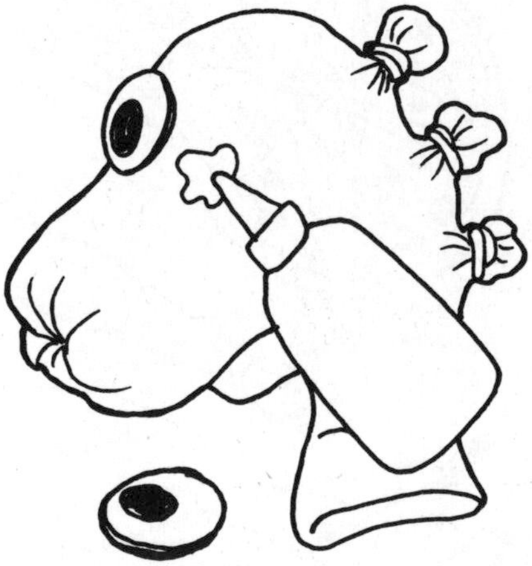

You will need

an adult sock

4 or more thin rubber bands

roly eyes

scraps of felt

scissors and white craft glue

5. From the felt, cut out long, thin triangular ears. Glue them in place.

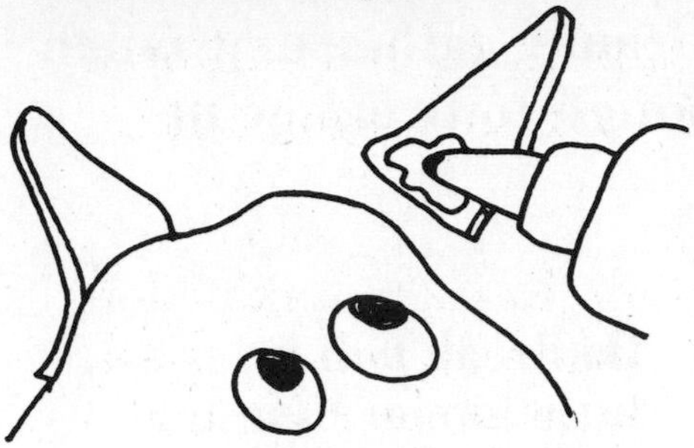

6. Cut out a long, forked tongue and glue it in the mouth.

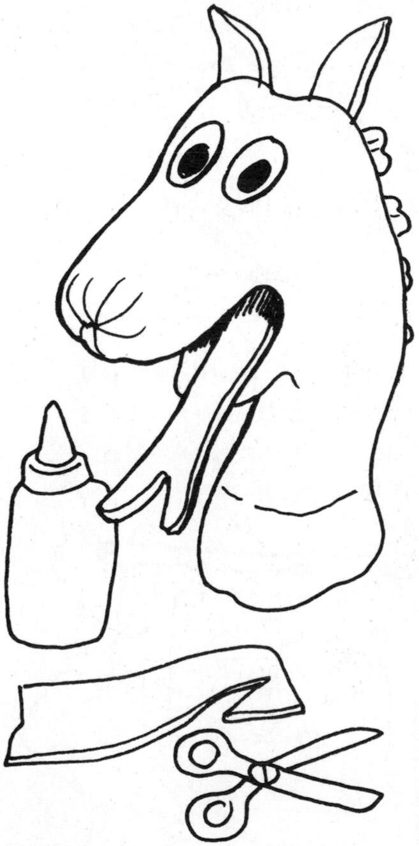

More sock ideas

Make a beanbag from a child-sized sock. Cut the sock down the center, through both layers, all the way from the ribbing to the middle of the foot. Spoon in some dried beans or plastic pellets. Tie the cut strips together very tightly in a knot. This beanbag should not get wet if you use real beans inside and it shouldn't be given to a baby. Use it for playing catch, for beanbag toss or for a hopscotch marker.

◎

Make smelly socks! Cut off the top part of a sock, put potpourri in the bottom part and tie it closed with a ribbon. Decorate the sachet with dimensional fabric paint, if you wish.

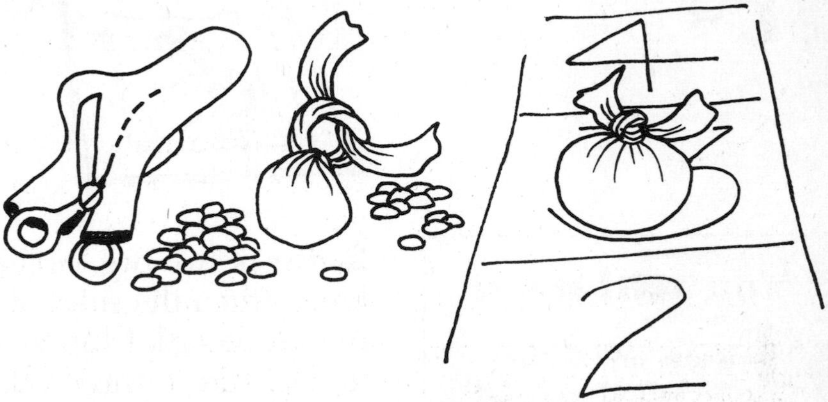

Stick frame

For this natural-looking frame, gather dry, fallen sticks and twigs small enough to break with your hands.

1. Cut a piece of cardboard a little longer and wider than your photograph or drawing. Cover the cardboard by gluing on construction paper.

2. Break two twigs a little longer than the sides of the cardboard. Glue them to the sides so they stick out beyond the cardboard on each end.

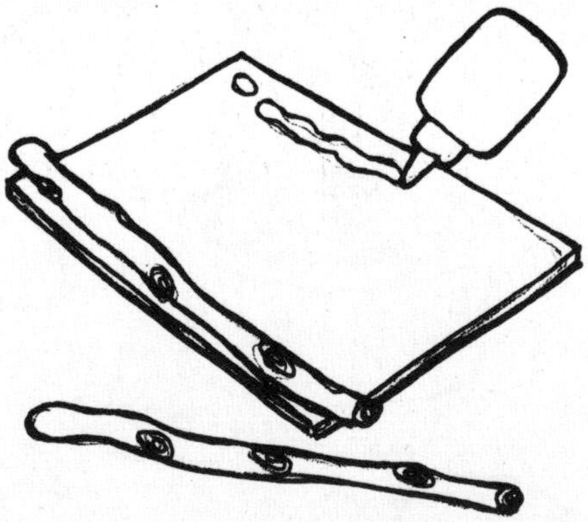

3. Break two twigs a little longer than the ends of the cardboard. Glue these twigs to the other twigs so they cross at the four corners of the cardboard.

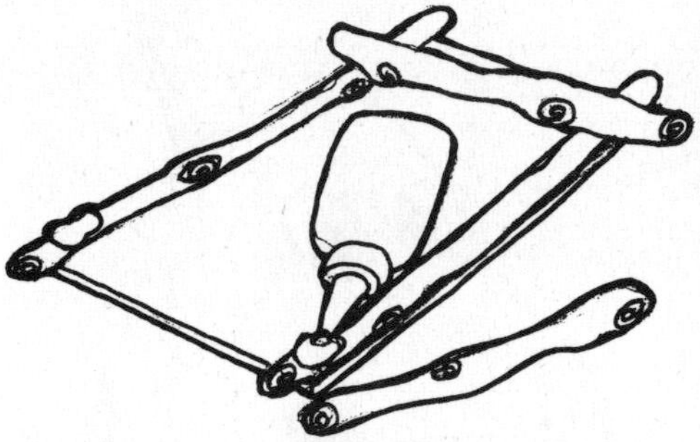

4. Glue the photograph or drawing to the center of the frame. Allow the glue to dry.

You will need

scissors and white craft glue
corrugated cardboard
a photograph or drawing
construction paper
twigs
twine or ribbon (optional)

5. To hang up your frame, tie a piece of twine or ribbon to the two top corners. If you'd rather stand the frame up, cut a strip of cardboard almost as high as the frame. Fold it about one-third of the way from the top. Glue the bent part to the center top area of the back of the frame.

More stick ideas

Sticks are terrific for making nature mobiles. Use twine or yarn to fasten two sticks together in an "X" shape. Hang shells, cones, feathers, leaves, seed pods and other found items from the sticks. To hang up interesting stones and other smooth things, try winding craft wire around the items first. This will give you something to tie onto so you can hang these items on the mobile, too.

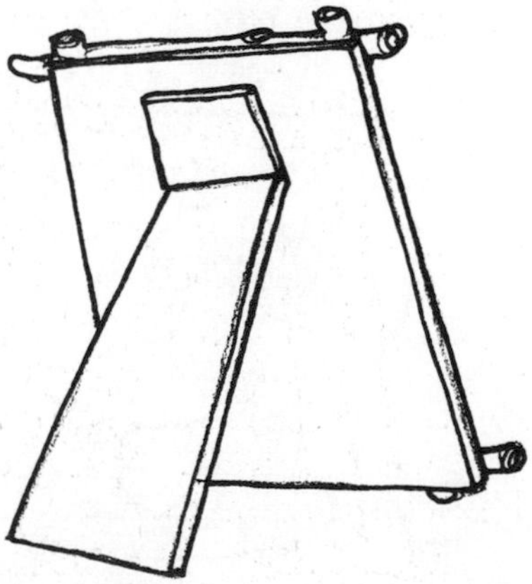

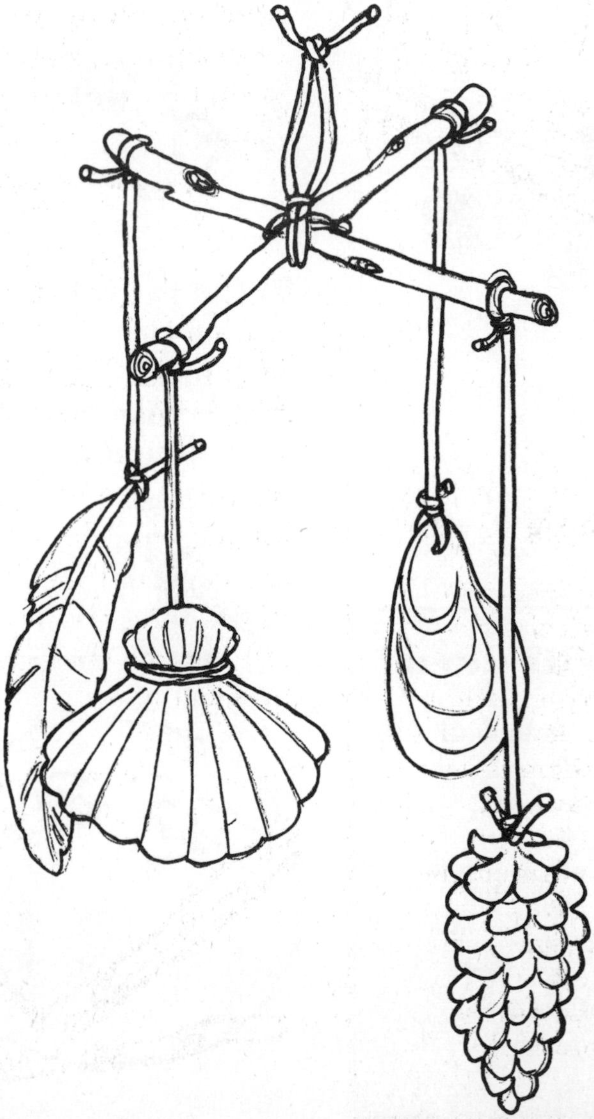

Styrofoam-ball bird

If you like, you can paint the Styrofoam ball before you begin. Slide it onto a Popsicle stick and stand it in a short cup to dry.

1. Draw eyes on the ball.

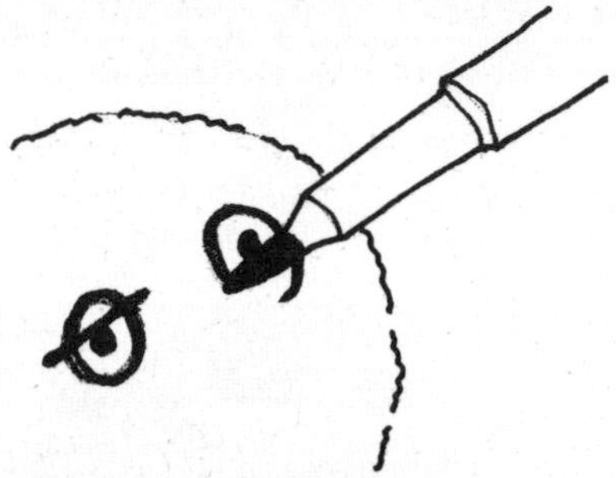

2. Cut two short pieces of pipe cleaner. Bend each into a tight "V" shape. Poke them into the ball to make a beak.

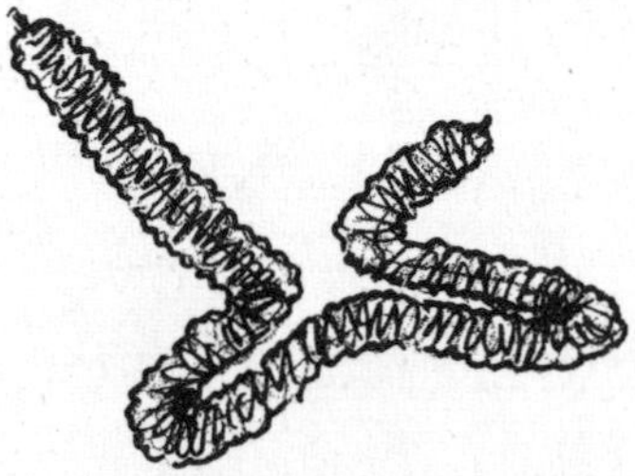

3. Bend two pipe cleaners into feet large enough to stand the bird up. Poke the two feet into the ball.

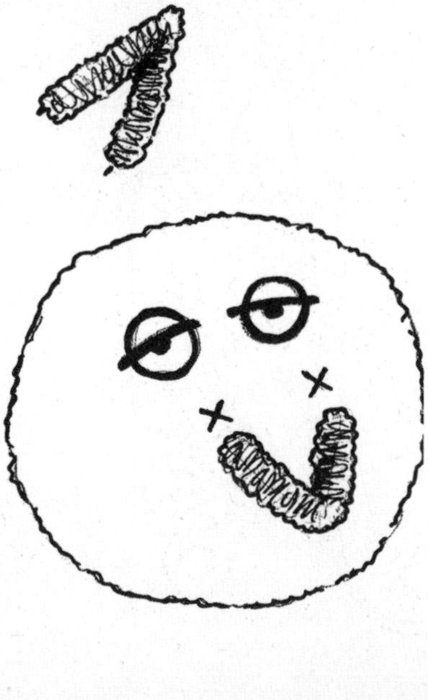

4. Poke many colorful feathers in a half-circle across the ball. You may need to adjust the feet so your bird can still stand up.

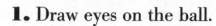

You will need

a Styrofoam ball
◎
a marker
◎
pipe cleaners
◎
scissors
◎
lots of colorful craft feathers

Wild thing pencil topper

If you want to be able to use your pencil eraser, don't glue the wild thing onto it.

1. Poke the eraser end of the pencil into the Styrofoam ball. Paint the ball. Place it in the cup to dry.

2. Cut many pieces of yarn, each twice as long as you'd like your wild thing's hair to be.

3. To make hair, use the toothpick to poke a small hole in the ball. Squirt in a dab of glue. Fold a piece of yarn in half and use the toothpick to push the yarn into the hole. Give your wild thing lots of hair.

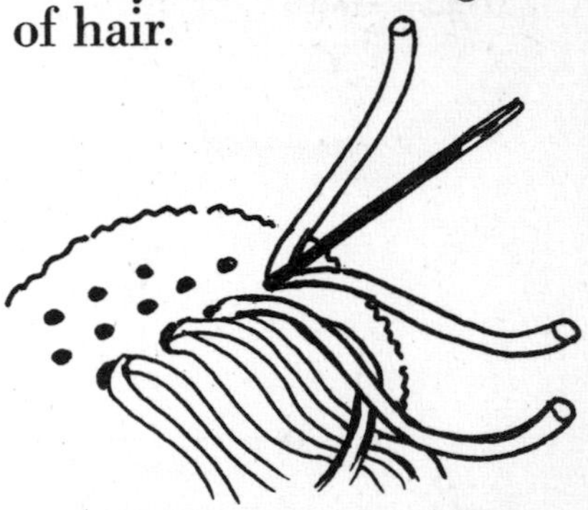

4. Glue on roly eyes or paint on a face.

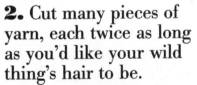

You will need

a small or medium Styrofoam ball

an unsharpened pencil

scissors and white craft glue

acrylic craft paint and a brush

a cup

a toothpick

yarn

roly eyes (optional)

Tin-can stilts

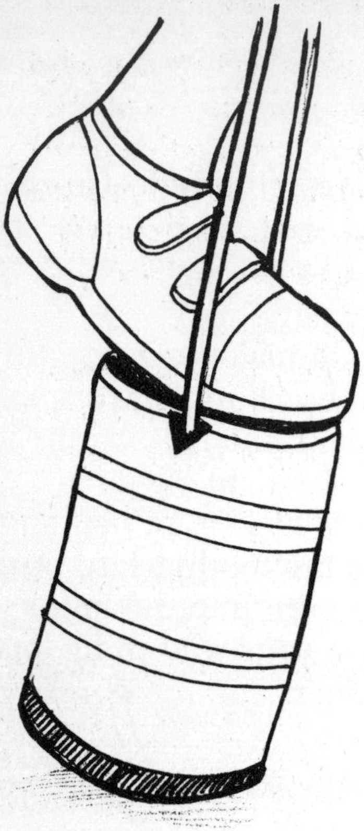

It's best to use these outside, but if that isn't possible, use them inside on carpet. Use cans from apple juice, coffee or canned tomatoes.

1. Tape around the rim of the open end of each can. (If there are jagged edges, you may need to tap them down with a hammer first.)

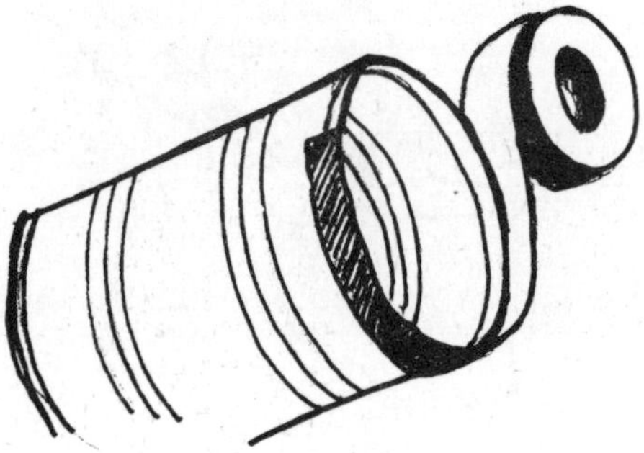

2. On the closed end of each can, position the can opener so that it cuts a triangular hole on the side rather than the top of the can. Make another hole across from the first.

3. Cut two pieces of twine a little longer than you are tall. Thread each end of twine into one of the holes in each can from the outside to the inside. Tightly knot the ends together inside the can.

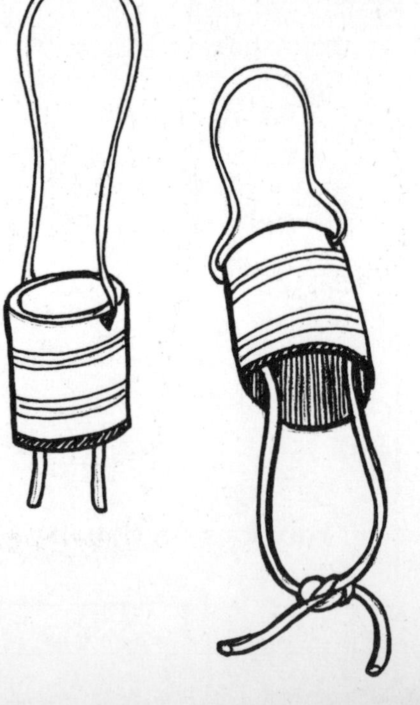

You will need

2 same-sized, clean tin cans, open on one end only

cloth or masking tape

juice can opener

twine, cotton rope or heavy jute

scissors

4. Wear rubber-soled shoes on the stilts so you don't slip off. Grip the ropes, keep your arms and legs straight and start walking. If the ropes are too long (they should be about as high as your mid-thigh), shorten them by re-knotting them in the can. It will take some practice to get good at walking on your stilts, but they're lots of fun.

More tin-can ideas

Use a tin can to make a pencil holder. Remove the label, and tape around the top rim of the can to cover any sharp edges. Glue felt, fabric, ribbon, yarn, self-adhesive vinyl or construction paper around it. Then you can glue on decorations, such as buttons, beads, shells, dried beans or colored pasta (see pages 158 and 159).

Make a desk organizer by decorating different-sized cans. Glue them together along the sides or tie them together with ribbon or a strip of fabric.

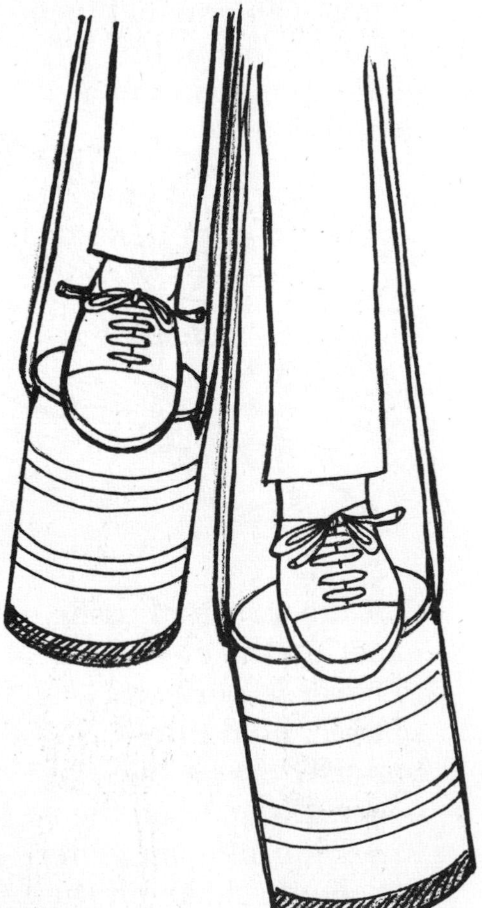

Tissue-paper butterfly

To display your butterfly, you can stick on a magnet and put it on the fridge or you can tie a string on it and hang it up. If you make a few butterflies in different colors, you could make a butterfly mobile (see page 191).

You will need

colorful tissue paper

◎

a ruler, scissors and white craft glue

◎

a clothespin with a spring

◎

half a tinsel pipe cleaner

◎

paper and glitter (optional)

1. Cut out three rectangles of different-colored tissue, each about 15 cm x 20 cm (6 in. x 8 in.) Gather all three rectangles together in the center to make a bow.

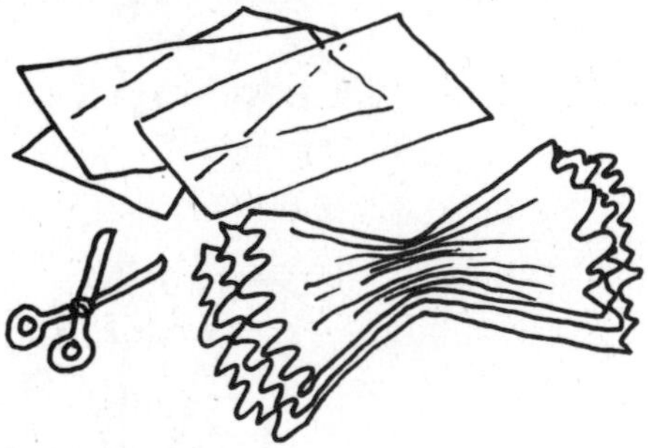

2. Open the clothespin and pinch the gathered tissue paper inside it.

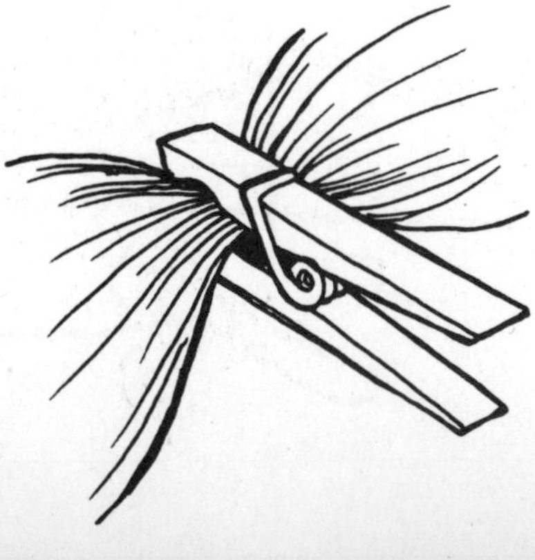

3. Bend the pipe cleaner in half and curl the ends to make antennae. Pinch the antennae in the clothespin, too. Add a dab of glue.

4. Glue a strip of tissue paper on the clothespin to cover it. For extra sparkle, hold the butterfly over a sheet of paper. Dot glue on the wings, sprinkle on glitter and gently shake off the extra glitter.

Tissue stained glass

Try this with a simple design, such as a heart, a large flower or the moon and stars.

1. Draw shapes onto one of the sheets of construction paper. Poke the scissors into the center of each shape so you can cut it out.

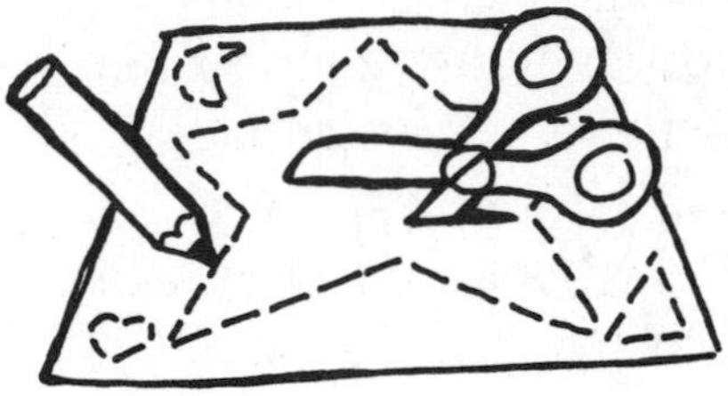

2. Hold the two sheets of paper together and trace the cutout shapes onto the uncut construction paper. Cut them out, too.

3. On one sheet of construction paper, glue a piece of tissue paper over each cutout.

4. Glue the two sheets together, matching all the cutouts. Hang your tissue stained glass in a window.

You will need

a pencil, scissors and white craft glue

2 sheets of construction paper

colorful pieces of tissue paper

Tissue-paper lei

For this lei, you can use store-bought beads as well as straw beads (see page 80) and pasta beads (see pages 158 and 159). Aloha!

1. Cut out many tissue-paper flowers in lots of colors, shapes and sizes.

2. Thread at least two arm lengths of yarn into the needle. Make a knot in the long end of the yarn.

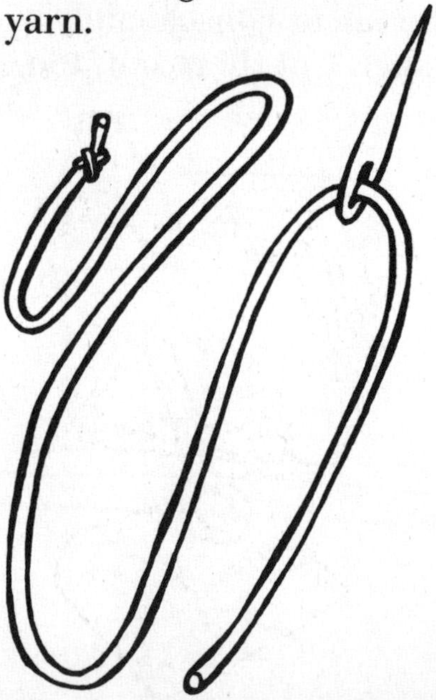

3. Thread on a couple of beads, tissue flowers, more beads, more flowers and keep going.

4. When your lei is long enough to fit easily over your head, knot the yarn together and trim the ends.

You will need

colorful tissue paper

scissors

yarn and a blunt needle with a large eye

beads

Giant tissue flower

These flowers make pretty party decorations. Also use one instead of a bow on a friend's gift. Make a whole bouquet!

1. Twist the two pipe cleaners together. Roll a small coil in one end.

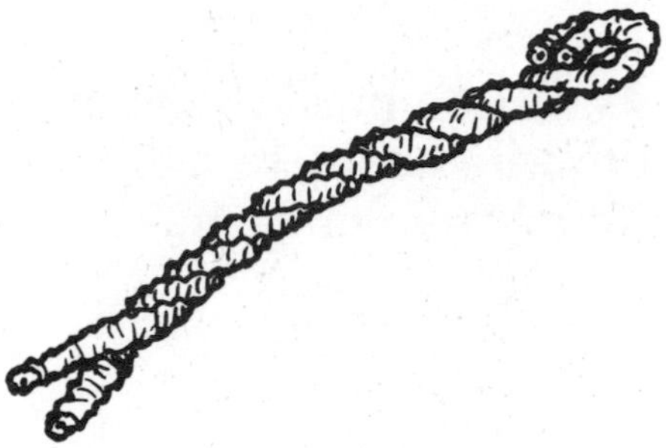

2. Cut 12 pieces of tissue, each about the size of a regular sheet of paper. If you'd like a flower with rounded petals, cut off the corners on each sheet of tissue.

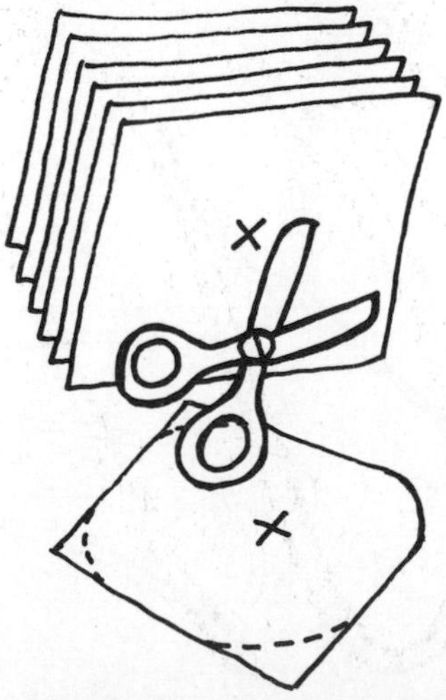

3. One at a time, thread the tissue sheets onto the straight end of the pipe cleaners. Make sure the edges of the tissue sheets do not line up.

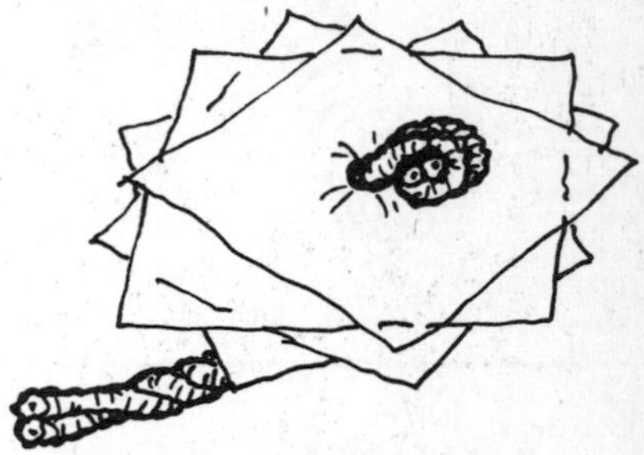

4. Pull up the tissue sheets by pinching them together at the base of the flower. Hold the tissue in this flower shape by fastening on a twist tie. Adjust and trim the petals, if you wish.

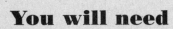

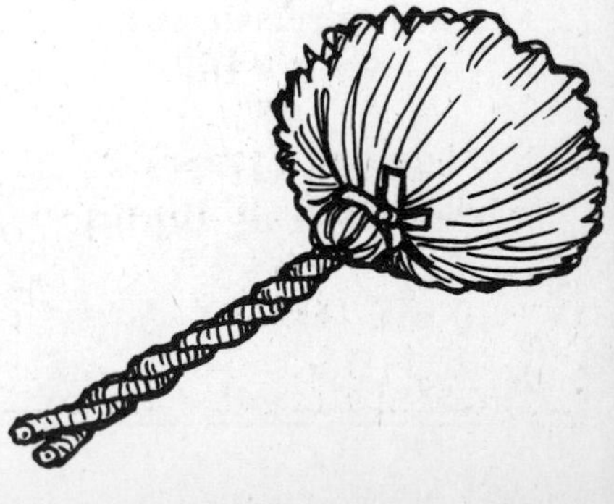

You will need

2 pipe cleaners
◎
tissue paper
◎
scissors
◎
a twist tie

Bubble blower and bubble mixture

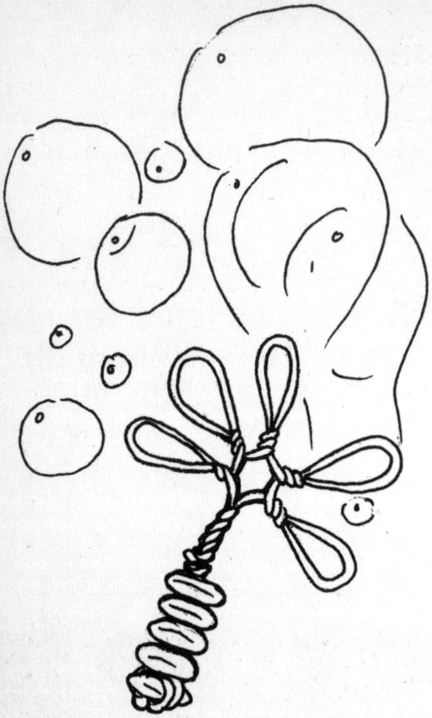

If you find it difficult to make bubbles or they don't last long, add 5 mL (1 tsp.) glycerin (available at a drugstore) to the bubble mixture. You can also use store-bought bubble liquid.

You will need

1 m (1 yd.) of 20-gauge wire (available at hardware stores)

wirecutters or old scissors

assorted beads with large holes

a margarine tub with a lid

50 mL (1/4 c.) dishwashing liquid

50 mL (1/4 c.) water

1. Twist a petal shape in the wire about 15 cm (6 in.) from one end.

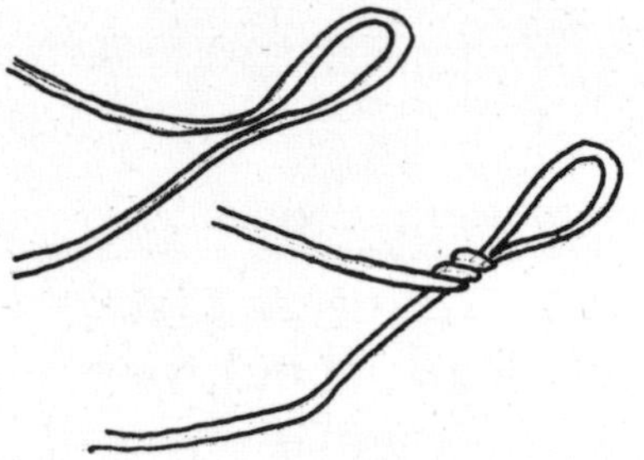

2. Using the longer end of the wire, make another petal shape beside the first one.

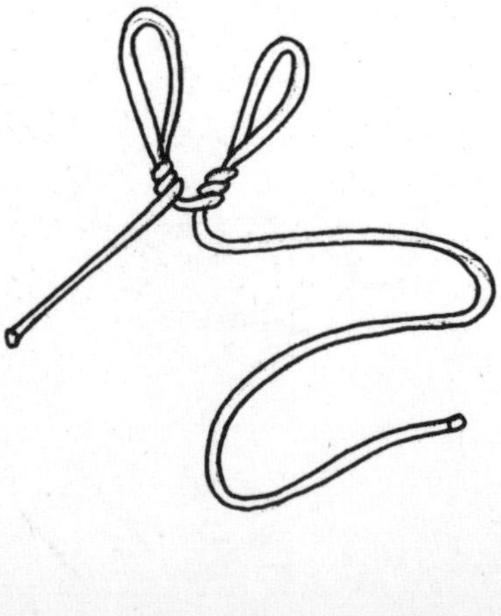

3. Keep making petals until you have five or six. The center of the flower may be a jumble of wire, but that's okay.

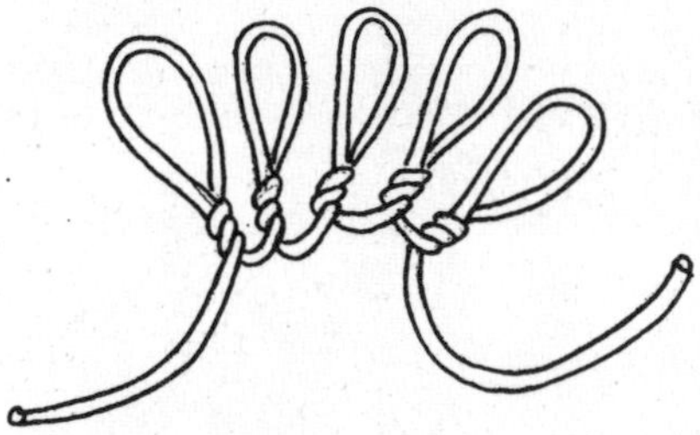

4. When you have enough petals, twist the leftover wire together with the piece you left at the beginning. Cut off any extra wire.

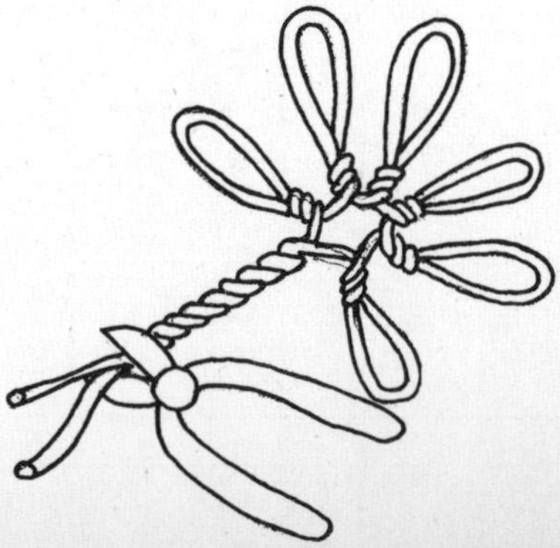

5. Thread on enough beads to cover about half of the handle. Bend up the wire ends and tuck them into the beads.

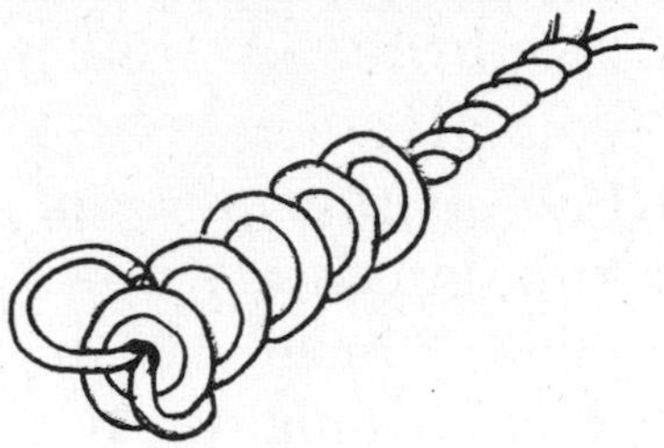

6. To keep the beads at the lower end of the bubble blower, bend a kink in the wire just above the beads.

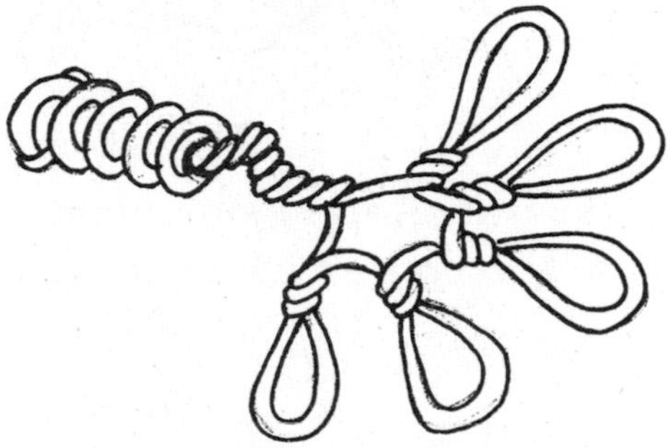

7. In the plastic tub, mix together the dishwashing liquid and water.

8. Dip the flower into the bubble mixture. Sweep the blower through the air, or blow gently for huge bubbles and blow hard for small ones.

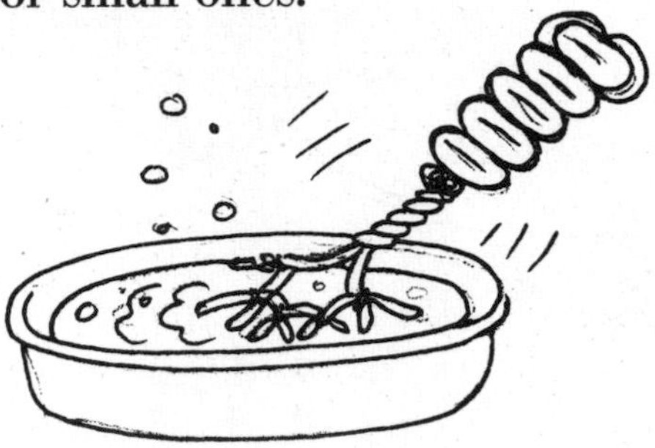

Yarn friend

To make this doll, choose a hardcover book that is as tall as you'd like your yarn friend to be.

1. Wind yarn around the book – about 20 times for very thick yarn and 50 times for regular yarn. Cut the yarn end.

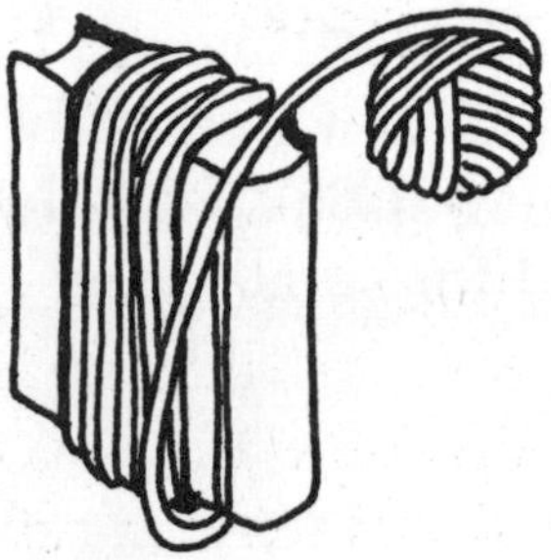

2. Cut an arm's length of yarn. Slide the wound yarn off the book and tie it together at the top with the cut piece of yarn. Knot the tying yarn ends together to make a loop.

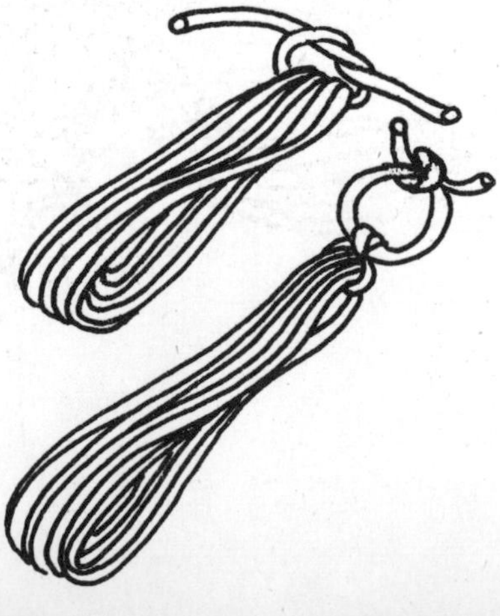

3. Tie another piece of yarn a little lower down to make a head. Let the yarn ends hang down the back.

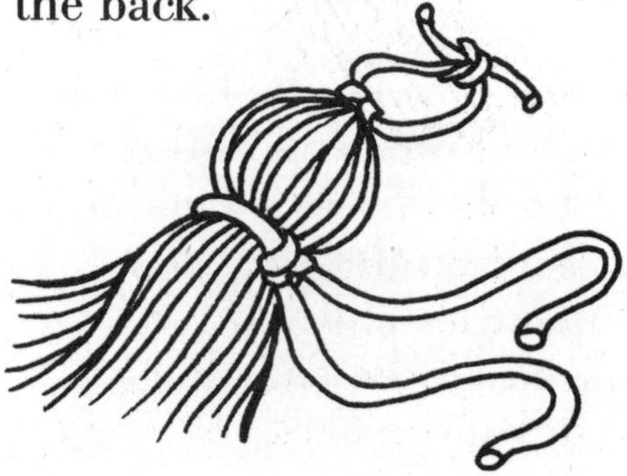

4. Cut all the looped ends at the bottom of the doll.

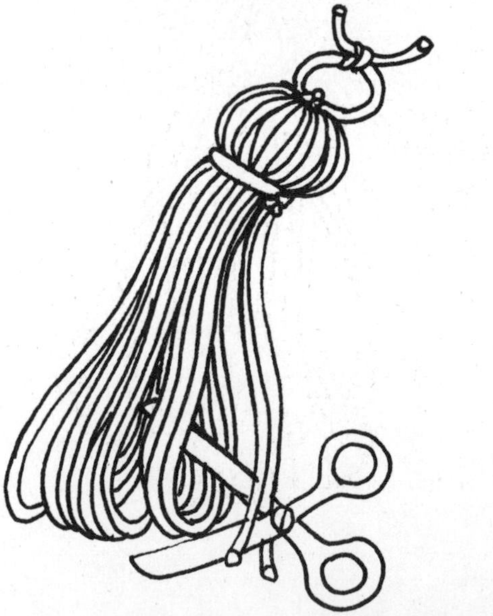

You will need

a hardcover book

yarn

scissors

roly eyes, beads, felt or other decorating supplies

5. Separate some strands of yarn from the doll's sides to make arms. Tie the strands in an overhand knot as shown and trim off the extra yarn.

6. Tie the waist with another piece of yarn and let the ends hang down the back.

7. Leave the rest of the yarn hanging loose for a skirt or separate it into two legs. Tie them at the feet. Trim off any uneven strands of yarn.

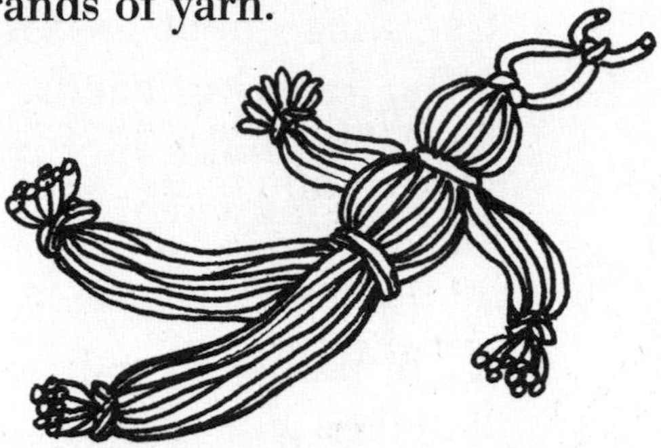

8. If you'd like to make hair, tie a few strands of different-colored yarn around the long loop on your doll's head. Create a face. Hang up your yarn friend or use the loop to make it into a marionette.

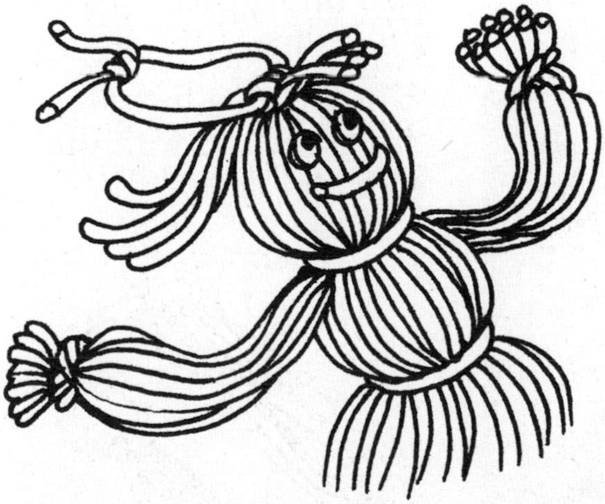

Gluey yarn creations

Use these neat-looking ornaments to decorate gifts, greeting cards, doorknobs or a tree. You can also make pictures by "drawing" on paper with gluey yarn.

1. In the plastic tub, stir together glue with enough water to thin it a little.

2. Cut about an arm's length of yarn and drop it in the glue mixture. Stir it around with the spoon or stick.

3. As you pull the yarn out of the glue, run it lightly through your fingers. Place the yarn on the cookie sheet.

4. Play around with the wet yarn until you're happy with your design. The yarn should be touching in many places. You may wish to include a yarn loop to hang up your creation. Allow the design to dry, then peel it off the waxed paper.

You will need

- a plastic tub
- white craft glue
- a plastic spoon or a Popsicle stick
- yarn and scissors
- a cookie sheet lined with waxed paper

Yarn greetings

Stitch up a simple greeting card for someone special.

1. Fold together the two sheets of construction paper.

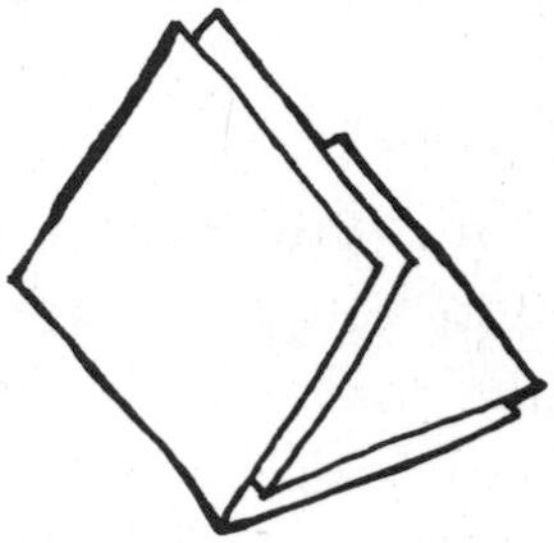

2. Open the sheets, keep them together and punch holes evenly all around the four sides.

3. Cut a length of yarn about three times the length of an adult's arm. Wind a little tape around one end of the yarn.

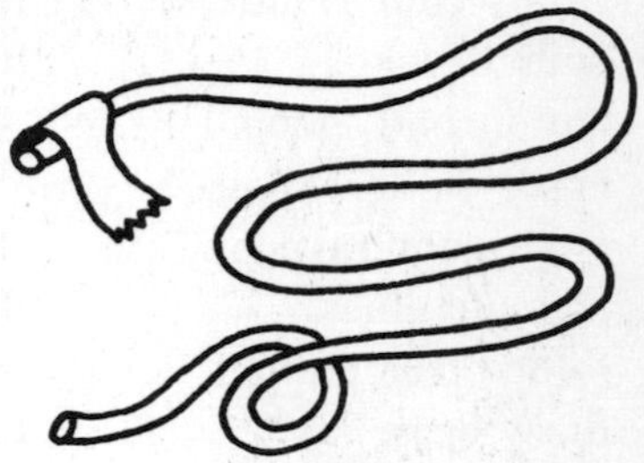

4. Leave a yarn tail in the bottom, right corner of the card and stitch it all around. When you get back to where you started, tie the yarn ends into a bow. Decorate the card and write a message in it.

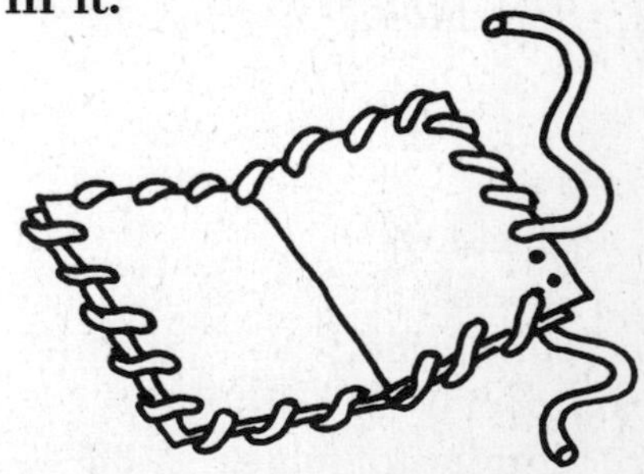

You will need

2 sheets of different-colored construction paper
◎
a hole punch
◎
yarn
◎
tape
◎
crayons or markers

Index